THE STUDENT VOICE HANDBOOK: BRIDGING THE ACADEMIC/PRACTITIONER DIVIDE

THE STUDENT VOICE HANDBOOK: BRIDGING THE ACADEMIC/PRACTITIONER DIVIDE

EDITED BY

GERRY CZERNIAWSKI AND WARREN KIDD

Cass School of Education, University of East London

United Kingdom – North America – Japan
India – Malaysia – China

Emerald Group Publishing Limited
Howard House, Wagon Lane, Bingley BD16 1WA, UK

First edition 2011

British Library Cataloguing in Publication Data
A catalogue record for this book is available from the British Library

ISBN: 978-1-78052-040-7

Printed and bound by CPI Group (UK) Ltd, Croydon, CR0 4YY

Emerald Group Publishing
Limited, Howard House,
Environmental Management
System has been certified by
ISOQAR to ISO 14001:2004
standards

Awarded in recognition of
Emerald's production
department's adherence to
quality systems and processes
when preparing scholarly
journals for print

INVESTOR IN PEOPLE

Contents

List of Figures

List of Tables

About the Editors

Gerry Czerniawski has passionately worked in the multi-cultural environment in the London Borough of Newham for over 10 years at secondary and post-16 levels before gradually moving into teaching within Higher Education within both the political sciences and education (The Open University, University of Northampton, London Metropolitan University and London University's Institute of Education). He is a senior lecturer in education at the Cass School of Education (University of East London) responsible for the education and training of teachers in the humanities and the social science disciplines. An experienced author, Gerry's research interests include teaching and learning, the identities of teachers and teacher educators, citizenship, comparative education, teachers' values, the impact of globalisation on the teacher profession and student voice. Gerry's latest book *Emerging Teachers and Globalization* (Routledge, 2011) is a European comparative study of teacher identities. Gerry has also co-written *Teaching Teenagers: A Toolkit for Engaging and Motivating Learners'* (Sage, 2011). Along with Warren Kidd, Gerry is the co-editor of this text.

Warren Kidd is a senior lecturer in education at The Cass School of Education, University of East London (UEL), where he is a teaching fellow of the university. He is the Cass School of Education's Leader in Learning and Teaching (LiLT). His interests include podcasting for learning, teaching and assessment; the use of Web2.0 tools for professional learning in teacher education; teacher identity and change; the adoption of student voice (and e-learning) as a means to 'train' Vocational Education and Training (VET) professionals. Previously, he has taught both sociology and psychology for 14 years in secondary schools and Sixth Form Colleges in Surrey, Kent and London. Warren worked for 8 years in the multi-cultural, urban environment of Newham in east London. He was the teaching and learning development manager of a large, diverse Sixth Form College, and was an advanced teaching practitioner. Warren is the co-author of *Successful Teaching 14–19: Theory, practice and reflection* (Sage, 2010) and *Teaching Teenagers: A Toolkit for Engaging and Motivating Learners* (Sage, 2011). Along with Gerry Czerniawski, Warren is the co-editor of this text.

About the Contributors

Julie Baldry Currens is the director of learning and teaching at the University of East London (UEL) where she leads the development and implementation of strategy, policy and practice with regard to the university's learning and teaching culture and the associated student experience. Her areas of particular interest, research and practice currently include: the rich and diverse methods by which students and colleagues support and enhance one another's learning as peers; student voice and student perception of their HE experience; professional standards in academic practice; the scholarship of learning, teaching and assessment and practice-based learning and curriculum design. Julie's doctoral dissertation explored student perceptions of peer learning and practice-based learning, and in 2007 she was awarded a HEA National Teaching Fellowship for her work in this area.

Ulrika Bergmark is a senior lecturer at the Department of Arts, Communication and Education, Luleå University of Technology, Sweden. Ulrika's research focus is mainly on learning issues explored from different perspectives. Areas of interest are ethics in school, student voice, strengths-based approaches, school improvement and qualitative methods. Ulrika is teaching at the master programme in education, as well as in programmes for in-service training for teachers. In her role as a senior lecturer, she is also facilitating school improvement processes within a municipality in the region where the university is situated. She is currently working with a research project with the purpose of exploring students' experiences of psychosocial well-being and learning in school. Together with her colleague Catrine Kostenius she recently published the book *The power of appreciation – learning, ethics and health* (published 2011 by Studentlitteratur, in Swedish).

Helen Bishton has been a teacher of over 20 years in special schools in the United Kingdom, the majority being schools for children with severe learning difficulties. She has developed a keen interest in children's voice activities, as an extension of her interest in how children make decisions and choices as part of their involvement and engagement in a school. As part of her studies for an EdD she carried out case study research with eight primary-aged children with severe learning difficulties in three variously inclusive schools; an important part of this research was eliciting the children's opinions. For the past five years Helen has been working at a school for secondary-aged students with complex social communication difficulties (ASD), where she is the headteacher; a context which, again, has provided Helen with another perspective on student voice.

Derek Bland is a lecturer in inclusive education at Queensland University of Technology. He was a secondary art teacher and has since had many years' involvement as a practitioner, researcher and administrator in programmes to find creative ways to improve educational opportunities and outcomes for socio-economically disadvantaged students. Derek also has an interest in the central roles of imagination and visual research methods in engaging marginalised students in education. He is currently working with students at schools that serve low-income areas in a series of participatory action research projects relating to educational engagement and tertiary aspiration.

Tony Breslin is chair of the charity Human Scale Education; director of the consultancy Breslin Public Policy Limited; and honorary research fellow at Birkbeck, University of London. He is also a member of the National Community Cohesion Panel, a Trustee at Speakers Trust, a non-executive director at Arc Theatre for Change and a vice-president of the Association for the Teaching of the Social Sciences. Between September 2001 and August 2010, he was chief executive at the Citizenship Foundation, the independent education and participation charity, and before this, he was general adviser, 14–19 Education, in Enfield, North London. Tony is an experienced teacher, trainer and examiner and a qualified Ofsted inspector. He has published and spoken widely, in the United Kingdom and overseas, on education and participation issues. His latest book, *Teachers, Schools and Change* (Trentham, 2011 – forthcoming) follows *Developing Citizens*, a collection of essays co-edited with Barry Dufour, published by Hodder Education in 2006.

Fiona Campbell is an academic developer, fellow of the Higher Education Academy and co-chair of the Staff and Educational Development Association Conference Committee. She has led two ESCalate-funded, inter-institutional Hearing the Student Voice projects which focused on capturing the student voice effectively to inform academic practice and curriculum development and has disseminated the outcomes through publications, conference presentations and the provision of project events. Fiona is Head of Professional Development at Edinburgh Napier University, where she enables the enhancement of academic practice across the university through the provision of developmental opportunities and support for staff.

Steve Cartwright began working at Trentham High School in November 2006 as science department subject leader. This was a promotion from assistant subject leader, a role he had held in two local schools previously. In 2006, THS was in special measures and the science department was in a difficult situation. From 2006 to 2008 the school improved its GCSE results and was then invited by the Local Authority to become part of a project with Cambridge University. Since this time, the school has continued using some of the strategies developed in the project. The science department has recently achieved 76% A*-C with 13% A*/A and the school has been given Specialist Science College Status.

Charlotte Chadderton is a postdoctoral research fellow at the Cass School of Education, University of East London. Before moving into Higher Education, Charlotte was an ESOL teacher and language support worker and taught in Berlin, St Petersburg and Manchester, and speaks fluent German and Spanish and some Russian. Alongside the teaching she worked as a volunteer with refugees in Berlin and Manchester. She gained her PhD in 2009 from Manchester Metropolitan University, which focussed on Citizenship Education, identities and race. Both at UEL and as research assistant at MMU, she has worked on several qualitative research projects in the fields of secondary education, lifelong and informal learning, vocational educational and race, using ethnographic, feminist, critical race and poststructural research methods. She has particular experience of research with disadvantaged groups and young people. Her current research interests include education for social justice, young people and control and surveillance, race, marginalised voices.

Rita Cheminais is a leading expert in the fields of Every Child Matters, Special Educational Needs and Inclusion. She has 33 years experience working in education as a teacher, SEN coordinator, an OFSTED inspector, a principal adviser for SEN and Inclusion in two local authority Children's Services. Rita is a respected author of many books and journal articles on Every Child Matters, Inclusion, and the SENCO role. Rita speaks regularly at national conferences and is an international trainer. Rita was commissioned by the DCSF/NCSS in 2009 to undertake project work on children's emotional health in two local authorities to identify good practice developments. Currently, Rita is a school improvement partner in Tameside, and a freelance education consultant and director of Educational Consultancy & Management (ECM) Solutions. Her website is www.ecm-solutions.org.uk where you will find more information about her current work.

Tina Cook, formerly a teacher of children with special educational needs is now a reader at Northumbria University. At the core of her work is a focus on inclusive practice in research. Using qualitative research, particularly collaborative action research, she seeks ways of facilitating the inclusion, as research partners, of those who might generally be excluded from research that concerns their own lives. Her methodological approach centres on ways of fore-fronting voices of those directly involved in a situation as a means of improving the quality of their lives. She has published on both methodological issues and issues related to research in practice.

Emily R. Crawford is a doctoral candidate in Educational Theory and Policy at the Pennsylvania State University. Her research interests include ethics in education, education policy, and immigration, particularly issues affecting the education of undocumented students.

Jenny Eland is a tutor for Educational Development at Birmingham City University. Initially a lecturer in Early Childhood Care and Education, Jenny moved into educational development, with particular interests in curriculum design, assessment and student-centred approaches. She is responsible for the University's Post Graduate Certificate Learning and Teaching in Higher Education and MA modules in course design and enhancement. To keep contact with undergraduates Jenny still teaches in a partner college. She is involved in policy development, project work and staff development, and is an active member of SEDA's Professional Development Framework Committee. She has participated in ESCalate-funded projects on using the Student Voice with Edinburgh Napier, Leeds Metropolitan and Westminster Universities.

Michael Fielding taught for 19 years in some of the UK pioneer radical comprehensive schools and for a similar period and with identical commitments at the universities of Cambridge, Sussex and London where he is currently emeritus professor of Education at the Institute of Education. Widely published in the fields of student voice, educational leadership and radical education, his latest book *Radical Education and the Common School – a democratic alternative* (Routledge, 2011) co-authored with Peter Moss seeks to reclaim education as a democratic project and a community responsibility and school as a public space of encounter for all citizens.

William C. Frick is an assistant professor in the Department of Educational Leadership and Policy Studies, Jeannine Rainbolt College of Education, University of Oklahoma. He holds a PhD in educational theory and policy from the Pennsylvania State University. His prior work experience includes 14 years in the public schools as a teacher, school counselor, principal and director of curriculum and instruction. Bill's research interests include valuation, ethics, and moral school leadership practices; school and community revitalization; and school reform at all levels. Among his publications are articles that appear in *Journal of Educational Administration*, *Journal of Beliefs and Values, Educational Policy* and forthcoming research in the *American Journal of Education*.

Su Garlick taught in the London Borough of Havering for 22 years, mainly in the fields of Design and Technology and Special Educational Needs. She is now a senior lecturer at the University of East London, training teachers in the area of Design and Technology. Her research interests are in Student Voice and she has been involved in a joint venture with a London secondary school for five years. Su is also keen to support her subject association and is currently contributing to a discussion document which will inform future ITT practice. Su is a fellow of the HEA, achieving Standard Descriptor 3 for her collaborative work with schools and other ITT institutions.

David Godfrey, until 2010, was an assistant director of Personalised Learning at the Sixth Form College Farnborough, Hampshire. He is now an educational consultant, continuing his student voice and action research work with the college. In previous roles, David worked at the University of Antioquia, Colombia, teaching psychology to prospective teachers; he has also worked as an associate lecturer for the Open University. Since returning to England in 1997, David has worked in the lifelong learning sector in the United Kingdom, much of which has been at the Sixth Form College Farnborough, where he started in September 2000 as a personal tutor and psychology teacher. Since September 2006, David has been responsible for action research projects at the college, organising an annual conference and editing an annual in-house research journal. David was a member of the Editorial Board for the

National Foundation for Educational Research (NFER) *pre* (Practical Research for Education) journal. David is currently a full-time doctoral researcher at the Institute of Education, University of London, looking into research engagement in schools and colleges.

Alia Islam was an A level student at Sir George Monoux College. She was a founder member of the Student Voice Team and is currently studying for a degree in Classics while being employed as the Study Plus Administrator at the college. She is particularly interested in ways of helping staff and students work together to improve the curriculum.

Bernadette Joslin, a history teacher by background, has worked in the learning and skills sector for over 20 years — most recently as a pastoral manager in a large FE college where she had a strong involvement with the development of the student union. Until May 2011 Bernadette was the programme manager of the highly regarded support programme for post-16 citizenship (PCSP) run by the LSN on behalf of the LSIS. The PCSP has made strong links between learner voice and citizenship education and has produced publications and runs event exploring this relationship. The ways in which learner voice can support skills for democratic skills of participation is an area of particular importance. The PCSP has also looked at new ways of strengthening learner voice, both individually and collectively.

Susan Kiragu (Kenya) is currently working as a research associate at the Centre for Commonwealth Education, University of Cambridge. She is involved in two qualitative projects in East Africa. The ASKAIDS project investigates how children's everyday and school sexual knowledges can be used in a HIV/AIDS curriculum and the Gender project is a longitudinal study exploring the reasons why some girls manage to stay in school despite facing socio-cultural and economic problems. Susan is also interested in the use of indigenous knowledges for curriculum development and teacher training. She strongly believes in research for social justice and intervention.

Joanne Kenworthy was a lecturer and researcher in Linguistics at the University of East London for over 30 years, specialising in sociolinguistics, bilingualism, discourse analysis and style in language and communication. Her other professional activities include consultancy and teacher training in the field of English Language teaching. She has been involved with Discover since 1997 in various roles, as a member of the Learning Advisory Group, as a trustee and as the lead evaluator of *Listening to Learn*. She is currently involved in the evaluation and development of Discover's *Catching Words*, exploring creative approaches to literacy in primary schools.

Rebecca Kirkman is a teacher of mathematics and started working at Trentham High School in 2005 as an NQT and is now head of the department. The school has been through a tumultuous time; special measures, to satisfactory, and most recently into the 'good category'. In addition, the school and local community successfully campaigned against closure under the BSF programme. Two years ago Rebecca was invited to work with the University of Cambridge in the 'Raising Achievement through Inclusive Contexts' in Stoke-on-Trent. This was a thought-provoking learning experience and the lasting effects of this relationship can be seen clearly within the school to this day.

Catrine Kostenius is a senior lecturer at the Department of Health Sciences, Luleå University of Technology, Sweden. Catrine's main research area is health promotion with focus on giving voice to children and youth and making something of their contributions. Areas of interest are the connection between health and learning, e-health, student participation and school improvement. She is teaching at the master programmes in health science and in education, as well as in programmes for health educators and teachers. Catrine is currently working with two research projects, one with the aim of developing a school health programme using mobile communication, and another with the purpose of exploring students' experiences of psychosocial well-being and learning in school. Together with her colleague Ulrika Bergmark she recently published the book *The power of appreciation – learning, ethics and health* (published 2011 by Studentlitteratur, in Swedish).

Geoff Lindsay is a director of the Centre for Educational Development, Appraisal and Research (CEDAR) at the University of Warwick and is a professor of Special Educational Needs and Educational Psychology. He was previously principal educational psychologist for Sheffield, LA, and before that a teacher in primary and special schools. His main research areas are SEND and inclusion, and the evaluation of new educational initiatives. He was a consultant to the Lamb Inquiry into parental confidence in the SEN system. He has led over 70 research studies, published extensively, and contributed to developments in a dozen other countries by consultancy and/or teaching, most recently Serbia as part of a UN-funded project on autism.

Tristan McCowan is a senior lecturer in Education and International Development at the Institute of Education, University of London. His research focuses on education, human rights and citizenship in an international context, and he is the author of *Rethinking Citizenship Education: a Curriculum for Participatory Democracy* (Continuum, 2009). His interests also include access to higher education, and he is currently undertaking a study of new socially engaged universities in Brazil.

Ros McLellan is a lecturer in Teacher Education & Development/Pedagogical Innovation at the Faculty of Education, University of Cambridge. Her research interests include achievement motivation, attitudes and perceptions, self-efficacy, creativity and issues related to gender and achievement. She has a background in teaching psychology and mathematics in the secondary school sector in the United Kingdom and is particularly committed to working collaboratively with schools to develop and refine strategies that make a real difference to teaching and learning in the classroom. She is currently working on a number of projects including an ongoing collaboration with Stoke Local Authority on raising achievement.

Colleen McLaughlin is a senior lecturer and deputy head of faculty at the University of Cambridge Faculty of Education, where she teaches and researches. She works in the fields of practitioner research, the personal, social and emotional aspects of education, including counselling. She has a particular interest in listening to the voices of children in education, in counselling and in shaping practice. She is currently researching adolescence, mental health and school experience; bullying and special educational needs and using children's sexual knowledge to shape sexuality and HIV/AIDS education. She is also very interested in the social and emotional aspects of collaboration.

Bev Millington, qualifying in 1982 and teaching both Religious Studies and English for the duration of her career to date, has held numerous posts of responsibility. These have included positions in both the curriculum and pastoral fields: subject leader, faculty leader, head of both Upper and Lower School, literacy coordinator, head of various year groups and transition. She joined Trentham High School — a Cooperative Trust, Specialist Science College in 2007 and is now assistant head with overall responsibility for Core and interventions at all levels. If asked to describe herself in relation to her vocation, she would say that she was a 'tenacious goal-driven visionary'.

Dana L. Mitra is an associate professor in the Education Theory and Policy Program at the Pennsylvania State University. She holds a PhD from Stanford University in Educational Administration and Policy Analysis. Her prior work experience includes teaching elementary school in the Washington, DC area and serving as the coordinator for two White House Conferences on Character Education. Dana's research interests include high school reform, student voice and civic engagement. Among her publications, she has published articles in *Teachers College Record* entitled 'The significance of students: Can increasing "student voice" in schools lead to gains in youth development?' and in *Education Administration Quarterly* entitled 'Adults advising youth: Leading while getting out of the way'. She also has published a book with SUNY Press entitled *Student voice in school reform: Building youth-adult partnerships that strengthen schools and empower youth.*

Bethan Morgan is a teaching associate at the Faculty of Education, University of Cambridge. She supports practitioner research within the Schools University Partnership for Educational Research (SUPER) and lectures and supervises on master courses. Her research interests include teachers' and pupils' perceptions of student engagement and teachers' continuous professional development. Since 2008, she has also supported teachers with school-based research in nine schools in collaboration with Stoke-on-Trent Local Authority. Before this, she taught for 17 years in secondary schools in Wales and the United Arab Emirates. Always passionately committed to pupil voice as a teacher, an MPhil course sparked Bethan's interest in research and led to an ESRC-funded PhD exploring pupil consultation under the supervision of the late Professor Donald McIntyre. Her research is featured in Rudduck, J & McIntyre, D (2007) *Improving Learning through Consulting Pupils* (London: Routledge) and published in the journals *Research Papers in Education* and *The Curriculum Journal*.

Joy Morgan has taught in inner London secondary schools for over 30 years with responsibilities ranging from head of faculty to head of year, gifted and talented coordinator to behaviour specialist. Joy's real passion lies in professional development for teachers and non-teaching colleagues at all stages in their careers. As part of this, she has developed innovative ways for students to make real and valuable contributions to the development of high-quality learning in trainee teachers' classrooms, producing measurable outcomes for teachers and students alike. Students have presented their Student Leadership initiatives at a number of conferences and have supported over 60 schools nationally in setting up similar projects, running advice sessions for teachers and students as well as providing training in both the state and private sector.

Gill Mullis is a deputy headteacher at Stocklake Park School, a member of the Vale Federation of Special Schools in Aylesbury. Before this she was Student Voice coordinator for the Specialist Schools and Academies Trust, where she provided training and guidance on how students and staff in schools can work together to develop principles, policy and practice in relation to student voice. She has also coordinated and contributed to national events, supporting student-led projects and student-authored publications based on maximising student participation in school improvement. Gill has enjoyed teaching in comprehensive schools in East Sussex, Milton Keynes and Bedfordshire, throughout this time working with others to define, develop and embed 'student voice'. She worked with students on the ESRC 'Breaking new ground' project, their research appearing in publications by Professor Michael Fielding and Professor Jean Rudduck.

Rob Pope has a long held interest in citizenship education and learner voice and has considerable experience in this field as a classroom practitioner and, until May 2011, in a national role as part of the post-16 citizenship team at LSN, in the United Kingdom. Rob has extensive experience of teaching and management in post-16 education, in particular at Richmond Upon Thames College where he taught sociology, was head of Social Sciences and Citizenship Project Manager. He has also been involved in teacher education as a course tutor at the Institute of Education, London University, has considerable experience in staff development work and of adult education, including tutoring for the Open University.

Anita Porter is a teacher of Sociology and Psychology at Impington Village College, an 11–19 Comprehensive School on the outskirts of Cambridge. She has Advanced Skills Teacher status for Citizenship and Student Voice. Her MA in Sociology and Gender Studies informs this work. She completed a Certificate of Further Professional Study at the Faculty of Education, University of Cambridge for which she investigated the ways in which membership of youth cults affected attitudes to learning. Further research on factors affecting achievement from the students' perspective, fuelled interest in her current work on the impact of student led research on classroom practice.

Ann Rumpus has just retired from Westminster University. Initially a lecturer in Biology, Ann moved into educational development, with particular interests in curriculum design, assessment and student-centred approaches. She was responsible for the University's education courses, (including an MA in HE and a Cert.Ed./PGCE(DTLLLS)) taught in partner colleges. She was involved in policy development, project work and staff development, Ann was co-director of the Westminster Partnership (a Centre for Excellence in Teacher Training), with Oxford Brookes University. She has participated in ESCalate-funded projects on using the Student Voice with Leeds Metropolitan, Birmingham City and Edinburgh Napier Universities.

Andy Samways is a deputy headteacher at a school in Suffolk. He has been involved in leading, coordinating and embedding student voice within the secondary schools he has worked in since 1993. In his previous post as deputy headteacher at the Sweyne Park School in Rayleigh, Essex he was influential in developing a range of innovative student voice opportunities that drew regional and national recognition. As a result of this he and groups of students have enjoyed sharing aspects of their student voice practice, presenting at workshops, conferences and through publications for the Specialist Schools and Academies Trust.

Corina Seal has taught Mathematics in secondary schools since 1980. As a senior leader at the Sweyne Park School in Essex, she oversees research activities, ITT, early career CPD and Training School outreach. The school has received national recognition for its innovations and success in areas such as Pupil Voice, coaching and mentoring, and personalised professional development. Corina has had several papers published on collaborative research as a form of CPD and has presented at a number of national conferences, including BERA 2008. She is a community leader for the Teacher Learning Academy and has worked with the National Teacher Research Panel, the National College, and CUREE.

Rai Shacklock is a head of Languages and English Language Teaching at Leeds Metropolitan University, UK. Rai was appointed to Head of Languages and English Language Teaching in August 2009. She has an MSc in Entrepreneurial Studies and a Bachelor of Education degree. Previously her background was in Events and Hospitality Management. Rai is a teacher fellow in the University and contributes actively to the Teacher Fellow Network. She has received a number of awards for teaching excellence. She acts as a paper reviewer for a number of publications and sits on the editorial board for the *Journal of Hospitality and Tourism Education*. Rai regularly presents at International Conferences on teaching, learning and assessment issues. Rai has participated in ESCalate-funded projects on using the Student Voice with Westminster University, Birmingham City and Edinburgh Napier University.

Raymonde Sneddon was a primary teacher in east London for 17 years, specialising in working with bilingual pupils, their families and communities. She was a teacher educator at the University of East London for 11 years with a special brief to incorporate the teaching of English as an additional language and issues around bilingualism, multiliteracy and equal opportunities into the Primary Curriculum. Raymonde is currently a research fellow in the Cass School of Education at the UEL and an honorary research fellow in the Department of Applied Linguistics and

Communication at Birkbeck College where she obtained her PhD. Raymonde researches and publishes in the field of bilingualism, multi-literacy, community languages and complementary education. She published *Bilingual Books – Biliterate Children* with Trentham Books in 2009.

Wes Streeting is the chief executive of the Helena Kennedy Foundation, an educational charity that supports disadvantaged college leavers to access higher education and the graduate professions. He is also an elected councilor in the London Borough of Redbridge, where he takes a particular interest in children services and leisure, particularly for children in care. Wes is a former president of the National Union of Students, representing millions of students in further and higher education across the United Kingdom. He has a particular interest in widening participation and youth citizenship, having served as a higher education ambassador for the Prime Minister's National Council for Educational Excellence under Gordon Brown and as a member of his government's Youth Citizenship Commission. He also played an active role in the European Students' Union (ESU) and represented UK students at the 2007 Bologna Ministerial Summit in London.

Pat Thomson is Professor of Education at the School of Education, the University of Nottingham. She is an adjunct professor at the University of South Australia and visiting professor at Deakin University, Australia. Her current research focuses primarily on arts, creativity and school and community change (see www.artsand-creativityresearch.org.uk). She is an editor of the international, peer refereed *Educational Action Research Journal* (Taylor and Francis) and the author/editor of 11 books, including, not the most recent of which are *Researching Creative Learning: Methods and Issues* (with Julian Sefton Green, Routledge 2010), *The Routledge Doctoral Students Companion: Getting to grips with research in Education and the Social Sciences* and *the Routledge Doctoral Supervisors' Companion: Supporting effective research in Education and the Social Sciences* (both with Melanie Walker, Routledge 2010).

Ian Wainer is the student voice coordinator at Sir George Monoux Sixth Form College, UK. He has been involved in education for over 40 years. He has been a practitioner, middle and senior manager in the Youth Service, FE Colleges and the Voluntary Sector. Ian's particular interest is how strategies and techniques drawn from informal education can be used to support students in their studies.

Martin Waller is an award-winning primary school teacher and educational researcher based in the United Kingdom. His main teaching and research interests are founded in multi-literacies, critical literacy, digital technologies and creative learning in relation to the curriculum and educational change. He is also fascinated by children's popular culture and how this can impact on learning. Martin currently coordinates creative learning across a large primary school and leads regular professional development events for other teachers. As a researcher he works independently through the Multiliteracies Learning Initiative, a non-profit research organisation which he founded in 2007. His professional blog is located at http://www.changinghorizons.net

Mick Waters has a range of career experiences that inform his work. Currently, a professor, he works with the schools in the Black Country Challenge in raising standards in the West Midlands. He works with schools in Sheffield in innovative approaches in learning and on several other initiatives to push the boundaries for making learning better. He is also president of the Curriculum Foundation, which seeks to promote a voice for the power and potential of the whole curriculum. He is the chair of 360 People, a company working to encourage young people to be involved in assessing their progress in the development of skills for adult life and employment. Mick is a patron of Heads, Teachers and Industry (HTI), which seeks ways to build reciprocal understanding between sectors, and a trustee of the Children's University which offers a range of learning opportunities beyond the school environment. He is the chair of Curriculum Enrichment for a Common Era, an organisation which promotes multi-cultural understanding through learning. Previously, Mick has worked at the Qualifications and Curriculum Authority as director of Curriculum taking a leading role in helping schools to rethink their approach to curriculum design and influencing national policy on aspects of the national curriculum.

Joanne Waterhouse was educated in London and gained a Bed (Hons) from London University. Her main subject was History. She taught in primary schools for 20 years culminating in serving as a headteacher of a large school in Havering. Before joining the Faculty of Education in Cambridge, Joanne worked as a schools' advisor for a Local Authority and her responsibilities included work as an Ofsted inspector. Joanne subsequently gained a master degree at Cambridge and is currently working to complete her doctoral studies. Her dissertation is focussed on trust and school leadership. As a member of the Faculty, Joanne has been a researcher with a long-term international project that required extensive travel and collaboration with school colleagues from seven countries, including Greece and Norway. She organised conferences for all participants and led seminars and workshops. Joanne also collaborated with Professor John MacBeath on a development and teaching project for youth leaders that was aimed at young people from several Arab countries. She designed and led two weeks of classes and workshops that took place in Cairo. Her work with the Faculty of Education in Cambridge includes (at present): senior tutor and course manager on two routes for the award of master degrees; Research collaborating with school colleagues to learn about pupil engagement and Research on school autonomy.

Wei Kan had been working as a teacher at a high school in Beijing for seven years before he obtained PhD at the University of Manchester, UK in 2007. He is currently working as assistant professor at Institute of Curriculum and Pedagogy, Faculty of Education, Beijing Normal University. He has worked as researcher fellow on a number of project, included teaching effectiveness and school-based curriculum design for Ministry of Education and Beijing Municipal Commission of Education since 2008. His main research interests lie in the comparative curriculum and pedagogy, pupils and teachers' narrative studies and most recently he has worked as an independent consultant to local authorities, and collaborated with colleagues at the Beijing Normal University, on a wide range of Classroom Improvement for secondary schools.

Emma Wisby, before joining the Institute of Education, University of London, worked as a researcher in the field of education and the labour market, conducting research for the UK education department and related government agencies. At the Institute her work has focused on schools policy, teacher professionalism and student voice. She has conducted a review of school councils for the UK government (*Real decision making? School councils in action*, 2007) and assisted with the development of national guidance on student voice (*Working together*, 2008).

This book is dedicated to the memory of Professor Peter Martin, 1949–2009.

Acknowledgements

With most books, it is usually difficult to pinpoint any one single moment or event which authors can say is the sole source of inspiration for the writing which comes out in print months or years later. However, it is clear to us as editors that the inspiration for this volume — for the desire to 'bridge' the academic/practitioner divide — comes largely from conversations (formal, informal and snatched rushed mutterings in busy corridors), planning meetings and working lunches building up to (and extending after) the *Listening to Learners: Partnerships in Action* event held at the Docklands campus of the University of East London (UEL) on Wednesday, 22 April 2009. The excitement of this event — of the mixture of colleagues, leading academics, practitioners, policy-makers and learners — and the vibrancy and diversity of the messages and debates triggered a 'what if' question: 'What if we edited a book of collected writings which continued on from the conference, bringing into print the diversity of voices around 'student voice''? This conference was a meeting point for many leading academics and practitioners — our first steps in *bridging the divide* that is the central characteristic of this collected volume, published two years later. Speaking at the event were some of the contributors to this volume. It was also, sadly, the last time we saw our now departed colleague, Peter Martin, to whom this book is dedicated. We would like to thank colleagues at Emerald for their support in putting this collection together; Ann Slater, Dean of School at the Cass School of Education, University of East London, and Professor Jean Murray, also at the Cass School of Education, for their continued encouragement and guidance; and to all our wonderful contributors for their patience, effort and extraordinary ability to write, to deadline, so impressively and so creatively. Most importantly, we would all like to thank our learners for their stimulating and at times challenging voices.

Foreword

It is more than a hundred years since the first Students' Representative Councils were first established by the Universities (Scotland) Act of 1889. Today, the concept of 'student voice' is no less contested than it was when it was first formally introduced to the ancient Scottish universities. But the context in which debates about the value and nature of student voice is changing rapidly — both within the United Kingdom and internationally — as this handbook demonstrates.

The character of the UK education system has undergone significant change and transformation over successive periods of political reform and, with it, we have seen the ascendancy of the notion of student voice as an expression of 'student consumerism'. For more than a decade, the public sector reform agenda under New Labour was designed to introduce a set of market incentives to drive up quality and standards, involving a radical shift of power from the provider to the user. Catherine Needham described this approach as 'marketplace democracy' in her paper on 'Citizen Consumers':

> The government's agenda for public service reform is concentrated on an objective of maximising "customer satisfaction" and expanding individual choice and competition. (Needham, 2003, p. 6)

In New Labour (and before it New Right) educational 'reforms', parental choice was designed to act as the market incentive for improvement — informed by league tables and underpinned by a diversity of providers from the traditional 'comprehensive' state school to a new breed of specialist schools and city academies. The further and higher education sectors also faced significant re-organisation along market-driven lines, primarily through reforming the funding arrangements for post-14 research, teaching and training to promote a system of 'demand-led provision'. This is not of course UK centric. The discourses and ideologies of marketisation, consumerism and 'choice' have also impacted in other education and other social welfare contexts globally.

Under New Labour, student voice and student consumerism were seen as one and the same — and an essential component of quality improvement. It was an intended consequence of the introduction of university tuition fees for full-time undergraduate students and the expansion of user charging models throughout the further education and skills sector that student consumerism was seen to 'higher standards'. However, it is not simply that students in the Higher Education and lifelong learning sectors pay more and therefore expect more from their experience. Education is increasingly 'sold' to students as an investment that pays dividends in financial and social benefits later on. The system of loans to cover tuition fees and maintenance costs are justified with 'buy now, pay later' messaging from the Government. An increasingly diverse range of state-funded and private providers market themselves to an ever-more discerning generation of students in more sophisticated ways. The notion of student consumerism may be seductive to some public policy makers, but it ultimately offers a reductive vision for our education system; one where students go simply to become certified, rather than educated; and one which leaves the educational process as little more than a commodity to be bought and sold in the market place.

There is an alternative.

This is where authentic student voice comes in. At every level of the education system, there is inherent value for the learner and the teacher in rejecting student consumerism without reverting to the traditional, paternalistic relationship where teacher always knows best and imparts his or her wisdom to the grateful recipient. In both models, students assume a passive role, stifling creativity and minimising opportunities for deeper learning.

In a paper for the Quality Assurance Agency for Higher Education in 2009, Graeme Wise and I argued for an approach to student voice based on the 'community of practice' model developed by Professor Frank Coffield for Learning and Skills Network (Coffield, 2008). Rather than seeing students as consumers or as equal partners — a notion heavily contested by some teaching unions and many academics including some of those writing in this book — learning is viewed as a process of induction. The strength of this model is the emphasis on relationships:

> not only between teachers and students, but between students and other students, at the same time and differing levels of study. It is an approach that calls for cross-disciplinary interaction to happen much more, and in ways that involves students at every level of study. (Streeting & Wise, 2009, p. 3).

Within this model, students are encouraged to become active participants, not only in learning but in the *process of learning*. It rejects individual utilitarianism and puts in its place an alternative model based on community participation and mutually beneficial outcomes. These principles are applicable at every level of the education system. School councils could, and should, be more than a series of discussions about school toilets, uniforms and whether detentions should be abolished. They should be about curriculum, pedagogy and extra curricular provision. This is the role and the value that authentic student voice work can bring: genuine and active participation, changing the nature of educational provision.

Education in the 21st century ought to involve active participation rather than the passive receipt — active in the sense that knowledge is not simply transmitted to students, but explored, shared and even produced through an academic apprentice-ship. It should also be engaging and challenging, rather than merely satisfying.

Learning is often a difficult and frustrating experience and we ought to foster a culture in which students demand an engaging and challenging experience.

As the many case studies in this handbook demonstrate, the debate about student voice and the tensions between the old orthodoxy of 'teacher knows best' and the emerging orthodoxy of student consumerism is not limited to the United Kingdom. But they also point to an emerging body of practice across diverse cultures and educational ecosystems that see student voice — and education itself — as much more than a means to an end.

At a time when education is increasingly valued in terms of its economic utility, there is an urgent need to restate the value of education for its own sake. By connecting students with their learning they are taught to connect with themselves and with others. Education should be personally liberating — not just an exploration of course material but of our individual and collective identities.

In a world still ridden with inequality, education is the best social leveller there is. For those whose beginnings have placed them at the greatest disadvantage, it is too often their first and only chance at breaking the cycle of poverty and deprivation. As Baroness Helena Kennedy QC wrote in her seminal report on lifelong learning, for too many students *if at first they don't succeed, they don't succeed.*

Those students, more than any other, deserve to be heard. A good education, that involves the active engagement and participation of students, can give them that platform.

Wes Streeting
Former President of the
National Union of Students (NUS)

References

Coffield, F. (2008). *What if teaching and learning were really the priority?* London: LSN.

Needham, C. (2003). *Citizen consumers: New Labour's marketplace democracy.* Catalyst Working Paper, London.

Streeting, W., & Wise, G. (2009). *Rethinking the values of higher education – consumption, partnership, community?* London: QAA.

Introduction: Outside Looking In and Inside Looking Out — Attempts at Bridging the Academic/Practitioner Divide

Although the Student Voice agenda gathers momentum in all sectors of education in the United Kingdom so too does the degree to which 'Student Voice' comes under the critical gaze of national and international commentators. Although the focus of Student Voice might have changed in policy, and as each successive government in the UK shapes the agenda as they see fit, the Student Voice movement itself continues to grow. Equally, international responses to Student Voice extend the debate and movement further. To acknowledge international and UK perspectives, this edited collection 'speaks' to both the practitioner and the academic alike. The Student Voice 'movement', is after all, in fact a broad church – it is multi-faceted, itself making inroads into a wide range of other educational practices and agendas from social justice education, concerns with citizenship-rich education and active citizenry, widening participation, safe guarding and action research to name but a few.

The term 'Student Voice' itself is highly contested. As Fielding (2009) suggests, 'Student Voice' is 'a portmanteau term'. In speaking and writing about 'voice' we recognize its role as a 'strategic shorthand' and its limitations (Robinson & Taylor, 2007, p. 6). Since the literature as a whole uses — often interchangeably — 'Student Voice', 'Learner Voice' and 'Pupil Voice' we have done so here, allowing our contributors to set the terms as they see fit. Despite the diversity of reasons why individuals, practitioners and institutions become interested in and involved with student voice work and research, the requirement for capturing and ulitilising voice remains, demonstrated here through a number of different practitioner case studies drawing on different local, national and international contexts. In presenting these different contexts, we are conscious that the Student Voice movement represents something rather special in the field of education — an opportunity for theory and practice, researchers, academics, practitioners, teachers and (most importantly of all) learners to co-construct the meanings of what they do and how, when and why they do it. What is exciting about the Student Voice 'movement' is the diversity of practice and the commitment of learners and practitioners to the principles of social justice, democracy, active citizenry and children's' rights. This diversity is reflected in the contributions to this volume, where we bring together leading national and international academics and practitioners — many of whom are first-time writers.

On some levels, Student Voice is itself fundamentally bound-up with social justice and democracy. On other levels, Student Voice can be seen as a mechanism for school and college improvement. Occasionally schools and colleges pay lip-service to Student Voice and in doing so construct a discourse of 'Student Voice' which operates as a controlling agent — *an additional mechanism of control* (Fielding, 2001, p. 100). Furthermore, some commentators suggest that Student Voice is a 'policy technology' (Ball, 2001) providing 'efficiency gains' which aid and legitimate competition between educational institutions leading to increased marketisation (Fielding & Bragg, 2003; Gunter & Thompson, 2007).

Student Voice that is authentic and inclusive has the potential to subvert, undermine and transform limiting and limited market cultures and this means that there is some genuinely exciting, diverse, radical and meaningful practice 'out there'. However, all too often educational practice is invisible — hidden away with academic and policy-makers' voices taking priority over the stories of teachers and learners themselves. In this volume we seek to readdress this invisibility of practitioners' work and make public the rich diversity of Student Voice practice in local contexts.

Aimed at policy makers and academics; teachers, teacher educators and trainee teachers and other learners in the schools, Further Education and Higher Education context this book offers multiple perspectives and 'voices', drawing on experiences and examples targeting educators and all stakeholders involved in Student Voice initiatives at local and international levels. It is through the combination of these perspectives that, as the title of the book suggests, the Student Voice movement can hope to *bridge the academic/practitioner divide*. Having said this, we recognise that, at times, this is an uneasy bridge, and moreover one built across an obstructive divide. In this volume we offer a number of different (and at times competing) theoretical frameworks and models; we also offer methodological guidance to researchers and practitioners keen to facilitate Student Voice in their work. The contributions in this volume draw on the myriad and over-lapping relationships between Student Voice and action research, citizenship, democratic education and students-as-researchers as well as locating these debates within international perspectives. In doing so, they situate Student Voice as a valuable and powerful mechanism for educational change.

In *Part One* of this book we explore the theoretical tensions and ambiguities in the Student Voice movement. This *Theorizing* (of) *Student Voice* offers a range of competing interpretations of the value and promises of Student Voice. Following on from the theoretical frameworks explored in Part One, in *Part Two* we consider *Student Voice in Practice*. In this section we explore a range of practitioner responses to Student Voice work from early childhood, through primary, secondary and lifelong learning as well as special education and Higher Education. In *Part Three* we consider the *Role of Student Voice in Informing Teachers' Professional Practice*. In doing so, we look at professional partnerships and learning partnerships between institutions, learners, teachers and learners and teachers. We explore how Student Voice can be used in such a way that teachers learn from learners. *Part Four* explores the *Capturing of Student Voice* so essential for the research enquiries that are at the heart of this volume. In this section we discuss the methodological, ethical and practical implications of Student Voice enquiry. Finally, in *Part Five* we turn our attention to *Student Voices Around the World* and offer a number of international and global perspectives from the United States, Kenya, Tanzania, South Africa, Australia, Sweden, China and Brazil.

Our contributors in this uneasy divide between 'academic' and 'practitioner' are both *outside looking in*, and, *inside looking out*. In the case of some contributors to this volume, their practice and research is fully integrated into the often closed worlds of educational institutions. For some of these practitioners this is the first public forum in which their work has been published and presented to an outside audience. The contributors to this volume are themselves varied — as are the contributions they have produced. The stories and voices in this volume are as varied as the movement itself. The contributions in this volume conceive and problematise Student Voice in the following ways:

- Student Voice is a means to institutional development, growth and evolution; involving learners in key democratic decision-making.
- Student Voice is radical and subversive; democratic and empowering, irrespective of government agendas, global market forces and neo-liberal agendas.
- Some commentators in this volume are highly critical of the claims made by Student Voice research to 'empower', whereas others are critical of the 'inauthentic' use of Student Voice — the construction of student voices within managerial discourses.
- For others still, Student Voice is a means to develop young people's citizenry and a means to ensure their safety, inclusion and participation in an ever-changing world. For these contributors, 'authentic' Student Voice has the power to enable learners and teachers to become co-conspirators in the meaning-making process that is democratic education. And this 'learning' extends way beyond the narrow confines of the classroom walls.

This is what we mean by an 'active-citizenship' (Ruddock & Flutter, 2000) in its broadest sense in order to develop learners who can participate in society in a socially responsible fashion we need to involve them in decision-making. We need to encourage and moreover 'allow' young people (and learners of, in fact, all ages) to have a voice as a means of educating them about their own role in the world, as much as their own role in their learning.

Developing research programmes and mechanisms through which voice can be captured is by no means simple. Some Student Voice practice comes with a warning (Ruddock & McIntyre, 2007; Fielding, 2004), namely that cynical attempts to capture learner voice for 'perfomativity' purposes alone end up perpetuating the cynical use of learners as 'objects' passive in their own educational journeys. As educators, we also must be prepared to hear things that we do not like. One thing is for certain, we are all enriched through the process of authentically listening — providing we not only *listen*, but also *hear* and *act*.

Gerry Czerniawski and Warren Kidd
May, 2011.

References

Ball, S. J. (2001). Better read! Theorising the teacher. In: M. Maguire & J. Dillon (Eds), *Becoming a teacher*. Buckingham: Open University Press.

Fielding, M. (2001). Students as radical agents of change. *Journal of Educational Change*, *2*(2), 123–141.

Fielding, M. (2004). Transformative approaches to student voice: Theoretical underpinnings, recalcitrant realities. *British Educational Research Journal*, *30*(2), 295–311.

Fielding, M. (2009). Listening to learners: Partnerships in action conference. *Student voice, democracy and the necessity of radical education.* [Key note presentation] April 22. London: University of East London.

Fielding, M., & Bragg, S. (2003). *Students as researchers; making a difference*. London: Routledge.

Gunter, H., & Thompson, T. (2007). Learning about student voice. *Support for Learning*, *22*(4), 181–188.

Ruddock, J., & Flutter, J. (2000). Pupil participation and the pupil perspective: Carving a new order of experience. *Cambridge Journal of Education*, *30*(1), 75–89.

Ruddock, J., & McIntyre, D. (Eds). (2007). *Improving learning through consulting pupils. Teaching and Learning Research Programme (TLRP) Consulting Pupils Project Team.* London: Routledge.

Robinson, C., & Taylor, C. (2007). Theorising student voice: Values and perspectives. *Improving Schools*, *10*(1), 5–17.

PART ONE
THEORISING STUDENT VOICE

Editors' Summary to Part One

In this first part of the book our authors introduce and explore some of the theoretical tensions and ambiguities within the Student Voice movement. Our first contribution from Michael Fielding reclaims and re-narrates the forgotten histories of Student Voice suggesting that the movement is at a crossroads requiring important choices of direction. Drawing on examples from within traditions of radical democratic education, Fielding presents two typologies in relation to renewed intentions and transformed set of practices associated with Student Voice. The next contribution (Pat Thomson, Chapter 2) examines the history of 'voice' and its association with the liberatory social movements of the twentieth century. Thomson addresses some alternatives to political conceptions of voice and concludes by offering some normative principles to underpin 'voiced' practices, principles which resonate with the origins of the term but which acknowledge the complexities and challenges now faced in the fast and complex twenty first century. Emma Wisby (Chapter 3) considers the drivers behind the recent interest in Student Voice among policy makers and schools and related analysis within the academic literature. The chapter identifies three main drivers in the latest wave of support for Student Voice: the children's rights movement; notions of active citizenship and a related emphasis on young people's development of 'life skills'; and school improvement. Wisby concludes by highlighting the challenges in enabling all students to participate in and benefit from provision for student voice. In the first of two contributions from Rita Cheminais, Chapter 4 examines the moral purpose and underlying philosophy of the British Every Child Matters initiative in relation to its influence in empowering and strengthening the voice of children and young people, and particularly that of the most vulnerable. Her chapter concludes by clarifying the English Coalition Government's policy on the agenda, with the replacement of Every Child Matters with *Help children achieve More*. Tony Breslin (Chapter 5) argues for a re-conceptualisation of school and college communities as both citizenship-rich and human scale — communities in which all voices are listened and to which all voices contribute. Drawing on the author's experience-gained in the classroom, in advisory work and in the leadership of two national charities in the field, Breslin provides an overview of both the history and the drivers of voice related initiatives in the English context and makes a particular connection between this and the emergence of Citizenship Education in English secondary schools. In the final contribution of the first part of this book Charlotte Chadderton draws explicitly on insights from poststructuralist theories in order to interrogate some of the theoretical assumptions which underpin the concern to privilege and capture 'silenced voices' in research with social justice aims. Chadderton concludes with some suggestions for a more complex understanding of student voice research based on these post-structural insights, and argues that this may help us both appreciate the potential of student voice initiatives, while being sensitive to the very real limitations.

Chapter 1

Student Voice and the Possibility of Radical Democratic Education: Re-Narrating Forgotten Histories, Developing Alternative Futures

Michael Fielding

Abstract

To more fully appreciate both the limitations and the range and depth of possibility student voice has to offer, we need to begin to reclaim and re-narrate its forgotten histories. Key examples from within traditions of radical democratic education remind us of alternative realities that prompt and inspire significantly different futures. The strength of the link between many of these alternatives and the quite different values and practices to those of contemporary neo-liberalism suggest the need to take stock of many contemporary preoccupations and assumptions. Two typologies are offered as an aid to a reconceptualised set of intentions and a transformed set of practices. The first typology — 'Patterns of partnership: A democratic alternative' — suggests ways of going beyond techniques of participation to a more fully acknowledged democratic aspiration. The second typology — 'Schools for democracy' — offers a wider institutional framework within which 'Patterns of partnership' can contribute to radical democratic practice. In conclusion, the chapter suggests student voice is at interesting crossroads that require important choices of direction.

Keywords: Radical; democratic; partnership; student voice

The Student Voice Handbook: Bridging the Academic/Practitioner Divide
ISBN: 978-1-78052-040-7

Introduction

The last two decades have seen student voice make enormous strides in many countries across the world in ways that are often interdependent and mutually enriching.

Such is the vibrancy of student voice and the range of research that seeks to deepen and extend its work, we may well be at the beginning of a new phase of its development. If this promise is to be fulfilled and if this new phase is to not merely excite us, but achieve substantial change that is of profound rather than peripheral importance, then we need to take stock before moving on. We need to acknowledge and more deeply understand where we have come from to make wise choices, not only about the kind of schools we want but also about the kind of society we wish to create together.

Forward to Fundamentals, Back to the Future

If we are to demonstrate and develop a belief in the possibility of intergenerational learning between adults and young people coming to understand the world anew in order to cherish and extend what is joyful, adventurous and expressive of a generously conceived common good, then we have to do more than applaud what is interesting and innovative in current work in the field.

We have to be able to make judgements about what is peripheral and what is of enduring value in student voice work at the beginning of this second decade of the 21st century, and we cannot do that unless we do at least two things with seriousness of purpose and hope for the future. Most importantly, we have to return to fundamentals, to our notions of education, not merely their incomplete realisation within the context of contemporary schooling. Schooling is never, and can never be, enough: its claims on our allegiance are necessarily partial and its legitimacy inevitably provisional and renewable. Historically it is a relative newcomer and prospectively its continuation in anything like its current form a matter of debate and contestation. We also have to resist the atemporal mindset in which we work and live, a mindset that insists, both implicitly and explicitly, that (i) There Is No Alternative (TINA) to the market as a guiding principle of our way of life and (ii) consequently consigns history to a market opportunity, or, failing that, an occasional, exotic footnote to the serious business of beatifying the present and sanctifying a future in which neo-liberalism will be more fully and more perfectly realised.

With regard to the first of these concerns — with education as the arbiter of schooling — readers will inevitably and properly have a range of positions on which they base their responses. The standpoint of this chapter is one that not only takes democracy as a pivotal preoccupation of education and schooling, but also further argues for a particular understanding of democracy. In sum, the understanding of education that animates my advocacy of student voice as part of a larger and more inclusive ideal of intergenerational learning, and ultimately of democratic fellowship, rests upon participatory rather than representative traditions of democracy.

With regard to the second concern — with the necessity of historical awareness in the formation of wise judgements about the worth of present developments and future possibilities — I share E. P. Thompson's (1968, p. 13) disquiet about 'the enormous condescension of posterity' that afflicts our wider society and so much contemporary work in the field of education. The consequences of such attitudes are profound. Russell Jacoby (1997, pp. 3–4) is entirely right in his judgement that our 'society has lost its memory, and with it, its mind. The 'inability or refusal to think back takes its toll in the inability to think'. As with fundamental views of education, so with its histories, our first task is to affirm the absolute importance of history as a voice in contemporary conversations about the nature and the future of education and schooling. Our companion task is to recognise and affirm that there is a plurality of histories reflecting particular standpoints, preoccupations and aspirations. Following the advice of Roberto Unger (1998, p. 235), we must *choose* our genealogies, not merely inherit them. For example, just as in her earlier work, Pat Thomson (2005) reminds us of the radical traditions of community organising in the United States, which have for too long been forgotten, so I am here reminding us of two radical examples from my own country, England, which have been subject to the same process of historical amnesia. Just as Pat Thomson chose Saul Alinsky as one of her inspirations, so have I chosen Alex Bloom and Howard Case as mine. The same is true for readers of this book — you must choose a historical narrative that expresses the kind of student voice work you admire and the kind of future to which you aspire. There is no neutral ground to occupy. Student voice is not a technique devoid of aims or purpose: those purposes exist, either explicitly or, more frequently, implicitly in the policy context or wider zeitgeist that gives energy and resonance to its contemporary appeal.

Radical Democratic Alternatives

Constraints of space and purpose forbid anything like an adequate history of student voice in England, let alone the UK, Europe or the wider world. Instead, I offer a preliminary sketch of a small number of radical alternatives that would merit a significant place in many narratives of education in and for democracy as a way of living and learning together. My purpose is to excite and encourage, to prompt a response that leads to radical thought and radical action, to energise an alternative to student voice as articulate consumers and in its stead insist on the necessity of democratic fellowship as both a worthy aspiration and a lived reality. All examples are deliberately taken from the maintained public sector, rather than the alternative private school tradition. This is not to demean the huge importance of pioneers in the radical private sector of education like A. S. Neill (1968) in England and James Aitkenhead in Scotland (Shotton, 1993). Their contributions are of enormous significance, regardless of time and circumstance. Rather, it is to encourage those working in the contexts of publicly funded education to reclaim and re-narrate a radical history of democratic education within the public sector.

The two examples I have chosen are intentionally quite different in terms of age group, everyday context and school population. St. George-in-the-East was a secondary modern school (i.e. a school catering for the vast majority of the state school population) in one of the toughest and poorest parts of London. Epping House School was a residential special school in rural Hertfordshire, England, catering for 'maladjusted' children between the ages of 5 and 12. However, both not only take democracy seriously as a way of living and learning together, the traditions of democracy they espouse and enact are participatory: their allegiance is to deep democracy, democracy that both requires and develops the active participation and responsibility of all, not the representative traditions that we currently presume and with which there is so much contemporary mistrust and disillusionment.

Epping House School — 'a vital, truly democratic community'

The remarkable head teacher of Epping House School in its radical heyday (1958–1974) was Howard Case. In many ways, his approach is best understood through its pivotal practice of the Daily Meeting attended by all staff and young people. Inspired and supported by the similar Weekly Meetings developed by A. S. Neill at Summerhill, the Daily Meeting at Epping House was the central feature of educational and community life of the school. It was here that all significant decisions about how students and staff lived, worked and learned together were taken on a daily basis. The Meeting was chaired by one of the children and normally lasted about an hour. Key elements included an agreed agenda preceded by a cultural activity of some kind such as a piece of music, a play, a talk or an exhibition of work chosen by staff or children (Case, 1966, pp. 133–134).

The order of items on the agenda was crucial. The constraining items, such as the Stop or Veto List in which children whose activities were restrained in some way by the will of the community as expressed in the Meeting, were dealt with first. This was followed by the negotiation of activities that staff were able to offer in the afternoon and evening, after the 11.00 am — 12.30 pm class groups, which the school expected the children to attend. Children were free to choose which activities they wished to take part in or to offer activities of their own or do nothing at all, a proviso Case (1966, p. 134) insisted 'is the most important of all, for a denial of this denies to the child the chance to stand and stare and wait for the welling up of energy'. Then came the allocation of voluntary communal work such as sweeping and cleaning and looking after the dogs and cats that had an important role to play in the emotional reparation and development of many of the children at the school. In Case's (1966, p. 136) view, 'The child must be offered the satisfaction of making a contribution to the community, of taking responsibility for a small area of community life, and of doing a job which is within one's capacity, well'. Then came the discussion/question time in which day-to-day issues were raised by children and staff. These together with Notes of Application with regard to the Veto and Privileges Lists were often 'the kernel of the Meeting' (Purdy, 1965, p. 12).

At its best, the Daily Meeting was seen by Howard Case as central to the kind of education, to the kind of human flourishing he was trying to encourage. In one of the key chapters of his book in which he reflects on the many detailed examples of community meetings, he pauses thus,

> I wonder if any society whose aim it is to produce a maturing membership can function without a meeting. The whole character of our community was noticeably different, I believe, because of it; there was the feeling as verbalised by one child to another in confidence, but overheard: 'We run this place.' In this remark, there was no feeling of: 'We run it against the adults or without adults.' 'We' meant 'all of us.' (Case, 1978, p. 71)

Rejecting the notion of 'self-government by children' as ridiculous on the grounds that he 'could not see why any community that relied heavily on adults should be run by children', Case (1978, p. 71) opted instead for 'shared responsibility', most prominently developed by David Wills (1948, 1966, 1970) in which, while the vast majority of decisions were indeed shared, adults retained control over a small number of key decisions, usually to do with matters of safety or health. Meetings were about the exercise of reasoned consent through the development of 'a fully participating community where each experienced the right to help, according to ability, in framing the laws or day to day arrangements' (Case, 1978, p. 71); a just community that encouraged 'the right to fullest self-realisation but not at the expense of others and the right of the community to restrain those who wished to destroy its institutions' (Case, 1978, p. 71).

St. George-in-the-East Secondary School, London — 'a consciously democratic community'

Despite the fact that he is virtually unknown today, Alex Bloom is, in many ways, one of the most compelling pioneers of radical secondary education we have ever had in England. After many years of what the *Times* obituary called 'quite orthodox school mastering' (Anon, 1955) on 1 October 1945 at St. George-in-the-East Secondary Modern School in Cable Street, Stepney in the East End of London, he set out to build what he described in his own words as 'A consciously democratic community ... without regimentation, without corporal punishment, without competition' (Bloom, 1948, p. 121).

This firmness of purpose and its pervasive coherence in all aspects of the school's structural organisation and cultural articulation was key to St. George-in-the-East's success. Equally important was Bloom's (1948, p. 120) commitment to exploring and developing with staff 'through peaceful penetration, courage and patience', an orienting set of perspectives that became known as 'Our Pattern'. Fundamentally, this was about the eradication of fear as the prime incentive to 'progress'. Thus, for

Alex Bloom (1952, pp. 135–136), 'Fear of authority [… imposed for disciplinary purposes]; fear of failure [… by means of marks, prizes and competition, for obtaining results]; and the fear of punishment [for all these purposes]' must be replaced by 'friendship, security and the recognition of each child's worth'. In his view, one of the main tasks of the school was to create a context for human flourishing that valued the contribution of each person and worked hard to develop a creative and responsive school community worthy of the loyalty and commitment of all its students.

The curricular and interpersonal opportunities the school offered, what one might call its existential framework of democracy, emphasised the importance of an approach to learning called the School Study in which the majority of the formal curriculum was co-constructed in each of the form groups within the context of thematic work, culminating in a School Conference in which work was celebrated and reviewed in both mixed-age and form groups. The remainder of the curriculum was negotiated through mixed-age Electives in which 'children make up their own timetable' (Bloom, 1953, p. 176). There was thus substantial emphasis, not only on communally situated choice exercised on a daily basis. There was also a recognition of the importance both of continuity of relationships with a class teacher and of multifaceted communal engagement with other students and staff. At the heart of these arrangements lay an immensely strong belief in what I have elsewhere called 'the insistent affirmation of possibility' (Fielding, 2008) and its resultant hostility to any kind of ability grouping or means of labelling children. Furthermore, students' own evaluations of their curricular experience in both its broad and narrow senses were sought and acted on through Weekly Reviews in which each student commented in writing on any aspect of learning and teaching they felt appropriate.

The formal democratic organisation of the school was imaginative, responsive and highly sophisticated (see Fielding, 2005, 2009, for a more detailed account). One of its most innovative features was the School Council and its attendant School Meeting. The first thing to be said is that it was a *school* council that involved all 10 teachers and 200 students gathering together in the hall to reflect on their work and lives together, a form of democratic engagement intended to promote intergenerational learning through lived, communal responsibility. Purposes and aspirations, the touchstones of meaning-making, framed the opening and closing of the event; a framework of reflection, dialogue, disagreement and celebration enabled contributions from all ages and identities in ways that challenged traditional hierarchies within the context of an insistent, demanding mutuality. A range of voices were heard, not only through the narratives of learning but also through the leveller of laughter and the eagerness of exploration. And through all this ran the excitement of the unpredictable and the reassurance of shared responsibility.

From the experience of School Meetings and the enormous range of democratic practices that informed the daily life of the school, 'a constitution (was) drawn up and accepted by the school' (Bloom, 1953, p. 175). For external legal reasons, Alex Bloom, as head teacher, had the power of veto over any decision made by the School Council/School Meeting. However, as he points out in a paper written two years before his tragic death at the school, 'I am required to explain to an extraordinary meeting of the School Council the reason for my use of it. So far the occasion has not arisen' (Bloom, 1953, p. 175). Summing up his reflections on the way the school lived and learned democracy on a daily basis he concludes thus,

> It will be seen that we, as teachers, have very little power. Nor do we need it. We are, by the nature of our work, in authority. Our School Council prevents us from being authoritarian. A large part of the school organization is in the hands of the children themselves, and the value of the experiences afforded by the School Council in responsible, democratic and constructive living is great. To the children the school becomes *our* school with a consequent enrichment of community feeling. (Bloom, 1953, p. 175)

Why Radical Traditions Matter

My hope is that in very briefly reclaiming and re-narrating these two remarkable examples of what I have elsewhere (Fielding & Moss, 2011) called 'prefigurative practice' — that is, grounded and inspirational practice that anticipates and develops more just, more humanly fulfilling future ways of being — I have, at least in part, justified my earlier insistence on our choosing radical genealogies, alternative histories that deny the dreary insistence of contemporary neo-liberalism that There Is No Alternative to an increasingly desperate *status quo*.

Before picking up on the kinds of values and purposes that animated these approaches and juxtaposing them with much contemporary student voice work, I want to reaffirm my insistence (a) that these inspirational examples both draw on and contribute to radical traditions of educational practice and aspiration that we have either forgotten about, marginalised or denied and (b) that these alternative traditions offer an important practical and intellectual resource for many adults and young people working in the field.

Thus, in coming to understand Alex Bloom's work more fully, we are naturally led to the writing of contemporaries like James Hemming (1948, 1980) who knew Bloom well; to the radical traditions of progressive state education that include companion pioneers like Teddy O'Neill (Burke, 2005) and to torch-bearing successors like Michael Duane (Berg, 1968), Bob Mackenzie (Murphy, 1998) and John Watts (1977, 1980) in the United Kingdom (see Berg, 1971; Shotton, 1993; Wright, 1989 for useful overviews of this tradition).

In coming to understand Howard Case's work, we are naturally led not only to A. S. Neill (whom he knew well) but also to Neill's predecessors in the radical traditions of therapeutic education like Homer Lane (Bazeley, 1928; Stinton, 2005) and to his contemporaries like Otto Shaw (1965) and David Wills (1948, 1960) (see Bridgeland, 1971; Shotton, 1993; Weaver, 1989, for useful over views).

These examples put much of our current work on student voice into a humbling and suitably modest perspective. They also contrast markedly with the corrosive nature of market-led approaches to education and schooling, which, insofar as they ever overtly approach matters of democracy, invariably reduce them to the querulous voice of customer and the hectoring collectivity of visceral self-interest. As Michael Sandel (2009, p. 4) so eloquently and so incisively reminds us,

> Democratic governance is radically devalued if reduced to the role of handmaiden to the market economy. Democracy is about more than fixing and tweaking and nudging incentives to make markets work better ... (it) is about much more than maximising GDP, or satisfying consumer preferences. It's also about seeking distributive justice; promoting the health of democratic institutions; and cultivating the solidarity, and sense of community that democracy requires. Market-mimicking governance — at its best — can satisfy us as consumers. But it can do nothing to make us democratic citizens.

Patterns of Partnership — A Democratic Alternative

The kinds of arguments that Sandel is seeking to make and the daily realities of democratic schooling developed by radical pioneers like Alex Bloom and Howard Case point to an approach to student voice that is still very much in the minority at the present time.

In what I call the high-performance, market perspective (Table 1.1) individuals are encouraged to see themselves as consumers or customers who are required to make choices, to constantly reinvent themselves in an unending pursuit of material and instrumental gain. Key drivers are individual ambition and aspiration. The institutional expressions of these orientations are found in schools that themselves seek an advantageous market position. Here, student voice is important because in listening to students, the school becomes a more accountable and more effective learning organisation and thus better at meeting its core responsibilities.

Table 1.1: High-performance schooling *through* market accountability.

Individual perspective **Personalised learning**	*Collective perspective* **High-performance schooling**
Driver Individual ambition	*Driver* Fully informed accountability
Dominant model Consumer choice	*Dominant model* Learning organisation

Key question
What job do I wish
    to have?
	Key question
	How can we learn from everyone to achieve
	    better outcomes?

Table 1.2: Person-centred education *for* democratic fellowship.

Personal perspective **Person-centred education**	*Communal perspective* **Creative society**
Driver Personal development	*Driver* Shared responsibility for a better future
Dominant model Relational dialogue	*Dominant model* Learning community
Key question What kind of person do I wish to become?	*Key question* How can we develop an inclusive, creative society together?

In contrast to a market-led, high-performance model, a person-centred, democratic approach to education presumes quite different intentions and processes. As illustrated in Table 1.2, key drivers are more holistic, inclusive and other-regarding in their orientation and more dialogic in their processes. At an individual level, the main concern is how one lives a good and fulfilling life; at a collective level, it concerns how best to co-create, with adults and with other young people, a good society, a democratic fellowship and a better world.

If we now apply these two contrasting perspectives to a typology of student voice that helps us to go beneath the surface of student involvement and begin to ask searching questions about the nexus of power and purposes that lie at the heart of these developments, we come up with two very different kinds of practice.

Acknowledging the groundbreaking work of people like Roger Hart (1992) and Harry Shier (2001) in the last decade, I have become increasingly convinced of the need to not only develop a tool for distinguishing different kinds of intergenerational partnership within the complexities and specificities of school based contexts, but also name and explore participatory democracy as a legitimate and increasingly urgent aspiration.

The typology — *Patterns of Partnership: How adults listen to and learn with students in schools* — (Table 1.3) suggests six forms of interaction between adults and young people within a school and other educational contexts.

Elsewhere (Fielding, 2011), I have illustrated and explored what each of these forms of partnership looks and feels like in practice. What is particularly pertinent here is to underscore the difference a democratic fellowship perspective makes to what actually goes on and the kinds of changes that result from this way of working.

Take, for example, the sixth pattern of partnership, *Intergenerational learning as lived democracy*. At classroom level, this might involve staff, students and museum staff planning a visit to a museum for younger students. At unit/team/department level, this might take the form of classes acting as critical friends to one another in the wider context of a thematic or interdisciplinary project within or between years. At whole school level, this might express itself through the development of whole School Meetings that are such an important iconic practice within the radical traditions of education.

Table 1.3: Patterns of partnership: How adults listen to and learn with students in school.

Instrumental dimension	6. **Intergenerational learning as lived democracy** • Shared commitment to/responsibility for the common good	*Fellowship dimension*
High-performance schooling *through* **market accountability**	5. **Students as joint authors** • Students and staff decide a joint course of action together	**Person-centred education** *for* **democratic fellowship**
	4. **Students as knowledge creators** • Students take lead roles with active staff support	
	3. **Students as co-enquirers** • Staff take a lead role with high-profile, active student support	
	2. **Students as active respondents** • Staff invite student dialogue and discussion to deepen learning/professional decisions	
	1. **Students as data source** • Staff utilise information about student progress and well-being	

It is, of course, possible to approach this sixth pattern of partnership from the standpoint of market models of democracy. Here, while plural in form, it is often individualistic in intent. Thus, planning a lesson for younger students or acting as critical friends for other classes could primarily be exercises in individual skill development rather than lived contributions to the common good. In contrast to this predominantly instrumental approach, the participatory traditions argue for democracy, not only as a way of meeting individual needs and arriving at collective decisions and aspirations, but also as a way of living and being in the world that intends an always open common good and the egalitarian freedom of democratic fellowship that shapes our daily encounters.

Fellowship readings of lived democracy foreground the importance of rich involvement of all participants in pursuit of communal aspirations. Thus, the kinds of School Meetings for which I am arguing are not those that attend with forensic energy to matters of procedure or the minutiae of form. Rather, they are those that acknowledge that democratic living requires more than procedural fidelity. It transcends justice: it is more-than-political; it is a way of life within which democratic fellowship is both the *raison d'être* and the means of its realisation. Democratic community, with the daily Meeting at its centre, is important because its explicitly egalitarian form enables a deep and demonstrable reciprocity, thereby providing both existential and practical testimony of the need for and presence, if not of love, then of care, of kindness, of human fellowship and the reciprocal needs of recognition. Indeed, for some key figures in the radical traditions, the main virtue of the Meeting with its egalitarian openness and mutuality had less to do with the procedural exploration of individual and collective intention than its capacity to enable us to engage the person behind the persona, to help us to 're-see' each other, to unsettle presumption and so reaffirm freedom as the centripetal value of democratic community.

Schools for Democracy

If *Patterns of partnership* point to various ways in which we can develop more democratic ways of working together in schools, my 10-point *Schools for democracy* suggests a wider institutional framework within which they can contribute to radical democratic practice (see Fielding & Moss, 2011 for a more detailed account).

1 *Education in and for radical democracy*
 • A proclaimed, not just an intended, democratic vitality, albeit one that bears in mind the constraints of context and circumstance.
2 *Radical structures and spaces*
 • Insistence on a permanent and proper provisionality.
 • Residual unease with hierarchy.
 • Transparent structures that encourage ways of working that transcend boundaries and invite new combinations and possibilities.
 • Interpersonal and architectural spaces that encourage a multiplicity of different forms of formal and informal engagement with a multiplicity of persons.
 • Preeminence of the General Meeting within which the whole community reflects on its shared life, achievements and aspirations. Here, young people and adults make meaning of their work together, returning tenaciously and regularly to the imperatives of purpose, not merely to the mechanics of accomplishment.
3 *Radical roles*
 • 'Role defiance and role jumbling' (see Unger, 2005) among staff but also between staff and students. See *Patterns of Partnership* earlier.
4 *Radical relationships*
 • 'Re-see' each other as persons, not just as role occupants.
 • Nurture a new understanding, sense of possibility and felt respect between adults and young people.
 • Joy in each other's being and a greater sense of shared delight, care and responsibility.
5 *Personal and communal narrative*
 • Multiple spaces and opportunities for young people and adults, to making meaning of their work, both personally and as a community.
 • Necessary connection with radical traditions of education.

6 *Radical curriculum, critical pedagogy and enabling assessment*
   The formal and informal curriculum must:
   - Equip young people and adults with the desire and capacity to seriously interrogate what is given and co-construct a knowledge that assists in leading good and joyful lives together.
   - Start with the cultures, concerns and hopes of the communities that the school serves.
   - Include integrated approaches to knowledge with students and staff working in small communities of enquiry.

   Critical pedagogy:
   - A reciprocity of engagement and involvement not only with the immediate community but also with other communities and ways of being, at local, regional, national and international levels.

   Enabling assessment:
   - Forms of assessment at both national and local levels that have the flexibility to respond to the particularities of context.
   - At classroom level — high levels of peer and teacher involvement through assessment-for-learning approaches and additional community and family involvement through public, portfolio-based presentations.

7 *Insistent affirmation of possibility*
   - A generosity of presumption that requires us to keep options open, to counter the confinement of customary or casual expectation.
   - Refuse ability grouping, promote emulation rather than competition and privilege intrinsic motivation and communal recognition over the paraphernalia of marks and prizes.

8 *Engaging the local*
   - Education as a lifelong process and the school a site of community renewal and responsibility in which young and old explore what it means to live good lives together.
   - School and community seen as reciprocal resources for broadly and more narrowly conceived notions of learning.

9 *Accountability as shared responsibility*
   - Democratic accountability better understood and enacted as a form of 'shared responsibility'.
   - Accountability as morally and politically situated, not merely technically and procedurally 'delivered'.
   - Develop new forms of accountability better suited to a more engaged understanding of democratic living.

10 *Regional, national and global solidarities*
   - Regional, national and global solidarities made real through reciprocal ideological, material and interpersonal support.
   - Value-driven networks and alliances that draw on and contribute to the dynamic of radical social movements.

Conclusion

Student voice is at interesting crossroads, and for those of us working in the field, there are some important choices to make about where we direct our energies and what view of society and human flourishing invites our commitment. Are we committed to a consumer-oriented, market-led approach that, as Gerry Cohen (1994, p. 9) uncomfortably reminds us, 'is typically some mixture of greed and fear' or are we prepared to reclaim and reimagine other approaches that presume quite different accounts of what it is to be and become more fully human?

It is time to take democracy seriously, and, in significant part, taking it seriously means reminding ourselves that representative — or, as they are sometimes called, elitist — approaches to democracy provide only one set of possibilities. For me, it is the alternative, participatory — or, as they are sometimes called, classical — traditions of democracy that suggest ways of living and learning together that offer a more inspirational, if more challenging, aspiration. The work of Alex Bloom and Howard Case, to which I referred earlier in this chapter, reminds us that these ways of working are not only possible within public sector schools: they, and the radical democratic traditions to which they belong, also develop a more worthy and more creative view of education than anything we are likely to find in market-led models currently benighting our daily work with young people in schools.

Unless schools themselves become more fully democratic institutions and unless democracy shapes the way we live and learn together, we will fail to achieve our wider democratic aspirations and continue to perpetuate the presumption of privilege and the smiling face of unguent condescension that so disgracefully disfigure our current political arrangements. In the resonant words of Shelia Rowbotham (1979, p. 140), 'Some changes have to start now, else there is no beginning for us'.

References

Anon. (1955). Obituary: Mr A.A. Bloom. *The Times*, September 24, p. 9.

Bazeley, E. (1928). *Homer lane and the little commonwealth*. London: Allen & Unwin.

Berg, L. (1968). *Risinghill: Death of a comprehensive school*. Harmondsworth: Penguin.

Berg, L. (1971). Moving towards self-government. In: P. Adams, L. Berg, N. Berger, M. Duane, A. S. Neill & R. Ollendorff (Eds.), *Children's rights* (pp. 9–53). London: Elek.

Bloom, A. A. (1948). Notes on a school community. *New Era*, *29*(6), 120–121.

Bloom, A. A. (1952). Learning through living. In: M. A. Pink (Ed.), *Moral foundations of citizenship* (pp. 135–143). London: London University Press.

Bloom, A. A. (1953). Self-government, study & choice at a secondary modern school. *New Era*, *34*(9), 174–177.

Bridgeland, M. (1971). *Pioneer work with maladjusted children: A study of the development of therapeutic education*. London: Staples Press.

Burke, C. (2005). 'The school without tears': E.F.O'Neill of Prestolee. *History of Education*, *34*(3), 263–275.

Case, H. (1966). A therapeutic discipline for living. *New Era, 47*(7), 131–136.

Case, H. (1978) Loving us: A new way of education. Privately published [copy held by London University Institute of Education Library, Classmark zz SA6390].

Cohen, G. A. (1994). Back to socialist basics. *New Left Review, 207*, September/October, 3–16.

Fielding, M. (2005). Alex Bloom: Pioneer of radical state education. *Forum, 47*(2&3), 119–134.

Fielding, M. (2008). On the necessity of radical state education: Democracy and the common school. *Journal of Philosophy of Education, 41*(4), 549–557.

Fielding, M. (2009). Public space and educational leadership: Reclaiming and renewing our radical traditions. *Educational Management, Administration and Leadership, 37*(4), 497–521.

Fielding, M. (2011). Patterns of partnership: Student voice, intergenerational learning and democratic fellowship. In: N. Mocker & J. Nias *Rethinking educational practice through reflexive research: Essays in honour of Susan Groundwater-Smith*. New York, NY: Springer.

Fielding, M., & Moss, P. (2011). *Radical education and the common school — A democratic alternative*. London: Routledge.

Hart, R. (1992). *Children's participation: From tokenism to citizenship*. Florence: UNICEF International Child Development Centre.

Hemming, J. (1948). Standards of social health in the school community. *New Era, 29*(6), 121–127.

Hemming, J. (1980). *The betrayal of youth: Secondary education must be changed*. London: Marion Boyars.

Jacoby, R. (1997). Revisiting 'social amnesia'. *Society, 35*(1), 58–60. [This article is the revised preface to the 1996 edition of his book *Social Amnesia*, first published in 1977].

Murphy, P. A. (1998). *The life of R.F. MacKenzie: A prophet without honour*. Edinburgh: John Donald.

Neill, A. S. (1968). *Summerhill*. Harmondsworth: Penguin.

Purdy, B. (1965). Epping House School — A study in the treatment of juvenile maladjustment. *Id* (15), 9–14.

Rowbotham, S. (1979). The women's movement and organizing for socialism. In: S. Rowbotham, L. Segal & H. Wainwright (Eds.), *Beyond the fragments: Feminism and the making of socialism* (pp. 21–155). London: Merlin Press.

Sandel, M. (2009). A new politics of the common good, Lecture 4, BBC Reith Lectures, 30 June.

Shaw, O. L. (1965). *Maladjusted boys*. London: Allen & Unwin.

Shier, H. (2001). Pathways to participation: Openings, opportunities and obligations. *Children and Society, 15*(2), 107–117.

Shotton, J. (1993). *No master high or low: Libertarian education and schooling in Britain 1890–1990*. Bristol: Libertarian Education. (see Chapter 8 'Free as a Bird').

Stinton, J. (2005). *A dorset utopia: The little commonwealth and homer lane*. Norwich: Black Dog Books.

Thompson, E. P. (1968). *The making of the English working class*. Harmondsworth: Penguin.

Thomson, P. (2005). Who's afraid of Saul Alinsky? Radical traditions in community organizing. *Forum, 47*(2&3), 199–206.

Unger, R. M. (1998). *Democracy realized*. London: Verso.

Unger, R. M. (2005). *What should the left propose?*. London: Verso.

Watts, J. (Ed.) (1977). *The countesthorpe experience*. London: Allen & Unwin.

Watts, J. (1980). *Towards an open school*. London: Longman.

Weaver, A. (1989). Democratic practice in education: An historical perspective. In: C. Harber & R. Meighan (Eds.), *The democratic school: Educational management and the practice of democracy* (pp. 83–91). Ticknall: Education Now.

Wills, W. D. (1948). Shared responsibility. In: New Education Fellowship (Ed.), *Problems of child development: A contribution to the understanding of children's needs* (pp. 79–83). London: New Education Fellowship.

Wills, W. D. (1960). *Throw away thy rod: Living with difficult children*. London: Gollancz.

Wills, W. D. (1966). Persuasive discipline. *War resistance*, *2*(18–19), 25–28.

Wills, W. D. (1970). Symposium on shared responsibility: An introduction. *Therapeutic Education*, Autumn, pp. 20–22.

Wright, N. (1989). *Assessing radical education: A critical review of the radical movement in english schooling 1960–1980*. Milton Keynes: Open University Press.

Chapter 2

Coming to Terms with 'Voice'

Pat Thomson

Abstract

Because the term 'voice' is now used to describe a range of very different processes in policy, research and practice, it is arguable that it has become almost meaningless — it works as an empty jug into which people can pour any meaning that they choose. In this chapter, I aim to support the recuperation of the term. I examine the history of 'voice' and its association with the liberatory social movements of the twentieth century. I discuss challenges to the notion of voice, for example, difference and plurality, bodies and actions, and (multi)-media for communication and meaning-making. I address some alternatives to political conceptions of voice and conclude by offering some normative principles to underpin 'voiced' practices, principles that resonate with the origins of the term but that acknowledge the complexities and challenges now faced in the fast and complex twenty-first century.

Keywords: Voice; social movements; consultation; democracy; appropriation

Introduction

Does the idea of 'voice' now mean anything at all? Policy-makers, practitioners and researchers around the world regularly refer to it; a myriad of documents suggest how 'voice' can be solicited and offer reasons that range from the utilitarian to the idealistic to say why it is important. One could be forgiven for thinking that 'voice' is now an empty jug into which any number of competing meanings can be conveniently poured for any number of contradictory ends.

The Student Voice Handbook: Bridging the Academic/Practitioner Divide
ISBN: 978-1-78052-040-7

I aim, in this chapter, to support more critical examinations of the multiple usages of 'student voice'. I first of all canvass the political history of the term 'voice' and its association with liberation social movements of the twentieth century. I discuss the challenges to this notion of 'voice' and consider what theorisations of 'voice' found in poststructuralist and literary traditions might have to offer political understandings. I conclude with a heuristic frame for examining 'voice'; this is intended to complement existing critical framings.

A Rough Guide to 'Voice': Political Voices

The notion of political representation was and is integral to struggles for universal suffrage. In the Western world, the women's suffrage movement for example had a strong focus not only on getting the vote but also on getting women into parliament in order that women's particular experiences, perspectives and needs could be reported and thus inform and change political agendas. This however was not generally called 'voice'; rather, the focus was on the parliamentary practices associated with citizenship and democracy.

The development of 'voice' as a discrete political category ascribed to an idea, and ideal practice, is strongly associated with the social movements of the post-war period. The civil rights (United States) and women's movements (Europe, United States, Australia and New Zealand), for example, mobilised a rhetoric of 'voice' to express the right to participate more broadly in public life. Both histories (herstories) were understood retrospectively as part of wider and longer-term social contestations for emancipation and the overthrow of exploitation and oppression and removal of discriminatory laws and practices — see, for example, Solomon's (1991) *A 'voice' of their own* about the role of the women's press and Hampton and Fayer's (1990) *'Voices of freedom'* on the life experiences of ordinary people in local settings. Social movements not only saw government and representation in all spheres of governing activities as important but also extended their concerns to all aspects of social and cultural life; they included not only leaders and notable figures as having 'voice' but also championed rights of 'the people' to 'voice' their everyday experiences.

'Voice' has thus come to be associated with a range of public activities and institutions. It still includes government and representation in governing but now goes much further. It covers media, for example, where concerns may be expressed about the ways in which 'voice' from socially powerful groups are privileged over other, less advantaged 'voice'. It covers historical events, where the 'voice' of victims of injustice become an anthology of stories, which changes the public record of past events; the Australian Stolen Generation Royal Commission and the Truth and Reconciliation Commission in South Africa are two examples of this kind of public 'voicing'. And it covers research, where social scientists are now often concerned to use methods that allow previously subjugated 'voices', and the knowledges that these carry, to become integral to the scholarly archive (e.g. Riley & Docking, 2004; Rubin & Silva, 2003; Smyth & Hattam, 2001).

Today, having a 'voice' is still associated with political activities in the public sphere, but this is associated with varying degrees of agency and rights. 'Voice' can be understood as a right to:

• an opportunity to express opinions
• access to events and people to influence decisions
• active participation in deliberation about decisions and events.

Political 'voice' thus sits on what is sometimes described as a 'strong or 'weak' democratic continuum (Barber, 1984), and what counts as citizens' activities varies accordingly. Furthermore, there are significant national differences in Western democracies that go to the degree of control that is exercised over the right to have a 'voice' and to speak out — debates about free speech and censorship, for example, are strongly connected to national constitutional and common law settlements that adjudicate different beliefs about the rights of the individual vis-à-vis the broader society.

'Voice' as a political concept brings together past and present, emotional and intellectual ways of knowing, public and private, various parts of social and cultural life, and truths and fictions. 'Voice' is inherently concerned with questions of power and knowledge, with how decisions are made, who is included and excluded and who is advantaged and disadvantaged as a result. Weak forms of 'voice' generally support the *status quo* or aim for modest reforms. The strongly democratic use of 'voice' equates to a call for a public sphere in which there is dialogue, reciprocity, recognition and respect. Reaching that utopian state is understood as a struggle to be heard, listened to and taken seriously. This kind of 'voice' continues in a direct line from its historical origins. Arguably, 'voice' is a concept that cannot be disconnected from concerns for a more just and equal society. It is not too much of a stretch to argue that weak versions of 'voice' that shore up the *status quo* are, in reality, re-writing history.

The 'Voice' of Children and Young People

Children however do not have the same rights to political 'voice' as adults. Whether they ought to have such rights is often disputed. Whereas some argue that children are the last group to be afforded suffrage, others suggest that children are not mature enough to even understand the issues at stake in public debates, let alone vote. There is considerable debate about the age at which children can assume adult responsibilities, and in most countries, there is a morass of different dates at which children can be tried in adult courts, make their own decisions about health issues, leave home, enter the workforce and so on. Nevertheless, there have been moves in most countries to extend to children the power to have some say in things that concern them.

One important contemporary indicator of the shift to acknowledge the importance of children's 'voice' can be found in the UN Convention on the Rights of the Child (United Nations [UN], 1989), which focuses on specific instances where children need to have a say; for example, it stipulates children the right to have some say about which parent they wish to live with (article 9). The Convention also asserts more general rights — to express views freely in all matters affecting them, be heard in legal proceedings and to enjoy freedom of expression and to 'seek, receive and impart information … orally, in writing or in print, in the form of art, or through any other media of the child's choice' (article 12). There are now, in countries that are signatories to the Convention, initiatives that follow these more general rights and there are official guides, advice and requirements for institutions and organisations to make provision for the 'voice' of children and young people to be heard.

This is the context in which 'student voice' has been promoted and contested.

Conceptual Problems with 'Voice'

Recent moves to support the spread of approaches to children's 'voice' have identified a number of problematic issues arising from the term itself as well as with the material ways in which the idea has been taken up. In this section, I focus on the former and take up the practical issues in the following section.

Concerns about the concept of 'voice' are numerous, but here, I focus on (1) singularity, (2) purpose, (3) embodiment, (4) authenticity, (5) language and (6) etiquette.

(1) *Singularity — 'voice' is a unitary noun; there is one 'voice' singular, not 'voices' plural*

Concern is often expressed that the use of the singular noun implies that what counts as children's 'voice' is a unified and single view — and that this is what is expected. Children and young people, just like any other social category, are of course not a homogeneous group; gender, religion, ethnicity and race, dis/ability and sexuality, location and participation in youth and other cultural pastimes are only some of the ways in which difference manifests within the social category. It is not only highly unrealistic to expect that there will be a simple and united 'voice' emanating from children but deeply problematic if differences are not encouraged and recognised. Children-as-researchers is often suggested as one way to allow the generation of multiple perspectives that are then rigorously analysed to arrive at a feasible explanation or action (Fielding & Bragg, 2003; Thomson & Gunter, 2008).

(2) *Purpose — children are asked, or choose to exercise 'voice' for different reasons*

A further concern is that 'voice' is elicited for a single purpose. Children do not always talk about the same kinds of things, any more than adults. Furthermore, adults may wish to engage children's 'voice' for different reasons. Some researchers have developed typologies of different types of 'voice' — Hadfield and Haw (2001) nominate authoritative (a representative 'voice' exercised in governance), critical (challenging the *status quo*) and therapeutic (discussing life circumstances); Bragg

(2007b) offers in addition the notion of a consumer 'voice' (responding to market research). These variations could of course be added to *ad infinitum*; the point is not to develop a complex typology of adjective + 'voice' to cover every conceivable situation, but to take account of the ways in which purpose and context require and produce different kinds of responses.

(3) *Embodiment — 'voice' is disembodied*

The concern here is that speech may be privileged over other forms of bodily expression. In the digital age, disembodied conversations are not unusual of course, but bodies in and of themselves can communicate — or 'give off' (Goffman, 1963) — important information. This can be in the form of what is often called non-verbal communication — gaze, expressions, stance and gestures — which can be either conscious or involuntary. But bodily communication includes other aspects, for example, adornment such as tattooing, or the wearing of particular kinds of clothes and symbols of attachment, which are intended to 'speak' and to indicate something of the chosen identity, attitudes, interests, pastimes and affiliations of the wearer.

(4) *Authenticity — 'voice' is understood as consistent and pure*

All 'voice'/s is/are situated, particular and partial; this is particularly an issue for researchers who must be wary of privileging 'voice'(s) over other forms of information and taking responses to questions as unwavering truth. People do not always behave in the same way. They may say one thing to one person and something different to another. They may feel constrained in some circumstances and offer what they think they are expected to say or they may be afraid of reprisals if they are honest. Or they may simply change their mind about what they think after having new information or as a result of reflection or because they just happen to feel differently. This means that those wanting to work with 'voice' ought neither to see it as a one-off event nor to think that what they hear is either a pure and unadulterated truth or a lie. As Bragg (2010, p. 31) points out, it is naïve to think that children can be given or find their 'voice', as if it is a pathway to some kind of authentic core being.

(5) *Language — 'voice' is expressed in words*

We are now immersed in a world of moving and still images combined with a variety of spoken and written texts; this pervasive digital media is now a dominant mode of communication yet is often not equated with the idea of 'voice'. The idea of 'voice' still seems to be connected with speech acts and events. This lens can exclude as many as it includes and narrow the range of what it is possible to discuss. A focus on 'voice' might deflect attention away from the reality that children use various forms of media and genres of expression. This is not the same as saying that children have preferences for visual or kinesthetic modes of communication, but rather it is that all of us live in multi-mediated worlds with various opportunities and affordances for expression. Additionally, many people, including children, often find aesthetic modes of expression — for example, through the performing and visual arts — a self-fulfilling and effective means of making sense of the world and communicating ideas.

(6) *Etiquette — 'voice' must be exercised in particular ways and at particular times*

There is a range of social rules about how 'good' communication happens. A well-mannered person speaks when spoken to, does not interrupt and says what they have to say succinctly and without giving offence. The corollary of this is that those who break these social rules are not regarded as exercising their right to speak appropriately; they are not taking responsibility for their speech actions. The history outlined at the beginning of this chapter suggests that political 'voice' is not always of the polite kind. Although social movements have attempted to use the 'right channels' through which to speak, they have also spoken up and out in ways that are confronting and challenging to those in charge. This antisocial 'voice' is an important option for those who find themselves without conventional avenues to have their say. Despite parenting being in part about the inculcation of manners and morals, children do not always exercise 'voice' in ways that are conformist, and it is often difficult for adults, particularly teachers who are charged with ensuring good social behaviour and etiquette, to understand a frustrated outburst expressed in the vernacular as a form of 'voice'. It is often easier to dismiss this as loutish behaviour, rather than allowing for the possibility that something is being said that deserves attention.

Given these problems that arise when using the terminology of political 'voice', are there any alternative ways of thinking that might assist, and any avenues of practical action, that might allow us to fulfil the aspirations embedded in the notion of 'voice'?

Practical Problems with 'Student Voice'

Student 'voice' refers to the processes through which schools and colleges ensure that children and young people, individually and collectively, are able to speak up about their education. Within the sector, it is argued that children and young people have specific perspectives on education derived from their particular experiences as students — they see the school as no adult does or can. These insights are crucial in the processes of change/improvement (Flutter & Ruddock, 2004; Pollard & Triggs, 2000; Ruddock, Chaplain, & Wallace, 1996). Exercising 'voice' — and working together in teams to make a case for something or to undertake an actual project — can also assist in the educative processes associated with leadership and active participation in work and civic life.

There is a range of openings for students to exercise 'voice' in schools, in matters of planning and review, pedagogy and curriculum, researching and making decisions. These may require them to act as representatives and advocates for peers or encourage them to engage in conversations about teaching/learning. Students can now be found involved in all facets of schooling, ranging from designing school building and hiring teachers to designing curriculum and evaluating teachers' performance. Specific structures — annual consultations, representative councils, student fora, membership of committees — are common approaches for soliciting students' views, needs and ideas.

However, in addition to the problems arising from the implications of particular theoretical interpretations of 'voice' outlined earlier, practitioners and researchers have noted a number of practical issues in educational applications of children's 'voice', for example,

- Student representation is often tokenistic and seems more about students being *seen* to be involved in school processes, rather than being active partners in change.
- Only some students are selected for representative activities, often those who are seen by staff as 'good' or as 'gifted and talented' or by their peers as 'popular'. 'Difficult' students are often not asked what they think.
- What students can discuss is limited. Some student councils are largely confined to discussions about fund-raising and social activities, whereas others are primarily ascribed the role of responding to policies and plans being developed elsewhere.
- Students are not supported adequately in their participation in governance. They are not given relevant background information or training in meeting procedures and receive no additional support in canvassing their electorates to ensure that what they say is representative.
- There is often little follow up to student 'voice' activities. Students are asked their opinions but their recommendations are acted on in a patchy fashion. It is as if the act of speaking is all that matters. This undoubtedly leads to cynicism about the democratic processes of participation.
- Governance conversations dominate school 'voice' activities. Teachers assume that what they do ordinarily equates to listening to students. Students are more likely to be asked about their learning preferences rather than open questions about knowledge, assessment and pedagogy. Children and young people are rarely involved in substantive and ongoing classroom conversations about pedagogy and knowledge.
- Students are not credentialed for participation in 'voice' activities. The learning is seen as extracurricular and does not constitute knowledge and skills important enough to be counted as school learning and achievement (Arnot & Reay, 2007; Bragg, 2007a; Fielding, 2001a, 2008; Lodge, 2005; Thomson & Holdsworth, 2003).

Many of these concerns relate not to policy but to the processes used in schools, and in performative times, it seems that their preference is for 'weak' rather than 'strong' forms of democracy. Schools are also tied into market processes and may often opt for practices that are more consumerist in orientation — asking students if they are satisfied or not, asking about preferences in provision and services and seeking their partnership in promotional activities.

Educational commentators propose avenues for stronger student democratic involvement, which entails them asking substantive questions, engaging in ongoing dialogue and using more participatory processes and structures (Fielding, 2004; Holdsworth, 2000). Exemplars of democratic schools and classrooms in action show that alternative approaches are possible and not only lead to the kinds of outcomes that are required by high-stakes policy regimes but also provide the basis for students to act as citizens now and in the future (Pearl & Knight, 1999; Thomson, 2007). Spreading and embedding such approaches remains a significant challenge.

Alternative Approaches to and Theorisations of 'Voice'

In this final section, I canvass some theoretical approaches to 'voice', which might assist in avoiding some of the difficulties associated with the concept of political 'voice'. I also develop a heuristic frame that might be used to support the evaluation of practical approaches in schools.

George Orwell's famous essay on the use of active and passive 'voice' in political rhetoric Orwell's famous essay (1946) points to additional theoretical resources to bring to the question of political 'voice'. These are found in language and literary fields. Here, I erect some signposts to theorisations of (1) authorial 'voice', (2) multivocality, (3) semiosis and (4) discourse, indicating how they might support more open ways of understanding 'voice'.

(1) *Authorial 'voice' — the way in which writers develop and become associated with a particular style through their choice of person, syntax, lexicon, punctuation, dialogue, description and so on*

This conceptualisation draws attention to the ways in which the 'voice' of children and young people will be expressed; their 'voice' may be expressed in a range of local and international accents and forms, use vernacular and creole languages and use metaphors and tropes drawn from youth, neighbourhood and family cultures. These are not only choices but expressions of particular identities and associations. Those seeking to work with children's 'voice' thus need to be receptive to a range of modes of expression and become multilingual and skilled at translating the messages for those who are not familiar with children's chosen communication forms.

(2) *Multivocality — literally refers to many 'voices'*

Political theorists often see multivocality as residing in conversations between groups and thus inevitably leading to relativism. However, literary theorists see multivocality as the presence of multiple influences, texts and experiences within one text, conversation or 'voice'. Bakhtin (1981), for example, argued that language was heteroglossic; there were specific dialects associated with particular places and occasions — for example, one spoke differently in church than in a law court. The implication of this idea is that children and young people need to acquire not so much etiquette but rather the dialects that are used in different places and understand the rationales for doing so.[1] Bakhtin also observed that conversations and single speech acts generally refer to other conversations, texts and cultural understandings. The words used are rich with meanings and with possible interpretations. 'Voice' is not transparent and about a single thing but rather always hybrid and interconnected. Those who work with children's 'voice' thus need to approach the act of interpretation of what is said as a self-conscious process requiring reflexivity to avoid a simplistic imposition of surface meaning.

(3) *Semiosis — refers to the process of making meaning from symbols and signs, including speech and images*

Linguistic and philosophical studies of meaning-making have been highly influential in the academy, yet seem to have had less influence among those who seek to work politically with 'voice'. Semioticians typically look at the way in which signs and symbols are decoded and how this activity is culturally and socially constructed and delimited. This perspective of course goes to the way in which children and young people might understand what is being asked of them when they are asked to 'do' student 'voice' — how they decode adult requests and what sense they make of it. It thus directs us to the kinds of intellectual resources children might need to make sense of the context in which they are being asked to speak.

However, concepts associated with semiology also apply to those who listen. One of the most influential contributions to semiology is that of Derrida (1976, 1978) who argued that there was no fixed meaning possible and that meaning-making was an endless play of *différence*. This perspective suggests that those who translate and interpret student 'voice' need to accept that what they think has been said may in fact be open to other interpretations. Their responsibility is therefore to make interpretation of children's 'voice' a shared act with an explicit process to ensure that there is at least some kind of agreement about what meanings have been intended — while at the same time recognising the impossibility of ever-reaching final and universal meaning and agreement.

Listening to voice may also mean listening to silence. Semiotic scholars concerned with the binary logic of Western thought would draw attention to the polar opposite of 'voice' — not-voicing. This highlights the right to silence and privacy and the ways in which silences and pauses in conversations also speak (Mazzei, 2007) as well as suggesting that there may be something embodied, which sits between and beyond 'voice'/not 'voice'.

(4) *Discourse — particular language usage attached to a specific practice, as in legal discourse, medical discourse and so on. This may or may not be codified but can be seen as an assemblage available for deconstruction and analysis*

---

1. The connection of Bakhtin's notion of 'voice' to political 'voice' is from as yet unpublished work by Janet Maybin.

Theories of discourse challenge the notion of language as neutral and context as unimportant. They suggest that all of us are located within discourses that shape and delimit what it is we can and do think, be and say (Foucault, 1972, 1980, 1981). Discourse is thus a very important counter to the notion of an authentic and pure 'voice', which can be taken at face value. It disrupts the notion that children just need to be asked to speak and they will, without fear or favour, as if there are no influences that shape what they say. It is always the case that children and young people will exercise 'voice' through and within a specific discourse community/ies. Their words, just like our own, cannot be seen as somehow separate from this cultural and social immersion. Schooling is riven with multiple discourses of development, of markets, of measurement, of progress and enlightenment, of what counts as a good and bad student, of gender appropriate behaviour and so on. The point is to understand that this is the case and to take this into account when hearing what is said and when analysing responses.

How then are these understandings, together with those outlined earlier in the chapter, to be made helpful to students 'voice' as a practice in schools?

Conclusion

There are already a number of helpful heuristics for thinking about 'voice'. Fielding (2001b), for example, offers a set of questions — Who is speaking, about what, who is listening, what happens as a result and in whose interests does this work? Hart (1997) offers a ladder of participation ranging from token participation through to reciprocal partnerships. There are useful outlines for ethical consultations (Alderson & Morrow, 2004), a growing compendium of texts, which address research processes with children and young people (Christensen & James, 2000; Kellett, 2005; Lewis & Lindsay, 1999), and several guides for practical methods for soliciting 'voice' (see Bragg, 2010, for a list).

As a complement to these resources, I offer in conclusion this set of questions drawn from the understandings of 'voice' canvassed in the chapter. These are intended to support more open and dialogic approaches to 'voice', congruent with political approaches to 'strong democracy'. They are intended for use as part of an evaluative approach to 'voice' activities. They are not intended to promote excessive introspection but, more simply, to act as reference points for some of the complexities that the notion of 'voice' brings.

- Who is speaking? Who do they represent? How many points of view will be brought into the conversation? Who and what might be left out? How could they/these be included?
- What counts as speaking in this context? What media, genres, dialects and accents are possible? What additional information and support might be needed to help speaking up and out? What happens to those who choose not to speak?
- How might speaking up and out be constrained by the context? by expectations? by allegiances and associations? by dominant ways of being, thinking and acting?

Do any of these need to be addressed or countered, and if so, who decides what and how this will be accomplished?

- How will 'voice'(s) be understood and by whom? What other conversations and texts are referred to in conversations? What steps need to be taken to promote shared processes of making meaning, translation and interpretation?
- Who decides what can be spoken about, in what way and for how long? Why is this so? How might this be different?
- Who does not want to speak? Where are the silences in conversations and how will we know what these mean? What is being said by bodies rather than through speech acts?
- In whose interests does 'voice' work? How do we know? What counts as evidence and what is omitted as evidence? What if this is unfair? How could this be changed?

References

Alderson, P., & Morrow, V. (2004). *Ethics, social research and consulting with children and young people*. Barkingside: Barnardo's.

Arnot, M., & Reay, D. (2007). A sociology of pedagogic voice: Power, inequality and pupil consultation. *Discourse: Studies in the Cultural Politics of Education, 28*(3), 311–325.

Bakhtin, M. (1981). *The dialogic imagination: Four essays*. Austin, TX: University of Texas Press.

Barber, B. (1984). *Strong democracy*. Berkeley, CA: University of California Press.

Bragg, S. (2007a). 'But I listen to children anyway' — Teacher perspectives on pupil voice. *Educational Action Research, 15*(4), 505–518.

Bragg, S. (2007b). *Consulting young people: A review of the literature: A report for creative partnerships*. London: Arts Council England.

Bragg, S. (2010). *Consulting young people: A review of the literature: A report for creative partnerships* (2nd ed.). London: Creativity, Culture & Education.

Christensen, P., & James, A. (Eds). (2000). *Research with children: Perspectives and practices*. London, New York, NY: Falmer Press.

Derrida, J. (1976). *Of grammatology*. Baltimore, MD: John Hopkins University Press.

Derrida, J. (1978). *Writing and difference* (1995 ed.). London: Routledge.

Fielding, M. (2001a). Beyond the rhetoric of student voice: New departures or new constraints in twenty first century schooling? *Forum, 43*(2), 100–110.

Fielding, M. (2001b). Students as radical agents of change. *Journal of Educational Change, 2*(2), 123–141.

Fielding, M. (2004). Transformative approaches to student voice: Theoretical underpinnings, recalcitrant realities. *British Educational Research Journal, 30*(2), 295–311.

Fielding, M. (2008). Interrogating student voice: Pre-occupations, purposes and possibilities. In: H. Daniels, H. Lauder, & J. Porter (Eds.), *The Routledge companion to education*. London, Routledge.

Fielding, M., & Bragg, S. (2003). *Students as researchers: Making a difference*. Cambridge: Pearson.

Flutter, J., & Rudduck, J. (2004). *Consulting pupils: What's in it for schools?* London: RoutledgeFalmer.

Foucault, M. (1972). *The archeology of knowledge* (1995 ed.). London: Routledge.

Foucault, M. (1980). *Language, counter memory, practice*. New York, NY: Cornell University Press.

Foucault, M. (1981). The order of discourse. In: R. Young (Ed.), *Untying the text: A poststructuralist reader*. Boston, MA: Routledge & Kegan Paul.

Goffman, E. (1963). *Behaviour in public places: Notes on the social order of gatherings*. New York, NY: Free Press.

Hadfield, M., & Haw, K. (2001). 'Voice', young people and action research: Hearing, listening, responding. *Educational Action Research*, *9*(3), 485–499.

Hampton, H., & Fayer, S. (1990). *Voices of freedom: An oral history of the Civil Rights movement from the 1950s through the 1980s*. New York, NY: Bantam Books.

Hart, R. (1997). *Children's participation: The theory and practice of involving young citizens in community development and environmental care*. London: Earthscan Publications; UNICEF.

Holdsworth, R. (2000). Schools that create real roles of value for young people. *Prospects*, *115*(3), 349–362.

Kellett, M. (2005). *How to develop children as researchers*. London: Paul Chapman Educational Publishing.

Lewis, A., & Lindsay, G. (Eds). (1999). *Researching children's perspectives*. Buckingham: Open University Press.

Lodge, C. (2005). From hearing voices to engaging in dialogue: Problematising student participation in school improvement. *Journal of Educational Change*, *6*(2), 125–146.

Mazzei, L. A. (Ed.). (2007). *Inhabited silence in qualitative research: Putting poststructural theory to work*. New York, NY: Peter Lang.

Orwell, G. (1946). Politics and the English language. Retrieved from http://bcs.bedfordstmartins.com/everythingsanargument/content/cat_010/orwell_politics_and_the.pdf. Accessed on January 11, 2011.

Pearl, A., & Knight, T. (1999). *The democratic classroom: Theory to inform practice*. Cresskill, NJ: Hampton Press.

Pollard, A., & Triggs, P. (2000). *What pupils say: Changing policy and practice in primary education*. London: Continuum.

Riley, K., & Docking, J. (2004). Voices of disaffected pupils: Implications for policy and practice. *British Journal of Educational Studies*, *52*(2), 166–179.

Rubin, B., & Silva, E. (Eds). (2003). *Critical voices in school reform*. New York, NY: Routledge.

Rudduck, J., Chaplain, R., & Wallace, G. (1996). *School improvement: What can pupils tell us?* London: David Fulton.

Smyth, J., & Hattam, R. (2001). 'Voiced' research as a sociology for understanding 'dropping out' of school. *British Journal of Sociology of Education*, *22*(3), 401–415.

Solomon, M. (Ed.). (1991). *A voice of their own: The women suffrage press, 1840–1910*. Tuscaloosa, AL: University of Alabama Press.

Thomson, P. (2007). Making it real: Engaging students in active citizenship projects. In: D. Thiessen & A. Cook-Sather (Eds), *International handbook of student experience in elementary and secondary school* (pp. 775–804). Dordrecht: Springer.

Thomson, P., & Gunter, H. (2008). Researching bullying with students: A lens on everyday life in a reforming high school. *International Journal of Inclusive Education*, *12*(2), 185–200.

Thomson, P., & Holdsworth, R. (2003). Democratising schools through 'student participation': An emerging analysis of the educational field informed by Bourdieu. *International Journal of Leadership in Education*, *6*(4), 371–391.

United Nations. (1989). Convention on the rights of the child. UN document A/44/25, UN, Geneva.

Chapter 3

Student Voice and New Models of Teacher Professionalism

Emma Wisby

Abstract

This chapter considers the drivers behind the recent interest in student voice among policy makers and schools and related analysis within the academic literature. While it takes its lead from developments in the United Kingdom, the wider policy trends that it discusses, which provide the context for student voice activity, are shared by many other countries. The chapter identifies three main drivers in the latest wave of support for student voice: the children's rights movement; notions of active citizenship and a related emphasis on young people's development of 'life skills'; and school improvement. It notes the neo-liberal framework that has underpinned much of the resulting activity, and the growing scepticism regarding the extent to which the 'transformative potential' of student voice can be realised in the current context. Yet, while it recognises the risk that student voice will simply further broader neo-liberal policies, policies that some claim to have de-skilled and de-professionalised teachers, it seeks to highlight the opportunities as well as the threats that student voice offers in this regard. In theory at least, the chapter argues, student voice could contribute to moves towards a democratic model of teacher professionalism, a model that offers more progressive potential than either conventional forms of professionalism or the managerial version that is currently to the fore. To achieve that, teachers have the opportunity to take the initiative and play their part in shaping student voice around collaborative cultures. An important aspect of democratic professionalism is the furtherance of social inclusion: the chapter concludes by highlighting the challenges in enabling all students to participate in and benefit from provision for student voice.

The Student Voice Handbook: Bridging the Academic/Practitioner Divide
Copyright © 2011 by Emerald Group Publishing Limited
ISBN: 978-1-78052-040-7

Keywords: Neo-liberalism; school improvement; teacher professionalism; democratic professionalism; social inclusion

Introduction

The provision for student voice that this chapter is primarily concerned with is that which enables students to initiate or input into decision making and see through change in their school: it is this provision that has the greatest potential to challenge the status quo in terms of teacher and student roles. One example of such provision is school councils, democratically elected groups of students who represent their peers to influence decisions in their school; another is 'students as researchers', whereby students identify an aspect of their schooling that in their view would benefit from investigation and are supported in conducting research around that topic and feeding back their recommendations to the school (for a fuller discussion of student as researcher and student as co-researcher models, see Fielding, 2004b). The chapter's interest is in the prospects for student voice activity such as this that moves beyond manipulation, tokenism and consultation with students to a shared dialogue between teachers and students and the role of teachers in supporting that agenda.

The past decade has seen a 'new wave' of interest in student voice among policy makers and schools in the United Kingdom, so much so that making provision for student voice has become almost a routine consideration for schools. This has generated attention from academic commentators regarding the drivers behind this trend, what it means for schools, students and teachers, and how provision for student voice might be further developed. Three main drivers are identified in this chapter: the children's rights movement; the encouragement of active citizenship and, linked to that, the development of young people's 'life skills'; and the school improvement agenda, with its interest in student behaviour and attendance, well-being and attainment and the relationship between them. Much of the related commentary in the United Kingdom has reflected on the dominant neo-liberal policy framework within which schools have long operated and the way in which this appears to have shaped interest in student voice and the form that provision has typically taken in practice. This framework is seen in many other countries — most notably in New Zealand, Sweden and the United States — characterised as it is by competition between schools, performativity and surveillance (see, e.g., Whitty, 2002; Whitty & Wisby, 2006). The concern within the literature is that, in these circumstances, the decision to promote and introduce provision for student voice will often be oriented around its potential to improve school performance as narrowly conceived. A further risk that commentators point to is that the very popularity of student voice at the current time generates a 'bandwagon effect' and, consequently, a tokenistic and possibly short-lived interest on the part of schools. In each case, the transformative potential of student voice is lost. Such a context obviously poses particular challenges to establishing what many commentators on student voice aspire to in the school system — dialogic models of student voice based in a concern for shared decision making and social inclusion. As typified by students as researchers, this would entail the active engagement of students and teachers working in partnership.

Drivers behind the Current Interest in Student Voice

This section outlines in more detail the aforementioned drivers for provision for student voice. It notes the reform agendas that underpin them, as well as their relative significance as indicated by the findings of a recent national survey of teachers in the United Kingdom.

Children's Rights

For some, student voice is about a moral commitment to giving children and young people a voice. This perspective is reflected in the United Nations Convention on the Rights of the Child (UNCRC), Article 12, which states that children have the right to express their views freely on all matters affecting them, the views of the child being given due weight in accordance with the age and maturity of the child. It chimes with new social studies of childhood, which argue that children 'should be recognised as competent agents, who are participants in and producers of, rather than passive recipients of, social and cultural change' (Bragg, 2007a, p. 15). It can also be linked to the movement for democratic schooling (see Apple & Beane, 1995).

While the UNCRC has precipitated related policies at national level in the United Kingdom (e.g. the requirement that local government bodies canvass the views of children and young people on policies that affect them), there is not a strong tradition of children's rights led provision in mainstream British schools. In a 2007 survey of 982 teachers in England and Wales, just 2% cited the UNCRC as a motivator for introducing provision for student voice (Whitty & Wisby, 2007a; see also Osler & Starkey, 2006). There are, though, pockets of provision that are ostensibly shaped by this agenda, the main example being those schools, albeit relatively small in number at present, that subscribe to UNICEF UK's Rights Respecting School Award (RRSA) initiative. Introduced in 2004, the RRSA encourages schools to use the UNCRC as their values framework. Important elements of this approach include teaching students about children's rights, modelling rights and respect throughout the school and students' active participation in school decision making (www.unicef.org.uk/rrsa).

Active Citizenship and Life Skills

Elsewhere, schools have been influenced by policy developments stemming from notions of 'active citizenship' and 'stakeholder democracy'. This reflects the efforts of successive UK governments to both develop individuals' political literacy and engagement and encourage them to participate in their local community (see, e.g., Adonis & Mulgan, 1994). Within the UK schools system, this agenda prompted the introduction of citizenship as a compulsory subject within the curriculum (see Crick, 1998). Students learn about their rights, responsibilities, duties and freedoms and about laws, justice and democracy. They learn to take part in decision making and different forms of action. School councils in particular have an obvious application in helping to develop students' understanding of democratic principles and processes. A closely related agenda has been the emphasis within the wider reform of the curriculum on developing students' learning and 'transferable' or 'life' skills (e.g. teamwork and negotiation skills). Again, schools have utilised student voice activity to support these objectives. In the aforementioned teacher survey, 17% of respondents cited enhancing their school's citizenship provision as the main reason for introducing provision for student voice; 21% cited developing students' social and emotional skills (Whitty & Wisby, 2007a).

School Improvement

A principal reason for UK policy makers' interest in student voice has been its potential to improve school performance (see, e.g., DfES, 2005). An associated strand of policy has sought to emphasise the link between student well-being and engagement and attainment (see, e.g., DfES, 2003). Another stems from the use of consumer choice and voice to bring about improvements in public sector provision. This includes the 'personalisation' of provision, whereby providers offer services that are more tailored to the needs of each user.

With regard to the former, the assumption is that giving students a greater sense of being trusted, listened to and of having a stake in their school will help to improve student behaviour and enhance students' engagement in their learning and, thereby, raise their attainment. Agreeing rules democratically and developing students' confidence and self-esteem as well as their skills in managing themselves and their relationships with others also play a part (for a discussion of the ways in which provision for student voice can support these outcomes, see, e.g., Davies, Williams, & Yamashita, 2006; Fielding, 2001; Frost, 2007; Shier, 2001). Personalisation offers a potentially more radical agenda — introducing choice for students across all aspects of school life. This could include giving students choice over the curriculum they follow and involving them in designing the curriculum, setting learning objectives and advising their school on, for example, how to use information technology. It could also include providing opportunities for students to give feedback on lessons (see, e.g., Hargreaves, 2004–2006, 2007).

Improving behaviour and attendance, well-being and attainment, as well as personalisation specifically, were all cited by a relatively small proportion of the respondents to the 2007 teacher survey (less than 10% in each case). This was, however, accompanied in the related case study research by teachers' frequent reference to using provision for student voice to give students 'a sense of ownership of their school' as per the assumptions outlined above. Improving the school's environment and facilities was by far the most popular reason given for having introduced provision for student voice, cited by 27% of the teachers. While this offers a more restricted form of improvement and sense of ownership, it can reasonably be viewed in the same way.

Responses to the Latest Wave of Interest in Student Voice

The three drivers and the associated reform agendas are not necessarily mutually exclusive — although that is not to say that in planning their provision for student voice schools are scrutinising these agendas to provide a clear and coherent rationale for that provision (see Whitty & Wisby, 2007b). What also stands out from these findings is the relative insignificance of the children's rights driver, the driver that places the greatest emphasis on reciprocal dialogue between students and teachers and on empowering students as an end in itself. One explanation for these findings is that the sheer popularity of student voice has led to a tokenistic and short-sighted approach to it on the part of schools. Another is that decisions to introduce student voice activity have become dominated by concerns about how it can support school performance in a more narrow sense.

The Dangers of Tokenism and Faddism

The immediate problem facing student voice is its frequent treatment by schools and teachers as a passing fashion. The result is, at best, a sense of obligation among school leaders to put in place some form of provision for student voice. Such provision may well be tokenistic and could even be harmful: students will tire of invitations to express their view that they see as restricted or as merely paying lip-service to the idea of consultation or participation, which could, in turn, generate cynicism about democratic processes. Indeed, such surface compliance is likely to lead to a focus on 'easy wins' in terms of the form that provision takes and the ends to which it is put. It is unlikely to foster a reflective review of the various reasons why a school might want to introduce provision for student voice in the first place. Fielding and Rudduck have written widely about the 'perils of popularity' in this regard:

> there is a worrying prospect that as more and more agencies become involved (which is of course a good thing in itself), as more and more pupil voice websites are set up, and as more and more 'how to do it' resources are produced, we may have 'mile-wide' promotions with only 'inch thick' understanding: schools need to take time to think why they want to develop student consultation and what the risks and benefits will be for them. (Rudduck, 2006, p. 133)

Ultimately, faddism risks the popularity of student voice burning out before its transformative potential has been understood (Rudduck, Demetriou, & Pedder, 2003).

The Emancipatory Critique

As Frost (2007) observes: 'Although student voice is enjoying another revival at present, each time it comes around it reflects the spirit of the educational age it inhabits, bringing with it old challenges and others unique to its time' (p. 354). Where once the latest wave of interest in student voice was regarded as a potential antidote to the neo-liberal agenda that has shaped education policy in the United Kingdom and elsewhere for the past three decades (see, e.g., Fielding, 2004a), more recent analysis has pointed to the degree of apparent alignment between the two. Bragg (2007b) makes this point forcefully:

> Now educationalists and others observing the implementation of student voice at school level — including those who are also its advocates — are surveying the field with some suspicion. The fact that student voice now appears to be fully compatible with government and management objectives and that senior staff are introducing it with the explicit aim of school improvement, causes disquiet, even concerns that it might be cynical and manipulative, intentionally or not masking the 'real' interests of those in power. (p. 344)

It is notable that even provision that is oriented around children's rights has come to be promoted on the basis of the potential benefits for schools in relation to external indicators. The aim of a recent three-year evaluation of the RRSA initiative was to assess the impact of the scheme on the well-being and achievement of children and young people in the participating schools, including measures of academic attainment and gains in social and emotional skills, knowledge and understanding (Sebba & Robinson, 2010). Headline findings were that, as well as building positive relationships across students and staff and active student participation in school life, participating schools had experienced reduced exclusions and bullying, improved student behaviour, improved attendance and a rise in attainment. The authors themselves concede that typical fluctuations seen in test results and changes in units of measurement for attendance and exclusions made overall trends in these data unclear.

On active citizenship, commentators distinguish between notions of citizenship as a set of ideas that adults instruct students about and notions of citizenship as relationships that students already experience in school teaching — between teaching about democracy as an investment for the future and enacting democratic principles in the daily life of the school (Rudduck & Fielding, 2006; Shallcross, Robinson, Pace, & Tamoutseli, 2007). The use of school councils to illustrate democratic principles and processes in support of the citizenship syllabus essentially falls into the former category, driven by external agendas and used selectively rather than as a means of changing school ethos.

On the development of students' transferable skills, as with school improvement, once again the risk is that the focus is on formal learning and raising attainment, rather than students' personal and social development or their active sense of membership of their school (Rudduck, 2006). Fielding (2004a) comments:

> student voice operating within this 'high performance' mode is largely an instrumental undertaking orientated towards increased measurable organisational performance. In its more extreme form it is about the use of student voice for particular kinds of adult purposes…. Student voice only has significance and is only legitimate insofar as it enhances organisational ends. (Fielding, 2004a, p. 211)

The suggestion, then, is that student voice has simply been harnessed to the 'machinery of the status quo' (Fielding, 2007).

Other commentators have taken a post-structuralist perspective in assessing current provision for student voice. Citing Foucauldian concepts of governmentality, concerned with instilling norms of individualism, self-reliance and self-management, Bragg (2007b) argues that student voice can be understood as a disciplinary device aimed at increased compliance and enhanced productivity. On this understanding, students who take part in provision for student voice become (unwitting) agents of government control. In the process, provision for student voice can serve to draw attention away from existing inequalities and may even serve to exacerbate them.

One charge from a post-structuralist perspective is that student voice might be reflective of and contribute to the responsibilisation of young people. Responsibilisation entails subjects seeing social risks such as illness, unemployment and poverty not as the responsibility of the state, but actually lying in the domain for which the individual is responsible and transforming it into a problem of 'self-care' (Lemke, 2001, p. 201). In this vein, Gustafsson and Driver (2005) draw on Foucault's concept of 'pastoral power' to examine whether public participation is better viewed as a necessary part of governance in modern Western democracies where subjects need to be recruited to exercise power over themselves (p. 529). Kelly (2001) for one has identified moves to 'normalise youth as rational, choice-making citizens, who are responsible for their future life chances through the choices they make with regard to school, career, relationships… ' (p. 30). Within a neo-liberal context, this appears to be the corollary of the aforementioned contemporary interpretations of childhood that argue for children to be recognised as competent agents and active participants in and producers of social change: students see themselves as individually responsible for informing themselves and maximising opportunities for themselves.

Of course, this is not about citizens exercising power in any absolute sense, but about them making the 'right' choices. Consequently, a particular anxiety of post-structuralist commentators is that student voice helps to incorporate students into managerialist rhetoric and 'corporate' ways of thinking and that the effect is to change orientations away from the peer group. Notably, this analysis has been used to raise reservations about what can be regarded as more developed forms of provision for student voice — in this instance, students as researchers:

> the freedom students as researchers offers ... comes at the cost of an intensification of relations of domination — the requirement (even if not fulfilled) to assent with heart not just body, to give an inner commitment not just outer conformity. (Bragg, 2007b, p. 356)

Bragg acknowledges from her own research with students the pleasure that they can derive from becoming more independent and taking their own decisions, as well as the opportunity student voice activity provides to escape, albeit temporarily, from the direct pressures of performativity cultures. She also acknowledges the use to which students will be able to put the skills and dispositions that they have developed through their participation, and their own recognition of those uses. Bragg's principal concern, on which she raises some searching questions, is the matter of which students get to realise those benefits. By introducing a social obligation to improve the self and the school, Bragg suggests, provision for student voice appeals more and is more easily accessible to some groups of students than others. This serves to create new — or rather simply reinforce existing — categories of problematic student, who in turn must take individual responsibility for the outcomes of their schooling. But how far can this critique inform practice? Schools can attend to the varying ability of students to access provision for student voice and the benefits that this can offer, but does the immediate work of publicly funded schools in a democratic society stretch beyond that? As Bragg herself comments: 'In one sense, schools are simply doing their job in preparing students to compete in a changed neo-liberal climate' (p. 353). That said, there is no reason why student voice activity, including students as researchers, could not be used at least in part to reflect critically on those very structures.

A remaining issue, as Rudduck and Fielding (2006) point to, is that of the capacity of provision for student voice to support the consumerisation of education. They ask:

> Are we creating a new order of experience for students in schools, new roles for teachers and students — or will the idea of consulting students prove to be little more than a ... nod in the direction of consumerism? (Rudduck & Fielding, 2006, p. 229)

The concept of personalisation provides a useful means of illustrating the spectrum along which a school's provision for student voice can sit in this regard, ranging from consumerism to the collaborative models of co-construction as set out by Leadbeater and found in certain forms of student voice activity:

> Many children feel education is something done to them.... An alternative is to paint children and parents as consumers, picking and choosing between different options in an education supermarket.... But this only engages users in choosing between different options

delivered to them. The point is to engage them far more in designing, producing and creating the learning they seek [based in an ongoing dialogue between the providers and users of a service]. (Leadbeater, 2005, p. 1)

A national survey of secondary school students, conducted alongside the teacher survey that has already been discussed, has pointed to the ambiguities inherent in current provision for student voice in this regard. It found that some students rejected a consumerist orientation altogether. Although there were other students who saw themselves as customers of their school, even they did not always feel they had a right to comment on every aspect of school life. Equally, none of the students had a strong sense of themselves as co-producers of teaching and learning provision as per the collaborative rather than consumerist model of personalisation (Whitty & Wisby, 2007a, 2007b). Deference among students and a more limited remit for student voice in some schools are explanations for this ambiguity. Another is the centre ground or 'third way' politics that has sat behind the interest in choice and voice as features of public sector reform, with its emphasis on pragmatism and 'what works' over ideology (for a fuller account, see Power & Whitty, 1999). This renders student voice as neither one thing nor another in terms of consumerism or collaboration: which inflection predominates will depend on how it becomes articulated with other policy developments — at the national level, but also within schools.

The Implications for Understandings of Student Voice

In contrast to the sometimes breathless enthusiasm for student voice within the policy literature and among advocacy groups, these various commentaries encourage a more considered and cautious approach to the concept. Still, they have their own shortcomings. One assessment might be that they pay insufficient attention to the 'realpolitik' of balancing what might be school and teacher priorities and external agendas. Another would be that, while advocacy of student voice has been 'too silent about the costs that accompany student voice', some emancipatory critiques have been 'too strident in their dismissal of the possibility of any significant capacity to challenge [the neo-liberal] hegemony' (Fielding, 2004a, p. 206). While running the risk of accusations of 'comfortable gradualism' (Fielding, 2007), the premise of this chapter is that the interest that has been shown in student voice, however rudimentary or apparently compromised, does provide important openings for wider changes in student–teacher roles and relationships. Crucially, teachers are the gatekeepers. If the wider potential of student voice is to be realised, teachers must exploit the ambiguities in relation to both student voice and contemporary understandings of teacher professionalism. First, that requires teachers to critically examine their attitudes towards student voice, including the status that they are prepared to accord it as well as the ends to which they would wish to facilitate it.

Student Voice and Teacher Professionalism

Those commentators arguing from an emancipatory perspective call for provision for student voice that is characterised by: care for students as persons, dialogue and partnership between students and teachers, a concern for social justice, a strong sense of solidary responsibility (e.g. acting on behalf of others), a clear sense of located identity (e.g. identification of and loyalty to marginalised groups), engagement with communities outside the school and an international rather than parochial orientation (Fielding, 2004a). The aim is to offer students a greater sense of ownership of their school (essentially as an end in itself), to strengthen young people's sense of themselves as confident learners and embed more exploratory forms of learning in schools. Such a view of student voice requires a revised understanding of what it means to be a student and what it means to be a teacher. The affinity with democratic models of teacher professionalism is strong.

Models of Teacher Professionalism

Teachers, as with most professionals, are employed or at least regulated by governments. Their professional status, therefore, is typically dependent on the sort of bargain they have struck with the state — their 'professional mandate'. The nature of teachers' professional mandate has become a key policy issue for governments in many countries, sometimes as part of a broader attempt to redefine professionalism, especially in the public sector, and sometimes as a specific aspect of education reform.

The teaching profession in the United Kingdom has never enjoyed the 'licensed autonomy' that occupations such as medicine and law have traditionally had, whereby they have been permitted by the state to regulate their own affairs. Nevertheless, from the 1950s until the mid-1970s, it experienced a considerable degree of de facto autonomy — the 'golden age of teacher control' (Le Grand, 1997). Parents were expected to trust teachers to know what was best for their children. Even though effectively the state paid most teachers' salaries, it did not intervene actively in the content of either teacher training or the work of teachers in schools. Particularly within the United Kingdom since the late 1970s, cultures of performativity and surveillance coupled with growing centralised prescription have eroded this traditional model of teacher professionalism (Whitty & Wisby, 2006). Critiques of such reforms suggest that they have resulted in a 'managerial' professionalism which accepts that decisions about what and how to teach are made at national or school level rather than by individual teachers themselves and that this has resulted in the de-skilling and 'de-professionalisation' of teachers (see, e.g., Furlong, 2005). However, sociologically, it is not necessarily appropriate to view such developments as an example of de-professionalisation, but rather as an attempt at *re*-professionalisation — that is, the construction of a different type of professionalism, perhaps more appropriate to contemporary needs. The 'traditional' model of teacher professionalism was not without its limitations: the 'old professions' have been variously characterised as elitist, paternalistic, controlling and detached (see Davies, 1995, 1996). It is also important to recognise that subsequent policy changes were based, at least in part, in a perceived failure on the part of teachers to deliver what society required of them (see Barber, 2005). Ironically, the managerialist attack on traditional models of teacher professionalism has contained some 'progressive moments', including the promotion of teachers' acceptance of accountability and transparency. This has opened up new possibilities, namely the furtherance of 'collaborative' and 'democratic' professionalisms.

Whereas collaborative professionalism refers to collaboration between different groups of professionals (e.g. teachers and youth workers), democratic profession-alism entails working in tandem with all relevant stakeholders: in the case of education that means relevant professionals, students, parents, families and communities (Whitty, 2002). Although this too represents a move away from a model of professional autonomy in which teachers make their own decisions about teaching quality, teachers can experience this positively as a move towards a dialogic, reflective model of professionalism, forged in alliance with students in the first instance. The benefits of student voice in this regard range from improved practice (e.g. better understanding of what leads to disengagement, or, more generally, seeing taken-for-granted aspects of teaching and learning from a different angle) to new ways of working through the harnessing of students' capacity for contributing constructively, to a sense of professional excitement and animation and to growing confidence to try to build more open working relationships (Ruddock, 2006, pp. 140–141). Arnot and Reay (2007) argue for a slightly different use of 'student voicings', one with more radical potential — the examination of what students say to gain new insights into the rules that govern the organisation of teaching and the social inequalities associated with learning (p. 318). Of course, to focus on student voice in this way, teachers need to feel that they too have a voice in their school and that their expertise is respected.

Involving all Students

First, it is necessary to recognise students' right not to participate in provision for student voice. That aside, the commitment to social inclusion and social justice inherent in emancipatory models of student voice and democratic models of teacher professionalism highlights the need to attend to the classed, gendered and raced aspects of student voice — aspects that risk being hidden in less reflective practice. This concerns participation and representation.

Consultation assumes a degree of confidence and a level of communication skills that not all students have or feel that they have. In that way, students are differently able to realise the promise of 'voice' as a result of the various subject positions they occupy beyond that of student. Added to this, the pressures to achieve quick results from consultation and participation may lead schools 'to listen most readily to the voices that make immediate sense' (Fielding, 2004b, p. 303).

For most schools, a significant proportion of their students will not be heavily engaged with provision for student voice. Those who are actively involved are more likely to be from relatively advantaged backgrounds, while disaffected students are no more likely to be attracted to student voice activities than to other school activities. In some instances research has revealed a significant 'excluded middle' within schools, with high achieving and disaffected students drawn into student voice activities (whether as a result of their own initiative or through encouragement by school staff) and other students being allowed to remain outside of such provision (Whitty & Wisby, 2007b). Schools must ask themselves which students are representing the student voice of their school, and whether the students who are best served by the current set-up of their school can serve the interests of students who appear least well-served? They must pay attention to finding ways of enabling all students to participate should they wish to do so and supporting students to that end. For representative provision, apparently fundamental critiques of the premise of provision for student voice need not be overwhelming. Just as there are difficulties in speaking about and for others, so there are difficulties in not doing so (see Fielding, 2004b, pp. 302–303). On this, Fielding points to the value of the act of dialogue itself as opposed to the content of what is said — in the sense that this process can be educative and empowering for the 'researcher' and those who are being researched. In many ways, students as researchers and democratic models of professionalism encapsulate the principle and process of speaking with (rather than about or for) others.

Conclusion

Given the broader policy context in which many schools operate, there is good reason to be sceptical about the extent to which the transformative potential of student voice can be realised. There is a very real risk that provision for student voice will simply feed neo-liberal agendas and further undermine teacher autonomy and authority. Yet, this outcome is arguably more likely if teachers resist student voice, whether actively or through tokenism.

Student voice opens up valuable possibilities, in terms of the student experience, but also in relation to moves towards democratic models of teacher professionalism. If this is to happen, teachers themselves need to take the initiative and play their part in helping to shape student voice around collaborative rather than managerialist cultures. This is not to underestimate the challenge that this presents to schools and teachers, not least in enabling all students to participate in and benefit from provision for student voice. The words of caution provided by the kinds of commentaries outlined in this chapter offer a valuable resource for practitioners and others in reflecting on the principle of and provision for student voice.

References

Adonis, A., & Mulgan, G. (1994). Back to Greece: The scope for direct democracy. *Demos Quarterly, 3,* 1–28.

Apple, M., & Beane, J. (1995). *Democratic schools.* Buckingham: Open University Press.

Arnot, M., & Reay, D. (2007). A sociology of pedagogic voice: Power, inequality and pupil consultation. *Discourse: Studies in the Cultural Politics of Education, 28*(3), 311–325.

Barber, M. (2005). Informed professionalism: Realising the potential. Presentation to a conference of the Association of Teachers and Lecturers, London, June 11.

Bragg, S. (2007a). *Consulting young people: A review of the literature.* London: Creative Partnerships.

Bragg, S. (2007b). 'Student voice' and governmentality: The production of enterprising subjects? *Discourse: Studies in the Cultural Politics of Education, 28*(3), 343–358.

Crick, B. (1998). *Education for citizenship and the teaching of democracy in schools: Final report of the advisory group on citizenship.* London: QCA/DfEE.

Davies, C. (1995). *Gender and the professional predicament in nursing.* Buckingham: Open University Press.

Davies, C. (1996). The sociology of professions and the profession of gender. *Sociology, 30,* 661–678.

Davies, L., Williams, C., & Yamashita, H. (2006). *Inspiring Schools — impact and outcomes: Taking up the challenge of pupil participation.* London: Carnegie.

DfES [Department for Education and Skills] (2003). *Every child matters: Change for children.* London: DfES.

DfES [Department for Education and Skills] (2005). *Higher standards, better schools for all: More choice for parents and pupils.* Norwich: HMSO.

Fielding, M. (2001). Beyond the rhetoric of student voice: New departures or new constraints in the transformation of twenty-first century schooling. *Forum, 43*(2), 100–109.

Fielding, M. (2004a). 'New wave' student voice and the renewal of civic society. *London Review of Education, 2*(3), 197–216.

Fielding, M. (2004b). Transformative approaches to student voice: Theoretical underpinnings, recalcitrant realities. *British Educational Research Journal, 30*(2), 295–311.

Fielding, M. (2007). Beyond 'voice': New roles, relations and contexts in researching with young people. *Discourse: Studies in the Cultural Politics of Education, 28*(3), 301–310.

Frost, R. (2007). Developing student participation, research and leadership: The HCD Student Partnership. *School Leadership and Management, 28*(4), 353–368.

Furlong, J. (2005). New labour and teacher education: The end of an era. *Oxford Review of Education, 31*(1), 119–134.

Gustafsson, U., & Driver, S. (2005). Parents, power and public participation: Sure start, an experiment in New Labour governance. *Social Policy and Administration, 39*(5), 528–543.

Hargreaves, D. (2004–2006). *'Personalising learning' (six pamphlets).* London: Specialist Schools and Academies Trust.

Hargreaves, D. (2007). *System redesign — 1: The road to transformation in education.* London: Specialist Schools and Academies Trust.

Kelly, P. (2001). Youth at risk: Processes of individualisation and responsibilisation in the risk society. *Discourse: Studies in the Cultural Politics of Education, 22*(1), 23–33.

Leadbeater, C. (2005). *The shape of things to come: Personalised learning through collaboration.* DfES: Nottingham.

Le Grand, J. (1997). Knights, knaves or pawns? Human behaviour and social policy. *Journal of Social Policy, 26,* 149–164.

Lemke, T. (2001). The birth of bio-politics: Michael Foucault's lectures at the College de France on neo-liberal governmentality. *Economy and Society, 30*(2), 190–207.

Osler, A., & Starkey, H. (2006). Education for democratic citizenship: A review of research, policy and practice 1995-2005. *Research Papers in Education, 21*(4), 433–466.

Power, S., & Whitty, G. (1999). New Labour's education policy: First, second or third way? *Research Papers in Education, 14*(5), 535–546.

Rudduck, J. (2006). The past, the papers and the project. *Educational Review, 58*(2), 131–143.

Rudduck, J., Demetriou, H., & Pedder, D. (2003). Student perspectives and teacher practices: The transformative potential. *McGill Journal of Education, 38*(2), 274–287.

Rudduck, J., & Fielding, M. (2006). Student voice and the perils of popularity. *Educational Review, 58*(2), 219–231.

Sebba, J., & Robinson, C. (2010). *Evaluation of UNICEF UK's Rights Respecting Schools Award*. London: UNICEF.

Shallcross, T., Robinson, J., Pace, P., & Tamoutseli, K. (2007). The role of students' voices and their influence on adults in creating more sustainable environments in three schools. *Improving Schools, 10*, 72–85.

Shier, H. (2001). Pathways to participation: Openings, opportunities and obligations — a new model for enhancing children's participation in decision-making. *Children and Society, 15*, 107–117.

Whitty, G. (2002). *Making sense of education policy*. London: Sage.

Whitty, G., & Wisby, E. (2006). Moving beyond recent education reform — and towards a democratic professionalism. *Hitotsubashi Journal of Social Studies, 38*(1), 43–61.

Whitty, G., & Wisby, E. (2007a). *Real decision making? School councils in action (DCSF research report 001)*. London: DCSF.

Whitty, G., & Wisby, E. (2007b). Whose voice? An exploration of the current policy interest in pupil involvement in school decision-making. *International Studies in Sociology of Education, 17*(3), 303–319.

Chapter 4

Every Child Matters, But Not Every Child is Heard

Rita Cheminais

Abstract

This chapter examines the moral purpose and underlying philosophy of the British Every Child Matters (ECM) initiative in relation to its influence in empowering and strengthening the voice of children and young people, particularly that of the most vulnerable.[1] It explores whether the ECM change for children programme truly increased the autonomy of the most vulnerable children and young people or merely became an over-bureaucratic controlling system, devoting little if any time to authentic listening of the voice of the child. The chapter highlights some of the most effective key drivers arising from the ECM initiative that really did have a positive impact on giving vulnerable children and young people a voice that was listened to and acted upon. The chapter concludes by clarifying the Coalition Government's policy on the agenda, when the term ECM has been replaced with *help children achieve more*.

---

1. Vulnerable children and young people include those with behavioural, emotional and social difficulties; those with learning difficulties and disabilities; those with special educational needs (SEN); those with life-threatening conditions such as cancer; those with chronic illness such as diabetes; children and young people with physical disabilities; those with sensory impairments; those with autistic spectrum disorder; those with communication difficulties; those with Down's syndrome; looked after children; children at risk of or who are being abused; those children and young people who are living in families under stress; those who have been bereaved; those in contact with the youth justice system; homophobic children and young people; children from black and minority ethnic groups; children and young people experiencing housing difficulties; children and young people seeking asylum; young people not in education, training or employment; young carers or young runaways.

The Student Voice Handbook: Bridging the Academic/Practitioner Divide
ISBN: 978-1-78052-040-7

Keywords: Every Child Matters; positive contribution; vulnerable children; marginal voices; children's commissioner

Introduction

Every Child Matters (ECM) was the most far-reaching government initiative in England and Wales in 2003, which, in response to the horrific death of Victoria Climbié,[2] brought about the most significant and radical change through an outcomes framework. This framework established closer joint partnership working and information exchange between education, health and social care in children's services to improve the lives of children.

Consulting and involving children and young people in having a much greater say about service design and delivery, and in decisions that affected them, was a key feature of the ECM initiative. This began to challenge the assumption that adults always know what is best for children. However, despite this aim, ECM was an adult-directed policy, owned and led predominately by adult professionals in children's services, which only began to touch the surface of real empowerment for children and young people in relation to enabling them to have a powerful and influential voice regarding their learning and well-being.

ECM, however, did prompt the government, through the ECM outcome *Make a positive contribution* to encourage schools in England to establish a school council, pupil forums and to use pupil questionnaires as part of their regular practice, in gathering the views of children and young people on aspects of learning and school life that directly affect them. Without the ECM change for children programme being implemented, pupil voice would not have gained as much popularity as it did from 2003 to 2010, under the Labour Government.

The Origin and Concept of Every Child Matters

The Labour Government in Britain, under the leadership of Tony Blair, published a Green Paper entitled *Every Child Matters*, in September 2003. This set out the government's ambitious plans to improve outcomes for all children and young people from birth to nineteen, including those of the most disadvantaged and those with additional needs. The key aim of the proposed initiative was to reduce the number of children and young people experiencing educational failure, engaging in

---

2. In the London Borough of Haringey, during 1999–2000, eight-year old Victoria Climbié was subjected to horrific and prolonged physical abuse and mental cruelty in the care of her great aunt and boyfriend Carl Manning, who both eventually murdered her. Up to the point of Victoria's tragic death, a number of services, which included the police, social services and the health service, had all noted the signs of abuse, but not one of them took sufficient action to prevent Victoria's death.

antisocial behaviour, suffering from ill health or becoming teenage parents. This was to be achieved by children's services and other agencies intervening early to prevent things going wrong in the first place.

The concept of ECM was similar to that of the US's initiative *No Child Left Behind*, which aimed to close the pupil achievement gap between white, black and Hispanic groups of children and young people.

The Every Child initiative was the Labour Government's response to Lord Laming's Inquiry[3] into the tragic death of Victoria Climbié, who suffered unimaginable cruelty at the hands of those relations entrusted with her care. This particular case highlighted the failings of a number of services, (police, health and social services) to protect and save Victoria's life on 12 occasions over 10 months, as a vulnerable child. These failings centred around services not intervening early enough, being poorly coordinated, not sharing information, lacking accountability, being poorly managed and being short of appropriately trained frontline workers. The report on the death of Victoria Climbié by Lord Laming in 2003 recommended services for children, young people and their families should be better integrated. It was for this reason that the UK Children Act 2004 legislated to establish a children's trust in every local authority in England, along with the move for integrated inspections of children's services, to safeguard the welfare of children and young people.

ECM, as a set of reforms, supported by the Children Act 2004, placed a moral obligation on maintained schools in England and Wales, in partnership with other services and agencies, to work together to improve the life chances of all children and young people, particularly those of the most vulnerable. It also acknowledged the rights, voice and choice of children and young people, irrespective of their social cultural and economic background.

In relation to pupil voice, the Labour Government had consulted with children, young people and their families on the outcomes that mattered most to them in their lives. This resulted in the identification of the five universal ECM well-being outcomes, which formed the outcomes framework comprising of the following:

- being healthy: enjoying good physical and mental health and having a healthy lifestyle
- staying safe: being protected from harm and neglect
- enjoying and achieving: getting the most out of life and developing the skills for adulthood
- making a positive contribution: engaging in decision-making, being involved with the community and society and not engaging in antisocial or offending behaviour
- achieving economic well-being: not being prevented by economic disadvantage from achieving their full potential in life

---

3. Lord Laming in 2001 chaired the public inquiry into Victoria Climbié's death. His final report, published on 28 February, 2003, resulted in improved child protection reforms in England and Wales. It also led to the ECM programme. In November 2008, Lord Laming was appointed to investigate social services nationally, following the death of Baby P in the same local authority, where Victoria Climbié had resided and died.

The Children Act 2004 placed a duty on governing bodies of schools in England, to promote the five ECM well-being outcomes. This also included the duty to cooperate with children's trusts and to have regard to the local authority Children and Young People's Plan. The Labour Government showed its commitment to supporting the 10-year ECM strategy (2003–2013) and the local integration of services by appointing a Minister for Children, Young People and Families within the Department for Education and Skills.

The Green Paper, *Every Child Matters* (2003), recognised that real service improvement could only be achieved by involving children and young people and by listening to their views. The first part of the Children Act 2004 provided for the establishment of a new Children's Commissioner for England to ensure children and young people's voices were effectively heard. Sir Albert Aynsley Green took up the post in March 2005. The commissioner acted as a champion for all children and young people, especially for those who were the most disadvantaged, whose voices were often unheard. He raised the awareness of the best interests of children and young people by drawing on their views locally and nationally, through commissioning The Children's Society to undertake a national survey the 'Good Childhood Inquiry' during 2007–2008, which sought the views of children and young people on six key topics: friends, family, learning, lifestyle, health and values. The outcomes from this inquiry along with the government's 'Time to Talk' consultation with children, young people and their families helped to inform the Labour Government's Children's Plan in 2007.

The Children's Commissioner reported annually to Parliament through the Secretary of State for Education and Skills on progress against the five ECM outcomes and the success or otherwise of policies in terms of what children and young people thought and actually experienced first-hand.

The Moral Purpose and Underlying Philosophy of Every Child Matters

The Labour Government's subsequent ECM change for children programme published in 2004 emphasised the underlying philosophy and moral purpose as being to protect, nurture and improve the life chances of all children and young people, including those of the most vulnerable with marginal voices.

ECM ensured that a holistic approach was adopted, which focused on the needs of the whole child or young person in relation to their learning and well-being. It acknowledged that learning could not take place effectively where a child or young person did not feel safe or experienced health problems, both of which could create barriers to learning. For example, vulnerable children experience barriers to learning resulting from emotional difficulties interfering with the motivation and attitudes to learning, due to them being in public care, moving between different foster parents and having little or no links with their biological parent(s).

Strengthening Pupil Voice through Every Child Matters

The Labour Government's ECM policy initiative attracted renewed attention in pupil voice. The Department for Education and Skills (DfES) Green Paper *Every Child Matters* called for children and young people to have more of a say in developing policies that affected them. It recognised the importance of children and young people having a voice and expressed a new seriousness in approaches to engaging with them.

The Children's Commissioner in England, through the ECM agenda and the Education Act 2004, had regard to the United Nations Convention on the Rights of the Child (UNCRC), which was adopted by the United Kingdom in 1991. In particular, to Article 12 of the Convention on the Rights of the Child, which states,

> State Parties shall assure to the child who is capable of forming his or her own views the right to express those views freely in all matters affecting the child, the views of the child being given due weight in accordance with the age and maturity of the child. (OHCHR, 1989, p. 4)

When determining what constitutes the interests of children and young people, the Children's Commissioner is committed to the principle of children and young people's views being actively sought, listened to, taken seriously and acted upon by services and agencies responsible for their welfare.

The Education Act 2002 placed a duty on schools and local authorities to consult pupils about decisions affecting them. The Office for Standards in Education, Children's Services and Skills (OFSTED) school inspection schedule before September 2011 required her majesty's inspectors to systematically seek the views of children and young people, against the five ECM outcomes. The Care Standards Act 2000, Schedule 1(10), provided for the appointment of the first Children's Rights Director for England, Dr. Roger Morgan OBE, in 2004. One of his core functions was to have regard to the views expressed by children and young people, particularly of those who were looked after and vulnerable, on issues relating to their rights, care, support and welfare. He conveyed their views to the government; OFSTED; the Children's Commissioners for England, Wales, Scotland and Northern Ireland; and to all the social care authorities in England.

In March 2007, the Commission for Social Care Inspection (CSCI) published 'Policy by children: A children's views report'. This report captured the ideas and views of vulnerable children and young people, which had been shared with the Children's Rights Director. Policy 12 in the report stated,

> Regularly ask children for their views and concerns, give children ways of saying their views and concerns at all times, take what they say as seriously as what adults say, take what they say into account in making decisions that affect children, and tell children what can or cannot happen in light of their views, and why. (CSCI, 2007, p. 11)

Policy 90 in the same report stated,

> Children should always receive feedback on what has been done with views they have given about important issues in their lives and future, and should always be given reasons for decisions and actions, including the reasons for deciding in a way that goes against their wishes. (CSCI, 2007, p. 41)

The Audit Commission (2008) in their report entitled *Every Child Matters — Are we there yet?* recommended,

> Children and young people themselves should have more say in how children's services are designed. (http://www.audit-commission.gov. uk/pressoffice/pressreleases/Pages/20081029everychildmatters.aspx)

The Children's Commissioner for England, Sir Albert Aynsley Green, felt that while there had been a plethora of surveys and focus groups seeking the views of children and young people on a range of topics relevant to their lives, at national, regional and local levels, it was important that these opportunities did not become one-off 'talking shops', with little further active participation.

Change for Children Programme: Poisoned Chalice or Children's Champion?

The ECM Change for Children programme was published in December 2004. It was accompanied by four documents: one for schools, one for social care, one for the criminal justice system and one for the health service. Each explained how the government's national framework for the local change programmes would help to build services around the needs of children and young people. One of the key actions of this programme was to listen to children, young people and their families when assessing, planning and delivering service provision. However, the programme was over-bureaucratic, composing of an ECM Outcomes Framework with numerous challenging performance indicators and targets for local authority children's services to aspire to. In addition, it brought in the National Service Framework for Children, Young People and Maternity Services, composing of 11 quality standards for health, social care and some education services.

Alongside these accountability frameworks, the Children's Workforce Development Council (CWDC) published the expected core skills and knowledge for the children's workforce. They also launched The One Children's Workforce Framework, which enabled senior managers of services to audit, develop and build the capacity of their frontline workers.

Schools in partnership with children's services were expected to offer a range of extended services. Sure Start Children's Centres were also established, in the most deprived areas, acting as service delivery hubs for children and their families. These were both viewed as being the vehicles to enable schools to meet the five ECM outcomes. There was too much change occurring all at once, creating a complexity of systems, such as ContactPoint, the electronic information sharing database utilised across children's services and by pastoral staff, and special educational needs coordinators[4] in schools.

The safeguarding procedures and protocols were equally complicated requiring endless form filling and tick boxes to be completed before any future action occurring. The 'team around the child' multi-agency meetings were also established, where all those professionals from the different services working with the child and their family would meet to discuss the nature and impact of the additional provision and interventions required to address the specific needs of the client. A nominated lead professional, who ideally would be a professional or practitioner who had the most frequent and best knowledge of the child and their family, was expected to coordinate, monitor, review and evaluate the impact of the additional support and interventions the child, young person and their family had received. This system placed an ever-increasing additional workload on an already busy professional from children's services or from within a school. The lead professional would act as the first point of contact for the child and their family. They would listen to any concerns raised by the child and their family and address these issues by coordinating extra support and interventions from relevant children's services.

On reflection, all these systems and procedures and protocols were taking frontline workers from health, social care and education away from direct work with children, because of endless form filling, report writing and attendance at numerous meetings. It became obvious from the critical case reviews being held in some local authorities across England that despite all these systems and procedures to improve outcomes for children and young people, vulnerable children were still continuing to die as a result of being abused by a member of their family and as an outcome of some children's services failing to intervene early and promptly enough, as in the case of Baby P[5] in Haringey local authority. Clearly, the voice of these vulnerable children and young people was not being heard or listened to by some frontline workers. School leaders were also becoming extremely frustrated by the lack of response from

---

4. All maintained schools in England and Wales must have a qualified teacher who takes on the role of special educational needs coordinator. They are responsible for coordinating, managing and evaluating the additional provision in school, for those children identified as having a special educational need, that is, pupils who have learning difficulties or disabilities, which make it harder for them to learn or access education in comparison to their peers of the same age.

5. Baby P (Peter Connelly), was a 17-month old boy who died in the London Borough of Haringey, after enduring more than 50 injuries over an 8-month period, while in the care of his mother and her boyfriend Steven Barker and his brother Jason Owen, who were all convicted of causing or allowing the death of Peter. The child protection services, the police and the health service in Haringey had once again failed to obtain an interim care order to remove Baby P from his home to a place of safety. Three inquiries and a nationwide review of social care services took place, following the conviction of Peter's mother, boyfriend and his brother.

some children's services, when they raised concerns about the welfare and safety of a vulnerable pupil.

Although the children's workforce subscribed to the philosophy of ECM, it was becoming an administrative nightmare for frontline workers to deliver in health, education and social care.

Seeking Children and Young People's Views

The Labour Government during 2008 focused on developing a children and young people's workforce fit for the 21st century, as part of the ongoing ECM change for children programme. This process involved consulting with vulnerable children, young people and their families, on what they considered to be the essential features of effective services and the important qualities for frontline workers in meeting their needs.

The government's report on the review of child and adolescent mental health services (DCSF/DH, 2008) captured the views of children and young people accessing their services, in relation to what they identified as being the key features of effective services. These included the following: greater continuity in the staff who are working with them; having an adult who they can trust in school to discuss problems with; receiving age-appropriate services in an accessible place; being provided with advice and information in a range of different formats and media; being listened to and given individual attention from a key adult; being spoken to in a non-patronising, straightforward way, free from technical jargon; having their insight and experience valued by professionals; having access to services as soon as the need first arises and having services who keep in touch following support and treatment. These views were taken into account by the government and children's health services to improve delivery of more accessible and appropriate child-friendly mental health services, with a focus on early intervention.

The DCSF in their 2020 Children and Young People's Workforce Strategy (2008b) identified the following views of children and young people, in relation to the frontline workers supporting them. These included explaining their role to the child or young person; be more approachable; have a positive attitude and a 'young' outlook; be at ease in working with children and young people; be open minded, fair and unprejudiced; be trustworthy and honest; keep promises; listen and act on what they hear; offer a range of options; enable other pupils to understand the child or young person's needs and, most importantly, never give up on a child or young person by believing in them. The Labour Government's commitment to ensuring the children and young people's workforce were ensuring the ECM outcome *Make a positive contribution* was realised, through frontline workers and service managers listening to and acting upon children's voice, clearly ensured they provided appropriate services to meet their needs.

Under the Labour Government, each year in the autumn term, pupils in years 6, 8 and 10 in maintained schools in Britain had the opportunity to participate in completing the Tellus Survey. This survey, which is administered by the National

Foundation for Educational Research (NFER), gathered children and young people's views on their life, their school and their local area. Findings from the survey were used to inform policy development at a local level and a national level, across the five ECM outcomes. One question on the survey asked pupils: *How much have your ideas about your school been listened to when you have given them to your school council or in other ways?* Pupils were offered six options to select one response from: 'a lot; a little; not very much; not at all; don't know; I haven't given my ideas'.

There are a number of different approaches and modalities that can be used by members of the children and young people's workforce to gather the views of those pupils who may not always wish to give their views in front of other peers and adults. The following list illustrates some of the most popular methods utilised, which can be tailored to suit the preferences of the children and young people:

- Play therapy
- Art and art therapy
- Story telling
- Using intermediaries such as toys, 'persona' dolls or puppets with young children
- Using technology such as text messaging, email, blogs, podcasts, digital camera and video recording
- Using talking mats, where the child or young person selects photographs and other visual methods to illustrate a view or raise a concern
- Making use of personal 'passports'
- Using symbols to communicate views or feelings, for example, PECS and Makaton
- Using circle time to share issues and raise concerns in front of other peers

In addition, maintained schools in England and Wales were also encouraged by the government, in revised guidance (DCSF, 2008a), to use their school council, pupil forums and pupil questionnaires, as part of their regular practice, to seek pupils views on aspects of school life and learning that directly affect them.

The Decline of Every Child Matters

The Conservative/Liberal Democratic Coalition Government took up office in the United Kingdom on the 11 May, 2010. Michael Gove, Secretary of State for Education, renamed the Department for Children, Schools and Families (DCSF) the Department for Education (DfE). ECM and its related systems have not featured in any Coalition Government educational policy documents or papers. An internal DfE memorandum issued in August 2010 advised on the preferred terminology to replace ECM and the five outcomes, which was *help children achieve more*.

Over the subsequent months during 2010, some of the ECM systems began to be dismantled or cease to exist, resulting in uncertainty about the future of this agenda existing among directors of children's services in local authorities and among head teachers of schools, commissioning services from local authority children's trusts. The Coalition Government's heightened focus on pupil achievement and academic attainment, and the move away from pupil well-being has resulted in a major shift in educational policy.

The following list of policy changes illustrates the rapid decline in the importance of ECM initiatives since 11 May, 2010:

- ContactPoint, the information sharing database on children discontinued
- The administration of the annual Tellus Survey to be discontinued
- £15 million budget cut for the CWDC, with the DfE taking on core workforce activities from the CWDC, which will cease to exist as a quasi-autonomous non-government organisation (QUANGO), from 2012
- Abolition of the Youth Justice Board.
- Review of the role of the Children's Commissioner, resulting in the incorporation of responsibilities of the former Children's Rights Director.
- Removal of the duty placed on schools and colleges to cooperate with children's trusts, along with removing the duty for schools to have regard to the local authority Children and Young People's Plan.
- Revised OFSTED school inspection framework from 1 September, 2011, focusing on just 4 instead of 27 key areas: pupil achievement, quality of teaching, leadership and management, and behaviour and safety
- Sure Start Children's Centres refocusing their work from universal to targeted services to meet the needs of the most disadvantaged children and their families
- Munro review of frontline social work and child protection procedures and practices to reduce bureaucracy, enabling social workers to have more time to work directly with children and families
- Downsizing and reducing the powers of the 'state' and local authorities, with a shift to outsourcing services to private companies, the voluntary community sector and social enterprises as part of the 'Big Society'[6]
- Local authorities no longer required to establish children's trusts or to produce an annual Children and Young People's Plan
- Introduction of the Pupil Premium, which brings schools additional funding for the most deprived pupils on free school meals or who are looked after children or children from armed services families

Clearly, the Coalition Government's focus is on pupil achievement and teaching in the continued drive to raise standards. ECM has been viewed by Michael Gove as a 'peripheral', distracting head teachers from their core purpose of raising academic standards. An 'arms length' approach to pupil well-being is the preferred option of

---

6. The Big Society, which is a Conservative notion promoted by the Coalition Government in England in 2010, is about devolving responsibility for people from central government to local communities. It includes three essential elements: voluntarism to facilitate charitable and social action in the delivery of public services; local civic involvement to encourage and empower individuals to effect their neighbourhood or community and association to encourage the formation of support groups and networks.

the current Coalition Government, giving head teachers greater autonomy. However, the recent White Paper published in November 2010 acknowledged the valuable role of pastoral care systems in schools in connecting with other services such as health, social care and other professionals to remove barriers to learning for the most vulnerable disadvantaged pupils.

Conclusion

Since the Coalition Government came into power on the 11 May, 2010, there has been less national consultation with children and young people. ECM is not a high priority for this government and as a peripheral or extra burden on teachers has taken the focus in schools away from pupil achievement and teaching. It was a Labour Government initiative, and for whatever reasons, this present government does not wish to continue to roll out the 10-year ECM strategy. No doubt the Coalition Government's comprehensive spending review has already highlighted the high-cost implications of continuing to move the ECM agenda forward. When the children and young people's workforce is being cut back in local authorities, it becomes very apparent that aspects of the initiative can no longer be realistically delivered.

References

Audit Commission (2008). *Every Child Matters — Are we there yet?* (Retrieved from http://www.audit-commission.gov.uk/pressoffice/pressreleases/Pages/20081029everychildmatters.aspx). London: Audit Commission.

CSCI (2007). *Policy by children: A children's views report*. London: Commission for Social Care Inspection.

DCSF (2008a). *Working together: Listening to the voices of children and young people*. Annesley: Department for Children, Schools and Families.

DCSF (2008b). *2020 children and young people's workforce strategy*. Annesley: Department for Children, Schools and Families.

DCSF/DH (2008). *CAMHS review. Children and young people in mind: The final report of the National CAMHS Review*. London: Department for Children, Schools and Families/Department of Health.

OHCHR (1989). *Convention on the rights of the child*. Geneva: The Office of the United Nations High Commissioner for Human Rights.

Chapter 5

Beyond 'Student' Voice: The School or College as a Citizenship-rich, Human Scale and Voice-Friendly Community

Tony Breslin

Abstract

Giving voice is the ultimate purpose of education: the educated individual is not simply literate and numerate — although those skills are, of course, vital. They are confident in their ability to speak up and speak out, concerned about the impact of their actions on others, engaged as problem solvers and team players who are willing to listen, reflect and learn at every opportunity, balancing assertiveness and empathy for the common good in the process.

Against this background, effective education communities, be these schools, colleges, training providers, youth clubs or adult education centres give voice not simply to those designated 'learners' — the pupils or students — but to all who come into their midst: teachers, youth workers, support staff, parents, employers and community elders. For these, in truth, are all learners, all part of a learning community. For this reason — and the focus of this text notwithstanding — there is a need to go beyond *student* voice and explore how the multiple voices of the school or college community can find expression, not in a competitive 'who shouts loudest wins' argument but in ongoing respectful conversation.

Drawing on the author's experience — gained in the classroom, in advisory work and in the leadership of two national charities in the field, the Citizenship Foundation and Human Scale Education, this chapter provides an overview of both the history and the drivers of voice-related initiatives in the English context and makes a particular connection between this and the emergence of Citizenship Education in English secondary schools following the publication of the late Professor Sir Bernard Crick's seminal report in 1998 (DfEE, 1998).

The Student Voice Handbook: Bridging the Academic/Practitioner Divide
Copyright © 2011 by Emerald Group Publishing Limited
All rights of reproduction in any form reserved
ISBN: 978-1-78052-040-7

In this context, the chapter that follows argues for a re-conceptualisation of school and college communities as both citizenship-rich and human scale — communities in which all voices are listened and to which all voices contribute. If twenty-first century educational organisations (or *associations*) are to truly leave the so-called age of deference behind, an age with its origins in the factory system of the nineteenth century, they need to go beyond the strengthening of student voice and have a sense of what citizenship-rich and human scale practice looks and feels like — and they need to know that such approaches build inclusion and widen and recast achievement in ways that are long overdue.

Keywords: Student voice; citizenship education; citizenship-rich schools; human scale education

Introduction

The campaign to develop student voice in English secondary schools is inexorably linked with a number of initiatives over the past 50 years: the emergence of new A level subjects such as Sociology and the growth of others such as Politics in the 1960s; the emergence of social studies curricula in the 1970s; the development of Personal and Social Education (PSE) in the 1970s and 1980s — and its subsequent growth into Personal, Social and Health Education (PSHE) and latterly Personal, Social, Health and Economics Education (PSHEE); the emergence of Integrated Humanities in the 1980s. Taken together, this package formed what two early proponents had framed as the 'new social studies' (Lawton & Dufour, 1973) and subsequently, more crisply and simply, the new social curriculum (Dufour, 1990).

Considered alongside developing work in areas as diverse as emotional literacy, pastoral support, economic awareness, enterprise education, Careers Education and Guidance and vocational preparation, these innovations in social and vocational learning — which often emerged from very different political and educational starting points — complemented more overt voice-focused work and helped to build the culture in which it might thrive. For instance, the Conservative government's Technical and Vocational Education Initiative (TVEI) of the 1980s and early 1990s with its focus on a broad, balanced curriculum that encompassed the vocational *alongside* (rather than *instead* of) the academic did much to introduce principles of equality of opportunity to a curricular and extracurricular discourse that was becoming increasingly 'voice-friendly' and on which the proponents of student councils and students-as-researchers programmes began to build. All of this served to inspire a new generation of teachers — some of whom had developed their own appetite and empathy for student voice on university campuses in the 1960s, 70s and 80s — who were keen to lend their support, not always with the endorsement of their senior managers or even their teaching union colleagues.

It is reasonable to contend, though, that it was the publication in 1998 of Sir Bernard Crick's seminal report *Education for Citizenship and the Teaching of Democracy in Schools* (DfEE, 1998) that both moved the issue of student voice to the centre stage and cemented its key relationship with Citizenship Education. It did so by making the case for placing matters of social and moral responsibility, political literacy and community engagement at the heart of both the statutory curriculum *and* the broader life of the school. Engaging students, both in their schools and in the wider community, was core to Crick's agenda — not because he was keen that young people should fill their time doing 'good' things but because he saw their active involvement at school and community level as a key means of developing their sense of political agency, their ability to think critically and with a healthy scepticism and their broader political literacy: this really was to be 'learning by doing'. Thus, Citizenship Education programmes had to provide young people both with the knowledge required for effective citizenship — how our legal, political, social and economic system works and how individuals and communities can impact on this system — and with the real experience of *doing* citizenship, within the parameters of their school and the expanses of their community.

Nearly 14 years on, almost 9 years after the addition of Citizenship as a statutory subject to the National Curriculum in England and following subsequent reports specifically concerned with student voice (Davies & Yamashita, 2007; Whitty & Wisby, 2007), we are gaining a grasp of its complexities and can point to the emergence of a specialist teaching community for whom the twin and symbiotic objectives of delivering Citizenship Education and building student voice are their passion and core expertise. We are also beginning to see where Citizenship Education and student voice might sit in the kind of new social curriculum for which earlier innovators had many of the parts but little of the connecting glue.

Crick and Beyond: Stronger Voices but Different Times

But we are also living in very different times; post-9.11 and the subsequent London bombings that we have come to refer to as '7.7'; post-banking crash and in the middle of an economic downturn and, in the United Kingdom, post-New Labour and in the middle of a review of the National Curriculum in which Citizenship — and its other partners in what might again be framed a 'new social curriculum' (Dufour, 1990) — is having its hand pressed firmly against the hot fires of curricular traditionalism, examination performance and 'hard' subjects.

Crick's report was about more than *just* a new subject though, as the wording in the title — education *for* citizenship — indicates. For Crick, the Citizenship initiative was primarily about developing political literacy in a society that was imperilling its democracy by ignoring it; Crick's deliberations were as much about educational purpose as curriculum content but, in a brilliant piece of policy scholarship (Grace, 1997), he recognised that the long absence of areas such as politics and the law from the school curriculum had contributed to this very malaise. Thus, as this author has previously noted and others have concurred (Breslin, 2004a, 2004b; Pattisson & Barnett, 2005), Citizenship was a new *type* of subject, one that made as much demand on pedagogy as it did on subject knowledge. Empowering and engaging with the voice of students is vital to this pedagogy, even if it is this spirit of innovation that leaves

Citizenship vulnerable in a policy context where pedagogy tends again to the didactic and where newer subjects are viewed as 'softer' and less academic. One cannot help but reflect that were the subject that we now know as 'Citizenship' to have been called 'Politics, Law and Economics', it might have found more favour in certain settings.

Whatever, though, the future for Citizenship Education itself, the prominence that it has been so vital in securing for student voice is unlikely to be ceded. As an American academic once remarked to me, 'trying to curb the voice of students once you have invited them to speak is like trying to put tooth paste back in the tube'; in the United Kingdom, conservative proponents of a 'Big Society', rich in civil engagement, might do well to ponder this: you cannot give people, especially young people, their voice but expect to be able to circumscribe what they might say; nor can you expect them to passionately engage in community life if their education has failed to prepare them to do so effectively and sufficiently. Those who have made the long march from voicelessness will want to put things — the things that matter to them — in their own words, as recent student protests have demonstrated in the United Kingdom and as the involvement of the young in reform movements in Tunisia, Egypt, Bahrain and elsewhere in the Arab world have shown in other settings. Schools, if anything, have been courageous in this respect; they have not wanted to 'put the toothpaste back in the tube'. Rather, they have been notable in forging progressively, albeit cautiously, towards greater student engagement. And those that have been most effective have worked broadly within a framework that might be described as 'citizenship-rich' (Breslin & Dufour, 2006; NFER, 2008).

In the remaining sections of this chapter, I want to do five things: first, I want to outline and explore the concept of the citizenship-rich school and the kind of human-scale community that it seeks to construct and renew; second, I want to reflect on how such practice might address the twin agendas that drive education policy — achievement and inclusion; third, I want to reflect a little more on matters of school structure and organisation and whether, especially in the context of the modern secondary school, arrangements are sufficiently 'voice-friendly'; fourth, I want to place student voice itself in a more critical spotlight and pose questions about which students get involved and in what ways and finally, in closing, I want to ask whether student voice itself, as currently construed, is too limiting a paradigm to work within and whether we need to reach beyond this to a broader concept of multiple voice — not only that of the student, of course, but also that of the parent, the teacher, the community member and the employer working together to generate the distinct and shared outcomes that each seeks and requires from our education system.

Clear in Voice and Human in Scale: The Citizenship-Rich School or College in Outline

The 'citizenship-rich' school or college — one that welcomes student and community involvement and is innovative and inclusive in the way that it does so — is a different kind of place in which to teach and learn, critically because the developing of citizens, rather than *just* the qualifying of learners, is at the core of its mission. In such a setting, children and young people are seen as much more than citizens of tomorrow. They are recognised — and given voice — as the learner-citizens of today, subject to and enabled by various laws and agreements, not least the United Nations Convention on the Rights of the Child (United Nations, 1989). Such a school or college has the following five defining characteristics:

1. Citizenship Education is clearly identified in the curriculum model, on the timetable, in assessment frameworks, in teachers' Continuing Professional Development provision and in the school's improvement and development plans.
2. It enables young people to develop their Citizenship knowledge through a skills-based and learner-centred pedagogy.
3. Citizenship learning, thus, takes place not only within designated timetable space — important as this is — but also through a range of opportunities and activities, on and off the school or college site, which are valued by students, teachers and the wider community.
4. It encourages and facilitates the active and effective participation of all — students, teachers, parents and the wider community — in its day-to-day activities.
5. It models the principles that it teaches about in Citizenship in the way that it operates as an institution and a community and proclaims this outlook in its documentation.

But why should a school or college seek to become citizenship-rich? Again, there are a number of rationales, but these might be summarised in terms of the following:

1. Justice: Schools and colleges seek to be just communities in which all are equally valued and given voice — a citizenship-rich perspective can help the achievement of this aspiration.
2. Effectiveness: Those schools and colleges that involve students, parents and the wider community so as to build a better understanding of the needs of each are better placed to meet these needs — a citizenship-rich perspective places the principles of student voice, community involvement, staff development and family learning at the core of school activity.
3. Achievement: Increasingly, research shows that a strong focus on these citizenship-rich principles brings returns in terms of student performance across the curriculum — voice-friendly citizenship-rich schools do not just raise citizens, they raise standards (Hannam, 2001).
4. Inclusion: The same principles deliver practical inclusion — the breadth of Citizenship learning is much wider than that of a conventional subject and reaches a broader range of learners including those often thought of as disaffected, disruptive or both.

In many respects, the citizenship-rich school has much in common with the Human Scale and Urban Village school traditions established by educationalists such as Theodore Sizer (1996) in the United States (Sizer, 1996) and Mike Davies (2005),

Mary Tasker (2003) and James Wetz (2009) in the United Kingdom. Similar commitments to inclusion, community and parental engagement and to social justice are evident as is a commitment to non-didactic and iterative pedagogies and to the child's personal and emotional development. Although the focus on some form of formal student democracy is written into the citizenship-rich model in a way that is not necessarily the case in purely human-scale settings, it is impossible to conceive of a human-scale school that does not embrace the voice of those in its care. Student voice emerges strongly in human-scale settings partly because of the concern for size (whereby the schools are either themselves small in scale or they are larger in size but arranged as a series of smaller learning communities) and, critically, because of the primacy given to the development of human relationships, not least between student and teacher, and the skills, dispositions and emotional literacy that support these. In the citizenship-rich school, student voice emerges for these reasons *and* because of the various conduits established for this, notably student councils and the like. It is important, though, that as much credence and prominence is given to student feedback that arises through informal voice channels (which provide a reflection of the extent to which pupils *feel* respected and listened to and the extent to which they are empowered deliberately to positively question *their* school) as those in the formal domain (such as the school council, student involvement on interviewing panels, surveys of student need, 'students as researchers' programmes and peer-to-peer support frameworks). Enabling voice is not just about creating structures; it is about the spirit and ethos of the school or college as a community.

Inclusion-First Policymaking: An Instrumental (and Moral) Rationale for Student Voice

Those that have used citizenship-rich or human-scale principles to change practice across their schools, enshrining student voice at the core of their practice, are rightly commended for their focus on matters of inclusion, social justice, community engagement, emotional literacy and the education of the whole child. It is less often the case that these school leaders and classroom practitioners are praised for their innovative approaches to building and widening achievement. Too often, matters such as student voice are seen as the 'fluffy' stuff, to be attended to after literacy and numeracy — or, more nakedly, examination scores — have been addressed, rather than as another means through which student achievement across a broader cohort can be raised. This is not to say that strategies around voice and engagement should become enslaved to the standards agenda. It is, though, to recognise their oft-ignored but potential contribution to it. With this comes a timely educational truth: the participative, community-engaged and community-engaging citizenship-rich or human-scale school builds inclusion; included students achieve.

By comparison, the kind of narrow 'achievement-first' strategy (where 'achievement' is measured largely or substantially by examination scores) typically favoured by policymakers of all persuasions risks contributing to exclusion. Herein is a tension that lies at the heart of the current educational agenda: the stress between raising achievement and maintaining inclusion. The common-sense response advanced by policymakers and politicians is that these two go hand in glove: raise achievement and inclusion takes care of itself. The reality is that this has never been the case. As any teacher in a 'challenging' school will testify, the more successful they are with the 60, 70, 80 per cent, the more excluded the 40, 30, 20 per cent become and, critically, in terms of the pervasive focus on 'school improvement', the more marginal the gains. In short, achievement creates its own exclusion; witness this in the living metaphor of our burgeoning gated communities where the 'successful' nervously secure themselves from their less successful peers with alarms, padlocks and security cameras. Citizenship-rich and human-scale perspectives — focused as they are around the primacy of the individual student's voice *and* the shared voice of the wider student body — are less about simple school or college improvement and more profoundly about school or college *transformation*: changing how schools operate as communities and as hubs *for* communities — giving these communities voice and producing sustainable gains in achievement in the process. Noticeably, and with the occasional noble exception (Ajegbo, 2007), 'closing the achievement-exclusion gap' has often been a more prominent feature in policy debates that are not centrally focused on education or that do not emerge from the educational domain. Closing this gap is, for example, a key objective of the range of reports in the community cohesion field (Cantle, 2008; CLG, 2007; Rowe, Horsley, Thorpe, & Breslin, 2011). It ought to have a more central role in educational thinking.

Strategies that give primacy to issues such as student voice are central rather than marginal to the standards agenda but start from a different place: the need for the school to work as an effective community and for the learner to develop as a confident, informed, effective, educated citizen. Such strategies might be defined as 'inclusion-first' (Breslin, 2007). The important drive to raise achievement — especially when characterised, as it is currently in England, by league tables, inter-school competition and the appearance of parental choice — has, after undoubted early gains, potentially added to the very exclusion that successful educational policy-making needs to challenge. When there is manifest underperformance across the education system, an all-out focus on levels of measured attainment is the right one. However, where low attainment is consistently located among certain, often voiceless, social groups and at certain schools (regardless of the frequency of inspections or changes to the leadership team), we have the educational version of market failure. In this kind of setting, new strategies are required. At such a point in the policy cycle, any new educational initiative should be appraised not simply on how effectively it can build the achievement of some but on how effectively it will deliver inclusion (and thence achievement) for all: the right kind of 'voice' frameworks can do so.

Institutional Barriers to Developing Schools that Are 'Voice-Friendly'

Likewise, however stabilising they might sometimes appear, our secondary school structures — as with our attainment-focused pedagogies — may be holding learning back, not driving it forward; they too might benefit from a little upheaval. Especially for those working in the most challenging schools, continual calls to 'improve' serve only to confirm the difficulty of their task, the absence of a level playing field and the organisational and operational straitjackets with which they are burdened. Far from 'underperforming', many of these schools are fighting against incredible socio-economic odds: poverty, family breakdown, community fragmentation, high levels of student and teacher turnover. Once any school is achieving the best it can with a given student intake, the requirement is for organisational transformation rather than simply a harder foot on the examination pedal — trying to achieve the latter without the former only results in teacher burnout and community disillusion. Here, the application of inclusion-first principles and citizenship-rich or human scale strategies offers the prospect of a way forward — and a strong sense of not just student voice but a full range of stakeholder voices provides a practical articulation of these principles and strategies.

But if our schools are going to become citizenship-rich, human-scale and voice-friendly, the extent of the institutional remodelling required should not be understated. The briefest look at the sociological literature on institutions tells us that the more structured (or in the jargon, 'total') the institution, the more likely that the institutional structure will militate against change. Indeed, total institutions struggle to distinguish between 'good' change — creative, innovative, transformational and enabling — and 'bad' change — poorly thought through, impractical and imposed (Breslin, 2007). In short, total institutions maximise the *feeling* of change — any change — while minimising its *impact* (Breslin, 2011b). Modelled on the early twentieth century manufacturing plant (if not the nineteenth-century psychiatric hospital), second-ary schools, in particular, are (perhaps necessarily) highly structured (and, therefore, fairly total) institutions. Might this explain why, as teachers, we feel that we are con-stantly dealing with change and yet, technology aside, we have much the same curriculum and classroom as we had 50 years ago? Might it also explain the dis-satisfaction and apparently low professional self-esteem expressed by teachers and evidenced by the relatively high numbers departing the profession year-on-year — the juxtaposition of bright, creative, socially motivated graduates and highly structured, risk-averse working environments that often deny the voice of the practitioner as surely as they do that of the student is a recipe for professional discord and institutional disharmony. It was surely one of the greatest policy oversights of recent years to have embarked on the most ambitious secondary school building programme in living memory without having a serious discussion about the kind of places we require schools to be in the twenty-first century. In truth, England's now abolished *Building Schools for the Future* programme risked building schools and colleges for the *past* — often stunning buildings but designed to support the teacher–learner relationships of the last century (and the one before that), rather than the century that we are now in.

Closing the Participation Gap: Reaching beyond the Usual Suspects

Cast an eye towards the make-up of our emergent political class and one gains a summary of the successes and failures of building youth engagement (and political engagement more broadly), certainly in the United Kingdom and across a number of other European democracies, in recent years. Here, there have been two issues, the first relating to the emerging disconnect between 'civil' society and 'civic' politics, a distinction that this author was first introduced to by three researchers prominent in the UK's voluntary sector (Jochum, Pratten, & Wilding, 2005); the second, a narrowing of the funnel into the civil and the civic spheres, especially the latter. These developments in the shape of civil society and the formal political realm have importance for any debate about student voice or youth participation because they serve to highlight the infrastructure in which we expect the young and others to find 'voice' and the challenges that they might face. But let me first spend a little bit of time articulating this distinction between the 'civil' and the 'civic'. In so doing, I draw heavily on an earlier paper (Breslin, 2008) produced for a pan-European discussion forum of which I was a part, *Res Publica*, convened by Diana Pinto (2007–2008), a title since adopted by an unconnected UK-based centre-right think-tank led by Phillip Blond (2010), author of *Red Tory* and one of the acknowledged architects of the Big Society framework cited earlier.

In discussions about how the individual or group interacts with the government and the state, it is common to use the terms 'civil' and 'civic' interchangeably, to consider them synonymous. This is an error; it is clear that the process through which individuals interplay with the state is mediated through two channels: a set of 'civic' conduits and institutions and a wider set of 'civil' relationships. Very broadly, the 'civic' conduits operate in the formal sphere, whereas the 'civil' domain describes a much more complex, untidier and informal space. At the school level, one might make a similar distinction, where those elected to the school council or student union executive or appointed to key status positions — such as prefect or head boy or head girl or union president — are part of the school's civic domain. By comparison, the group of 'self-starters' who launch a campaign to open school or college facilities to the community in the evening are operating in something more akin to the civil realm.

In the wider context, we would, therefore, think of the 'civic' as constituting formal politics — locally, regionally, nationally and, increasingly, beyond — and we might also think of longstanding organisations linked in to formal politics: political parties, trade unions and chambers of commerce. Finally, we might include larger 'voice of the sector' bodies such as, in the United Kingdom, the Trade Union Congress (TUC) and the Confederation of British Industry (CBI). Those that operate in the civic sphere are either a part of the apparatus of state or they are hardwired into that apparatus by virtue of their influence, status and, perhaps, longevity. By contrast, 'civil' society consists of a myriad of usually smaller organisations and campaigning groups that range from locally based tenants' action groups and community support networks to nationally prominent charities and campaigning bodies, broadly defined in the United Kingdom as the 'third sector'. In terms of student voice, a campaign to change the school uniform or to raise funds for an earthquake abroad that emerges from the student body (rather than as a project of the school council) would constitute activism that has its base in the school's civil society.

Against this background, I want to suggest three things: first, that, beyond the school or college gates, civil society is in better health than the civic frameworks with which it, from time to time, works; second, that, again beyond these gates, the civic and the civil spheres are becoming increasingly separated and that this is problematic for the future health of our democracies and third, that at the level of the school or college and more widely, we need to do better in reaching and including a far greater range of participants. There is nothing new in these concerns — as noted earlier, a concern about the health of the 'civic' sphere formed much of Crick's staring point almost a decade and a half ago, and this specific worry permeates a range of more recent reports (Goldsmith, 2007; NFER, 2008; Power, 2006). An initial response to this situation was to cast the problem as one of apathy. However, the relative healthiness of the 'civil' sphere is a challenge to this analysis — in the United Kingdom, the numbers of (especially young) people active in a range of campaigns and campaigning bodies, across the past decade, that span the political spectrum — from the Countryside Alliance through Make Poverty History to the Stop the War Coalition and the current student loans protests — are hardly an indicator of apathy, although, as I shall outline later, the apparent narrowness of the demographic involved in these campaigns is a cause for concern. Nonetheless, whether their schools, colleges and universities capture it or not, these young people are keen to get their voice across; they are interested in overtly *political* issues. Indeed, the increasingly global popularity of youth-focused 'vote-them-off' television programmes such as *Big Brother* and *The X Factor* suggests that voting itself is not the problem — the way we 'do' formal politics is. Moreover, the apparent mood among media commentators and activists in the civil sphere that formal politics lacks the wherewithal to demonstrate relevance to the issues that protestors raise evidences the kind of separation between the civil and the civic domains claimed here (Breslin, 2008; Neil, 2011).

Of course, some civil society activists have always questioned the value of formal politics — such a question, whether reasonable or not, has been posed by just about every major protest movement. I want to suggest, though, that the separation between the two spheres, at least in the United Kingdom, is in danger of becoming entrenched and that this entrenchment results from two related dynamics. The first of these dynamics relates to the long-term decline of those organisations that bridged the civil and the civic spheres, creating reasonably clear route-ways from community- or workplace-based civil participation to a place in the civic realm. Thus, the decline in the power, influence and profile of organisations such as the trade unions (which, for instance, saw their UK membership decline from 13.2 million members in 1979 to 6.4 million in 2005) has a direct impact on the ability of these bodies to prepare activists not just for *civil* engagement but also for political participation in *civic* life. The young car factory apprentice encouraged (or sometimes obliged) to first join a trade union, then to attend union meetings and then to stand for some minor office has set out on a path that may subsequently lead to an invitation to join the local Labour Party — and standing for election to the local council at some later point. Until recently, this was not an uncommon biography for a Labour activist seeking nomination as a parliamentary candidate to bring to the selection process but a range of changes — notably in our industrial infrastructure, our methods of manufacture and the nature of our local communities — have unwittingly conspired to being this particular production line to a close, and they have been helped by an additional dynamic: the professionalisation of the routes into formal politics.

This second dynamic has done much to contribute to the separation between the civic and the civil spheres, and it has implications for the young people now emerging from our schools and colleges. When a recent and comparatively youthful English Secretary of State talks of being 'the first Labour MP in my constituency not to have worked down the mine', he tells a story not just about industrial decline but about the changing ways in which those with political aspirations are recruited into formal politics — much earlier and following a very particular induction that serves as preparation for a life in formal politics. Today, such an induction might typically involve a period working as an MP's researcher, a period in the employment of a prominent think-tank and a spell as a 'Special Adviser' to a senior political figure, all preceded by a degree in politics, philosophy and economics from one of a handful of elite universities. Of course, much of this is good for the efficiency of politics, and it attracts many of the best young brains (and young voices) into the formal political infrastructure. The risk, though, is that it recasts political representation as a full-time, lifelong, graduate-entry career, by definition impacting on the diversity of backgrounds from which candidates are drawn and the breadth of experience that they are able to draw on from outside, what is increasingly referred to, somewhat pejoratively, in the United Kingdom as the 'Westminster village' — a difficult village for the experienced civil society campaigner or the community or workplace activist to enter and one that can appear irrelevant, aloof and self-serving to those more distant from the political process. Meanwhile, the civil society workforce itself is increasingly graduate educated (often to second degree), tightly networked, white and usually of middle-class origin. In short, the internal diversity of third sector bodies is rarely as rich as the diversity that these bodies rightly campaign for externally. At a time when, at least in the United Kingdom, a commitment to social mobility is one of the few uniting narratives across political parties (Milburn, 2009), it is ironic that our parliamentarians have barely taken a glance at the diversity and heritage of those in their own profession.

But where is the relevance of all of this to debates about student voice and the development of voice-friendly schools and colleges? The argument is that these problems have been accentuated by some of the initiatives designed to encourage wider youth participation and learner or student voice. As I have argued elsewhere (Breslin, 2008, 2011a), these well-intended initiatives have tended not to broaden the numbers involved but, instead, have opened up further opportunities for those already expert in participating, widening the 'participation gap', rather than closing it, in the process (Breslin, 2008). Thus, in the school or college setting, it is too often the case that it is the same students who sit on the school council, act as student researchers, gain appointment as prefects and lead charitable campaigns, each participation experience further honing their engagement skills, their ability to get *their* voice across. And it is these students who are most likely, on the one hand, to come from middle-class backgrounds and, on the other, to proceed to the kind of careers now open to bright, confident and much better prepared young people in civil society and in the slipstream into formal politics. To reiterate, the crisis in social mobility is as pertinent to those young people entering politics or civil society as it is to those seeking a career in medicine or law. While this should never be its sole or main purpose, opening up student voice opportunities to more students will ensure that more are prepared to subsequently take their proper place in public life, just as Crick had aspired for them to do.

Widening and Redefining Voice: A Challenge for the Voice-Friendly School or College

Against this backdrop, the challenge to schools and colleges is threefold and clear. First, if we accept the premise that particular students and student clusters are, in a sense, overactive within the school community, we need to think seriously about redistributing existing participation or 'voice' opportunities across the school or college; second, we need to substantially increase the range and number of opportunities available so that students are exposed to 'voice' opportunities that genuinely stretch and challenge them, as we would expect learning activities anywhere else across the life of the school or college to do and third, we need to think about stretching the concept of the voice-friendly school or college beyond the student body. Before closing, let me say a little more about each of these challenges.

(1) *Sharing voice: Redistributing the participation opportunities available*
    Schools and colleges should review their 'voice' arrangements to ensure that participation opportunities — or the best opportunities — are not dominated by a small group of students, even where these are bright, confident and able volunteers. Every student has the right to have their voice developed and heard and to rehearse the skills of effective citizen engagement and political participation — whether this is chairing a meeting, making a speech or taking part in a debate — and should be given the chance to do so. This implies that schools and colleges should evaluate their 'voice' policies and strategies frequently, monitoring who takes part, how often and how they are elected or selected, and intervening to strengthen participation skills in areas such as public speaking and negotiation.

(2) *Raising voice: Increasing the number and diversity of participation opportunities available*
    Too often, those participation opportunities that schools and colleges offer tend to one kind of civic participation — serving on a formal committee, typically the student council but sometimes (and this is to be encouraged) serving as an associate member of the governing body. We need to be bolder, though, in what we think of as a formal or informal participation opportunity and where we find them: in community settings, through volunteering programmes, on social action projects, through the local youth council or election to a youth parliament. We also need to think about how they relate to curriculum learning and what skills they develop in which young people, taking time to push learners beyond their comfort zones and into the kind of participation settings that they would not ordinarily choose.

(3) *Widening voice: Moving beyond notions of 'student' voice*
    In developing voice programmes and participation frameworks, schools and colleges are emphatically right to start with the voice of the learner, but in itself,

this is insufficient. In poorer communities, in particular, we need to give voice to these communities as a whole, not simply to young people. In fact, through family engagement programmes and by enabling all who work in these schools and colleges and with these young people to find (or re-find) their own voice, we can challenge the current barriers that prevent active citizens having their say in a wide range of settings, breaking the cycle that can see parents, teachers and mentors as demotivated as the young people they teach or support. A concern for social justice — and for the health of our democracy — dictates that we cannot allow such a situation to sustain.

None of this is easy but it is a moral prerequisite that students and others in the school or college community should be able and encouraged to express themselves; that they should have the knowledge, skills and confidence to do so effectively and that the nature of their interventions should be purposeful, respected and, where possible, acted upon. As the colleagues contributing to this book and many others, especially in the Citizenship Education community, can demonstrate, there is a wealth of good practice to learn from — and a clear sign that when schools and colleges embrace the voices of their students and the wider communities that they serve, they are more effective in the task traditionally ascribed to them by those communities, by parents and by policymakers — delivering an excellent education. Perhaps that is why schools and colleges rarely unravel participation frameworks once these have been put in place; perhaps, it is why they do not want to put the toothpaste back in the tube; perhaps, it is why so many are now going a little further, a little quicker. We should commend them for doing so.

Conclusion

As was contended in the Abstract at the head of this chapter, giving voice is the ultimate purpose of education: the educated individual is not simply literate and numerate — although those skills are, of course, vital. They are confident in their ability to speak up and speak out; concerned about the impact of their actions on others; and engaged as problem solvers and team players who are willing to listen, reflect and learn at every opportunity, balancing assertiveness and empathy for the common good in the process.

Raising Voice, Raising Citizens, Raising Standards

Against this backdrop, there are several good reasons for schools and colleges to think more positively about matters of 'voice', but three are perhaps especially pertinent:

- The more effectively that schools and colleges draw on voice across the student body and various stakeholders, the more that they will understand the needs of those students and other stakeholders and the better placed *they* will be to serve them.

- The greater the variety of formal and informal voice opportunities that schools and colleges open up, the wider the range of meaningful opportunities that they will create for *all* students to develop the communication, negotiation and listening skills vital for their self-esteem, their future employability, their political literacy and their capacity to genuinely make an impact in their communities and beyond.
- The more that these opportunities are opened to other stakeholders, the more that communities themselves will be engaged in this capacity building and in the creation and renewal of the educational and community infrastructures that serve them.

Those familiar with the UK's recent policy history will be aware of the impact of the 'Every Child Matters' narrative on practice in the education and children's services sphere under the last Labour government. In the context of the discussions laid bare in these pages, we need to move beyond a paradigm in which every *child* matters to one where every *voice* matters. That really would bring the impact that Crick's report on Citizenship Education sought — it would 'change the political culture' of our society, permanently and for the better; it might also give us the much-needed building blocks for the 'Big Society' that the current UK administration is so keen on.

References

Ajegbo, K. (2007). *Curriculum review: Diversity and citizenship*. London: Department for Education and Skills.

Blond, P. (2010). *Red Tory: How left and right have broken Britain and how we can fix it*. London: Faber & Faber.

Breslin, T. (2004a). Citizenship: New subject, new TYPE of 'subject'. *Teaching Citizenship*, (8), Spring, 38–45 (Association for Citizenship Teaching, London).

Breslin, T. (2004b). Citizenship, 'subject building and the rethinking of 'subject'. Careers Education and Citizenship: An inclusive approach, Occasional Paper, Lent 2004, pp. 17–25, Canterbury Christ Church University College — VT Careers Management, Kent Breslin, T. and Rowe, C. (2011, forthcoming) Set of news and journal articles currently in development in partnership with Navigate Education, Deddington.

Breslin, T. (2007). Inclusion-first and citizenship-rich: A glimpse of the future of schooling. *Transformation*, (7), Autumn, 4–8 (Capgemini — National School of Government, London).

Breslin, T. (2008). *The state and civil society: Issues of relevance and problems of access*. Unpublished seminar paper. Res Publica, Paris.

Breslin, T. (2011a). Fostering youth civic engagement: Reflections from the UK. In: K. Plehwe (Ed.), *Demokratie Leben Lernen*. Berlin: Hanseatic Lighthouse.

Breslin, T. (2011b). *Teachers, schools and change*. Stoke-on-Trent, UK: Trentham Books.

Breslin, T., & Dufour, B. (2006). The way forward: Building the citizenship-rich school. In: T. Breslin & B. Dufour (Eds), *Developing citizens: A comprehensive introduction to effective citizenship education in the secondary school*. London: Hodder Murray.

Cantle, T. (2008). *Community cohesion: A new framework for race and diversity*. Basingstoke: Palgrave Macmillan.

CLG (2007). *Our shared future: Report of the commission on integration and community cohesion*. London: Department for Communities and Local Government.

Davies, L., & Yamashita, H. (2007). *School councils-school improvement*. University of Birmingham, with the support of the Esmee Fairbairn Foundation and Deutsche Bank.

Davies, M. (2005). *Less is more: The move to educate on a human scale*. Bristol: Human Scale Education.

DfEE. (1998). *Education for citizenship and the teaching of democracy in schools*. London: OCA.

Dufour, B. (1990). *The new social curriculum: A guide to cross-curricular issues for teachers, parents and governors*. Cambridge: Cambridge University Press.

Goldsmith, P. (2007). *Citizenship: Our common bond, Lord Goldsmith's citizenship review*. London: Ministry of Justice.

Grace, G. (1997). Critical policy scholarship: Reflections on the integrity of knowledge and research. In: G. Shacklock & J. Smyth (Eds), *Being reflexive in critical educational and social research*. London: Falmer Press.

Hannam, D. (2001). *A pilot study to evaluate the impact of the student participation aspects of the citizenship order on standards of education in secondary schools*. London: Community Service Volunteers.

Jochum, V., Pratten, B., & Wilding, K. (2005). *Civil renewal and active citizenship: A guide to the debate*. London: National Council for Voluntary Organisations.

Lawton, D., & Dufour, B. (1973). *The new social studies: A handbook for teachers in primary, secondary and further education*. London: Heinemann.

Milburn, A. (2009). *Unleashing aspiration: The final report of the panel on fair access to the professions*. London: Cabinet Office.

Neil, A. (2011). Posh and posher: Why public school boys run Britain. BBC1 Television Programme (broadcast 19th February 2011), London: British Broadcasting Corporation.

NFER. (2008). *Citizenship education longitudinal study (CELS): 6th Annual Report: Young peoples' civic participation in and beyond school: Attitudes, intentions and influences*. Department for Children, Pinto Schools and Families, London.

Pattisson, P., & Barnett, A. (2005). *A school for citizenship* in *teaching citizenship*. Issue 10. Association for Citizenship Teaching, London.

Pinto, D. (2007–2008). *Voices for the 'res publica': A series of reports on the national roundtable seminars*. Unpublished data.

Power (2006). *Power to the people: The report of power — An independent enquiry into Britain's democracy*. York, UK: Joseph Rowntree Charitable Trust/Joseph Rowntree Reform Trust.

Rowe, D., Horsley, N., Thorpe, T., & Breslin, T. (2011). *School leaders, Community Cohesion and the Big Society*. CfBT Education Trust, Reading, UK.

Sizer, T. (1996). *Horace's hope: What works for the American high school*. New York, NY: Mariner Books.

Tasker, M. (2003). *Smaller structures in secondary education: A research digest*. Bristol: Human Scale Education.

United Nations (1989). *The United Nations Declaration on the rights of the child.* New York, NY: United Nations.

Wetz, J. (2009). *Urban village schools.* London: Calouste Gulbenkian Foundation.

Whitty, G., & Wisby, E. (2007). *Real decision making? School councils in action.* London: Institute of Education/Department for Children, Schools and Families.

Chapter 6

Not Capturing Voices: A Poststructural Critique of the Privileging of Voice in Research

Charlotte Chadderton

Abstract

This chapter makes a contribution to the debate on the potential, or otherwise, of student voice research to have a social justice impact. It draws explicitly on insights from poststructuralist theories to interrogate some of the theoretical assumptions that underpin the concern to privilege and capture 'silenced voices' in research with social justice aims. Most of the poststructural theorists whose work is referred to have not written specifically for the field of student voice, rather they engage more generally with the question of marginalised voices in research. The chapter discusses the impact of poststructural notions of truth, subjectivity and power on issues such as voice, representation and empowerment in research and draws on data from a recent ethnographic study of Key Stage 4 (aged 15–16) students' experiences of education in secondary schools in Manchester, England, to illustrate some of the tensions that arise. It is argued that a more complex notion of voice as shifting and fluid should be adopted, as well as a notion of researcher as unreliable narrator, to try and avoid naive or even potentially damaging research being conducted in the name of student voice research. It concludes with some suggestions for a more complex understanding of student voice research based on these poststructural insights and argues that this may help us both appreciate the potential of student voice initiatives, whilst being sensitive to the very real limitations.

Keywords: Poststructural voice; plural and shifting voices; power and representation; the unreliable narrator

The Student Voice Handbook: Bridging the Academic/Practitioner Divide
ISBN: 978-1-78052-040-7

Introduction

Academic research has been implicated in the continued oppression of many social groups through the silencing of subjects' voices (Bishop, 2005; Tuhiwai Smith, 1999). Marginalised groups such as women; non-white people; lesbian, gays, bisexuals and transsexuals (LGBT); young people and people with disabilities have been, and continue to be pathologised, dominated and even exploited through both qualitative and quantitative research. Whilst this does not happen in the same way or to the same extent with each group, the fact remains that research plays a role in the marginalisation process. Many recent studies therefore privilege the notion of 'capturing' participants' voices to render their perspectives heard (Orner, 1992; Solorzano & Yosso, 2002, p. 37) and allow subjects to self-define (Ladson-Billings & Donner, 2005, p. 283), with the aim of challenging this pathologisation. In such research, the experiences and perspectives of marginalised groups are accepted as the foundation of knowledge (Delgado Bernal, 1998, p. 558). Such studies tend to be driven by concerns to promote social equality, challenge objectification and stereotypes, make the research process more democratic and contribute to the empowerment of participants. This attempt to challenge marginalisation and empower can be seen in many aspects of what might be called the student voice movement, which encourages young people to share their own ideas about their educational experiences to bring about transformation in terms of school improvement or active citizenship. These claims to capture voice and empower are, however, contested and problematic.

Although some critiques of the call for student voice have been made in the field of student voice (see, e.g. Bragg, 2007; Ellsworth, 1989; Fielding, 2004; Orner, 1992), this chapter draws explicitly on insights from poststructuralist theories to interrogate some of the assumptions that underpin the concern to privilege voice. Most of the poststructural theorists whose work is referred to have not written specifically for the field of student voice, rather they engage more generally with the question of the voices of the marginalised in research. Whilst the author is aware that much is omitted from this discussion, and the critique could be expanded, this chapter is intended as a contribution to an ongoing debate, and a call for more complex notions of voice to inform educational research.

Some Poststructural Insights

Poststructuralist theorists have critiqued the notion that the researcher is able to render participants' voices heard in research, arguing that it is naïve and ultimately impossible (e.g. Mazzei & Jackson, 2009). This view is based on three main features of poststructural thought. First, the notion of a universal 'truth' has been problematised. Poststructural theorists argue that reality can be plural, can have conflicting meanings and meanings vary according to context (Weedon, 1997, p. 24). It has also been shown that language does not accurately reflect reality (Peters & Burbules, 2004; St. Pierre, 2000). Second, poststructural theories challenge the notion of a unitary subject (Lenzo, 1995) and a stable, coherent self (St. Pierre, 2000). Rather than being seen as the fixed essence of an individual, identities are seen as socially produced, negotiated and performatively and discursively constituted (Butler, 1993, 2004). Subjectivity is considered to be influenced by several competing discourses and therefore as contradictory and shifting. Indeed, the subject is viewed as the site of the battle for power between competing discourses, which the subject always has to negotiate (Weedon, 1997). Third, poststructural theorists have a complex under-standing of power as 'pervasive, productive, positive' (Peters, 2001, p. 13), rather than just oppressive. Power is seen as multidirectional, not just unidirectional.

These developments in theory have had a significant impact on the way in which the notion of 'voice' can be understood in research; this chapter discusses just some of them. My aim with this discussion is not to dismiss the notion of privileging voice in research, rather to problematise and complicate it.

Complicating Notions of Voice

Notions of 'voice' tend to privilege experience as a source of knowledge, a stance that has been challenged by poststructuralists. The privileging of experience was part of a move to expand and disrupt the traditional notion of universal foundations of knowledge (Delgado Bernal, 1998). Women have been at the forefront of the move, arguing that theories that stem from patriarchal perspectives are inadequate to address notions of gender, or more broadly, difference (Flores, 2000). Feminists have suggested that women bring different perspectives based on their experiences of oppression. Instead, there has been a recognition that what counts as knowledge counts as such because of the power (based on position in society) of those creating it-thus knowledge is created, and situated, not inherent or based on reason (Lenzo, 1995; St. Pierre, 2000). More recently, feminists from minority backgrounds have argued that the influence of race, class or sexuality, would lead to more diverse perspectives (Flores, 2000). Race theorists have also argued that experience of racism creates a common awareness or viewpoint (e.g. Tate, 1997, p. 210). Some thus claim the existence of a 'racial consciousness' (Barnes, 1995, p. 341), based on a shared, voiced experience of oppression (Calmore, 1996), which shapes people's perspectives. Advocates of student voice claim similarly that young people have a unique perspective stemming from their experiences as students (Fielding, 2001; Mitra, 2003).

However, the automatic linking of voice or perspective to experience or identity has been called into question by poststructuralists, on the basis that experience becomes linked to notions of 'authentic' knowledge (Lather, 2009; Mazzei, 2009; St. Pierre, 2000) 'expressed through a transcendental voice that reflects a direct and unmediated consciousness of experience' (Jackson, 2003, p. 703). They argue that the privileging of experience is underpinned by the belief that the subject has access to a single coherent reality and that the subject can both interpret and express this reality. As Jackson (2003) argues

> [The] romanticisation of voices leads to emancipatory researchers' tendencies to idealise and totalise their participants' experiences,

> ignoring the messiness of their multiple subjectivities and contextual
> realities. (Jackson, 2003, p. 697)

It has also been argued that to assume a unified experience can lead to the essentialisation of individual experience (Peters & Burbules, 2004). The notion of an 'authentic voice' is seen to ignore different and shifting experiences, as well as the complexity of the intersection of various factors that shape both experiences and perceptions of these, including class, age, gender, race, religion, origin and biography. Furthermore, it has been pointed out that experience does not automatically equal awareness, nor does it equal any kind of wider understanding or an automatic ability to locate the experience in a wider context (Weiler, 2001; Crozier, 2003). Moreover, experience can be informed by, for example, racism or sexism, and therefore be used to oppress, rather than to emancipate (hooks, 1994, p. 85). Thus whilst I am not arguing that lived experience does not offer an important perspective, the notion of fixed links between experience and knowledge needs to be problematised (Weiler, 2001). There is a problem, then, with student voice programmes that are — implicitly or explicitly — underpinned by the notion of voices as 'authentic', unitary or singularly representative.

The second point concerns self-definition. The right to, and possibility of, self-definition has been seen by many of those privileging voice as empowering. However, poststructuralists have challenged the notion that a subject *can* actually self-define (Pillow, 2003, 2007). Poststructural theorists such as Judith Butler (1993, 1997, 2004) have argued that identity categories do not reflect identities; they create them. Discourses do not describe (pre-existing) subjects as is widely believed, rather they shape and produce them. This approach challenges the liberal humanist belief that the subject is the author of the discourse she speaks (Weedon, 1997). A person is rendered a subject through discourse, in a process referred to as subjectification. Butler argues that the subject cannot pre-exist its subjectification. The individual subject is therefore both constituted and constrained by discourse. As Mercer (1994, cited by Bhattacharyya, 1997, p. 241) asks, 'Having come to voice, what and whose language do you speak? What or whose language speaks you?' Again, this challenges notions of 'authentic' voice. An understanding of the poststructural subject as discursively constituted, multiple, dynamic, unknowing and unknowable means subjectivity can never be totally understood or captured. While this does not mean the call for self-definition should be dismissed, it does mean that the notion itself should be problematised (Lather, 2007, p. 38). Thus any student voice programme that is based on the belief that when students offer a perspective, that this is necessarily representative of an essential, unmediated self, which the students themselves are able to understand and express, needs to be complicated.

It has also been argued that meaning can be voiced in other ways besides speech. Different aspects of voices, such as silence or humour, body language or dress, can tell us something (MacLure, 2009). In interviews and meetings, research participants may resist certain avenues of questioning, leave their meanings unclear, contradict themselves or hide things. In addition, the data can 'speak' to a researcher emotionally or politically (Walkerdine, Lucey, & Melody, 2001), and she can read into the words and reactions of participants things that are not spoken explicitly. Indeed, a focus on student voice as that expressed through speech alone, or which only takes into account perspectives offered in student voice discussions, can mean that important aspects are easily missed.

Furthermore, it is argued that research is inevitably a representation of others; rather than a reflection of their reality (Pillow, 2003). Even studies that claim to represent the voices of others do just this — they provide a representation. As Walkerdine et al. (2001) argue, research is therefore inevitably subjective,

> no matter how many methodological guarantees we try to put in place
> in an attempt to produce objectivity in research, the subjective always
> intrudes. (p. 84)

The story the researcher tells has inevitably been filtered through her own beliefs and values and is therefore to a large extent 'dependent upon our prior understandings of the subject of our observation' (Siraj-Blatchford & Siraj-Blatchford, 1997, p. 237), and second, the way the participants position her will influence the data (Siraj-Blatchford & Siraj-Blatchford, 1997). Therefore, it could be argued that she does not collect data as much as generate it through her own involvement. Any student voice projects that claim to be a true presentation of a single reality at a specific school, or of a specific situation, need to be questioned.

Much social justice research, including student voice programmes, has empowerment or emancipation of marginalised participants as a main aim.

> It is assumed that uncovering what is 'silenced' can and should lead to
> emancipation or empowerment for those whose voice is captured in the
> display of research data. (McWilliam, Dooley, McArdle, & Tan, 2009, p. 63)

Qualitative methods are often seen as more appropriate than quantitative for accessing people's perspectives and feelings. They are thought to be better able to create a non-hierarchical relationship, break down barriers and relax participants by conversing with them rather than interrogating them (Gunaratnam, 2003, p. 87; Wong, 1998).

However, simplistic views of empowerment have been critiqued, including the view that any student voice project will automatically empower the participants. Much has been written about the ways in which power relations affect the research process itself (e.g. Ellsworth, 1989; Gunaratnam, 2003), including in the specific field of student voice (e.g. Orner, 1992). There is therefore, a growing awareness that different researchers will generate different data from the same participants, due to the influence of factors such as race, gender, age and class. Equally, the intended aim for empowerment has been criticised as patronising. Britzman (1997, cited by McWilliam et al., 2009, p. 1) refers to it as a 'wish for heroism'. Marker (2003) points out that many people do not see themselves as powerless and thus in need of emancipation. Moreover, it has been argued that viewing research as empowering is naïve, as all research can be seen as exploitative and thus involving a power imbalance (Kvale, 2006). This is because the researched always give much more than the researcher — at least while the research is being conducted. What respondents tell researchers is ultimately data (Kvale, 2006). In most cases, key decisions are ultimately taken by the leading researchers rather than the participants or student researchers (Crozier, 2003; Jackson & Mazzei, 2009; Marker, 2003). When research is written up, participants do not have the opportunity to influence directly the way they are represented. Even where respondents or student researchers are involved in the interpretation of the data, this still does not mean their voices are 'authentic' (Lather, 2001). Attempts to make research more democratic cannot alter the fact that voices are inevitably changed in some way by the research process (Jackson & Mazzei, 2009). It could be argued then, that research actually recentres researchers' voices, rather than enabling participants' voices to be heard (Chadderton, 2009). Any student voice project, then, which fails to acknowledge the politics of representation, or the role of the researchers/organisers, needs to be challenged.

However, whilst power relations do impact upon research projects, poststructuralists argue this is complex, inconsistent and unpredictable (Archer, 2003). Respondents can also resist the research process, by resisting certain avenues of questioning, leaving their meanings unclear, contradicting themselves and hiding things, telling different stories to the ones for which they are asked. In doing so, they challenge the role of research to fix meaning about their lives. Again, notions of authentic voice are brought into question. Some participants might take more control of the research, politicising it and pushing it towards activism (Gunaratnam, 2003, p. 121). They might also challenge the convention of research to safeguard anonymity, trying to control how their voices are heard. Thus the notion of interviewing being either emancipatory or oppressive (Kvale, 2006) is perhaps misleading. Rather it can be seen as a constantly shifting interplay of dominance and resistance. Student voice projects that aim to further democracy thus cannot only afford to ignore power relations, but also need to take a more complex view of power and empowerment.

The Difficulty of Fixing Meaning

The following example shows how research studies are inevitably a combination of diverse and shifting narratives and subjectivities. Lack of space dictates that I employ a single example, but this example allows a discussion of many of the issues discussed in the first half of this chapter. I draw on data from a recent ethnographic study of Key Stage 4 (aged 15–16) pupils' experiences of education in secondary schools in Manchester, England, which aimed to render the young people's voices heard to challenge dominant discourses around young people's disengagement. The data were generated at a comprehensive school for girls aged 11–18, where the proportion of students eligible for free school meals is well above average. Students are from a diverse range of ethnic backgrounds. The example comes from a discussion led by me (female, late 20s, white) with a group of girls (all of south Asian descent) about their relationships with teachers:

> Rahula: All he [Mr Perry] says is ... hearts and kisses on everything.
>
> Sadiya: We were doing algebra, on the board, you know, it said x, whatever, I didn't know what it was. It said x times and I go "I don't understand" and he said, "Are you confusing your x's with boys' names, you're right loved up." And I said, "You know what, fuck off, I hate you".
>
> Naseema: Kick him where it hurts! Mr Perry goes red when any girl talks to him, even though this is a girls' school.
>
> CC: Right, so what's he doing here then?
>
> N: I know! He goes bright red, like tomato, proper red. And once, you know when we were doing electricity and you have a rod and you have to rub it? (Laughter) All the girls were laughing and he goes, "Girls, this is not a dick!" And then he goes bright red.
>
> (Everyone collapses in giggles)
>
> CC: How do you feel when he says stuff like that to you?
>
> Kalila: I think it's funny! (Laughs) Cos like, it's coming from a man. Our teacher.
>
> N: It's embarrassing!
>
> S: ... yeah, he's got this pervy smile (Does some heavy breathing) When we were arguing with him outside, he goes, "There's no arguing, I'm gonna win this argument." I said, "Sir, I'll batter you!" and he went, "I'm 15 stones, I'll crush you!"(Laughs)
>
> S: And I went, "Yeah, whatever." But why are you telling me that you're 15 stone, like I wanna know? That he's gonna crush me?
>
> N: That's assault, you know. Is that assault, "I'm gonna crush you?"

In this example, we only have the girls' description of what happened. We cannot check the accuracy of the account, we cannot know if it really happened like this, or even if it happened at all. The girls may have exaggerated the stories, may have told different stories or different versions of these stories to a male researcher, or an Asian researcher. The way this discussion is represented when I write up the research — and indeed, whether this discussion is mentioned at all — depends to a large extent on my interpretation of it.

Although the girls do not explicitly say so, it seems to me the data suggest that some male teachers sexualise them. Others may argue that this extract represents an example of harmless banter, or they may argue that the students have as much power as the teacher. Because of my feminist politics, because the discussion resonates with my own experiences of implicit sexualisation from male teachers at school, and because it could be argued that the teachers would not talk like this to male pupils, I interpret it as sexualisation. I read the accounts through the lens of my own subjectivity.

The girls seem to be suggesting that they are erotically marked as 'Other' by some male teachers, whose comments 'call up longstanding stereotypes' (Ikemoto, 1995, p. 307) of a sexual nature. The girls' strong language suggests that these stories have meanings for them beyond the individual incidents. By making references to the body and physicality, the teachers reinscribe the female students into the female stereotype, which views females as defined by their bodies and sexual objects for the male gaze. The use, for example, of the word 'crush' by one teacher, carries overt sexual connotations of male control and female submission. The structure of dominant male and submissive female is potentially rendered more unequal by the fact that the teacher is white and the girl is Asian. Although this is my interpretation, it is supported by other literature: as Pillow (2004) points out, there is a history of eroticising female and raced bodies.

In choosing this specific example, and giving the interpretation above, as a researcher I am therefore complicit in constructing these individuals' subject positions (Alcoff, 1991; Pillow, 2003), as I am representing them and their stories. My voice is therefore dominant, and presenting this discussion as a reflection of a single reality and the girls' authentic voices would be misleading. It cannot be claimed that these are the girls' true subject positions, that their words represent a single reality, nor that this research allows us direct access to their perspectives. If, however, the data are so unreliable, this begs the question: is it useless to conduct the research in the first place? How does the researcher escape from a kind of paralysis? (Jackson & Mazzei, 2009) How can research based on the principle of foregrounding student voices make a contribution to social justice?

Voices as Plural and Shifting

The issues outlined above should not lead us to conclude that voices are unimportant. On the contrary, the voices of marginalised groups can and should still be foregrounded in research. The narratives of participants should indeed be the starting point for enquiry (Leonardo, 2004), as an insight into the ways in which individuals understand their lives is crucial to inform an investigation of the oppressive structures in society (Weedon, 1997, p. 8). However, it should be emphasised that voices should not be viewed as representative of any one group, 'authentic', or as reflections of a person's 'true' identity or reality (Jackson, 2003, p. 704). Not only is this naïve, it can also be dangerous, in that it risks reinforcing existing stereotypes of oppressed groups by suggesting homogeneity or essential links between (perceived) identity and experience. Instead, research should explicitly acknowledge that voices are plural, dynamic, contradictory and incomplete (Flores, 2000).

> This does not mean that voices are incapable of expressing truth; instead voices only partially tell stories and express meaning since they are bound by the 'exigencies of what can and can't be told ... Narratives of lived experience are always selective, partial and in tension' (Britzman, 1991, p. 13). This tension comes from the struggle to express meanings that are difficult to pin down, irreducible to one essential source, historically contingent, contextually bound, and socially constructed. (Jackson, 2003, p. 704)

Research that aims to privilege marginalised voices should be explicitly acknowledged as a combination of participants' perspectives and the researchers' standpoints — both plural and shifting. The role of the researcher, then, cannot be any more than an unreliable narrator — although this should not be considered a disadvantage. As an unreliable narrator, the researcher presents no single 'truth', only located and partial truths, but perhaps therefore more credible (DeVault, 1995, p. 628) and less potentially damaging?

Not Capturing Voices: A Poststructural Approach to Student Voice

Whilst this chapter only touches on a few of the assumptions underpinning many student voice initiatives, a poststructural understanding of some of these issues may help us both appreciate the potential of student voice initiatives, whilst being sensitive to the very real limitations (Fielding & McGregor, 2005). An understanding of truths as shifting, of subjectivities as dynamic, fluid, and discursively constituted, and of power as productive as well as oppressive, gives researchers the opportunity to think a little differently about projects or initiatives that aim to privilege student voices.

Most important to any project that privileges student voice is an approach that is explicitly underpinned by an understanding of the plurality and shifting nature of voices. This allows for an awareness of several important factors. For example, it would value student perceptions without seeing these as representative or universal and would explicitly reject notions of authenticity. It would avoid homogenous notions of the student body and would also mean that research would be less likely to stereotype or essentialise student perceptions. A poststructural approach then would have the potential to open up spaces for different or contradictory voices. This offers researchers and practitioners, for example, an awareness of different kinds of non-verbal communication, which would allow research to take into account wider perspectives of the students, expressed in different ways, for example, dress, arts, and identities. It would challenge an 'easy' view of school realities as static and universal. Such an approach would also challenge the privileging of only specific voices — normally the most conformist, the 'good' students, the more verbally articulate are those which are heard. An awareness of power relations as complex would allow us to question the oft-made assumption that student voice projects automatically empower the students — but would also banish the view that students are totally powerless. It also has the potential to help researchers and practitioners avoid a situation where privileging student voice is tokenistic, or themes that might bring about real change for social justice are ignored in favour of 'less threatening' topics.

A poststructural approach would acknowledge explicitly that any research inevitably involves representation and subjectivity, that voices do not necessarily 'speak for themselves', nor can they be unproblematically captured or heard, nor can any project make feasible claims to neutrality or objectivity. Keeping in mind the notion of researcher as 'unreliable narrator' would help to avoid such claims. Such an approach might allow for a deeper engagement with democratic notions of student voice, projects that aim not for consensus but ongoing debate, in order that the data gathering processes and the results may possibly be more democratic and participatory. A poststructural approach to student voice research, then, would require a complex understanding of the issues involved, and would not provide any 'easy' answers. However, this more democratic and perhaps less grand approach may be more likely to move towards providing a deeper challenge to growing social inequalities in this neo-liberal age.

Conclusion

This chapter makes a contribution to the debate on the potential, or otherwise, of student voice research to have a social justice impact. I have drawn on insights from poststructuralist theories and interrogated some of the theoretical assumptions which underpin the concern to privilege and capture marginalised voices in research. Although most of the theorists whose work is mentioned have not written specifically for the field of student voice, I have argued that their work is highly relevant for this field, as they engage more generally with the question of marginalised voices in research. I have discussed the impact of poststructural notions of truth, subjectivity and power on issues such as voice, representation and empowerment in research, and argued that a more complex notion of voice as shifting and fluid should be adopted, as well as a notion of researcher as unreliable narrator, to try and avoid naive or even potentially damaging research being conducted in the name of student voice research. A more complex understanding of student voice research based on these poststructural insights may help us both appreciate the potential of student voice initiatives, whilst being sensitive to the very real limitations.

References

Alcoff, L. (1991). The problem of speaking for others. *Cultural Critique, 20*, 5–32.
Archer, L. (2003). *Race, masculinity and schooling*. Berkshire: Open University Press.
Barnes, R. D. (1995). Politics and passion: Theoretically a dangerous liaison. In: R. Delgado (Ed.), *Critical race theory: The cutting edge*. Philadelphia, PA: Temple University Press.

Bhattacharyya, G. (1997). The fabulous adventures of the mahogany princesses. In: H. S. Mirza (Ed.), *Black British feminism: A reader*. London; New York, NY: Routledge.

Bishop, R. (2005). Freeing ourselves from neocolonial domination in research. In: N. Denzin & Y. Lincoln (Eds.), *The Sage handbook of qualitative research* (3rd ed.). Thousand Oaks, CA; London; New Delhi: Sage Publications.

Bragg, S. (2007). 'Student voice' and governmentality: The production of enterprising subjects? *Discourse: Studies in the Cultural Politics of Education*, 28(3), 343–358.

Butler, J. (1993). *Bodies that matter*. New York, NY; London: Routledge.

Butler, J. (1997). *The psychic life of power*. Stanford, CA: Stanford University Press.

Butler, J. (2004). *Undoing gender*. New York, NY; Abingdon: Routledge.

Calmore, J. O. (1996). Critical race theory, Archie Shepp, and fire music: Securing an authentic intellectual life in a multicultural world. In: K. Crenshaw, N. Gotanda, G. Peller & T. Kendall (Eds.), *Critical race theory: The key writings that formed the movement*. New York, NY: New York Press.

Chadderton, C. (2009). *Discourses of Britishness, race and difference*. Unpublished PhD thesis, Manchester Metropolitan University.

Crozier, G. (2003). Researching black parents: Making sense of the role of research and the researcher. *Qualitative Research*, 3, 79–94.

Delgado Bernal, D. (1998). Using a Chicana feminist epistemology in educational research. *Harvard Educational Review*, 68(4), 555–582.

DeVault, M. (1995). Ethnicity and expertise: Racial-ethnic knowledge in sociological research. *Gender and Society*, 9(5), 612–631.

Ellsworth, E. (1989). Why doesn't this feel empowering? Working through the repressive myths of critical pedagogy. *Harvard Educational Review*, 59(3), 297–324.

Fielding, M. (2001). Students as radical agents of change. *Journal of Educational Change*, 2(2), 123–141.

Fielding, M. (2004). Transformative approaches to student voice: Theoretical underpinnings, recalcitrant realities. *British Educational Research Journal*, 30(2), 295–311.

Fielding, M., & McGregor, J. (2005). Deconstructing student voice: New spaces for dialogue or new opportunities for surveillance? Paper presented to the Symposium, Speaking up and speaking out: International perspectives on the democratic possibilities of student voice, Annual Conference of the American Education Research Association Montreal, April.

Flores, L. A. (2000). Reclaiming the 'other': Toward a Chicana feminist critical perspective. *International Journal of Intercultural Relations*, 24, 687–705.

Gunaratnam, Y. (2003). *Researching race and ethnicity: Methods, knowledge and power*. Thousand Oaks, CA; London; New Delhi: Sage Publications.

Hooks, B. (1994). *Teaching to transgress*. New York, NY; London: Routledge.

Ikemoto, L. C. (1995). Traces of the master narrative in the story of African American/Korean American conflict: How we constructed 'Los Angeles'. In: R. Delgado (Ed.), *Critical race theory: The cutting edge*. Philadelphia, PA: Temple University Press.

Jackson, A., & Mazzei, L. (Eds). (2009). *Voice in qualitative inquiry: Challenging conventional, interpretive and critical conceptions in qualitative research*. London: Routledge.

Jackson, A. Y. (2003). Rhizovocality. *Qualitative Studies in Education*, 16(5), 693–710.

Kvale, S. (2006). Dominance through interviews and dialogues. *Qualitative Inquiry*, 12(3), 480–500.

Ladson-Billings, G., & Donner, J. (2005). The moral activist role of critical race theory scholarship. In: N. Denzin & Y. Lincoln (Eds.), *The Sage handbook of qualitative research* (3rd ed.). Thousand Oaks, CA; London; New Delhi: Sage Publications.

Lather, P. (2001). Postmodernism, post-structuralism and post (critical) ethnography: Of ruins, aporias and angels. In: P. Atkinson, A. Coffey, S. Delamont, J. Lofland & L. Lofland (Eds.), *Handbook of ethnography* (pp. 477–492). London: Sage.

Lather, P. (2007). *Getting lost: Feminist efforts towards a double(d) science*. Albany, NY: State University of New York Press.

Lather, P. (2009). Against empathy, voice and authenticity. In: A. Y. Jackson & L. A. Mazzei (Eds.), *Voice in qualitative inquiry: Challenging conventional, interpretive and critical conceptions in qualitative research*. Abingdon; New York, NY: Routledge.

Lenzo, K. (1995). Validity and self-reflexivity meet poststructuralism: Scientific ethos and the transgressive self. *Educational Researcher*, *24*, 17–23.

Leonardo, Z. (2004). The color of supremacy: Beyond the discourse of 'white privilege'. *Educational Philosophy and Theory*, *36*(2), 137–152.

MacLure, M. (2009). Broken voices, dirty words: on the productive insufficiency of voice. In: A. Y. Jackson & L. A. Mazzei (Eds.), *Voice in qualitative inquiry: Challenging conventional, interpretive and critical conceptions in qualitative research*. Abingdon; New York, NY: Routledge.

Marker, M. (2003). Indigenous voice, community and epistemic violence: The ethnographer's 'interests' and what 'interests' the ethnographer. *Qualitative Studies in Education*, *16*(3), 361–375.

Mazzei, L. A. (2009). An impossibly full voice. In: A. Y. Jackson & L. A. Mazzei (Eds.), *Voice in qualitative inquiry: Challenging conventional, interpretive and critical conceptions in qualitative research*. Abingdon; New York, NY: Routledge.

Mazzei, L. A., & Jackson, A. Y. (2009). Introduction: The limit of voice. In: A. Y. Jackson & L. A. Mazzei (Eds.), *Voice in qualitative inquiry: Challenging conventional, interpretive and critical conceptions in qualitative research*. Abingdon; New York, NY: Routledge.

McWilliam, E., Dooley, K., McArdle, F., & Tan, J. P. (2009). Voicing objections. In: A. Y. Jackson & L. A. Mazzei (Eds.), *Voice in qualitative inquiry: Challenging conventional, interpretive and critical conceptions in qualitative research Abingdon*. New York, NY: Routledge.

Mitra, D. L. (2003). Student voice in school reform: Reframing student-teacher relationships. *McGill Journal of Education*, *38*, 289–304.

Orner, M. (1992). Interrupting the calls for student voice in 'liberatory' education: A feminist poststructuralist perspective. In: C. Luke & J. Gore (Eds.), *Feminism and critical pedagogy* (pp. 74–89). London: Routledge.

Peters, M. A. (2001). *Poststructuralism, Marxism and neoliberalism*. Lanham, MA; Oxford: Rowman and Littlefield Publishers.

Peters, M. A., & Burbules, N. C. (2004). *Poststructuralism and educational research*. Lanham, MD; Boulder, CO; New York, NY; Toronto; Oxford: Rowman and Littlefield.

Pillow, W. (2003). Confession, catharsis or cure? Rethinking the uses of reflexivity as methodological power in qualitative research. *International Journal of Qualitative Studies in Education*, *16*(2), 175–196.

Pillow, W. (2004). *Unfit subjects*. New York, NY: Routledge.

Pillow, W. S. (2007). Past the post or after postmodernism: Working the limits of voice in qualitative research. Working draft presented at British Educational Research Association Annual Conference (BERA), Institute of Education, London, September.

Siraj-Blatchford, I., & Siraj-Blatchford, J. (1997). Reflexivity, social justice and educational research. *Cambridge Journal of Education*, *27*(2), 235–248.

Solorzano, D. G., & Yosso, T. J. (2002). Critical Race methodology: Counter-storytelling as an analytical framework for educational research. *Qualitative Inquiry, 8*(1), 23–44.

St. Pierre, E. A. (2000). Poststructural feminism in education: An overview. *International Journal of Qualitative Studies in Education, 13*(5), 477–515.

Tate, W. F., IV. (1997). Critical race theory and education: History, theory and implications. *Review of Research in Education, 22*, 195–247.

Tuhiwai Smith, L. (1999). *Decolonizing methodologies.* London; New York, NY: Zed Books.

Walkerdine, V., Lucey, H., & Melody, J. (2001). *Growing up girl: Psychosocial explorations of gender and class.* Basingstoke: Palgrave.

Weedon, C. (1997). *Feminist practice and poststructuralist theory* (2nd ed.). Malden, MA; Oxford, Victoria: Blackwell Publishing.

Weiler, K. (2001). Introduction. In: K. Weiler (Ed.), *Feminist engagements: Reading, resisting and revisioning male theorists in education and cultural studies.* New York, NY: Routledge.

Wong, L. M. (1998). The ethics of rapport: Institutional safeguards, resistance and betrayal (feminism and fieldwork). *Qualitative Inquiry, 4*(2), 178–200.

PART TWO
STUDENT VOICE IN PRACTICE

Editors' Summary to Part Two

In this part of the book we consider some of the research stories from practitioners, making clear their practice and the challenges they have confronted when adopting student voice strategies. Some of these practitioners are first time researchers and writers. We take the contributions in this second part in a rough chronological order of the schooling sectors — starting with early childhood (Joanne Kenworthy, Chapter 7), moving to primary (Martin Waller, Chapter 8), secondary (Ros McLellan and colleagues, Chapter 9; Bethan Morgan and Anita Porter, Chapter 10; Andy Samways and Corina Seal, Chapter 11) and post-compulsory education (Rob Pope and Bernadette Joslin, Chapter 12; Ian Wainer and Alia Islam, Chapter 13) before then considering specialist and inclusive education (Helen Bishton and Geoff Lindsay, Chapter 14) and finally Higher Education (Julie Baldry Currens, Chapter 15). What unites these contributions is the value practitioners place on student voice work. In these various practitioner contributions the structures of how voices are captured and utilised are very different. Different again are the political and institutional dimensions behind why student voice agendas are engaged with in the very first place.

Chapter 7

'We're the Ones Who Are Going to Live Here': Children's Voices in the Regeneration of Their Local Area

Joanne Kenworthy

Abstract

The rights of children to participate in decisions that affect them have been enshrined in international conventions and national policy statements. In terms of the scale of social and physical impacts on the lives of children and their families, urban regeneration ranks highly. This chapter reports on two projects run by *Discover*, a creative arts and learning center for children. The projects set out to develop participation models to enable young people's voices to be heard in the context of regeneration. *Discover* worked in partnership with a primary school adjacent to a large-scale regeneration area in London, a local authority, and the development companies contracted to deliver the redevelopment. Facilitation as a key role in consultation processes is discussed and the dynamics of the interactions between the adults and the children are explored. Some of the impacts on the regeneration professionals working with children are examined, and the children's reflections on their experiences are documented.

Keywords: Children's rights; regeneration; facilitation; consultation; *Discover*

The Student Voice Handbook: Bridging the Academic/Practitioner Divide
Copyright © 2011 by Emerald Group Publishing Limited
All rights of reproduction in any form reserved
ISBN: 978-1-78052-040-7

Introduction

In the early years of the twenty-first century, a unique constellation of events and agencies emerged, which would lead to two action-research projects exploring children's voices and visibility in the context of the regeneration of their local area. Plans had been approved for the largest retail-led, mixed-use urban regeneration project ever undertaken in the United Kingdom. The 73-hectare site was in an area of east London north of the Thames, Stratford, in the London Borough of Newham. Using criteria such as income levels, barriers to housing and services, and environmental factors, Newham is the sixth most deprived borough in England. It has one of the most ethnically and culturally diverse communities in the United Kingdom. With its complex history of industrial decline in the mid-twentieth century, depopulation and sporadic rebuilding after World War II, and as the point of arrival of successive waves of immigration, east London has long been a focus for growth and regeneration.

From 2006, this site overlapped with the construction site of the 2012 Olympic and Paralympic Park. In London's bid for the Games, the decision to site the Olympic Park in Stratford was envisaged as a means of ensuring an "enduring legacy of the Olympics ... the regeneration of an entire community for the direct benefit of everyone who lives there" (House of Commons, 2007; http://www.publications. parliament.uk/pa/cm200607/cmselect/cmcumeds/69/69i.pdf). The large development companies leading the regeneration were responding to new agendas for consulting with communities. Local government officers in Newham were developing strategies for consulting with local residents about the massive changes to come. A common concern of these commercial and governmental agencies was that, in the context of urban development, children[1] are a section of society which has been "voiceless."

Discover,[2] a Story Center for Children

Discover, the UK's first hands-on creative story space for children, had opened in Stratford in 2003. *Discover's* purpose is to provide creative play and learning opportunities for children and their carers, particularly targeting families living in social and economic disadvantage. In *Discover's* programs, activities structured around story-telling and story-making engage children's curiosity and imagination, and the arts are used to enable them to explore and express their ideas, emotions, and aspirations. *Discover* has a strong ethos of advocating children's rights and an equally strong record of working in its community to ensure that children are listened to and consulted about issues that affect their lives.

---

1. The word "children" is often used for those under 12 and "young people" for the age range of 12–18 years. In this chapter, they will be used interchangeably.
2. *Discover* is a registered charity number 1070468. For more information, see http://www.discover.org.uk.

The Genesis of "Listening to Learn"[3]

An action-research project, "Listening to Learn," was designed by *Discover* to address the common interests and goals of these very different agencies. Partnership was a cornerstone of the initiative. *Discover's* commercial partners were *Westfield*, the developers of the retail center, and *Lend Lease*, responsible for the residential developments. The local government partner was Newham. There were two "educational" partners, a local primary school and the University of East London. The school was located in the regeneration area, adjacent to the Olympic Park construction site. The daily lives of its pupils would be affected by the disruptions of construction work, and their life chances and experiences would be shaped by the changes to their local area. The university's role was to evaluate the project. I led the evaluation team and was also involved in disseminating the findings of the project through seminars held throughout the United Kingdom and in producing a toolkit as a resource for practitioners and professionals working in regeneration contexts.[4]

"Listening to Learn" in Action[5]

"Listening to Learn" ran from 2006 to 2009. The first two years were based in the school and in *Discover* and were designed to explore models of consultation between regeneration professionals, for example, architects, designers, local government planning officers, managers of development companies, and children and their families, which were genuinely collaborative and long-term, rather than "one-off." A key aim was to investigate the role of the arts as a tool for children to communicate their ideas. A range of participation methods were used, which required "information-sharing and dialogue between children and adults based on mutual respect and power-sharing" (Lansdown, 2004).

From 2006 to 2008, 200 children in the school worked with artists to learn skills in photography, film, drama, and visual arts. The regeneration professionals visited the school to talk about the proposed changes to the area. With the artists' support, the children identified a set of themes, for example, "Outdoor Spaces," and used their art skills as a tool to communicate their views. In July 2007, their perceptions about their area and their aspirations for its future were presented at an exhibition of the children's art work, "Listen to Our Stratford," attended by the development and

---

3. "Listening to Learn" was supported by the National Endowment for Science, Technology and the Arts (NESTA); the East Foundation; Sir John Cass's Foundation; the London Borough of Newham; and two development companies: *Lend Lease* and *Westfield*.

4. The toolkit took the form of a website, which can be found at http://www.designmatters.org.uk.

5. In the following sections, comments from the participants are taken from interviews with the children and adults, evaluation and feedback sessions, and audio and video recordings made to document the projects. Italics indicates strong emphasis by the speaker. The names used are not the children's real names; their ages at the time are given in brackets. The full evaluation report of "Listening to Learn" can be found at http://www.designmatters.org.uk/why/project_evaluation/.

local government partners, the children's families, and their teachers. There were group discussions based on questions that the children wanted to ask their adult partners. During these discussions, it was clear that the children's participation needed to be facilitated by *Discover* staff, to ensure that adults did not dominate the talk or focus on their own agendas.

Toward the end of the second year, the *Discover* team explored a different model that would involve a group of about 10 pupils working collaboratively with local government officers for two months. This "mini-project" was structured to promote equality of roles and responsibilities: the officers identified a planning issue that the children could help them with; the children identified issues that they wanted their adult partners to address. The participants had opportunities to discuss issues together, then work independently on their "assignments"; then meet again to present findings and discuss and evaluate outcomes.

Supporting the Participants

Facilitation is essential to enable children to participate in public decision-making. Adult professionals who have the power to effect change in children's involvement may have high commitment but little understanding of key factors or practical issues. Young people may not expect opportunities to participate to be available to them and may not understand the purpose of what they are being asked to do.

Early on in the project, there were sessions with the children to explain the ideas behind "Listening to Learn." Throughout the project, *Discover's* team reiterated the purpose of the project through comments such as "they [the planners and developers] tend not to ask kids about this stuff ... that's why we are a useful tool for them" (said by the film artist). Adults' confidence in the children's abilities was also continually emphasized. For example, in introducing the children to the mini-project, the project leader said, "really it's about working together ... they know you're very capable and you're really creative."

Artist facilitators are primarily "creative enablers" in that they can design arts activities to stimulate the expression of the children's ideas and guide them to create artifacts that will communicate those ideas. They need to nurture children's creative responses and "give them space to play, engage and reflect on their activities" (Pringle, 2010). The working principle of the artists' sessions was that they allowed the children's impulses and imaginations to direct the work.

In interactions with regeneration professionals, facilitators need to constantly monitor the progress of the talk, because "how speakers adopt roles and assign them to each other in dialogue" (Martin & Rose, 2003) is an indicator of their notions of their interlocutors' rights and competencies. If adults assume that children are not intellectually able to understand how planning decisions are made, or should only be consulted about issues relating to playgrounds or schools, children's contributions will inevitably be restricted.

Throughout the mini-project, there were regular meetings between the participants. In these meetings, a pattern of interaction emerged in which the adults allocated speaking roles to the children that put them at the center of the discussion. The children would be asked "open questions," for example, "What do you think should happen?" Such questioning can be essential not only to discover children's perspectives but also to enhance their participation. The children's views were treated very positively, and the adults often deferred to the children before expressing their own views.

At end of this mini-project, the children were asked about their experiences. Vladko [aged 9] thought the project was "good" because "I could say what I wanted to say about our area, and they (the officers) are serious." When asked what happened when they met together to discuss their issues, he replied "we showed them and they showed us." His comments reflect important dimensions of listening to children: the opportunity to express their ideas to listeners who are genuinely interested ("serious"), in contexts where all speakers have equal roles and rights. In the next section, we look at how the second project, "Building the Future"[6] developed these dimensions further.

"Building the Future"

Discussions between *Discover* and *Westfield London Shopping Center* about the findings of "Listening to Learn" led to the idea of children taking on the role of "consultants" for development companies. The outcome of these discussions was a three-year project at whose center was the creation of a group of 26 children aged 4–13 years recruited from local schools to act as "young consultants."

The young consultants were supported by *Discover's* facilitators and staff from two architecture firms. The group first met with members of *Westfield's* team to discuss aspects of the design of public spaces in their "brief." These included public art, street furniture, and water features. For each area, the children went on field trips to research existing public spaces; these were followed by design sessions using art forms as a platform to express their ideas. In a series of workshops, they presented and discussed their findings and ideas with their *Westfield* partners.

The children understood that they were being approached both as young people and as residents of their local area. They developed a clear notion that one aspect of their role was to carry out research: "[our job is] to gather ideas and other people's opinions including ourselves and put it together to tell *Westfield*" [Sunita, aged 12]. Their input would contribute to the design process: "[we'll be] giving them ideas of what they should do and what they should change" [Ivan, aged 13]. Children need to be involved: "we know more about children because we *are* children" [Penelope, aged 12]. Children's contributions can compensate for gaps in adult thinking: "being adults themselves they'll be thinking more about the adults" [Ivan]. Fatima [aged 13] echoed this idea, but also emphasized local children's rights: "maybe some of the

---

6. "Building the Future" was supported by *Westfield*.

things we're thinking about *they* haven't thought about ... we're the ones who are going to live here (in Stratford) and we'll be using the space."

The workshops focusing on water features are a particularly striking illustration of the mode of working and the dynamics of the interaction between the children and the adult professionals. The group was asked to investigate elements of water features, for example, still or moving water, use of sculpture, and report back to *Westfield's* design team. They visited various water features in London, using video to interview one another about their own responses and understandings and how these differed from those of adults. One theme that emerged was "interactivity." For example, Ivan thought that "small people ... like small children under the age of 10 like to *interact* with water because they really like it ... older people sometimes like to relax and calm themselves." Twelve-year old Melanie's interpretation of interactivity seemed to have more to do with engagement: "[a water feature] needs to be something people get interested in and stop and look at it." Benjamin [aged 9] said he liked the sight and sound of water because "it soothes my mind."

Following the field trip, they discussed their design ideas with their *Westfield* partners. The children presented their ideas using models and drawings. The *Westfield* team then showed them the latest design brief that used "digital water" (digital displays on surfaces in the proposed public square). Melanie was among those who thought that "for children it's better to have real water because they can play and stuff." However, some children were attracted to the possibilities of digital water. Sunita described how the discussion developed: "our thoughts kind of changed as they were telling us because at first we were all for real water but when they started explaining why digital water would be better some people kind of changed their thoughts and said digital water instead."

In follow-up sessions, a film artist worked with the children to create their own digital water designs using stop frame animation to show to *Westfield*.

Being a "Young Consultant"

During and after the workshops, the children were asked to reflect on their experiences. Sunita referred to their status as stakeholders in the future of their local area: "our say is as important as everyone else's say." She hoped their ideas would be used: "[our ideas] are quite sensible so they might add them," but she was also aware of how consultation processes worked: "you kind of have to accept the fact that some of your ideas won't be used because there's loads of other people's opinions everywhere and we're not the only ones." Fatima talked about benefits: "we benefit because we understand now how children's opinions really do *count* and other big companies like *Westfield* realise that the ideas that children have are sometimes better than the ones they have."

Two comments highlight the impacts of the way children and adults worked together: "at first you're quite ... really nervous because they are a lot older than you ... [you] are like quite young ... but as you get to talk to them you find out that they really *do* listen to your ideas and it becomes a lot easier" [Sunita]. Christina [aged 12] described how "you kind of get more confidence and you present your ideas really good … because you've got to know them more."

It seems that these young consultants have developed strong notions of the "rightness" of children being consulted. They believe that their ideas are of real value to the design process and are keenly aware of the benefits of working collaboratively.

Adults Learning to Listen

In these two projects, children worked with many different regeneration professionals, including designers, senior directors, housing officers, senior retail managers, as well as community relations staff. Regeneration professionals may have little or no experience of working together with children in their professional lives. Their engagement needs to be supported. The provision of training programs is one obvious response. However, the experience of these projects points to the impacts of working together with professionals whose role is to promote and facilitate the participation of children. One *Discover* team member reported her occasional "frustration" when mentoring adults who were "novices." Although they "really tried to answer the children's questions," they were sometimes unable to interpret their underlying messages about the built environment, issues such as accessibility, safety, and respect for public places. At other times, she had to explain why a particular question had (probably) been asked. However, it was extremely gratifying to observe adults getting better at establishing a rapport with children and learning how to listen to and encourage children's contributions.

For the regeneration professionals, the impacts of working on the projects included changes in their views of children's capabilities and the "fun and innocence," "enthusiasm," "positivity," and imagination they bring to the consultation process. Significantly, their experiences had impacted on their views of what consulting with communities should be like: consultation requires continuity, space for feedback and an intermediary to make the process work. Listening to children is not asking them to tell you "what they want." It needs sensitive interpretation of their ideas and willingness to explore what seem to be "simple messages." One of the local government officers said that he had learned that it is essential that adults be open to various ways of communicating and interacting: "you need to be able to converse at their level   it's no good me going in with lots of jargon or technical terms, and you have to have a sense of fun … it's not very strict, very formal … it's not talking *to*, it's talking *with*."

Conclusion

Both these projects were designed to move away from types of interactions where it is exclusively adults who initiate action, set agendas, and determine the ways of communicating. Their focus on the processes of adult–child interaction offers valuable insights into how to move toward models characterized by "attentive and respectful adults and children working collaboratively" (Hay & Fawcett, 2010). The keys to success are not only commitment to children's right to participate and the use of methods that play with children's strengths and predilections as communicators but also getting the interaction right. "Interaction between young people and adults ... is at the heart of their relationships and therefore fundamental to enabling young people's participation in decision-making" (Kirby & Bryson, 2002).

"Children's participation offers the possibility of realising a sense of citizenship and inclusion through active involvement in local decision-making" (Percy-Smith & Thomas, 2009). When Fatima said, "we're the ones who are going to live here," she was not only stating her position as a stakeholder but also alluding to her rights as a citizen. One has a sense that she is learning what "doing citizenship" feels like. The children on these projects had opportunities to give their views, think deeply about how changes in the area might affect them, work with those whose responsibility is to bring about those changes, and develop the skills needed to influence the future of their local area. In discussing what "real participation" is, Percy-Smith and Thomas (2009) emphasize the need for children to be "active citizens." These projects have contributed to the development of models and approaches that can support the establishment of benchmarks of good practice and thereby promote and enable "real participation."

References

House of Commons. (2007). London 2012 Olympic Games and Paralympic Games: Funding and legacy. Retrieved from http://www.publications.parliament.uk/pa/cm200607/cmselect/cmcumeds/69/69i.pdf. Accessed on 4 March 2011.

Hay, P., & Fawcett, M. (2010). Family learning in 5 × 5 × 5 = creativity. *Engage*, *25*, 83–90.

Kirby, P., & Bryson, M. (2002). *Measuring the magic: Evaluating and researching young people's participation in public decision-making* (Retrieved from http://www.participation.ro/resources/library/2643_measurethemagic_001.pdf). UK: Carnegie Trust for Young People.

Lansdown, G. (2004). Participation and young children. *Early Childhood Matters* (103), 4–14.

Martin, J. R., & Rose, D. (2003). *Working with discourse*. London: Continuum.

Percy-Smith, B., & Thomas, N. (2009). *A handbook of children's and young people's participation: Perspectives from theory and practice*. London: Routledge.

Pringle, E. (2010). Families and creative learning in art galleries: Setting the scene. *Engage*, *25*, 7–18.

Chapter 8

'Everyone in the World Can See It' — Developing Pupil Voice through Online Social Networks in the Primary Classroom

Martin Waller

Abstract

The use of online social networks in society has presented many challenges, questions and concerns for parents and educators in recent years. Moral panics surround the safe use of such technologies and the so-called toxic nature of Internet practices on childhood as well as safety both in online and in offline worlds. However, many young people and adults use online networks as a way of participating and communicating. As a result, social networks have become part and parcel of how many people live and work in the world. However, the use of systems in schools has remained sporadic with little emphasis on pupil voice.

This chapter explores how the use of a social networking site (Twitter) can be used as a safe way to support pupil voice as well as the development of both traditional and digital writing in a year 2 classroom. Children in 'Orange Class' use Twitter as a way of documenting, reflecting and sharing their learning with a global audience. Many 'followers' choose to respond to the children's learning and offer feedback; as a result, communication skills are developed through the interactions with users on the website. Adults in the classroom moderate communications between the children and the outside world. Subsequently through a managed, yet real-world environment, the children are able to amplify their voice to the world, while developing safe practices within an online social network.

Keywords: Pupil voice; social networking sites; Twitter; digital technologies; Web 2.0; literacy; reading; writing

The Student Voice Handbook: Bridging the Academic/Practitioner Divide
Copyright © 2011 by Emerald Group Publishing Limited
All rights of reproduction in any form reserved
ISBN: 978-1-78052-040-7

Introduction

Pupil voice has many benefits to the education system and affords young people the opportunity to talk about what helps and what hinders their learning (Rudduck, 2005). Such an approach does indeed 'bridge the gap' between pupil and teacher understanding of the curriculum and learning process. The methods and approaches to which pupil voice can be promoted are vast. However, the approach I describe in this chapter harnesses a popular channel of communication of many young people — social networking sites. Communicative practices within such networking systems are characterised by instant channels such as newsfeeds and messaging systems where voice is shared in an increasingly diverse and globalised manner. In the past, there has been a dissonance between such systems and the education system (Davies, 2006). This has been due to increased scrutiny from the press and privacy advocates focused on the safety of young people (boyd & Ellison, 2008). However as Davies and Merchant (2009, p. 111) state,

> Much of the moral panic around new media focuses on the idea that they distract the attention of children and young people from engaging with print literacy practices and are a causal factor in failing standards in literacy in schools.

The aim of this chapter, however, is to explore how the use of new social networking sites can be harnessed to amplify pupil voice and enhance learning in the classroom through shared dialogue and reflection. I will explore the nature of social networking sites before linking their safe use within an educational context. I will then build on findings from my previous research (Waller, 2010), which explores how I have used Twitter with my year 2 class (Orange Class)[1] as a means of developing pupil voice and shared learning on a global scale. My role in the research process is that of a teacher–researcher where I am primarily a classroom teacher who uses research to explore new ways of learning and promoting pupil voice and creativity in my classroom.

Social Networking Systems

Social network sites (SNS) such as Twitter, Friendster, MySpace, Bebo and Facebook allow young people to present themselves, articulate their social networks and establish connections with others within different contexts, while at the same

---

1. Children in year 2 in the public education system in United Kingdom are generally aged 6–7 years. The research site for this project is a year 2 classroom in a suburban primary school (ages 3–11 years) in the United Kingdom.

time presenting their voice in diverse ways (Ellison, Steinfield, & Lampe, 2007). boyd and Ellison (2008, p. 221) define SNS as,

> Web-based services that allow individuals to (1) construct a public profile or semi-public profile within a bounded system, (2) articulate a list of other users within whom they share a connection, and (3) view and traverse their list of connections and those made by others within the system.

Through the use of SNS, literacy practices and pupil voice are encoded in the construction of personal profiles, discussions of participants and the forging of friendship links by either following a profile or requesting a friendship connection. Users of such websites represent themselves digitally using text, images, video, links and quizzes to express how they see themselves (boyd, 2007, p. 2). As a result, social networking systems can become embedded in participants' lives through the 'collecting' of online friends (boyd & Ellison, 2008, p. 216). These 'public displays of connection' serve as important identity signals to validate young people's identity and voice in online profiles (Donath & boyd, 2004, p. 72).

Twitter

As a result of their popularity, new social networks continue to be developed and used by different communities. One such SNS that has received an influx in media attention is Twitter. This SNS takes a different approach to other more established networks as it limits communication to 140 characters. This has led to the term 'micro-blogging' where users create a limited profile and begin sending short messages known as tweets (Galagan, 2009, p. 28). Twitter incorporates the directed friendship model of choosing accounts to 'follow' and gaining 'followers' in return. It also borrows features from blogging platforms in that it allows dynamic, interactive voice and identity presentation to unknown audiences through ongoing tweets and conversations with others. It is through these ongoing tweets that self-presentation takes place and voice is developed, thus creating a 'twitter stream' of information (Marwick & boyd, 2010, p. 3).

The @ClassroomTweets Project

Twitter was chosen as the SNS to explore in the classroom because it was an open system but did not require the construction of a detailed profile to participate in the environment. This meant that children's identities were not exposed and privacy issues could be addressed through a very basic biography. Furthermore, Twitter allows us to 'approve' any followers to our online social network before they can view any tweets from the account. My role within this process is to act as the link between the children and the wider Twitter network. This includes managing the users who follow the account as well as occasionally tweeting alongside the children.

The motivation towards using a Twitter account addresses many areas such as the development of digital literacy skills, promoting pupil voice, encouraging disengaged writers and the evaluation and reflection of learning. A single account was set up (@ClassroomTweets[2]), which allows children to 'tweet' and contribute towards the shared twitter stream. Figure 8.1 shows a collection of tweets made by members of the classroom. It represents both teacher and pupil voice in unison across a shared twitter stream.

Figure 8.1: Orange Class Twitterstream [@ClassroomTweets].

The children control what is posted to the Twitter stream. They regularly choose to support one another in writing tweets to create a shared dialogue. Indeed as Robinson and Fielding (2007) attest, pupils believe working together with peers supports their learning. Furthermore, Marsh (2010, p. 29) suggests that

---

2. Twitter users are required to place an '@' symbol before usernames when tweeting to another person's account.

> Reading in this context means not simply decoding, but involves the taking part in the construction of social networks in which knowledge is co-constructed and distributed.

Within this context, the children feel comfortable at experimenting with language. Furthermore, the stigma of getting something 'wrong' is removed, and the encouragement the children receive when tweeting from their peers promotes a culture of collaboration and reflection. This is a stark contrast to existing pupil voice research by Robinson and Fielding (2007) who state that children are apprehensive to share their work as they are worried about the consequences of 'getting it wrong'.

During the project, Twitter has allowed the children to share their voice with a dynamic and global audience as well as engaging in powerful writing, which is partly driven by the potency from the immediacy of publication (Davies, 2006, p. 60). The children are not fully aware of who their audience actually is, but they have created their own imagined audience (boyd, 2007). Such an audience is ambiguous (but still exists), and different children choose to use Twitter in different ways and share different information with their audience. For example, some children enjoy demonstrating their understanding of topics covered in class to solidify their understanding and receive feedback from the social network (Waller, 2010). This is evidenced in Figure 8.2 where a child has demonstrated to their network that the class is learning about riddles.

```
I am little.I have courls like a parrot. What am i?
10.33 AM Apr 28ᵗʰ via blu

I am smaller than your hand but bigger than a tiny seed. The famers hate it
when I go and eat there cabbige. I start of like an agg
10.28 AM Apr 28ᵗʰ via blu
```

Figure 8.2: Extracts from @ClassroomTweets.

In this example, the child is reaching out to the social network to answer the riddle, which would subsequently demonstrate the effectiveness of the work. As a result, the child received many responses, most of which included the correct answer to the riddle. Twitter in this context not only allows the child to communicate with a community that extends beyond the classroom walls but also share and celebrate their own learning and understanding (Waller, 2010). Such tweets also allow me as the class teacher to capture useful instances of pupil voice and learning interactions that can inform future classroom activities. This is consistent with pupil voice research by Robinson and Fielding (2007) who assert that when pupils are listened to on teaching and learning issues, teachers can gain insights into what motivates, hinders and helps learning (p. 3).

As the children continued to tweet about their work, they began to receive replies to their writing. Audience participation operates on many levels, with most followers choosing to simply read the children's twitter stream. However, while using Twitter, the children have developed a network within their imagined audience, which includes people who they communicate with on a regular basis and whom the children class as online 'friends' in the context that boyd and Ellison (2008) describe. The children choose to communicate with these followers and in this sense are shaping and creating their own personal learning network.

Some of the members of the children's social network choose to interact with them to begin a dialogue. This counters the ongoing issue of authenticity with pupil voice projects where sometimes there can be a lack of genuine interest in young people's views (Rudduck, 2005). For example, Figure 8.3 highlights one follower's response to a child's tweet asking about the weather in different parts of the world. In addition, from the children's previous tweets, they recall that they have been learning about describing words in their writing.

> Good Morning @classroomtweets! I am in Madrid, Spain and it's a very
> warm, sunny, blue-sky day here! What is your weather like today?
> 11:00 AM Apr 26th via web

Figure 8.3: Extract from @ClassroomTweets Follower.

In this example, the follower decided to include detailed descriptions in their tweets. The children were then able to respond to the tweet and share information with a member of their network who lived in a different country. Not only does this help the children's learning but also provides an authentic dialogue between the children and the follower.

Other followers take an interest in the children's work by asking them to describe and elaborate on their learning. In Figure 8.4 one of our followers has responded to a tweet about finding a treasure chest.

> @ClassroomTweets How exciting about that treasure chest. I live on an
> ancient mound which people think has Roman remains. Tell me more
> 8:44 AM Feb 24th via web in reply to ClassroomTweets

Figure 8.4: Extract from @ClassroomTweets Follower.

Such a response can be classed as a literacy event (Heath, 1983) as it instigated a discussion as to what words such as 'ancient' actually mean and what Roman remains were. The fact that the follower also prompted the children to 'Tell me more' led to the children creating a more detailed account, which was emailed to the follower. This meant that the children understood that Twitter was not the best medium to send a more detailed reply and an email was more appropriate. Such exchanges with members of the children's social network not only involve pupil voice, but as Marsh (2010, p. 30) suggests,

> Reading is, in this example, a social practice that extends beyond the walls of the classroom and enables children to engage in forums in which inter-generational literacy is commonplace.

Within this context, children are not patronised or treated as inferior to the adults in their social network, rather they are recognised as co-constructors of meaning through pupil voice. There is mutual respect between the children and their followers. Furthermore, when the children engage in conversation with users to exchange ideas, it mirrors the uses of technology they will encounter in both leisure and employment in future years (Marsh, 2010, p. 30).

Twitter has also been instrumental in developing other practices with digital technologies. For example, when the children were learning how to draw pictures of fish in a lesson, they tweeted about the activity and received a request asking the class to publish a photograph of their work (Figure 8.5).

> @ClassroomTweets great fish! Can you twitpic one of your drawings?
> 1:56 PM Oct 14th from web in reply to ClassroomTweets

Figure 8.5: A follower asks for examples of the children's work.
From Waller (2010, p. 16).

> @ClassroomTweets what a wonderful drawing! I love all the spots. Thank you for sharing that with me! Your tweets make me smile.
> 2:17 PM Oct 14th from web in reply to ClassroomTweets

Figure 8.6: A follower provides feedback on the children's learning.
From Waller (2010, p. 16).

This literacy event (Heath, 1983) led to the children taking a photograph of one of their drawings, uploading it to the Twitpic[3] (http://www.twitpic.com) service and then adding it to the twitter stream. They then received feedback on their learning from the original tweeter (Figure 8.6).

Exchanges such as these have engaged the children in their work and allowed them to share it with a global audience. Furthermore, this was an authentic assessment practice where the children demonstrated that they had met the objectives and received feedback from an independent user. Existing pupil voice research has already highlighted that children gain great satisfaction when they are praised for their achievements and increased motivation when their voice is heard (Robinson & Fielding, 2007). This work was not only praised by their class teacher but also by a wider social network of people from across the globe.

---

3. 'Twitpic' is a photo uploading service that allows users to upload digital images and automatically post them to their Twitter account.

e-safety

The rise of social networking systems in society has attracted increased scrutiny from the press and privacy advocates, primarily focused on the safety of school-aged users (boyd & Ellison, 2008). However, as boyd (2007) suggests, a large proportion of adults panic because they simply do not understand the shifts in terms of the changing communications landscape. SNS simply amplify pupil voice in the context of children's offline worlds, and if children are engaged in risky behaviour online, it is typically a sign that they are engaged in risky behaviour offline (boyd, 2007). What is clear is that just like the offline world, there are dangers and risks that cannot be completely eliminated (Byron, 2008). Furthermore, boyd (2007) also argues that the technology is too often blamed for what it reveals and suggests destroying the technology will not solve the underlying problems that are made visible through mediated spaces like SNS (boyd, 2007, p. 5).

At the start of the @ClassroomTweets project, the safety implications and a set of rules were discussed with the pupils. However, such issues were discussed in an open and contextually driven manner (Davies & Merchant, 2009), with the children realising why such precautions were needed. Three primary rules (Waller, 2010) were discussed with the children:

1. Children must not mention their name or any of their friends by name in tweets under any circumstances.
2. Children must not check for replies or messages (this prevents the possibility of them seeing any inappropriate material that may be viewable).
3. Children must not navigate away from our Twitter stream page and look at other people's profiles (in case of inappropriate content or language use).

These rules were discussed with the children in the context of real-world use of social networks and the e-safety implications of not following them. Subsequently, the children have always chosen to follow them. Replies to children's tweets are always checked by adults before they are discussed with the children as there is always the possibility of inappropriate messages being sent due to the open nature of Twitter (Waller, 2010). As a result, children are not able to engage in 'private' discussion with any members of the social networking site.

Conclusion

As Davies and Merchant (2009) suggest, embedding Web 2.0 practices in school involves a focused look at how different kinds of services relate to educational objectives. In this case, @ClassroomTweets promotes pupil voice as a vehicle for evaluating and reflecting on current learning, which in turn informs future learning. In addition, it also allows children to engage in meaningful dialogue with an online social network to develop competencies with spoken, written and digital literacies. Projects such as @ClassroomTweets also demonstrate that open Web 2.0

technologies can be used in schools to support meaningful engagement in the construction of social networks as well as amplifying pupil voice to the world in a relevant and authentic manner.

References

boyd, d. (2007). Social network sites: Public, private, or what? *Knowledge Tree, 13*. Retrieved from http://kt.flexiblelearning.net.au/tkt2007/?page_id=28.

boyd, d., & Ellison, N. (2008). Social network sites, definition, history, and scholarship. *Journal of Computer-Mediated Communication, 13*, 210–230.

Byron, T. (2008). The Byron review: Safer children in a digital world. Crown Copyright.

Davies, J. (2006). Escaping to the Borderlands: An exploration of the Internet as cultural space for teenaged Wiccan girls. In: K. Pahl & J. Rowsell (Eds), *Travel notes from the new literacy studies: Instances of practice* (pp. 57–71). Clevedon: Multilingual Matters.

Davies, J., & Merchant, G. (2009). *Web 2.0 for schools: Learning and social participation.* New York, NY: Peter Lang.

Donath, J., & boyd, d. (2004). Public displays of connection. *BT Technology Journal, 22*(4), 71–82.

Ellison, N., Steinfield, C., & Lampe, C. (2007). The benefits of Facebook "Friends:" Social capital and college students' use of online social network sites. *Journal of Computer-Mediated Communication, 12*(4), 1143–1168.

Galagan, P. (2009). Twitter as a learning tool. Really. *American Society for Training & Development, 63*(2), 28–31.

Heath, S. B. (1983). *Ways with words: Language, life, and work in communities and classrooms.* Cambridge: Cambridge University Press.

Marsh, J. (2010). The ghosts of reading past, present and future: The materiality of reading in homes and schools. In: K. Hall, U. Goswami, C. Harrison, S. Ellis & J. Soler (Eds), *Interdisciplinary perspectives on learning to read: Culture, cognition and pedagogy* (pp. 19–31). Oxon: Routledge.

Marwick, A. E., & boyd, d. (2010). I tweet honestly, I tweet passionately, Twitter users, context collapse, and the imagined audience. *New Media & Society, Online Early Edition*, 1–20.

Robinson, C., & Fielding, M. (2007). *Children and their primary schools: Pupils' voices (primary review research survey 5/3).* Cambridge: Faculty of Education, University of Cambridge.

Rudduck, J. (2005). "Pupil voice is here to stay!" for QCA futures. Retrieved from www.qca.org.uk.

Waller, M. (2010). It's very very fun and ecsiting – using Twitter in the primary classroom. *English Four to Eleven*, Summer, pp. 14–16.

Chapter 9

Student Voice in the Secondary School Context: A Case Study of the Benefits of Schools, Local Authorities and Higher Education Institutions Working Together

Ros McLellan, Rebecca Kirkman, Steve Cartwright and Bev Millington

Abstract

There is a well-established research tradition relating to student voice at the Faculty of Education, University of Cambridge due to the work of internationally renowned authors such as Jean Rudduck and Donald McIntyre. Although we mourn their loss, their legacy lives on in a vibrant research culture that strongly values consulting students, acknowledging that they are experts about their own learning and working in partnership with schools to promote this message. In this chapter, we report a case study that illustrates these values. Ros McLellan has been working in partnership with Stoke Local Authority over the past three years to help to raise achievement in Stoke secondary schools. Trentham High School participated in the first phase of this project and implemented a three-pronged intervention strategy to raise achievement by providing assertive mentoring, extension lessons and a befrienders scheme to promote positive attitudes to learning. Rebecca Kirkman, Steve Cartwright and Bev Millington are the teachers at Trentham High School who put these interventions in place. This chapter tells the story of their experiences and what they learned by talking to the young people involved in the research. We finish with a reflection on the value of schools within a local authority working in partnership with Universities to promote student voice.

Keywords: School–local authority–university partnership; secondary school context; educational intervention; critical friendship; interviewing students

The Student Voice Handbook: Bridging the Academic/Practitioner Divide
Copyright © 2011 by Emerald Group Publishing Limited
All rights of reproduction in any form reserved
ISBN: 978-1-78052-040-7

Introduction

The authors of this chapter are a university lecturer at the Faculty of Education at the University of Cambridge (Ros) and three secondary school[1] teachers from Trentham High School in Stoke-on-Trent, UK (Rebecca, Steve and Bev) who worked together as part of a Local Authority[2] (LA)-sponsored project to raise achievement. In this chapter we demonstrate the value of partnerships between higher education institutions working with schools within particular LAs to promote student voice, by presenting a case study of the work done at Trentham High School as part of the Cambridge Stoke Raising Achievement in Inclusive Contexts (CS-RA) Project.

Ros starts the chapter, contextualising the background to the CS-RA Project and discussing the role of student voice within this. Rebecca, Steve and Bev then present an overview of the project work at Trentham High School. We finish with a joint reflection on the value of schools within a LA working in partnership with a university to promote student voice.

The Cambridge Stoke Raising Achievement in Inclusive Contexts Project

The CS-RA Project developed out of a large-scale national raising achievement project: The Raising Boys' Achievement (RBA) Project, funded by the DfES[3], and conducted between 2000 and 2004 by a team based at the Faculty of Education, University of Cambridge (Younger & Warrington with Gray et al., 2005; Younger & Warrington with McLellan, 2005). The RBA Project was a three-phase research and intervention project involving over 60 primary, secondary and special schools across England. Schools worked together in learning triads comprising a school that had had some success in closing their gender gap with two partner schools, to share and develop strategies to raise boys' achievement, and were supported by a critical friend (Swaffield, 2003, 2004) from the Faculty. Four different categories of strategies were

---

1. In the United Kingdom, students typically attend a relatively small (one or two class entry, i.e. 30–60 children per cohort) primary school between the ages of 5 and 11 where they are usually taught by a single class teacher for all curricular areas. At the age of 11 they usually transfer to a much larger secondary school (six to eight form entry) for the rest of their compulsory education to the age of 16 and whilst they will have a form tutor they see on a daily basis, they are timetabled to have lessons with subject specialists and hence are taught by up to a dozen different teachers.
2. For the purposes of management of public services including education, the country is divided geographically into a large number of local authority areas. In rural areas these often align with county boundaries, but in urban areas they more usually equate to either part of, or, in the case of Stoke, the entirety of an urban conurbation.
3. Central government's Department for Education and Science (DfES). The department's name was changed from DfES to DCSF (Department for Children, Schools and Families) and then, most recently, to DfE (Department for Education).

identified that have the potential to raise achievement of all students (and boys in particular), and those that are pertinent to the case study of Trentham High School are outlined below. The findings of the project were widely publicised through the DfES website and fed into the most recent DCSF gender achievement gap awareness-raising work in their 2007–2009 'Closing the Gaps' programme, and the project team have been invited to speak at numerous meetings to academic and practitioner audiences both in the United Kingdom and overseas. It is fair to say, therefore, that the findings from the RBA Project have had a considerable impact.

It was in this context that a senior member of Stoke-on-Trent Local Authority approached the Faculty in early 2008 to ask whether members of the RBA team would be prepared to work with Stoke LA to help to raise achievement in Stoke secondary schools. Overall GCSE[4] performance in Stoke was considerably lower than the national average in England at this time, with 34.8% of students attaining the benchmark 5 or more A*–C grades,[5] including mathematics and English, in the summer of 2007 compared with the national average of 46.8% (Department for Education, 2007), and boys' performance was perceived to be a particular issue. Ros, who had acted as the critical friend to nearly half of the secondary school triads in the RBA Project, was asked to lead this work, and the CS-RA Project was born.

The CS-RA Project was originally conceived as a one-year research and intervention project for the 2008–2009 academic year modelled very closely on the approach adopted during the RBA Project.[6] This would entail a small number of Stoke secondary schools working together as a group; the rationale behind this being the extensive research indicating that teachers' professional development, and learning is enhanced by undertaking research in their own contexts (Campbell & Groundwater-Smith, 2010; Stenhouse, 1975, 1983) particularly when supported in communities of practice (Hargreaves, 2003; Lave & Wenger, 1991; McLaughlin, Black-Hawkins, & McIntyre, 2007). Hence, it was critical that school colleagues researched their own contexts and were supported in this endeavour by, not only Faculty and LA colleagues, but also each other to develop practice and ultimately help to raise achievement. This philosophy underpins much of the professional development work undertaken by the Faculty, for instance in the SUPER partnership that Ros is also involved with (McLaughlin, Black-Hawkins, Brindley, McIntyre, & Taber, 2006), work within which is represented elsewhere in this volume.

---

4. GCSEs are public examinations set and externally marked by national examination boards and are taken by all students at the end of Year 11 (students aged 15–16 years), the final year of compulsory schooling. Schools' performance is judged by GCSE results, and data are available in the public sphere through the Department for Education website at http://www.education.gov.uk/researchandstatistics/attainmenttables.

5. A* is the highest grade awarded at GCSE, with a C grade being the minimum grade required in mathematics and English for entry to higher level study and for some career options.

6. The project has subsequently been repeated with new cohorts of schools in 2009/2010 and 2010/2011, and although the aim is still to raise achievement, the focus has changed each year to reflect current needs in the LA. For instance, the focus is Foundation Learning for 2010/2011.

The other main principle on which the Project was premised was the importance of consulting students about their learning as part of the inquiry process, in recognition of the fact that students are expert witnesses in providing insight into the facilitators and hindrances of their learning (Rudduck & Flutter, 2004). This is a key Faculty value, and there is a strong tradition of student voice research lead by two pioneers in the field; Jean Rudduck and Donald McIntyre (see for instance Rudduck & Flutter, 2004; Rudduck & McIntryre, 2007). Sadly, Jean and Donald have passed away in recent years, but Jean, who was a co-director of the RBA Project, ensured that students were asked for their opinions and experiences of the strategies participating schools were putting in place to raise boys' achievement in that project, which Ros had first-hand experience of from her critical friend work. She was therefore keen that schools in the CS-RA Project would also consult students and regard this as an important source of information when evaluating the success of their work.

In practical terms the CS-RA Project was run through a series of conferences where school colleagues met LA and Faculty staff to learn about the process of inquiry, and principles and practicalities of action research, as well as the work of the RBA Project; share ideas and progress, and plan for intervention and research to be conducted before the next conference based on feedback given during the conference. Financial support was given to enable three members of staff from each school to lead the project in their context, and various resources were made available through a project virtual learning environment (VLE), which also facilitated communication between everyone involved. In between the approximately termly conferences, each school was visited on separate occasions by the LA coordinator (who had recently completed an EdD and aligned with Faculty values regarding research) and a Faculty critical friend appointed to this role. The critical friend[7] is highly committed to the principle of consulting students, having completed her PhD under Donald McIntyre's super-vision. Hence, we have strongly promoted the value of student voice, provided practical support for schools to enable them to consult students (see MacBeath, Demetriou, Rudduck, & Myers, 2003) and ensured opportunities for the collection of testimony from students occurred during critical friend visits. How this has worked in practice can be seen in Steve, Rebecca and Bev's account of the work at Trentham High School, to which we now turn.

The CS-RA Project at Trentham High School

At the time of this project, Trentham High School was undergoing significant change. Having been judged as unsatisfactory in March 2006 by the government inspection service, Ofsted, it had begun a journey of improvement and had just been re-judged as a 'rapidly improving school' with a 'clear, common purpose' and 'good capacity to make further improvements' and satisfactory overall (Ofsted, 2007).

---

7. Bethan Morgan is the co-author of *Student Researchers Exploring Teaching and Learning: Processes and Issues* that appears in Chapter 8 of this book.

Table 9.1: Trentham High School intervention strategies.

Strand	Description	RBA classification type
Master Classes	Identified cohort of 25 potential A/A* students in core subjects invited to attend weekly after school class to extend learning in English/maths/science	Pedagogical/ organisational
Assertive Mentoring Scheme	Master class cohort allocated mentor. Fortnightly meeting to agree plan of action (recorded). Mentor actively intervenes on behalf of and has high expectations of mentee	Individual
Key Leader Befriender Scheme	Six highly influential (in terms of sway over peers) Y11 students identified (key leaders). Allocated a key befriender-a senior member of staff — who informally encourages and aims to get key leader onside with school aims/learning. Key leaders unaware they are being 'befriended'	Socio-cultural

Keen to maintain this momentum, the project appeared timely to help the school improve further and working with Cambridge University seemed appealing.

Rebecca, Steve and Bev were asked to lead the project as they were Head of the three core departments (mathematics, science and English, respectively), and it was felt that involvement of these departments would potentially maximise benefits for the school. Having reviewed the 2008 GCSE results, underachievement by some highly able students,[8] particularly by boys, was identified as a particular concern. Hence, the school decided to focus its work on raising achievement of students predicted multiple A/A* grades. Having been introduced to strategies identified during the RBA project, a three-strand approach was adopted (Table 9.1).

Although improved performance at GCSE was the ultimate aim of the project's work, various data sources were available to evaluate the project's success including records from mentor meetings, the key befrienders' logs, feedback from master class teachers and actual GCSE data. However, one data source that was regarded as particularly important was the testimony of participating students. Hence, it was agreed that half a dozen students participating in the master classes and assertive mentoring programme (representing the diversity of the group) should be interviewed to ascertain their experiences and views on these strategies, and volunteers were sought[9]. The critical friend was asked to conduct the interviews as it was felt that the students would be more likely to give honest answers to an unfamiliar person; if they

---

8. Based on projections from prior attainment at national public examinations at the end of years 6 and 9.
9. As students involved in the Befrienders scheme were not aware that they had been targeted, it seemed inappropriate to interview any of the key leaders.

Table 9.2: Areas covered in student interviews.

Issue	Sample question(s)
Overall perception of being part of the Cambridge Project	• What do you think the teachers are trying to do in the Cambridge Project? • How do you feel about being part of the Project?
Perceptions of master classes	• Have the master classes helped? • How? Why not?
Perceptions of mentoring	• Has the mentoring helped? • How? Why not?
Impact of Cambridge Project	• What part of your learning is the Cambridge Project helping you with • Has the Cambridge Project affected your confidence in tackling higher level work?
Suggestions for improvement	• Is there anything you haven't liked/found useful? • Can you suggest any improvements to the master classes/mentoring?

talked to a teacher they might give answers they thought the school would want to hear. An interview schedule was developed with the critical friend and Ros' help, and the areas covered are summarised in Table 9.2. Students were interviewed on a one-to-one basis for approximately 20 minutes. Conversations were recorded with students' permission and transcribed. Students were aware that Rebecca, Steve and Bev would read the transcripts but were assured that they would not be identified by name. The importance of being candid to help the school learn from their experience was strongly flagged, and it was also made clear that there wouldn't be any adverse consequences from making critical comments, and they could withdraw their testimony at any point.

The students who were interviewed were generally very enthusiastic about the project. This positive feedback coupled with analysis of the other data sources has convinced the school that the master classes and assertive mentoring are worth continuing with.[10] Students particularly liked the fact they were publically identified as being part of the 'Cambridge Project' so references to this remain although CS-RA

---

10. The Befriender scheme appeared to have less impact and was discontinued but what was learned from the experience of befrienders was incorporated into the mentoring scheme.

Project finished in September 2009. Students spoke positively about how the master classes had helped their learning:

> Its just the deeper knowledge of each subject because in class we have to cover each topic in a certain amount of time and if you don't get it then we just move on but now I can actually understand it more. [Student E]

> It helped quite a lot because we have been covering stuff we did quite a long time ago so it's just like recapping and going over it. [Student D]

Comments like this indicate that the master classes were effective in reinforcing the more challenging aspects of the syllabus. However, students also had suggestions for improvements:

> A lot of people did struggle with it so if we could have an input you could take a group off somewhere and do what they are struggling with and then do a little bit of something else. [Student F]

> Maybe some of the things like science some do triple science and some do double award. I'm doing triple so sometimes I'm going over what I did in the double it wasn't time wasted because it may still come up in the exam I'm not sure but I kind of already knew it so it wasn't as interesting. [Student B]

Remarks like these indicate that students felt the master classes would have been more useful if they had been given more of an input into the content of these lessons. In addition, a number of students felt that some of the work that they had covered in science was not sufficiently geared towards the triple science course. The school has since taken these comments 'on board' and decided to give students more choice of topic matter. The issue raised by having double and triple science students within the same group has been discussed and the school is considering splitting the group for science master classes to enable the focus to be targeted more appropriately to students taking different science routes in the future.

Students who had had one-to-one meetings with a mentor were also positive about the mentoring programme:

> It genuinely helps keep you organised and focused and it's if you have got any problems with anything, you can raise that. [Student A]

> If you are underachieving in any subject then they will talk to you and find out if you need any extra help. [Student D]

> Well we normally have an Achievement Manager ask us how we feel about the subjects and any issues we have she will raise with the teachers so it does help with the learning and like if we don't like

something or other in a particular she will mention that to them and she will sort it out. [Student B]

The mentor meeting records together with comments made during interview indicated that some students did not meet their mentor very frequently, whereas others had met their mentor in a group with other students involved in the CS-RA Project. In these cases mentoring appeared to have been less effective as students were more ambivalent about the helpfulness of these sessions, suggesting, for instance, that one-to-one sessions would be better as 'some people don't like talking in front of others' (Student F). Overall, this implied that mentoring had not been implemented as envisaged in all cases, but where it had been, it had generally worked well. The school has acted on this feedback. The Deputy Headteacher[11] now has responsibility for assertive mentoring and has refocused and slightly expanded the scheme to involve around 30 students who are underachieving and in danger of not achieving the benchmark 5A*–C grades at GCSE[12]. Mentors have been trained and the paperwork developed to record meetings has been streamlined. The scheme is closely monitored to ensure mentoring takes place and so that students who start to meet targets can leave the scheme, providing opportunities for others who are struggling to join.

The school went through a further government Ofsted inspection in January 2010 and achieved a 'good' in most areas with an overall 'good' designation (Ofsted, 2010), and there seems no doubt that the CS-RA Project has contributed to this success.

Reflections: The Value of Schools Working through Local Authorities in Partnership with Higher Education Institutions to Promote Student Voice

From Rebecca, Steve and Bev's perspective, the project offered exciting new ideas, as 'student voice' was a relatively new idea at Trentham High School. They believe that consulting students was invaluable in judging the success of the strategies put in place. Having a critical friend from the University, who spent time in school, was vital, as it enabled students who were not used to their views being sought directly by teachers to be interviewed by an outsider, and this generated a large amount of data that were extremely useful for evaluation and future planning. Furthermore, the fact that the critical friend was an expert in student voice was helpful, as she was able to help them craft suitable interview questions.

---

11. Although UK schools are governed by a governing body, responsibility for the day-to-day running of a school is delegated by the governors to the Headteacher, who is supported by a small group of senior teachers including one or more Deputy Headteachers.
12. That is, the focus has expanded beyond the A/A* cohort and now only includes students who are underachieving based on comparisons between performance on the half-termly standard assessments and predictions based on prior achievement.

The school is now deploying student voice systematically. The mathematics department, for instance, incorporates a student questionnaire into its monitoring and evaluation process. This is conducted by the learning support worker attached to the department and is confidential. The senior leadership has introduced a new quality assurance programme whereby each half-term a specific department is internally reviewed using the Ofsted model. As part of the process, a cross-section of students are interviewed to gather data on students' views and opinions. An important aspect of the legacy of the CS-RA Project, therefore, is the integral role of student voice in the self-evaluation process of the school at all levels.

For Ros, working with a group of schools in an identified project supported by an LA not only financially but also in terms of shared values, has been a rewarding way of disseminating the research and philosophy of eminent figures in the student voice field. Although the structure of the project has been refined slightly for later cohorts of Stoke schools to involve the LA coordinator more and increase the frequency the schools come together to promote the idea of a community of inquiry, she is convinced that this partnership model offers a useful way forward for academics and practitioners to work together to promote student voice in schools.

Conclusion

Although the partnership developed during the CS-RA Project between school, LA and university colleagues has been extremely rewarding and productive in terms of introducing successful research informed interventions to raise achievement in a range of secondary schools in Stoke LA that have been effectively evaluated affording student voice a prominent role; our experience of working together to introduce student voice in the secondary school context outlined in this chapter has suggested a number of issues need to be considered for the potential benefits of collaboration between school and university colleagues to be realised. We would like to conclude by raising three issues.

First, university and school colleagues need to have a shared understanding and expectations about what each can offer and the role each should fulfil. Working on a *research* project with a prestigious university, such as the University of Cambridge, can initially appear daunting for school colleagues who, in our experience, do not initially perceive themselves as researchers. Launching the Project with a residential conference in Cambridge, where university, LA and school colleagues ate and relaxed together was extremely important for building relationships, as well as providing quality time and space to discuss, think and plan and, in general, demystify the research process and school and LA colleagues' role in this. University colleagues also need to be sensitive in supporting school colleague's development as researchers. Colleagues from Trentham came away from our first Stoke conference, having presented the first phase of their work, dissatisfied that university colleagues had provided limited formative feedback to help them move forward, whereas university colleagues had been concerned not to appear to be too critical. Relationships and good communication are key but difficult to develop when in real terms contact between busy school, LA and university colleagues is restricted.

The second issue relates to the practicalities of working together so that school colleagues can benefit from university colleagues' research knowledge. Although school, LA and university colleagues came together for a number of conferences over the year to share ideas and progress and to plan, the actual time available for university colleagues to introduce and develop new ideas, such as student voice work, was somewhat limited. Materials such as the 'Consulting Students Toolkit' (MacBeath et al, 2003) were made available through the Project VLE and school colleagues encouraged to engage in email dialogues with university colleagues and each other, but school colleagues in reality made little use of this resource as they found it difficult to find time to explore what it offered and reflect on how it might be used to support their research in school. We have planned the Project slightly differently with schools that have joined in later cohorts so that LA colleagues have a much more prominent role running twilight sessions with school colleagues utilising resources on the VLE to further develop knowledge and understanding in between the conferences attended by school, LA and university colleagues.

The final issue pertains to cultural issues in school contexts relating to student consultation. Student voice was a somewhat new initiative at Trentham School and students were not accustomed to be asked about their learning. In this situation, school colleagues felt that questions would be better posed by an outsider, the university critical friend. This proved to be effective, as students were forthcoming about the initiatives the school had put in place. The challenge is to create a culture where students and staff feel student consultation is worthwhile and valuable after the end of the Project when the outside critical friend is no longer available for this role. Transforming culture takes time but systemising student consultation by making it part of monitoring and evaluation and acting on student suggestions is certainly helping to effect the desired changes.

References

Campbell, A., & Groundwater-Smith, S. (Eds). (2010). *Connecting inquiry and professional learning in education*. Routledge: London.

Department for Education. (2007). Secondary school achievement and attainment tables 2007. Retrieved from www.education.gov.uk/researchandstatistics/attainmenttables. Accessed on January 11, 2011.

Hargreaves, A. (2003). *Teaching in the knowledge society: Education in the age of insecurity*. Maidenhead: Open University Press.

Lave, J., & Wenger, E. (1991). *Situated learning: Legitimate peripheral participation*. Cambridge: Cambridge University Press.

MacBeath, J., Demetriou, H., Rudduck, J., & Myers, K. (2003). *Consulting pupils: A toolkit for teachers*. London: Pearson Publishing.

McLaughlin, C., Black-Hawkins, K., Brindley, S., McIntyre, D., & Taber, K. (2006). *Researching schools: Stories from a schools-university partnership for educational research*. Abingdon, Oxon: Routledge.

McLaughlin, C., Black-Hawkins, K., & McIntyre, D. (2007). *Networking practitioner research.* London: Routledge.

Ofsted (2007). *Trentham high school inspection report.* London: Ofsted.

Ofsted (2010). *Trentham high school inspection report.* London: Ofsted.

Rudduck, J., & Flutter, J. (2004). *How to improve your school: Giving pupils a voice.* London: Continuum.

Rudduck, J., & McIntryre, D. (2007). *Improving learning through consulting pupils.* London: Routledge.

Stenhouse, L. (1975). *An introduction to curriculum research and development.* London: Heinemann.

Stenhouse, L. (1983). *Authority, education and emancipation.* London: Heinemann Educational.

Swaffield, S. (2003). The role of a critical friend. *Managing Schools Today, 12*(5), 28–30.

Swaffield, S. (2004). Critical friends: Supporting leadership, improving learning. *Improving Schools, 7*(3), 267–278.

Younger, M., & Warrington, M., with Gray, J., Rudduck, J., McLellan, R., Bearne, E., Kershner, R., & Bricheno, P. (2005). *Raising Boys' Achievement* (No. 636). DfES.

Younger, M., Warrington, M., & with McLellan, R. (2005). *Raising boys' achievement in secondary schools.* Maidenhead, Berkshire: Open University Press.

Chapter 10

Student Researchers Exploring Teaching and Learning: Processes and Issues

Bethan Morgan and Anita Porter

Abstract

This chapter presents an example of student voice work currently in progress at Impington Village College, a state 11–18 school near Cambridge, United Kingdom. In partnership with the Faculty of Education, University of Cambridge, the school is researching student engagement. Wishing to build on the existing history of, and strong emphasis on, student voice at Impington, the college Senior Leadership Team is exploring the following question: 'Will student engagement be raised if research resulting in change is led by students rather than staff?' We outline the steps a group of Year 10 students (age 15–16 years), supported by teachers, have taken to design and lead a research project. We describe the students' decision to focus on teaching and learning, their research training and how they chose the POD (a small space with recording equipment) as an innovative method of gathering data from fellow students. We consider the opportunities this research is providing students and conclude by considering issues for student voice that are highlighted by this project.

Keywords: Student-led research; student voice; student engagement; secondary school context; school–university partnership; teacher–student collaboration

Introduction

This chapter presents an example of student-led research at Impington Village College (IVC) in the United Kingdom. The project is currently in progress (2010–2011) and students are not yet in a position to report on actual results and outcomes. Our aims,

The Student Voice Handbook: Bridging the Academic/Practitioner Divide
Copyright © 2011 by Emerald Group Publishing Limited
ISBN: 978-1-78052-040-7

therefore, are to describe the processes involved in the research and raise issues of the role and involvement of students in school-based research that we suggest are useful for academics and practitioners interested in student voice work to consider. We also highlight some complexities of student voice work amid the realities of school life.

IVC is a state funded school providing education for children aged between 11 and 18 years. The school is located in the villages of Histon and Impington (population approximately 8,500), two miles from the university city of Cambridge in eastern England. The school admits students from a diverse range of socio-economic backgrounds, with a catchment area that covers five local villages and a section of the north of Cambridge, both containing private and social housing. Approximately 6% of the main school (students 11–16 years) receive free school meals and 6% are students from ethnic minority backgrounds. The school also contains a specialist centre for students with a range of disabilities.

IVC has a tradition of student voice and has had a strong Student Council for the past decade. The work of the council was part of research carried out by the University of Birmingham (Davies, Williams, Yamashita, & Ko Man-Hing, 2006) and also featured in an article in the Times Educational Supplement in 2004.[1] In addition, two Year 10 student members presented on the effective development and organisation of student councils at a Teachers' conference organised by the Citizenship Foundation.[2] This was followed by the two students being invited to take part in a live BBC[3] phone-in providing advice to schools. Currently, student voice at IVC is formally represented by the Student Council, a non-elected group which aims to be inclusive and representative of all students. Anita, co-author of this chapter, is an Advanced Skills Teacher[4] responsible for supporting and developing student voice at the college.

IVC is also a member of the School–University Partnership for Education (SUPER) with the Faculty of Education, University of Cambridge (see McLaughlin, Black-Hawkins, Brindley, McIntyre & Taber, 2006). Bethan, co-author of this chapter, is a teaching associate at the Faculty of Education, University of Cambridge and part of her role in the SUPER partnership is to provide critical friendship (Swaffield, 2007) to IVC to support and develop practitioner research. Within this partnership, since 2008, IVC has been part of a research project exploring teachers' and students' perceptions of engagement in school and classroom learning. This has involved research led by Bethan on behalf of the school–faculty partnership and also research, such as featured in this chapter, initiated by college staff and students. Support from Bethan, in her role

---

1. http://www.tes.co.uk/article.aspx?storycode=389570.
2. http://www.citizenshipfoundation.org.uk/.
3. BBC: The British Broadcasting Corporation
4. Advanced Skills Teacher 'is a role in a state school in England and Wales. Advanced Skills Teachers are judged through external assessment against a range of criteria to demonstrate excellent classroom teaching practice. They are employed in Advanced Skills Teacher posts in roles which include an element of work dedicated to supporting teaching colleagues in their own schools, and other schools in the area, to improve their own practice. The role was introduced in 1998 to reward excellent teachers who chose to stay working in classrooms, rather than following other routes to promotion through leadership.' Source: http://en.wikipedia.org/wiki/Advanced_Skills_Teacher.

as critical friend, also includes school visits and access for practitioners such as Anita to academic research literature on student voice (e.g. Flutter & Rudduck, 2004; Morgan 2009; Rudduck & McIntyre, 2007; Thomson & Gunter, 2006) and student engagement (e.g. Morgan, McLaughlin, McLellan, & Waterhouse, 2009). Anita and colleagues also present and share school research with other partnership schools at the annual SUPER conference hosted by the Faculty of Education.

With student engagement highlighted as a result of these varied school–university partnership activities, the IVC senior leadership team (SLT), encouraged by the Headteacher, posed the question: 'Would student engagement be raised if the research resulting in change was led by students rather than staff?' They then asked Anita, in her role as student voice co-ordinator, to approach the Student Council to find out if students would help to explore this question by researching a topic of their choice. Both the SLT and Anita were interested in the role of students as active participants and collaborators in research rather than passive respondents (Cook-Sather, 2002, 2009).

It is within the context outlined earlier that the project featured in this chapter takes place. Bethan and Anita, in their respective roles, have collaborated in reporting on it. After describing key stages in the students' research, the chapter concludes by reflecting on opportunities it has provided for students and issues it has raised for students and teachers.

The Student Researchers' Project

In this section, we outline the steps a group of Year 10 students (age 15–16 years), with Anita's support, took to plan and investigate their research. We describe the recruitment of the student research group, the students' decision to focus on teaching and learning, their research training, project design and project pilot.

Recruitment of the Student Research Group

To investigate the question originally posed by the SLT, Anita took several steps. First, she approached Year 10 Student Council members to ask if they were interested in conducting research. Some students (who were also part of the college's Gifted and Talented programme[5]) volunteered immediately. However, Anita also encouraged others to take part so that the group represented the diversity of student council members.

---

5. 'Gifted and Talented' is a policy implemented in UK schools which aims to identify and support students with an ability to develop to a level significantly ahead of their year group (or with the potential to develop those abilities): 'gifted' learners have abilities in one or more academic subjects, like Maths and English; 'talented' learners have practical skills in areas like sport, music, design or creative and performing arts. For further information, see: http://www.direct.gov.uk/en/Parents/Schoolslearninganddevelopment/ExamsTestsAndTheCurriculum/DG_10037625.

The final group involved 12 students (8 boys and 4 girls). Second, Anita asked students to select a subject to research. They chose 'The opinions of Year 10 students with respect to teaching and learning in the College'. The group felt this was a legitimate topic to engage with since as students they had had extensive experience of teaching and learning. This project, they decided, would be an excellent opportunity to discover students' views and convey these to the SLT.

Training

Anita next facilitated research training for the student group. This involved four one hour sessions during lessons allocated on the school timetable to students' Personal Development. As the sessions were during school time, parental permission was not sought. Anita trained the group to understand the requirements of sociological research in education drawing on her own knowledge and experience of teaching sociology and psychology. This included introducing students to, for example, positivist and interpretivist perspectives on research, discussion on the uses of quantitative and qualitative data, sampling frames and notions of validity, representativeness and reliability. The sessions also involved discussion and the use of scenarios where the students could make informed decisions with respect to the most appropriate methods to use for their research topic. Using this information, the group discussed and debated the various options available to them:

> It would be most useful if we could collect both quantitative and qualitative data
> [Year 10 Student Researcher]
>
> I realise that the choice of methodology depends on the researcher's theoretical perspective
> [Year 10 Student Researcher]

With Anita's support, the group discussed issues that could arise when students conduct research with other students as the participants, for example peer group pressure and the idea that the interviewees' responses may be influenced by the interviewer's presence. They also considered issues surrounding written answers in surveys, for example the fact that some students might find this uncomfortable due to literacy difficulties. The group realised that if this was the situation, the validity of the research findings and the depth of the students' responses would be affected.

Research Project Design

With these limitations in mind, the group developed the idea of gathering data by giving students the opportunity to talk in a 'POD': a small enclosed comfortable space which would contain recording equipment. A sound-proofed library office was available, along with music practice rooms. The group especially hoped this would give students who might otherwise remain silent, or lack confidence to speak in a group situation, an opportunity to voice their opinions. The group also hoped that the POD method would overcome the ethical issue of safeguarding students' anonymity. Another ethical consideration the group noted, with Anita's guidance, was that of the potential for students in the POD to disclose sensitive information. In light of this, all those taking part were briefed and reassured in advance that if any issues of concern were disclosed then these would be handled according to school policy.

The group decided that the question list to prompt students in the POD should include both structured closed questions and open questions to gather quantitative and qualitative data. The group believed this would give students the opportunity to give their opinions and at the same time would allow for some numerical data to be gathered which could also be useful if the research was repeated with another Year group.

Pilot

For their pilot study, the group initially selected a random sample of 20 Year 10 students to individually spend time in the POD recording answers to the questions. The group then listened to the recordings, evaluated their methodology and adjusted the question list accordingly (e.g. it was obvious some questions were not clear or too long). The pilot prompted a lively discussion about how essential it was to have a representative student sample to enhance validity; the group were keenly aware they needed to gather data from as diverse a range of students as possible, namely, students perceived as highly engaged in school and disengaged or disaffected. As a result, they decided the research must be open to include all the students in Year 10 who were willing to take part. The group hoped this would guarantee that all the students in Year 10 would experience ownership of the project findings, hopefully leading to greater engagement in the research process.

The student research group are still gathering data for their project. Next steps will be to finish analysis of the data and present findings to the Year 10 cohort, the SLT and college governors. A research report will be written by Anita and the student group. However, the issue of how realistic it will be to expect students in the research group to commit time to continued data analysis and writing in light of how busy they are with revision for external examinations, now that they are in Year 11, is one that Anita is keenly aware of and sensitive to.

Reflections on the Project

We conclude by reflecting on opportunities involvement in this project has given the student research group. We then consider issues for students and teachers that the project has highlighted.

Opportunities for Students

Involvement in this project has provided the student research group with opportunities to work with adults, collaborate with peers and develop research skills.

Opportunity to Work with Adults

The student research group has been provided with the opportunity to take ownership of a substantial project. The group has had the opportunity to work alongside Anita and the Senior Leadership. Throughout the process the group has been set deadlines by the college's SLT member responsible for teaching and learning. Other less significant deadlines for stages of the research have been set through discussion between Anita and the student research group. The expectations of staff involved in the project have been high. These expectations have focused on the student researchers meeting deadlines, presenting their research proposal to the college's teaching and learning group, the whole college staff and the Governing Body and being able to justify their choice of methodology and answer impromptu questions.

Opportunity to Collaborate with Peers

Throughout all project phases, the student researchers have needed to work as a group, using skills of negotiation as they express their views and listen to others, often having to compromise and adapt their original aims. They have discussed the strengths of individual members of the group, allocating tasks and roles appropriately.

Opportunity to Develop Research Skills

The student group has demonstrated evidence of acquiring skills of evaluation and analysis with respect to research methodology as displayed in comments made to Anita during the process, for example:

> In order to ensure representativeness our sample must include the whole Year group [Year 10 Student Researcher]
>
> A small sample will lack validity [Year 10 Student Researcher]
>
> Our quantitative data will be high in reliability and therefore we can make comparisons [Year 10 Student Researcher]

Selecting the appropriate methodology has involved careful evaluation of the pilot study. The pilot enabled the group to detect potential barriers to their research aim;

students were quick to search for adaptations and feasible alternatives. For example, when evaluating the pilot, the students realised that barriers to their research aim were the inclusion of too many questions; this had caused confusion for some of the students taking part. Following this discovery, the group deleted three questions from the list. Two questions focusing on similar themes, shown up by repetition in the students' answers, were amalgamated. The vocabulary used in two of the questions had obviously been unclear for some of the participants so the team simplified the wording using more accessible vocabulary. Finally, the research group realised how interesting the responses from all the students were, regardless of their attitude to school. This confirmed their decision to give the whole Year cohort the opportunity to take part in the research rather than selecting a sample.

The process of analysing the recordings has required the group to develop a number of skills. Verbatim typed transcriptions are not possible due to issues of time and resources. However, the group has taken a rigorous approach to data analysis, sharing the process of listening to recordings in groups of three, making notes of key points, then discussing and comparing their findings.

> There have to be at least 3 people at a time listening to the tapes otherwise it's easy to miss important stuff [Year 10 Student Researcher]

There has been a great need for trust, a high level of consistency and a collective understanding of material relevant to their research aim. Anita's training has stressed the requirement to detect themes that are emerging from the participants' recordings. This has involved the students selecting what they consider to be the most relevant material while mindful of issues of bias. Collating the findings has also demanded patience and focus.

> You've really got to look out for the different themes that come up on the tapes, you can't write everything down [Year 10 Student Researcher]

> At first I couldn't get a grip of all the research words but now I feel that I really know what I'm on about [Year 10 Student Researcher]

> Sociology really appeals to me now, I've never done anything like this before [Year 10 Student Researcher]

Inclusion has been a strong theme with respect to the whole Year cohort taking part and every student being provided with the opportunity to have a voice. This has involved careful consideration of wording and expectations of students' literacy skills when devising and evaluating the question list. In addition, a discussion with the special needs staff team was arranged to ensure that the students in the Year cohort who have speech disabilities have also been able to take part.

Through discussion, and Anita's careful intervention, the students have achieved clarity as to why making their research open to all individuals in the Year group is the only way to value all opinions and gain a valid picture of students' perspectives.

Issues for Students

We highlight here issues that have arisen for students during this process revolving around the research group's assumptions of other students in their cohort and the Year 10 cohort's perceptions of the research group.

The Research Group's Assumptions of Other Students in Their Cohort

Initially some students in the research group could not see the relevance of interviewing students who they assumed had a negative attitude towards school. They saw the process of interviewing, for example, students from the college's Gifted and Talented programme as potentially more valuable; they assumed these students would achieve an immediate understanding of the aim of the study and provide articulate answers.

At this stage, while students were designing their research project, Anita felt it was appropriate to intervene and introduce students to certain sociological ideas such as differential educational achievement based on the socio-economic background of students. The group discussed the difficulties of defining social class and the inherent dangers of making assumptions about other students concluding how important it was to be inclusive in their approach. As one student commented: 'The process of researching our Year cohort has been more challenging than I expected'. Through such discussion, the group has recognised that providing a voice for students who dislike school may lead to gaining valuable insights into reasons behind their disengagement:

> I realise now why it's essential to include everyone or you could miss something crucial [Year 10 Student Researcher]

The group see this as an excellent example of qualitative research, providing them with the opportunity to discover how marginalised students, in their own words, really feel.

From these enlightening discussions, several group members have become particularly focused on gathering the views of students perceived as disengaged, realising that an understanding of their perspectives has the potential to lead to change:

> It's really interesting, people have said stuff that I wouldn't have thought of ... I suppose that shows that we all have different experiences of school [Year 10 Student Researcher]

If an increased focus on their needs could lead to more engagement from these students within the classroom, this would benefit all students and teachers. For example, some of the students in the Year cohort have behaviour support plans. This is possibly due to the fact that they may have difficulty engaging in the classroom. The feedback from these students could provide teachers with further information on what it is specifically within the classroom that leads them to become disengaged and what methods these students believe help them to achieve engagement. This data could then inform the lesson planning of both individual teachers and departments, with a view to further inclusion and support of these students in their learning. Further engagement of these students would then affect the teaching and learning environment for all in the classroom.

The Year 10 Cohort's Perceptions of the Research Group

When reflecting on the project the student research group felt that initially some of their peers had possibly viewed them as an elite group aligned with teachers:

> At first I thought that people would think that we were real geeks and I didn't want them to think I was any more geeky than they think already but actually it's been alright, people seem to have got really in to it [Year 10 Student Researcher]

However, as this comment suggests, the Year 10 cohort began to see the student researchers as representing their views; student participants who had appeared disengaged at the beginning of the work began to relate to the project as they valued their experience of the POD and any initial wariness in attitude changed as the following comments illustrate:

> I can't believe that we can speak into a recorder and what we say might affect what happens in school [Year 10 student research participant]

> I didn't think I'd like speaking into the recorder but actually it was really great to be able to say whatever you want [Year 10 student research participant]

> The fact that students in my Year group are organising this makes it feel really different somehow [Year 10 student research participant]

> It was good to just talk into a microphone. I hate writing down what I think. I never know how to describe it [Year 10 student research participant]

The student research group believe this is due to the students' unusual experience of being able to make honest comments about teaching and learning in the College in the POD's safe environment:

> I've been really honest-a lot of good stuff though. I felt I could because no one else was listening and sometimes it's a bit embarrassing saying what you think in front of your mates like in other research things [Year 10 student research participant]

Another interesting factor noted by the student researchers has concerned the composition of their group:

> I really think that the fact that student x and student y were involved has made a real difference to how the other students have seen the project. I mean they're into dance and performance and stuff and other kids already thought they were alright [Year 10 Student Researcher]

> The fact that x and y were on the research team meant that other kids were up for being involved at the beginning [Year 10 Student Researcher]

Certain members of the research group are popular with fellow students and student researchers feel this has contributed to getting students to participate in the research.

Issues for Teachers

This project has highlighted a number of issues for us to consider and explore regarding future student voice research within the college and the partnership. To conclude, we suggest issues of the selection of student researchers and collaboration between teachers and student–researchers are relevant for all schools engaged in student-led research to reflect upon.

Issues of Selection of Student Researchers

Powerful and valuable as this project has been (and continues to be) we are mindful of issues surrounding selection of the student research group. Involvement in a research project is a worthwhile activity for students providing opportunities for working alongside adults, collaborating with peers and acquiring research skills. To be truly inclusive, such research opportunities would ideally be open to all students from a year cohort, regardless of their membership or not of the School Council. We are aware of the potential dangers of this kind of work, in creating an elite group of students and privileging some students at expense of others, if not guided and supported sensitively (Mullis 2002; Thomson & Gunter, 2006). How can such opportunities be extended to any students who are interested irrespective of membership of the school council or a 'gifted and talented' group within schools? This is a question we are keen to explore.

Issues of Collaboration between Teachers and Student Researchers

The role of the SLT in this project is crucial. It has raised the status of the students' research by asking students to carry out research on their behalf. Students feel that the SLT in this way are giving them the opportunity to formally include student voices to contribute to potential change and formulation of school policies:

> It's good to think that when we've left there might be changes that this research led to [Year 10 Student Researcher]

The requirement for presentations to different adult groups has also helped students justify their research proposal and through questions reflect further on their research methods.

In reflecting on such collaboration between teachers and students, we suggest that two models from the student-voice literature are helpful here so that adult involvement in student voice research is mindful of dangers of tokenism and manipulation, namely: Hart's (1992) 'ladder of participation' (p. 8) and Fielding's (2001) nine questions (p. 110). Roger Hart (1992) drew on his extensive experience of researching young people's participation in a range of environmental and community projects in many countries on the behalf of UNICEF and designed a 'Ladder of Participation' as 'a beginning typology for thinking about children's participation in projects' (p. 9).[6] Michael Fielding (2001) drew on his extensive experience of student voice initiatives (and in particular those of students-as-researchers) to propose nine 'clusters' of questions that can be applied to examine 'arrangements and practices which seek to both acknowledge and promote student voice' (p. 133). What these models have in common are increasing levels of pupils as active, not passive, participants in their education. Such models help us to continually reflect on ways in which student-led research is initiated and owned by students.

Conclusion

This chapter has reported on student led research that is in progress at IVC. We have described the various stages of the research and have suggested involvement has

---

6. Hart (1992) emphasises that his typology, while useful for supporting thinking about children's participation, 'should not be considered as a simple measuring stick of the quality of any programme' (p. 1). Hart also proposes that 'it is not necessary that children always operate on the highest possible rungs of the ladder' (*ibid.*).

provided the student research group with opportunities to collaborate with teachers and fellow students. We have reflected on issues of students' perceptions and assumptions of each other. We have highlighted how a teacher (Anita) has facilitated the students' research through training, support and sensitive intervention. Eliciting student voices on teaching and learning can be a challenge — even for student researchers who are their peers. However, as this project illustrates, the role of a skilful and supportive teacher in guiding students to explore preconceived assumptions is invaluable in facilitating and developing student voice. Finally, we highlight two issues — those of the selection of student researchers and collaboration between teachers and student researchers — that we feel are important to continually reflect on in student voice work.

The original question posed by the IVC senior leadership team that sparked this student research project was 'Would student engagement be raised if the research resulting in change was led by students rather than staff?' Although this question has yet to be answered, we feel our student researchers have demonstrated that when given opportunity, support and responsibility, they have a key role to play alongside teachers in harnessing research to release the voices of their peers.

References

Cook-Sather, A. (2002). Authorizing students' perspectives: Towards trust, dialogue and change in education. *Educational Researcher*, *31*(4), 3–14.

Cook-Sather, A. (2009). *Learning from the student's perspective: A sourcebook for effective teaching*. Boulder, CO: Paradigm Publishers.

Davies, L., Williams, C., Yamashita, H., & Ko Man-Hing, A. (2006). *Inspiring schools: Case studies for change-taking up the challenge of pupil participation*. Esmee Fairburn & Carnegie UK Trust. Available to download from: www.esmeefairbairn.org.uk/pdf/InspiringSchools_P31.pdf

Fielding, M. (2001). Beyond the rhetoric of student voice: New departures or new constraints in the transformation of twenty first century school? *Forum*, *43*(2), 100–110.

Flutter, J., & Rudduck, J. (2004). *Consulting pupils: What's in it for schools?* London: Routledge Falmer.

Hart, R. A. (1992). Children's participation: From tokenism to citizenship. *Innocenti Essays No.4*. Unicef, United Nations Children's Fund. Available to download from: www.unicef-irc.org/publications/pdf/childrens_participation.pdf

McLaughlin, C., Black-Hawkins, K., Brindley, S., McIntyre, D., & Taber, K. (2006). *Researching schools: Stories from a schools — University partnership for educational research*. London: Routledge.

Morgan, B. (2009). Consulting pupils about classroom teaching and learning: Policy, practice and response in one school. *Research Papers in Education* (First published on: 11 November 2009 (iFirst)).

Morgan, B., McLaughlin, C., McLellan, R., & Waterhouse, J. (2009). *Pupil engagement in schools and classrooms: A literature review*. Unpublished Report for the Schools-University Partnership for Educational Research (SUPER), Faculty of Education, University of Cambridge.

Mullis, G. (2002). 'Is this a good idea?' 'It's a great idea'. *Communicating (The newsletter of the Consulting Students about Teaching and Learning Project), 6,* 2–3. Available from: http://www.consultingpupils.co.uk/

Rudduck, J., & McIntyre, D. (2007). *Improving learning through consulting pupils.* London: Routledge.

Swaffield, S. (2007). Light touch critical friendship. *Improving Schools, 10*(3), 205–219.

Thomson, P., & Gunter, H. (2006). From "consulting pupils" to "Pupils as researchers": A situated case narrative. *British Educational Research Journal, 32*(6), 839–856.

Chapter 11

From Ethos to Practice — Pupil Voice at the Sweyne Park School

Andy Samways and Corina Seal

Abstract

The Sweyne Park School is situated in South-East Essex, England, and has a roll of 1300 pupils aged from 11 to 16 years and 180 staff. Pupil voice activities are an established and integral aspect of life at the school. Creating the time and space for formal and informal opportunities for dialogue between staff and pupils has been at the heart of school improvement activities. A wide variety of opportunities are facilitated to capture pupil perceptions of learning, teaching and a wide variety of aspects of school life. Within the ethos of 'respect', insightful feedback is channelled into learning, teaching, evaluation and hence school improvement. As practices continually evolve and move up the rungs of Hart's 'Ladder of Participation' (1992), so pupils themselves are involved in planning how we might get the best out of pupil voice activities. From targeted groups through to pupil volunteers, all pupils within the school community are encouraged to believe that their opinions matter. In this piece we explore our mechanisms for pupil voice and the impact the work has on the school community. Three activities will be discussed in detail: these are e-mentoring, Headteacher's Achievement Time and pupils' input into Self Review.

Keywords: Respect; opportunities; pupil perceptions; school improvement; evolving practice

Introduction

A highly successful community comprehensive secondary school, Sweyne Park has 1300 pupils and 180 staff, and was created by an amalgamation of two schools in 1997, The Sweyne School and Park School in the town of Rayleigh in South East

The Student Voice Handbook: Bridging the Academic/Practitioner Divide
Copyright © 2011 by Emerald Group Publishing Limited
All rights of reproduction in any form reserved
ISBN: 978-1-78052-040-7

Essex: it is both a Specialist Science School and Training School. Pupils at the school are predominantly white British and come from a wide range of socio-economic backgrounds.

At the heart of life at Sweyne Park is the school's 'Respect' Code of Conduct. It is the first aspect of school life that pupils and families are introduced to when considering whether to come to the school. Open Evening presentations, school tours and primary school visits all highlight the importance of respect to school life. The Code of Conduct is that respect is fundamental and that as a pupil you:

- Respect yourself
- Respect others
- Respect the environment

The code influences all aspects of school life, from promoting and recognising positive behaviour to unpicking and giving sanctions for unacceptable behaviour, as Headteacher, Andy Hodgkinson, notes:

> 'Respect' has been the single most important guiding principle throughout our journey to create a community where everyone is a learner and to 'secure pupil success'. Pupil voice has therefore been a logical extension of this principle and the benefits to school improvement have been enormous. Not only do our pupils feel a genuine sense of pride in their school but through their ideas we have been able to shape teaching and learning, the curriculum and our overall provision to improve pupil outcomes. Their feedback and views never cease to surprise and impress us and certainly leave us no room for complacency!

Many pupils also recognise its importance:

> Respect is such an important thing in school life. Because of the simplicity of the code, it's been easy to follow since year 7. I think respect helps pupils to get their voice heard. Respect covers all aspects of life so I'll continue to use it in anything I decide to do in the future. [Female School Council member in year 10, aged 15]

Out of the Ethos, the Vision for Pupil Voice

The overriding view of staff at Sweyne Park School is that pupil voice is not an addition to the curriculum but a part of everything pupils do throughout the day. The founding Headteacher, Kate Spiller, established the importance of respecting pupil feedback when the school was created in 1997. She believed, like Rudd, that pupil voice involves 'Empowering learners by providing appropriate ways of listening to their concerns, interests and needs in order to develop educational experiences better suited to those individuals' (2007, p. 8). The school's leadership team was keen to use pupil voice not only as a means for improving teaching and learning (Flutter & Ruddock, 2004) but also to foster the pupils' sense of being part of a new learning community where they could 'develop a genuine appreciation of democracy and a sense of their own competence and responsibility to participate' (Hart, 1997, p. 3). As new members of staff join the school, they are introduced to the ethos of respect as a key element of all relationships in the school. Many new staff will have had first-hand experience of meeting with a pupil panel as part of their interview process. Modelling of respect by staff on an everyday basis is encouraged so as to embed and share the ethos with pupils in a very practical way. Staff development activities, the weekly staff bulletin and briefings all regularly highlight and focus on pupil voice feedback.

The school's vision is for every child to be a confident learner, able to adapt the way they think, the skills they utilise, and to embrace innovative approaches to learning. In this way, every child is encouraged to develop autonomy as a learner, develop their talents and help create choices that open doors in their future.

Pupils are encouraged to play an active role in their education; their views are listened to and influence many aspects of school life. As a result, pupils are given many opportunities to develop transferable skills in learning, leadership capabilities and the qualities that will facilitate lifelong learning through:

- *Engagement*: feeling fully involved in learning and the life of the school
- *Responsibility*: having control over their learning and behaviour
- *Independence*: being able to make decisions within their own learning
- *Confidence*: feeling good about themselves, their progress and achievements
- *Maturity*: being open, honest and able to work together within a culture of respect
- *Interdependence*: working with others

The leadership of Sweyne Park School strives to create and maintain an open and trusting atmosphere between staff and pupils and to encourage pupils to play an active role within learning and the life of the school.

From Vision to Practice

A key priority in establishing the opportunities for pupil voice at The Sweyne Park School has been the high regard for pupil feedback and the recognised importance (learned from experience!) of communicating to pupils the impact that their feedback has had in changing the school. Throughout the academic year both formal and informal opportunities for pupil feedback to staff are recognised and inform school development. All opportunities are viewed as a way of gauging pupil perception on a whole range of aspects of school life; from Year 6 Induction to the Year 11 Leavers' Ball, conversations on school trips to the School Council and thinking about options choices to learning in the classroom. In all cases, pupil voice provides a wealth of feedback with which to better plan for next steps and school improvement.

In the following sections we outline three particular activities that have evolved and provide invaluable insights. The activities are e-mentoring, Headteacher's Achievement Time and pupils' input into School Self Review.

E-Mentoring

The transition from primary (KS2) to secondary school (KS3) at age 11 is a daunting time for many pupils and families – the school is all too easily seen as bigger, more confusing and full of big people! Real worries, anxieties and a whole host of misconceptions exist. The quotes below are a snapshot of reflections by Year 7 pupils (first year in secondary school) on how they felt as Year 6 pupils before joining Sweyne Park. The real fears and serious misconceptions they held are clear:

> The night before, I was very worried about getting lost and teachers being cross with me because I did not know where to go in the new school. [KS3 girl, aged 11]

> I was the only one coming from my primary school and I was really concerned about being lonely and not having any of my friends around me. [KS3 boy, aged 11]

> I was a bit worried about getting a detention for speaking when I was not supposed to speak and how much homework I was going to get. But I was also looking forward to meeting new mates, having new lessons and new teachers. [KS3 boy, aged 11]

A highly successful e-mentoring scheme has been running since 2008. It aims to support transition from primary (year 6) to secondary (year 7), helping pupils understand their new school before they start and so feel more confident about life at secondary school. Pupils are integral to the process as outlined below:

- Year 7 pupils volunteer for the scheme.
- A team of 20 pupils is selected and meets the member of staff responsible for co-ordinating the scheme.
- The team is provided with training on key matters such as Internet safety and e-mail etiquette.
- Team members create a bank of appropriate key messages to convey to the new intake (i.e. correcting their misconceptions!).
- Members of the team visit the primary schools to introduce themselves and the scheme to Year 6 pupils.
- Year 6 pupils send their questions, concerns and so on to the dedicated school e-mail address.
- Once a week the team meets with the co-ordinating member of staff in an ICT room.

- In small groups they talk about each of the e-mails received and how they might reply and respond to the e-mails received.
- The Year 6 pupil receives their e-mail at their primary school.
- Once transition has taken place and with the first term of the year completed, a new team is created with 'old e-mentors' involved in the training of the 'new team'.

An example of an e-mail received from a Year 6 pupil together with the reply from a Year 7 mentor is given below:

> Dear mentor
>   What are the school dinners like and what's the homework like?
>   From Adam, Year 6 [aged 10]

> Hi Adam I'm Lily and I used to go to your school.
>   The school dinners at Sweyne Park are nice — we have a variety of foods like the meal deal, paninis, rolls, pasta and fruit. They don't cost a lot. We have swipe cards. I get given £10 a week for my card and this is definitely enough. When you first come to Sweyne Park you get given a homework booklet by your tutor. Two weeks later you start class homeworks. Don't worry — I thought homework would affect my social life but it certainly doesn't!
>   Hope this helps!
>   From Lily [aged 11]

The impact of this simple but highly influential scheme is seen on many levels. First and foremost: it goes a long way to reassure new pupils (and their families) about starting at a new school. For our pupils involved it is a fantastic opportunity for them to reflect on their experiences, communicate effectively to help others and rise to the challenge of responsibility. The scheme also provides staff involved in the transition process a window into the specific concerns, anxieties and questions of the new intake; this in turn provides a valuable opportunity to tailor communication, information and planning so as to best suit the individual pupils and groups concerned. A highly sustainable process, this scheme continues to be one of the most rewarding of pupil voice activities for all concerned and sees pupils playing a crucial role in the life of the school.

Headteacher's Achievement Time

At 8.20 am each Tuesday morning. Headteacher's Achievement Time takes place in the Parents' Meeting Room at Sweyne Park School. Embedded into the school week, it is an opportunity for nominated pupils to share their work, progress and successes with the Headteacher and members of the Leadership Team. The calendared event allows every Department and Year Team an opportunity to highlight and formally recognise pupils' achievements. The reasons for nomination are varied — excellent progress, great determination and persistence or outstanding attainment: to name but a few. As well as providing an excellent opportunity to recognise achievement, the weekly event also provides a valuable way for senior staff to get to know about the individual successes of pupils right across the school and a great way to sample feedback from pupils in a more informal way. Their views on learning, classroom activities and school life provide a regular and valuable reminder of current pupil perceptions and concerns. In the selection of short pupil quotes below, the impact and value is very apparent:

> I went in Year 7 and it was the best thing in the world – I felt really good. [KS3 boy, aged 13]

> You might think you are not doing well but when you know you are it's like "Yes!" [KS3 boy, aged 12]

> I felt special and important because I had been selected to show my work. I also felt privileged. It's really recognising and rewarding us for how well we are doing and it tells us we are doing well. [KS4 boy, aged 14]

> I liked the fact that my work was actually being seen. It shows me that teachers know you are progressing in subjects you are doing. [KS4 girl, aged 14]

> In textiles I thought I was doing all right but when I did get invited it was a massive confidence boost. [KS3 boy, aged 12]

> I was asked to go for my Food Technology work which surprised me because I have never been good in the kitchen. The postcard was a surprise too – Mum made me cook dinner after that! [KS3 girl, aged 12]

Pupils share their achievements through conversation, presentations, movie clips, performances, the showing of coursework and exercise books and demonstrations. Over the course of the year, a wide selection of pupils attend, are presented with a special pen and have a postcard sent home to further recognise their achievements. With insight and thought, the motivational effect of this opportunity can really be used to recognise pupils' talents, especially those who might not recognise it in themselves. At the same time the conversations provide such a rich source of pupil perception for staff to reflect on – what does learning look like in the school, what is going well, how would they suggest it could be even better, and how does it feel to be a Sweyne Park pupil at the moment?

Pupil Voice within Self-Review

Departmental Reviews are a key element of the school's self review process. These planned reviews focus on aspects of teaching and learning within a department (or focus on whole school matters or specific year group). Evidence is sought in various forms including lesson observations, consultant interviews with pupils, pupil questionnaires and data analysis. Pupil voice once again forms a valuable source of feedback and opinion. Every lesson observation finishes with a pupil feedback session. Pupils are selected (at random, e.g. 2nd and 7th boy/girl on the register or targeted through prior attainment) and asked a series of planned questions to elicit their opinions on the lesson just observed.

A further development over time has been the creation of a team of consultants who regularly work for the school. The team at present is made up of a retired headteacher, retired deputy headteacher and an ex-assistant headteacher. They have been recruited to work with the school on an annual basis and bring with them a wealth of experience and specialisms. Over the course of a year, they visit the school in different amounts of time ranging from a day a week to twice a term. Within the review process, small groups of pupils (maximum 6) spend up to an hour with one of the consultants. The focus for the dialogue is planned and agreed by Leadership and department members at the outset of the review. It can also evolve through the process and therefore respond to previous findings and pupil feedback. Pupils are often asked to rate both their enjoyment and the challenge of the subject using a simple 10 point scale (1 = low, 10 = high). By using post-it notes the individual pupil's opinion is captured, free from the influence of their peers. Exploratory questions can then delve into considerable depth and highlight fascinating perceptions, issues and misconceptions. In this way, quantitative and qualitative data are generated and add to the findings and hence planning of next steps. Pupils are used to seeing the consultants around school and value the opportunity to feed back on their experiences.

> We know it is important for you (the consultant) to get our views because you are taking us out of lessons and not talking to us in our own time. I would not be as keen to say some things to teachers-here you can be more open and actually give opinions and not hide them. I also think you get us to go into more depth. [KS4 girl, aged 15]

> It feels a more formal way of sharing ideas and I think that more will be done with the feedback I give. I think I was more honest. [KS4 boy, aged 15]

> Because I was selected out of the whole group I felt important because I'd been chosen. It's also like time out-instead of learning we are doing something to improve the school. [KS3 boy, aged 13]

The consultant findings are a rich source of feedback and over time have highlighted subtle aspects to take account of in future planning. Memorable insights have been gleaned from comments such as those quoted below:

> I don't think teachers know how far we can go – we can do more! We feel passionate about this subject and want to be challenged further [KS4 boy, aged 16]

> Instruction time and the teacher talking is often too long – it leaves us with less time for the activity and takes away motivation. [KS4 girl, aged 15]

> I love PE because it's the one subject when I can run around, let off steam and get really muddy and no-one tells me off! [KS3 boy, aged 12]

Consultants themselves enjoy the experience and are skilled at managing these sessions. They feed back to the Leadership Team, Head of Department or specific staff as required:

> It's always fascinating to carry out pupil voice work at Sweyne Park. The children are very responsive and love to have their say. They are always honest but respectful: it's part of the ethos to give feedback on school life and they know that. They have such insight into the complexity of the institution – it's a pleasure and a privilege to hear their ideas about how we can make the school better. [Sweyne Park Consultant]

Challenges

The development of pupil voice at The Sweyne Park School has not been without challenges. Considerable time was invested in building up an ethos conducive to pupil voice at the time of the amalgamation of Sweyne and Park Schools in 1997. From the outset, staff were extremely proactive in using and modelling the Code of Respect, and actively engaged pupils in dialogue about lessons and learning. In the following years, some new members of staff, on joining Sweyne Park from other schools, found it difficult to adjust to the expectations of pupils who were used to having a voice. Once this problem became apparent, the induction programme was adjusted to ensure that staff were prepared for what was to some a significant culture change.

Another issue that became apparent was that whilst pupils' views were being sought, listened to and acted on, the outcomes and impact of the pupil consultation were not always clearly communicated back to the pupils themselves. This led to instances of pupils feeling that their influence was less than in reality. Once this problem came to light, it was addressed by more visible celebration of the successes and impact of pupil voice through assemblies, the weekly pupil newsletter and a plasma screen set prominently opposite the pupil entrance.

In the early years of pupil voice at the school, there were some particularly able pupil speakers who came to represent the School Council and pupil voice on numerous occasions. It soon became apparent, resonating with observations made elsewhere by Hadfield and Haw (2001), that this small group of pupils was being viewed as a favoured 'elite' by some others in the pupil body, and so actions were taken to ensure that there was a wider spread of involvement. Now an Enrichment

Database is used to keep track of the activities individual pupils are involved in. It allows staff to get a better understanding of pupils' skills, interests and involvement. The database can also be used to understand if the activities available are excluding any pupils or particular group of pupils.

During the development of the school and year councils, there have been times when the drive and commitment of coordinators has been inconsistent from one year group to another. To ensure that all pupils have equal opportunities in this area, a payment was made available for a member of staff to coordinate all year councils.

Conclusion

The respect code of conduct underpins all Sweyne Park life. In so many instances, the opportunity for pupils to contribute to discussion about school improvement highlights the maturity, responsibility and understanding of pupils. In recognition of this, in rounding off the process, feedback is given back to the pupils (through the weekly newsletter, assemblies, etc.) to share outcomes, action and appreciation.

Hart (1992) describes eight levels of participation in his ladder metaphor. At the Sweyne Park School, the majority of pupil voice activity is adult-initiated with decisions shared with pupils (level 6 of the ladder): however, just as leadership among staff is moving toward a 'bottom-up' model, so are developments in pupil voice. The Sweyne Park School seeks to create a community where people are keen to get involved in activities that benefit both the school and themselves. What underlies this is the school's ethos, but on a practical level the range of opportunities offered to the pupils enables it to happen. Pupils believe that the school listens to them, respects their opinions and that they have a voice within the organisation and future planning of their school.

> Without pupils the school would not be a school and our view is really important! [KS3 girl, aged 13]

References

Flutter J., & Ruddock, J. (2004). *Consulting pupils: What's in it for schools?*, London: Routledge Falmer.

Hadfield, M., & Haw, K. (2001). 'Voice', young people and action research. *Educational Action Research, 9*(3), 485–499.

Hart, R. (1992). Children's participation: Frp, Tokenism to Citizenship (Innocenti Essays; No 4; No inness 92/6). Florence: UNICEF International Child Development Centre.

Hart, R. (1997). *Children's participation*. London: Earthscan.

Rudd, T., Colligan, F., & Naik, R. (2007). *Learner voice: A handbook*. Bristol: Futurelab.

Chapter 12

Improving Quality, Developing Citizens: Learner Voice in Post-Compulsory Education and Training

Rob Pope and Bernadette Joslin

Abstract

National policy, together with committed effort on the ground, has led to student, or learner voice[1] becoming a high priority in English post-compulsory education and training. Providers should have a learner involvement strategy in place and the Common Inspection Framework makes clear they will be judged on how well they engage with learners to improve the effectiveness of their organisation and provision. There is still ambiguity, however, around what learner voice means and what effective practice looks like. Many providers find it challenging to move beyond 'lists' of things that they are doing to hear the voice of learners, to establish coherent whole organisation approaches to learner voice and citizenship education more broadly, with a culture that allows everyone to be genuinely listened to. The argument developed in part reflects the authors' experience in running the national Post-16 Citizenship Support Programme. However, they write here in their personal capacities.[2]

Keywords: Learner voice; post-compulsory; involvement; citizenship; quality

1. Across the sector different terms are used — 'pupil', 'student', 'trainee', 'inmate', etc. Consequently we mainly use the widely accepted generic term 'learner', except in quoting others or when referring to a particular context.
2. Bernadette Joslin, until May 2011, was the Programme Manager and Rob Pope the Development Manager in the Citizenship Team at LSN, an educational charity which, from 2006 to 2011, has, on behalf of the Learning and Skills Improvement Service (LSIS) run the Post-16 Citizenship Support Programme. This provides citizenship curriculum materials and staff training throughout the post-compulsory sector in England. For further information see www.post16citizenship.org.

Introduction

In referring to the post-compulsory education and training sector in England we include a wide variety of organisations, including colleges of general further education, sixth form colleges, work based learning (or training) providers, sixth forms in secondary schools, specialist colleges of various types, youth and community groups, offender learning institutions and adult and community education providers. All these organisations cater for people aged 16 and above, although in some instances younger learners can also be included.

Clearly this is a very diverse sector in terms of the organisations themselves, the pathways and courses they offer and the groups of learners involved. We might expect, then, considerable variation in responses to the concept of learner voice and in implementation strategies. It is beyond the scope of this chapter to look at each different type of organisation separately. That said the overall policy context and the key questions we raise are relevant for every organisation in the sector: what do learners gain from being given a voice and why is it important to listen to learners? How can we ensure that staff and learners have trust in learner voice strategies? What structures and processes need to be put into place to make an impact on the ethos and culture of an organisation? How far should we go with learner voice, in sharing decision making with learners?

In particular we question whether the link that is often made between quality improvement and learner voice takes us far enough. Seeking the views of learners about their education and training provision is essential but providers may be highly successful on some measures, yet have under-developed learner voice structures and not see the need for them. We argue for a more rounded view of learner voice and representation, where a strong link is also made with the citizenship curriculum and there is development and empowerment of learners for effective democratic participation both now and in the future. We illustrate general points of argument with examples of learner voice practice from a range of organisations together with comment from learners themselves on the value of involvement to them. In conclusion, on the further prospects for developing learner voice in the post-compulsory sector, we briefly look at conflicting influences at work in a period of spending cuts and contradictions running through government ambitions for a Big Society.

Impetus from National Policy: A Brief Context

We begin by considering some key issues in the national policy context for learner voice in post-compulsory education and training.

Although learner voice is not a new idea in the post-compulsory sector it has had fresh impetus in the past decade — part of what Michael Fielding (2004) calls a *new wave* of student voice which has influenced not just schools but all phases of education. This renewed interest in involving learners in their organisations comes from many sources — 'above' and 'below' — but a climate of encouragement, and in some cases requirement, from national policy in the period of the Labour

Government (1997 to May 2010) had a significant impact. Clear expectations of the sector have been set and much good, innovatory practice has been established.[3] However, in a large and diverse sector implementation is still patchy and genuinely effective processes which impact significantly on the experience of most learners in an organisation are not yet commonplace.

Following recommendations in the Foster review of Further Education Colleges to increase responsiveness to students and promote the learner voice, the government White Paper, *Further Education: Raising skills, improving life chances* (DfES, 2006), set out the requirement that all providers of further education should develop a strategy to involve learners. This located the purpose of the exercise very much in service improvement and the personalisation of learning — where learning is a more tailored experience and learners have the status of partners or co-producers of the whole process. The White Paper stated:

> When learners participate in decisions affecting their learning experience, they are likely to play a more active role in the provider's quality improvement processes — a key lever of service improvement ... We will encourage more learner representation in all aspects of the system from national policy making to course content and delivery. (DfES, 2006)

Following the White Paper the government ensured that all governing bodies of further education colleges should include at least two student governors, thus making a strong statement about the inclusion of learners in college decision-making structures. Also in 2006, at the national level, Bill Rammell, the Minister for Lifelong Learning, Further and Higher Education, took the initiative to establish a National Learner Panel (NLP). This would meet regularly to provide government with direct access to learners from a wide range of backgrounds with the aim of ensuring that the voice of the learner could impact on national education and training policy. The first panel members ranged in age from 17 to 75 and were drawn from further education colleges, work-based learning and adult and community learning (LSC, 2007).

Meanwhile all the public bodies charged with funding, inspecting and improving the post-compulsory sector were in the process of stepping up the priority afforded to learner involvement and voice and we turn now to the part they have played.

Role of the Learning and Skills Council: Learner Involvement Strategies

Until 2010 the Learning and Skills Council (LSC) had responsibility for funding and planning Post-16 education and training (other than Higher Education) in England.

---

3. For documentation of emerging good and interesting practice examples see endnote 6 and references LSC (2007) and LSC (2009).

As part of this brief the LSC was pro-active on learner voice and, attempting to give further effect and substance to the intentions of the 2006 White Paper, published a handbook of guidance *Developing a learner involvement strategy* (LSC, 2007). This document explained the requirement for all LSC funded colleges and training providers to have an organisational learner involvement strategy in place by 2007/ 2008, and provided a wide range of good practice examples and a set of key principles to follow. The handbook suggests that learner involvement strategies should always cover the involvement of learners individually, strengthening teaching and learning and responsiveness to individuals, and collectively, promoting participation and representation. It also suggests that strategies should include the development of the organisation and creation of a culture of learner involvement.

These are key principles which rightly point to the importance of providers avoiding reliance on just one or two mechanisms for learner voice — the learner satisfaction survey or traditional college student union, for example, are valuable in themselves, but are unlikely to be sufficient to ensure effective voice for all learners. Instead, as a strategic priority, it is important to integrate learner voice systematically into all quality improvement systems and decision-making processes — relating to the life of the classroom and the organisation as a whole. This suggests the need in most cases, and certainly in large organisations, for a wide range of mechanisms to make a reality of learner voice and representation — if the participation needs of all groups and individuals are really to be met.

And indeed, colleges and other providers have responded variously with forums, councils and parliaments; advisory panels; shadow leadership groups; working groups on specific issues; classroom discussions; debating societies; faith groups; conferences and special events; use of mobile technology and creative media; involving learners in lesson observation and learner researchers — to name just some of the vehicles in place for voice and representation. One vital challenge for providers is to develop the particular approach — the combination of structures and processes — best suited to their own circumstances and needs. One size certainly does not fit all in post-compulsory education and training. This is well illustrated in the three examples described in Table 12.1.

Role of Inspection and Improvement Bodies

In terms of inspection, the *Common inspection framework for further education and skills* makes clear that providers will be judged on how well they engage with learners to bring about improvements, with inspectors evaluating 'the extent to which the provider implements and monitors an effective strategy to involve learners ... in the decision making of the organisation' (Ofsted, 2009).

Further education providers are also required to submit the results of the annual Framework for Excellence Learner Views survey. Responses across a number of standard questions, including how far learners feel listened to and how far they feel their views are acted upon, are published on-line and users are encouraged to compare answers when assessing overall provider performance (Skills Funding Agency, 2011).

Table 12.1: Three case studies of learner voice in post-compulsory education.

1. *Lewisham College* in South East London is a Beacon college with a very diverse student population numbering over 13,000. Lewisham has well-developed formal structures for listening and responding to the learner voice including a student charter, course representatives who attend a school forum and the larger overall college forum. Also there are student governors and a directly elected student union president and executive. Other processes include learner surveys, comments cards, focus groups and user surveys. Feedback is publicised through 'you said, we did' posters. In an important further development, as part of the personalisation of learning, the college is moving towards an ethos of contribution. This is called 'the breaking voice' and aims to involve learners in developing a sense of contribution to the community, 'becoming givers as well as takers' and providing solutions to problems (LSIS, 2009b).

2. *At Chichester College*, students became involved in reviewing a new whole college learning model developed by staff. What emerged from this dialogue was a simpler and more learner-friendly model, based on the question 'Has the penny dropped?' The model, which came into use throughout the college, offers the following questions for learners to review their learning: Was the aim of your lesson explained? Was it connected to your previous lesson? Were the teaching and activities interesting? Did the teacher or trainer check that you understood? Did the penny drop? — Yes — I know more than when I came into class (LSC, 2007).

3. *National Star College* caters for 160 young people with severe disabilities through specialist education in a residential setting. Here, citizenship is an important element in the curriculum and learner involvement is seen as a crucial mechanism for strengthening the learners' capacity to engage as active citizens. Key aspects of this include course and residential representative structures, making up a student union executive and a student parliament; a taught citizenship programme promoting integration into the wider community; and an Envoys programme where young people are trained in how to be effective participants in meetings and working parties on specific issues. Feedback from learners is also gathered through personalised learning mentors. Learners have been able to influence decisions on a range of issues from course content (such as the taught citizenship programme) to college facilities (LSIS, 2009b).

The national bodies responsible for promoting quality improvement in the post-compulsory sector have also been very active in promoting learner voice and continue with this work. The Learning and Skills Improvement Service (LSIS) runs a programme of support for learner involvement practitioners across the sector and has published an extensive range of useful learner voice resources for staff and learners.[4] LSIS has also funded the national programme to support Post-16 Citizenship; this has identified and supported six main approaches[5] to citizenship learning across the post-compulsory sector, including 'citizenship through learner voice and representation'.[6] As we argue below citizenship and learner voice share important common ground in learner empowerment and much can be gained by explicitly linking the two areas.

Before the establishment of LSIS, one of it's predecessor organisations, the Centre for Excellence in Leadership (CEL) also had a strong track record in prioritising the learner voice as a key strategic commitment. CEL instigated the 'Leading the Learner Voice Awards', which recognise learner leadership and celebrate new forms of student representation across the further education system, and also sponsored a practitioner research programme, 'Leadership and the Learner Voice'.[7]

Citizenship Education and Learner Voice — Making the Connection

Citizenship enables young people to learn about their rights and responsibilities, about power and how society and political systems work. It also enables them to discuss and develop knowledge and understanding of topical and often controversial social, political, environmental and economic issues. It encourages learners to express their views and have a voice in democratic processes, for example within their schools, colleges, training organisations and other places of learning. The most successful citizenship learning is active, reflective, learner-led and community-focused. It enables learners to work with others to take action for change on issues of concern and to make a difference locally and more widely in a variety of contexts (LSIS, 2009a).

Citizenship and learner voice — while not synonymous — share important common ground and can be mutually reinforcing. Both emphasise learner autonomy, the skills of negotiation, advocacy and responsible action, an interest in improving things and understanding decision-making processes. Effective, active citizenship learning is not possible without good learner voice and opportunities for appropriate action. In turn citizenship knowledge and skills can help to build a strong basis for learners' understanding of, and involvement in, learner voice structures and processes. Both citizenship and learner voice depend for full effectiveness on a wider culture of inclusion and a democratic ethos in classrooms and across whole institutions.

---

4. Includes notably the Toolkit for learner representatives (http://tlp.excellencegateway.org.uk/tlp/xcurricula/toolkit/) (QIA, 2006).

5. The six approaches are, citizenship through: learner voice and representation; qualifications and personalised programmes; group tutorial and enrichment programmes; voluntary and community-based activities; single citizenship events and projects (LSIS, 2009a).

6. For an exploration of this approach see in particular *Listening to learners? Citizenship and learner voice (a pack of training and development activities with DVD-ROM video clips)* (LSIS, 2009b).

7. Resulting in series of research reports on the themes of learner voice and quality improvement and learner voice and equality and diversity programmes (Collinson, 2007).

Learning may be deepened if practical learner voice work is explicitly linked with other dimensions of citizenship education. In building democratic involvement, for example, there is likely to be considerable value from taking part in an election for a learner forum — with learners experiencing a variety of roles, including those of elector and elected representative. However, this learning can be enhanced if there is an opportunity to reflect on the experience and relate it to wider knowledge of representative and other forms of democracy and how the roles in question might be fulfilled in other contexts. This blend of practical experience and academic knowledge is a feature of some very successful citizenship programmes — both non-accredited and accredited — including mainstream qualifications such as the General Certificate of Secondary Education (GCSE) in Citizenship Studies and Advanced Level in Citizenship Studies. It is also an approach endorsed by successive inspection reports from the Office for Standards in Education (Ofsted) on citizenship education (Ofsted, 2006, 2010) and the Qualifications and Curriculum Development Agency (QCDA) guidance for providers of Post-16 Citizenship (QCDA [formerly QCA], 2004).

Benefits of Learner Voice and How Far Should It Go?

In national policy statements, among those in the field and from learners themselves there is a degree of consensus that the benefits from learner voice and representation may include some or all of the following: a more engaging and higher quality learning experience — even a transformation in the role of the learner; improved motivation and better learning outcomes; better understanding of barriers to participation and success; better relationships between learners and staff with more mutual respect and understanding — perhaps a more equal and democratic relationship; personal development — greater learner self-awareness and responsibility for their learning; boost to learners' confidence and self-esteem; enhanced learning for effective citizenship and democratic participation — immediately and in the longer term; increased learner retention, achievement and progression; contribution to staff development and organisational quality improvement.

Some of these benefits are clearly evident — in rather different ways — in the observations of two learners shown in Table 12.2.

Notwithstanding such powerful testimony, the assessment of benefits to be expected or actually gained from learner voice strategies is complex and influenced by many factors, including views taken about the fundamental purpose of post-compulsory education and training, the role and other interests of those involved and the particular techniques and processes under consideration.

In particular, there are different views about how far learner voice and participation in decision-making in the sector should go. Understandably there will be resistance from *some* staff and senior leaders to the prospect of change, especially radical change in the direction of learner led participation. Decision-making shared can be seen as power lost and professional status undermined. There is much further to go with the argument that power shared can lead to gains rather than losses for everyone involved. There is also a big need for staff at all levels to be fully included in

Table 12.2: The benefits of learner voice work in the post-compulsory sector.

---

1. *A student from a South London college, on being a member of a student working group on an issue of particular concern to herself and her peers:*

I have enjoyed the privilege of being a member of the 'Respect and Protect' group in which I was able to interact and work alongside enthusiastic youths like myself who want to be heard and accounted in making a difference to society. Joining this group has enabled me to voice my opinions and be heard and valued. It has enabled me to voice my thoughts, opinion and comments to influential authorities that can help me make a difference. This group has also gave me a sense of belonging; it has been apart from the streets a place where I can voice my opinions and conduct real life work that will have affect on me and future generations to come. This work has engaged me in a positive way and, made me look at crime in a different perspective other than that gained from several years on the streets. I thank this group for changing my mindset and teaching me how to use my street skills wisely in order to help others [Author interview with student at the College, following the project in 2008]

2. *A sixth form student from a school in Hertfordshire comments on the experience of being part of a consultation about the development of the citizenship curriculum:*

The actual consultation itself, I thought that was really good because it made me feel a bit more respected; and I thought that was good because it meant that when you were learning, it was like you knew that it was going to be relevant. And you knew that even if you didn't like it, or you didn't think that really worked, and, like, next year they probably wouldn't want to know about it, you felt like you could go to (staff member) and say, oh, that didn't really work, or that really worked. It meant that you felt like you had a say. [LSIS, 2009b (transcript from DVD-ROM)]

---

the making of change towards greater learner participation in decision-making and quality processes. Michael Fielding puts the point well:

> You need to start with values and purposes. Why are you doing this? Be clear what your values are. Share those with students. Share those with colleagues. Talk them through. So the starting point isn't about what kind of structures do we need to have, though that's very important. Our starting point must be, why are we doing this work and what are we trying to achieve? If you're inviting colleagues to work in a different kind of way, say this is what we believe in (at) the college, this is what we aspire to … can we think together about how we might approach this differently in order to achieve what we want to achieve? There needs to be an understanding by the college leadership that you need to create the structures and cultures to enable this to happen. And it probably will mean a significant change in existing practices. [LSIS, 2009b (transcript from DVD-ROM)]

Table 12.3: Questions to stimulate development and reflection on practice.

Questions to stimulate development and reflection on practice
- What do we mean by 'learner voice'?
- Why is it important to listen to learners — what are we trying to achieve?
- What do learners gain from being given a voice?
- How can we ensure there will be equality of opportunity for all groups of learners to be represented and have a voice?
- What are the links between citizenship education and learner voice?
- How can we ensure that staff and learners have trust in the learner voice strategies?
- How can we involve learners and staff fully in developing the learner involvement strategy?
- What training and support will be needed for learners and staff?
- Which learner voice strategies will be most effective?
- How to impact on the overall ethos of the organisation?
- How do we know we are succeeding in listening well to learners?
- How should we feed back action to learners?
- How should organisations reflect on their strategy, and who should be involved in this process?

Source: Adapted from LSIS (2008).

In a similar vein, the questions in Table 12.3 can be a useful catalyst for stimulating discussion and reflection among staff, at all levels, and learners on a wide range of issues concerning learner voice in an organisation.

Models of Learner Participation

Discussions, policy-making and training sessions in the post-compulsory sector have sometimes benefited from a consideration of typologies or frameworks depicting different types of learner involvement in decision-making. For example, Hart's 'Ladder of Participation' contains eight rungs or levels of participation from 'manipulation' at the bottom to 'young people initiated, shared decisions with adults' at the top (Hart, 1992). Similarly, John Shuttle, for research on learner representation in further education and adult education institutions in the South East of England, used an adapted version of a five-level spectrum of engagement developed by the International Association for Public Participation (IAP2) (Table 12.4). The model spans the whole range of participation and decision-making from institution-led to student-owned.

The results of Shuttle's small scale research study must be treated with caution as only 29 responses were received from 180 organisations initially approached. Nonetheless the analysis and findings are still of considerable interest, especially as we lack evidence of this depth about the types and levels of learner voice processes

Table 12.4: Process of learner engagement with student voice.

Level of participation	Processes and activities
Inform: learners informed of decisions — they receive regular information, are notified of their rights and ways of participating	Presentations; meetings and forums
Consult: learners consulted to support decision-making views taken into account by institution, then informed of decisions made	Views gathered through tutorials; consultation workshops and learners as research respondents
Involve: input from learners into decision-making process ensures that learner views are included	Learner governors; student councils; focus groups and learner representatives on various panels
Collaborate: decisions shaped by learners in a partnership arrangement	Learners as co-researchers; learner-led consultations; learner-shaped policy making and learners on management committees
Empower: ownership of decisions by learners towards full learner control with planning and other management activities given over to learners	Students as researchers; learner managers; learner-managed activities and consultation; delegation by learners nad policy formation by learners

Source: Adapted from Shuttle (2007).

for organisations across the sector as a whole. Although Shuttle found only one institution 'had empowered learners to take high levels of control that could be identified as being learner-led' he is positive about the overall progress made in the respondent organisations (as demonstrated in Table 12.4), concluding that:

> The results demonstrate a high-level of student engagement across the respondent sample ... (indicating) the emergence of institutions that appear to work in partnership with learners and demonstrate that they listen to students and reflect the decision making process back ... so (learners) feel they are heard. (Shuttle, 2007)

Conclusion

Learner voice and representation generally seems not to be a priority with the UK conservative-led government (in office from May 2010) in the way it was with the previous administration, and there are specific indications of this in the post-compulsory sector. In the last year the NLP has been discontinued, with the possibility that an online panel may be used instead. Had the NLP been maintained it would have provided a forum for ministers to discuss directly with panel members the implications of recent controversial decisions regarding further education, including the withdrawal of the Education Maintenance Allowance (EMA) — which, together with the tripling of maximum university tuition fees, prompted so much student protest across the country at the end of 2010.

Other aspects of the Conservative led government's education policy also give rise to concern in relation to the prospects for learner voice. The curriculum review recently announced by the department for education (DfE) puts under threat the continuation of citizenship as a statutory subject in the school curriculum from 2013 — which may have eventual knock on effects for the offer and take-up of citizenship in the post-compulsory sector.

Spending cuts in the sector may also impact negatively on work for learner voice and participation. One immediate example concerns the recently announced 75% cut (114 funded hours per learner down to 30) in 'Entitlement' funding, which all further education providers receive for each learner, and covers areas including pastoral tutorial support and 'extra-curricular' enrichment activities. These are all important 'spaces' where colleges and other providers are likely to locate citizenship programmes and other activities central to the maintenance of learner voice and representation. At the present time all post-compulsory providers are absorbing the implications of this government funding decision and considering how best to respond.

Prospects for Learner Voice in the Post-Compulsory Sector

In some ways, then, the current UK government stance on learner voice and citizenship education appears indifferent at best and hostile at worst. On the face of it though there is a conspicuous contradiction in government thinking — as the much heralded agenda for the creation of a Big Society is predicated on the development of an 'empowered citizenry' willing and able to undertake volunteering and social action projects in local communities. As yet, though, there is no indication that the government sees a role for schools — or the institutions of the post-compulsory sector — in contributing in explicit ways to the development of active, empowered citizens; or at least not through learner voice or citizenship education.

That said other indications are more promising for the health of learner voice and involvement in the sector. At present the inspection requirements, referred to above, for providers to have strategies for taking account of learner views remains in place — as does the momentum from various national agencies and many individual providers to strengthen this work. An evaluation in 2008 of the impact of the first year of the learner involvement strategy found that 65% of further education providers had a programme of learner involvement 'fully in place', and that both learners and providers reported benefits (LSC, 2009). The position is likely to have improved further since then. Despite other conflicting forces, this constitutes a relatively strong position from which to build further.

References

DfES. (2006). Further education: Raising skills, improving life chances, Cm 6768, Norwich, www.dfes.gov.uk/publications/furthereducation

Fielding, M. (2004). 'New wave' student voice and the renewal of civic society. *London Review of Education*, *2*(3), 197–217.

Hart, R. A. (1992). Children's participation: From tokenism to citizenship. Innocenti Essay 4, UNICEF International Child Development Centre, Florence, Italy. Retrieved from http://www.unicef-irc.org/publications/pdf/childrens_participation.pdf

LSC. (2007). Developing a learner involvement strategy: A handbook for the further education sector. Retrieved from www.lsc.gov.uk/news/latestnews/news-27022007.htm

LSC. (2009). Evaluation of the impact of the learner involvement strategy. Retrieved from http://readingroom.lsc.gov.uk/lsc/National/nat-lis_year_two_final_report-june2009-v1-1.pdf

LSIS. (2008). Citizenship staff development quick steps 4: Learner voice. Retrieved from http://www.excellencegateway.org.uk/page.aspx?o=242762

LSIS. (2009a). Getting started with post-16 citizenship. Retrieved from http://www.excellence-gateway.org.uk/page.aspx?o=242762

LSIS. (2009b). Listening to learners? Citizenship and learner voice. Retrieved from http://www.excellencegateway.org.uk/page.aspx?o=246142

QCA [now QCDA]. (2004). Play your part: guidance for providers of post-16 citizenship. Retrieved from http://www.excellencegateway.org.uk/page.aspx?o=242762

Ofsted. (2006). Towards consensus: Citizenship in secondary schools. Retrieved from http://www.ofsted.gov.uk

Ofsted. (2009). Common inspection framework for further education and skills. Retrieved from http://www.ofsted.gov.uk

Ofsted. (2010). Citizenship established? Citizenship in schools 2006/9. Retrieved from http://www.ofsted.gov.uk

QIA. (2006). Toolkit for course representatives. Retrieved from http://excellence.qia.org.uk/reps/index.html

Shuttle, J. (2007). 'Learner involvement in decision making', Brighton and Hove City Council Learning Partnership, in Collinson, D. (2007) 'Leadership and the learner voice', Collinson, D. Centre for Excellence in Leadership, Lancaster University, pp. 30–48. Retrieved from http://www.excellencegateway.org.uk/media/post16/files/David_Collinson_Leader-ship_&_LV.pdf

Skills Funding Agency. (2011). Framework for excellence: Learner views. Retrieved from http://ffe.skillsfundingagency.bis.gov.uk/pi/learnerviews/

Chapter 13

'They Could Run this Place Without Us!' Using Student Voice to Improve Teaching and Learning in a Sixth Form College

Ian Wainer and Alia Islam[1]

Abstract

This chapter written by Ian Wainer, a member of staff, and Alia Islam, a student, relates the journey the college has made in establishing the Student Achievement and Learning Team (SALT). The SALT Team is made up of students who represent their subject and discuss teaching and learning issues with teachers and staff. Our students are all 16–19-year olds.

We hear about the genesis and development of the project and insights are offered into the dynamic of change when all partners in the education process have their assumptions challenged and learn to relate to each other in a different way. Ian is an ex-youth worker and brings an informal education perspective to the work. The core issues of student empowerment and partnership are discussed along with the insights gained by students into the nuts and bolts of teachers work. Student Voice initiatives are reflected through the prism of adolescent development and through the narrative we hear how the programme meets the needs of teenagers and in so doing provides the college with invaluable feedback. We also hear how Student Voice can increase the organisation's capacity to deliver services. Finally the piece examines the impact on teaching and learning and the organisation generally and indicates plans for future development.

---

1. Alia Islam was a student at Sir George Monoux College 2009–2011. She is now employed by the college as the Study Plus Administrator and is pursuing a degree in History at Birkbeck College.

The Student Voice Handbook: Bridging the Academic/Practitioner Divide
Copyright © 2011 by Emerald Group Publishing Limited
All rights of reproduction in any form reserved
ISBN: 978-1-78052-040-7

We took the decision in principle that every conversation at the college should be a dialogue with students, and in that spirit, this chapter is written as a reflective conversation between a teacher and a student.

Keywords: Informal education; FE; mission; identity; impact measurement

Introduction

Sir George Monoux Sixth Form College is situated in Walthamstow, East London. It is part of the post-compulsory Further Education sector, and its cohort are 16–19-year olds drawn from North and East London. In common with many institutions in this sector, we offer a mix of vocational and academic courses although as a sixth form college we do only cater for 16–19-year olds. The vast majority of our students progress to university. There are just over 2000 young people attending, and they are fairly equally split between academic vocational courses.

There has been an educational institution on the site for nearly 500 years, and the Sir George Monoux College today comprises a wide mixture of young people from a range of ethnic and religious backgrounds with Pakistani Muslim and Afro-Carribean young people being well represented. In addition there are Turkish, Kurdish and East European as well as White English students in the mix.

Ian: Out of these ramblings an interesting and effective student voice approach evolved. We talk about how the project got started. How we laid down the main elements of how students and staff would work together and how we seemed to be inhabiting a hinterland between formal and informal education. We also report the impact, on staff, students and the work of education. We then look at how there are usually often unforeseen positive outcomes when embarking on student voice work before finally thinking about capacity and sustainability.

How the Project Began

Ian: My background is in youth work within the Jewish community and the City of Westminster. Originally trained as Drama teacher, I have mainly taught Health and Social Care within colleges and have worked as both a senior and middle manager with both formal and informal education.
I was asked by the principal to initiate a student voice project within the college paying particular attention to including the student perspective in the improvement and evaluation of teaching and learning. There has been an active Student Union at the college for many years, and I decided to ascertain the level of student support and interest and I arranged an introductory meeting in May 2009. I was delighted that over 60 students attended, and they

were keen to get involved. We looked at how they felt about their education and how it could be improved. It became clear that two students, Alia Islam and Alyaa Khogali, were particularly passionate, articulate and anxious to get involved. I will be writing a little later about the leadership role played by young people in this project, but what is fascinating to me as how, if the environment is set up appropriately, a leadership emerges, unbidden and self selecting.

Project Formation

Ian: It was time for some research. There are many models of student voice operating in the field it was crucial that whatever model we developed was effective and took into account our history, ethos and current situation. A guiding document was 'Pupil voice: comfortable and uncomfortable learning for teachers', McIntyre et al. (2005), University of Cambridge. This report gave us an important perspective. I realised quite early on that power is an issue in Student Voice. Yes, young people can attend meetings, give their opinions and happily go on their way. I had seen plenty of that in the youth service, but if students were to become genuine partners in their education, respected as experts and influential in curriculum development, implementation and evaluation, then there would have to be a transfer of power. It is a maxim that no one gives up power without a struggle. Would staff at Monoux be any different?

Alia: This is what we wanted to avoid when setting up Student Achievement and Learning Team (SALT), a power struggle. On one side we didn't want the teachers to feel threatened or lose control; however, we DID want to successfully implement the changes we wanted.

We decided to find some practitioners who were ahead of us, actually not a very difficult challenge as we were really just getting started. We discovered that on our doorstep, George Mitchell School was involved in some excellent work in this field. The school is a neighbour of ours and has a broadly similar cohort. It is a comprehensive secondary mixed ability co-educational school.

We met with Matthew Savage the Deputy Head, and he told us of their 'Making Learning Better' (MLB) project. On their website they describe their project thus, All staff meetings, training and in-house INSET have a unique flavour at GM: they all play host to large numbers of MLB consultants. Whether allocating departmental capitation, debating the merits of different student grouping arrangements, or participating in training on whole school literacy, we value our students' opinions on everything in our school which directly affects them and that is pretty much everything.

Ian: Each curriculum area has a small team of MLB consultants, whose key role is to observe lessons and feed back to the teacher afterwards. MLB lesson observations are central to the success of MLB, as they provide a constant mechanism for improving lessons through a challenging, learning-focused dialogue between teacher and student. Good practice is then shared fortnightly through the MLB forum and blog.

In an extremely helpful conversation, Matthew pointed out to us a couple of issues. The one that really made an impact on us was the need for pupils who had a good level of academic and interpersonal skills as the MLB role was complex and sensitive. Our next visit was to South Camden Community School where we saw the teacher responsible for the SLAT and we learnt how it took about a year to establish trust between the SLAT members and the teachers and how this was a process and not achieved overnight. This was very helpful and provided a useful template for our SALT project.

The SALT Protocols

Ian: Back at college we held a couple more meetings with students and the group delegated Alyaa and Alia two 17-year olds, to sit with me and figure out how our student voice was going to work at college. The students then wanted to ratify what was decided. We developed a document which was named the SALT Protocols. Partly I think because it sounds like a Robert Ludlum novel and also we wanted a name that was different to the SLAT project at the school.

Alia: I'd just like to add here, that out of the group that gathered, some people wanted to call it the 'Student Learning and Achievement Group' which if you abbreviate…doesn't exactly read very well. We wanted to make an impression…but the right kind!

Ian: The guiding principles were that each course should have a Subject Explorer, drawn from the course, attending the first 20 minutes of every course team meeting to give the student perspective on teaching and learning. I say student perspective and not students' perspective with a particular emphasis, as the intention was not to elect this young person but to have them apply for the role and be interviewed and appointed. We had a successful representative body in the Student Union, and here we were looking not for the most popular young person but for the one with the most developed set of skill. At the same time a job description, person specification and application form were written. Our original group liked this idea, and it was ratified and agreed by them and then this 'steering group' was disbanded.

At the same time we embarked on a round of meetings with managers and staff to market SALT and get a commitment from the college to implement it. What was immediately apparent was the plan was championed by Alia, Alyaa and a small group of 10 students. So the young people were actually explaining the ideas and negotiating with the management team. This core group became the SALT executive whose task was to provide the student perspective on college wide teaching and learning issues. It struck me what a powerful voice young people have and how they could be far more articulate and convincing then I could ever be. They were however pushing against an open door. With OFSTED looming we needed a convincing Student Voice strategy in place, but above and beyond this, there was clearly a real and principled commitment to the scheme. In May 2009 we received a major boost as the OFSTED monitoring visit report noted that we had made significant progress in leadership and management including student voice. They were impressed with the range of initiatives to include students in the planning, delivery and evaluation of services. Student ambassadors and the student union were included in this and they noted that at this stage, it was too early to discern the impact of the SALT project.

Formal and Informal Education Strategies

Ian: The new academic year of 2009/2010 came as it always does with alarming rapidity and I found myself in a new Student Voice co-ordinators office in the 'Zone' the main college thoroughfare. The Zone is the central meeting place in the college. The student information centre is located there as well as the office of the enrichment officer. It is a large space with sofas, chairs and tables to work on and a large screen TV. It is a bustling busy environment and is always full of students working, relaxing or meeting their friends between lessons. Organically a team was developing. There was a sense of mission in these student voice pioneers, not only that but a sense of community was developing apace. My original background in education was within a Jewish youth movement in the late 1960s and early 1970s. I learnt some basic lessons about working with groups of young people. First, some young people have a dissatisfaction with the status quo, a feeling that things could be done better, fairer and in a more productive and enjoyable way. Second that adolescence is a search for identity and that identity is often found within the group, and third, many adolescents seem to be always hungry. A sense of community, actually more than that, an actual community began to coalesce around the SALT team. An important aspect of this was having a physical base for student voice activity. I share this office with Bryony, a trainee youth worker on a Youth Work Diploma course. Tea and coffee are on tap and Bryony has a delightful approach to working with young people. The office soon became a meeting place to plan, plot, discuss, gossip and generally move the project forward. So the two factors here are space and time. We had a space that the students felt some degree of ownership over, and I was given a generous allocation of remission, time off of teaching to concentrate on student voice activities. Another factor though it sounds somewhat facile is a common lunch hour. All students and staff were available at the same time every day. This type of activity is not possible without a sound, friendly and supportive relationship between staff and students where all players are aware implicitly and explicitly of the nature of the work and the boundaries. Bryony and I were also able to offer educational and personal support to the SALT team and within a matter of weeks it felt as if SALT had always been a feature of life at Monoux.

Alia: Thinking back to that time, I realise how important having the office was to us as a developing group but also to 'us' as individuals. It gave us — me certainly — a sense of belonging, and often I would find myself simply going into the office to talk about things totally unrelated to SALT. Also many times I went in talking about things such as how rubbish the canteen food was and came out planning our next project/goal.

Ian: Seeing the energy and the involvement and passion of the young people, it occurred to me that perhaps what I was witnessing was that two potent features of adolescent development were combining, the need for friendship groups and socialising and a sense of mission. I mentioned hunger, not necessarily for knowledge, and we had two guiding principles for our activities. One, that our approach to student voice should not be tokenistic but a real and authentic attempt to realise the potential of young people acting as partners in their own education and secondly that at every meeting there should be pizza. In addition we thought that branding the project was important and hooded sweatshirts more generally known as "hoodies" were produced with a logo proclaiming Monoux Students Seen and Heard emblazoned on the front. I hope what is clear is that we were using some of the techniques of informal education to complement the informal curriculum.

I had witnessed in other settings how young people attending meetings can often be window dressing for young peoples' voice, and because of a lack of preparation, training and contextualisation, the young people would suffer a sense of anomie sitting silently through interminable agenda items about arrangement for petty cash payments and rotas. I was determined that this would not happen at Monoux, and we would avoid the cynicism and disillusionment that follows. We held two very successful training events for subject explorers, the name for SALT members, unpacking educational jargon and explaining how course team meetings run. The central activity and the most important was a small group meeting with a teacher. The teachers were asked to talk openly and honestly about how they felt about their jobs, the good things and the frustrations. Open and honest conversations ensued, and students were shocked at the constraints and pressures that staff operate under.

Backstage Pass

Ian: In retrospect what was happening and it was a by product of the success of the initiative was that certain students were issued with a figurative "back stage pass" to the management and operations of the college. They were starting to attend a range of meetings and heard things that surprised, delighted and sometimes shocked them. Their perspective was refreshing and enlightening. For me I was able to see the processes of the college and the dynamics between staff with fresh eyes. I write this section with bated breath to hear Alia's reflections on how she viewed these meetings.

Alia: Until having attended these meetings, I did not fully appreciate the strain and pressure of being a teacher. Before, sitting in the classroom, it would not have weighed upon my conscience to irritate and provoke the. It was only after I attended the meeting that I realised something: the teachers have it harder than us. When they push us into doing work, and constantly nag and repeat the same thing over and over again — they do it because they have to. If they didn't, the student's grades would be bad, resulting in more pressure on the teacher from senior members of the college to do better. The meetings displayed the sheer amount of out of class preparation a teacher had to do, so it follows on that by the time they were actually teaching, they might be a little worn-out and unwilling to spend as much time and effort explaining and breaking down the work to students.

It's frustrating to think about teaching and education from a teacher's perspective. While the teacher may initially begin their career determined to help students succeed, the daily grind of administration and performance monitoring takes its toll on their enthusiasm for teaching, their willingness to teach to the best of their ability as a student and on their patience and time for students.

As students, you enter education believing that the teachers are there for YOU. Then you start to realise that they are not; they first have to manage to keep their job. After the meetings I realised that although the teacher may desperately want to help you, they may desperately want to spend extra time with you explaining work to make sure you succeed but they can't — they have to complete various reports and prepare lesson plans. In this regard, SALT is unable to do anything — these changes must come from the government and OFSTED — the group who monitor and assess institutions on their ability and capability to provide an education to student. At the moment our impact and focus are limited to individual subject classes and teaching and learning.

Ian: I have been party to many meetings both in the youth service and in colleges where youth participation is high up on the agenda, but it takes a degree of confidence by the institution to open up the doors in this way. There is no doubt that at Monoux we had in Kim Clifford the then Principal and Paolo Ramella, the current Principal senior managers that enjoyed listening to and working with young people. Increasing the SALT executive met with the managers without me. There is the issue of modelling here. My youth and community work background had schooled me in the paramount importance of empowerment and to be aware of dependency. By operating independently of me in my role as Student Voice co-ordinator, the students were taking real ownership of the scheme. Ultimately I am looking for a degree of role reversal where my job is enabling and facilitating the project rather than controlling it. At the time of writing in the second year SALT, this has indeed become the case. A new teacher who came to see me mistook, Jalal the chair of the SALT

executive, for a member of staff. He was busy in the office organising
meetings, and I took this as a major indicator of success.

Relationship with the Student Union

Ian: When we started SALT, there was already in existence an active Student Union.
More concerned with ensuring that students had what they needed in college,
lockers, canteen prices and organising the prom, there seemed to be a gap in the
student voice market. There is an issue here that is practical and operational
and borders on the ideological. The Student Union is an elected, representative
body, whereas SALT is unelected. The Student Union exists in a well-
understood democratic paradigm, whereas SALT is something else. It is based
more on a meritocratic business model where the best person is appointed for
the job. With these two student structures existing side by side and existing in
different paradigms, the opportunity for misunderstanding and conflict is rich.
Indeed there was some though most of it was played out by staff rather than
students. In fact there was a cross over in roles and activities and the young
people seemed less concerned than the staff. By amending the Student Union
constitution so that SALT becomes a sub-group of the union the needs of
democracy are served and we are able to continue with a winning formula. It is
well to consider the impact of new structures on what already exists.

Alia: I would just like to say, that when the student founders of SALT (i.e., myself and
Alyaa) found out about this — becoming a sub-group of the Student Union —
we were furious! SALT was supposed to be a completely different entity that
was concerned with the teaching side of college, rather than recreational aspect,
which the Union had control over. The original idea was that we were to have
equal power — over different aspect of college, not that we subservient to the
Union. However, because Alyaa and I were no longer involved in the daily
running of SALT, we could do nothing in protest (except imagine horrible
things happening to the Union members who proposed the merge!).

The Road to Damascus

Ian: So while all this was happening, what of staff? I would be lying if I said there was
a total absence of cynicism. Some teachers told me that this was just window
dressing for OFSTED and others thought that this represented a world turned
upside down. I think these attitudes were on the periphery and most people were
taking a wait and see approach. A breakthrough came after the first Information
Technology course team meeting. I received a memo from Steve, one of the IT
teachers sent me this email with the a copy of the minutes:

> I must admit that I was very sceptical of this and thought it to be
> no more than Ofsted fluff, but the 20min session we planned

> lasted over an hour and produced some excellent insights into the student experience. A lot that they had to say we had identified as areas for improvement, but included some outside of our control. They also made some very reasonable and well reasoned suggestions. [Steve, FE teacher]

The suggestions included access to computers, the structuring and timing of assignments and the number of print credits available.

The students were marketing the scheme without us realising it, and teachers were surprised to find the small and sometimes major, encumbrances to teaching and learning were shared by the students. The subjects ranged from the practical, problems with software and print credits, to the pedagogic, students feeling too much emphasis was placed on assessment and not enough on learning and the frustration of disruptive students. Actually the anticipated resistance from staff never materialised and most became supportive of the scheme. Indeed working closely with students seems to have had a beneficial effect on both parties. There is no doubt that the idea of having student voice as the first agenda item at course team meetings was extremely helpful as was posting the minutes on Moodle the VLE. As the year progressed we reached about 70% coverage of the courses. There is still a need for staff training. A simple 'so how is it going' may not illicit the quality of feedback we are looking for. As the role of Subject Explorer has become more understood, the useful nature of the feedback obtained has improved. Be aware however that in a college of over 2000 students the best laid plans of men and women may go awry. The loss of a common lunch hour has been a blow but making sure that the students know when and where the course team meeting has also been problematic. We have posted the meeting schedule on Moodle, the colleges Virtual Learning Environment, but a simple change of room and time can be enough to throw the system.

Impact

Ian: The college has spent money, time and effort on student voice but how do we measure the impact. I don't believe there is a statistical tool sophisticated enough to determine the impact of the programme in isolation from the myriad of influences on results, although the college has had better results of late, and I am happy to take credit for this. So we needed an index of what curriculum changes had happened as a result of the project and how the individual subject explorers had benefitted. Alyaa and I trawled through the minutes of the course team minutes, and we found some interesting information. The feedback is too detailed and rich to give much more than a flavour here but here are some examples:

> More information needed on careers and higher education courses, work experience, trips, further assistants with editing, more camera

tripods and equipment are needed, more subject workshops, more details about critical perspectives, poor equipment, information on how editing is used to construct representation, more workshops. [A level Media Studies students]

Students unhappy about Print credits, clarify assignments in more detail, subject workshops, Extension tasks to help prepare for University, Stronger sanctions for disruptive students, too much emphasis on results, too much emphasis on meeting criteria rather than gaining knowledge, more trips and speakers, limited disk space hindering learning, print credits, not enough free computers, college should be wireless, one and a half hour lessons too long, break in the wrong place, lunch is too short, high proportion of timetable clashes and errors, internet blocking .g. ASDA computer blocker are locked, software that is used in IT rooms not available elsewhere in college, no pre-installation for office 2007 and CS4. [Btec National Business students]

Topic work needed to complete assignment not completed before deadline, textbook not very useful, revision sessions, each lesson should have more focus, and key points summary and exam questions, students own revision recourses should be shared on Moodle, some confusion between those shown in class and in text books, enjoy practices but not too many, more workshops, tie during lessons for questions about assignments, hour and a half lessons to long [A Level Statistics students]

And the list goes on. We also documented the teacher's responses and in most cases the concerns are addressed and if not, an explanation given. Looking back over the student's feedback I can see a host of suggestions and recommendations that are sensible, well thought through, achievable and absolutely grounded in the day by day experience of attending five lessons a day. The students seem to be experts in their learning. They are on the teacher's side and understand the frustration of disruptive students and are well aware of the damaging effect on their own learning. They understand the problem of resources and their requests are measured and realistic. I was also fascinated to see the instinctive grasp of pedagogy that can only come after years spent in education as a consumer. We are trying to achieve a virtuous circle, well informed and co-operative students enjoying and benefitting from their lesson, feeding back to staff, staff improving the quality of the provision and students who can see the impact of their feedback, they have a sense of involvement, ownership empowerment, which is fed into their lessons, leading to more effective and motivated staff, better lessons and better results. Not bad for a few sweatshirts and a few pizzas! Most interesting of all is that the expected resistance from teachers never materialised, and they welcomed the students input.

Impact on Student's Development

Alia: There are several aspects of the development of SALT Explorers to consider, the first being personal development. As a student coming to a mixed, buzzing environment like Monoux for the first time it was slightly overwhelming and I was unsure if I would fit in anywhere (as you generally are!). Being a part of SALT and becoming involved in the making of it gave me a sense of community and belonging (as cheesy as it sounds). Through SALT I made friends with people I would never have talked to. Another aspect of my personal development was the exposure to senior members of the Staff body, including the principal, vice principal, senior managers, governors and senior leadership team. This allowed me to not only develop my interpersonal skills, but it also enabled me to see how the other side lived! (The answer to the second part is: very nicely!) As part of the program to advertise and feedback our activities and outcomes, SALT members participated in a wide variety of meetings. I have to admit that standing up and doing presentations in front of people who decided the fate of SALT was daunting and mostly terrifying with a hint of excitement thrown into the mix, although overall they were good experiences.

    The meetings with the senior management provided not only good experiences but also ways to put our training into action. Through the discussions and the presentations, they helped forge positive relations between us (the students) and the senior management that then further enabled us to make positive improvements in learning. Once we had their support it became easier to implement changes to the teaching methods, it also felt as if we had some kind of impact on their thoughts and decisions which to students who were used to have virtually no power or say in how they were taught was a huge matter. To summarise, for me SALT changed my outlook of college, and life in general, honestly, I would not be where I am today without it. It provided a social scene, something to look forward to whenever I was reluctant to come in, and an actual working method to have our voices heard and implement change.

The World of Unforeseen Consequences

Ian: At the OFSTED visit in September 2010, the UK body for inspecting 'standards' in all levels of the UK educational system before higher education, the following appeared in the report:

> Considerable work and effort have gone into consulting students both at curriculum and whole-college level. Focus groups, subject explorers and SALT consultations have provided teachers and managers with valuable insights from students into the way the college runs, the way students feel and barriers to progress. In addition, these initiatives provide the college with a valuable means by which young people can take advantage of wider social

and work-related skills as well as being a way in which the college
can celebrate success

When we make our plans and set our targets, we are predicting if not
fantasising the future. In an informal setting the students may develop the
curriculum themselves guided and facilitated by the youth worker. In the early
days of the project our marketing manager asked me whether I could give her
some ideas about running focus groups. This early conversation led to the
formation, drawn from the SALT of a group of 15 student focus group
facilitators. These students, trained by an external professional, now run
regular focus groups on issues commissioned by teachers and managers. They
have produced reports on ethnicity gender as well as reports on curriculum
issues and staff are using the data gathered in their self-assessment reports. No
member of staff is ever present at the focus group sessions, and the reports are
produced in a timely and professional manner. We have also been the hub for
the UK Youth Parliament and there is an online emagazine on Moodle about
all the student voice activity in college. Together with the Union a student
teaching and learning conference 'The Learner's Wave' was organised at the
end of last term. The administration, planning and delivery were all
implemented by the young people with minimal support from staff. These
initiatives were not planned for but arose out of the enthusiasm of the young
people. Part of my work is to make sure there is synchronicity between the
machinations of the colleges' management processes and the speed that
the young people work at. The college's decision making is far slower than the
young people's, and this can lead to misunderstanding and frustration, and I
have to mediate between the two, sometimes encouraging the college to work
faster and the young people to be more patient.

Capacity and Sustainability

Ian: What is clear is that the college by involving young people more in its
operations has increased its capacity to deliver. A campaign on Homophobia
is being run by the Student Union, reports and quality processes are carried
out by students, students help with interviewing new staff and they are helping
to improve the quality of teaching and learning. I wonder how far this can be
exploited, some institutions have students observing lessons, leading small
groups or delivering parts of the curriculum all seem desirable and achievable.
What are the benefits and what are the potential problems? We hear more
about co-leadership, do we want a student shadow Head of Department?

This whole project came into existence because of OFSTED's emphasis on
student voice. In my career I have lost count of the number of initiatives that
have come and gone. The management in my college have been supportive

and enthusiastic but when budgets are cut will they consider that my energies are more fruitfully spent in the classroom. Time will tell.

Conclusion

Ian: So where next for SALT? At the time of writing we are amazed at the take up for the programme. We had 80 Subject Explorers or as the seemed now to be known as Salties, or Salt reps, at our first training meeting, the executive trebled in size, and we have more focus group facilitators than we know what to do with. We are working on a range of activities to make sure that we have not raised expectations that we cannot fulfil including working more closely with outside agencies. At the heart of these endeavours is the student attending the course team meeting and taking an increasing role in curriculum planning, delivery and evaluation and we must not lose sight of this fundamental.

So what of this journey? The college has in its staff and students the capacity to develop this project further, how far can we take this partnership with students. Could they teach part of the curriculum, could they inspect lessons, where are the boundaries. So often they are both financial and political, time will tell. We have now a functioning student voice operation with clear protocols, The last 18 months has been one of improvement. Improving results, improving relationships, improving inspection reports, and an improving learning environment. I think my skills and ability as an educator have also improved. Not as a result of a training course delivered by an older and wiser colleague, there are plenty of wiser, somewhat fewer older, but by working closely with the young people whose perspectives on education and the world are, cogent insightful and ultimately life enriching.

Worried about the future, not me.

Chapter 14

'What About What I Think of School?' — Student Voice in Special and Inclusive Education: A Practitioner and Personal Response

Helen Bishton and Geoff Lindsay

Abstract

Listening to pupils' opinions is a human rights issue whatever the age or ability of the pupils. There are also educational arguments that capturing pupils' opinions enhances their learning. This chapter is based around findings of research carried out with pupils with severe learning difficulties attending variously inclusive primary schools by one of us (HB). Methods of eliciting opinions from pupils with limited communication abilities are explored. Links are made with other pupil voice methods used in her current position of working at a secondary school for pupils with Autistic Spectrum Disorder/Asperger's Syndrome (ASD). The use of puppets and visual cues are explained to add a further dimension to interviews with the pupils. 'Diamond Ranking' and the use of photographs were also used to elicit opinions. These techniques were drawn from research by Ann Lewis (Lewis et al., 2005). The variety of methods that were used to gain the pupils' views was important to the breadth and depth of the opinions expressed. The pupils expressed opinions about how they felt about school, their friends and hopes for the future. Whichever school setting they attended pupils were overwhelmingly positive about their experiences. The majority of what was disliked in school involved relationships rather than specific activities or subjects. Friends were equally important and available to the pupils in different settings and adults were equally unimportant. Examples are also given about how these techniques and others have been used in an individual school setting with ASD pupils to build up a school culture of consultation with pupils and a shared vision for the school.

The Student Voice Handbook: Bridging the Academic/Practitioner Divide
ISBN: 978-1-78052-040-7

Keywords: Special educational needs; inclusion; schools; autistic spectrum disorder; friends

Introduction

This chapter has been co-authored although the research was carried out by one of us (Helen Bishton) and the chapter is therefore written from a personal perspective and in the first person. As a teacher of over 20 years experience in special schools, the majority being schools for children with severe learning difficulties (SLD), I have always found that giving children choice and control was a vital part of their learning. In this chapter I explore this in more detail, not only drawing particularly on my research project but also referring to my current practice as a headteacher. This chapter will explore issues of eliciting *pupil voice* in school settings. I will explore the theoretical methods I used in the research project and then give practical examples as to how I have used these methods in my current school. I am providing both a practitioner and personal view which includes recollections from teaching.

In the United Kingdom there has been a move away from teaching children with SEN in segregated special schools where all children with similar needs are taught. Parents can choose to have their child attend a mainstream (local neighbourhood) school which is obliged to meet the child's SEN. Some local authorities (LAs) choose to give considerable extra resources to one mainstream school in an area and this school becomes an enhanced resource school, which will have a specific number of places for children with significant SEN which are funded accordingly. Inclusion is the move towards all children being given the opportunity to be accepted and take their place in their local area where they live.

In my early years as a teacher I found that giving children with very limited communication skills the opportunity to exercise some control of their environment and have a choice as to what they would experience was an extremely powerful tool in developing their communication skills. This could simply be choosing between orange or blackcurrant squash or being able to control the environment in the sensory room through the use of electronic switches. Recently I have expanded this use of giving the students control by a keen interest in pupil voice activities. As part of my studies for an Educational Doctorate I carried out case study research with eight primary-aged children with SLD in three variously inclusive schools. Listening to the children's opinions was an important part of this research. For the past five years I have been working at a school for secondary-aged students with complex social communication difficulties (ASD) and this has given me a totally different perspective on student voice.

The usefulness of listening to pupil voice was vividly illustrated on my first pupil day at my new school. As the new headteacher I had carefully prepared a presentation to make to the whole school the first time it would be gathered to pass judgement on me, my first assembly. Coming from the headship of a primary school for children with SLD it turned out to be a very odd experience as everyone was quiet, looking at me and seemingly paying attention. After the assembly I was sitting in my office contemplating how well it had all gone when my secretary rang to say that Ben and Tom (two Year 11 boys) would like an appointment to see me. I told her they could come right in, as I wanted to demonstrate the open door policy I had told them about in assembly.

Ben and Tom proceeded to tell me how awful my assembly had been. They said they knew that I had come from a primary school and they understood that that was the problem but that I had to change. I thought 'It can't all be bad' so went through each element of the assembly to ascertain what the problem was. I was told the music was OK, the way I spoke was too babyish, the way I used props was too babyish, pictures and videos were fine but not objects, and the use of candles and having a 'quiet time' was complete rubbish. I listened and then replied 'I will continue to use the music. I would like you to help me make the talk part of the assembly more suitable for secondary-aged pupils. But the 'quiet time' stays as it is an important part of what I think assembly is about, having time to reflect as a community.' Ben and Tom seemed satisfied with this, they helped me understand what were important issues for the pupils that they would like to hear about in assembly and they also met me briefly after assembly for the next few weeks to pass their judgement, they were very fair and encouraging. By the time it got to half term they said I seemed to have learnt how to do assemblies in a secondary school!

Issues

Rights and Efficacy

Due to the practical experiences of working in a school setting, as described earlier, I was determined to include children's perspectives in any research that I carried out. My doctoral research studied children's experiences of inclusion. In this research I drew on the experience of two very different groups of pupils with special needs and three different types of school organisation: special, (where all children have SEN), mainstream (local neighbourhood school) and enhanced resource (mainstream school with additional specialist provision). The debate within inclusive education focuses mainly on children's rights but it is also important to consider the question of the best way of helping children's development in different educational settings. There is a strong human rights lobby that advocate inclusion for children with SEN (CSIE, 1997) although my interest in inclusion is based on whether it is a more effective way of educating children (Lindsay, 2003, 2007). Inclusion over the years has been characterised as the right of all children to attend their local mainstream school, however more informed thinking is interested in the actual experiences of the child and are they truly included in all aspects of school life (Ainscow, 2002). The physical place is of minor importance compared to the educational experience of the child.

Likewise there is a children's rights argument for listening to the opinions of pupils. The United Nations Convention on the Rights of the Child (1989) gave children the right to express their views and this was further enshrined in UK law by the Children Act (DoH, 1989). Increasingly, UK legislation is requiring children's views to be sought and acted upon (Valuing People DoH 2001; Education Act DfES, 2002):

> Decisions made about or on behalf of a child are better informed and more likely to produce positive outcomes if she or he is involved in the process. (UNICEF, 2007, p. 31)

In my experience listening to pupils' views is also extremely effective practice in engaging pupils, motivating them and involving them in the learning process. Ultimately what is important is the learning relationship between teacher and pupil and what actually happens in that relationship to aid the pupils' development. The act of asking the child their opinion is of less importance than the results of having that opinion heard. Pupils do have the right to have their say but if they do not see the results of their input, if they are not listened to and empowered to have an influence, then the real power of pupil voice is lost. This is the downfall of some of the large consultation exercises that take place with children nationally or on a local authority (LA) basis. The children are asked their opinions but they never see the change that is as a result of their opinions.

We recently had an Her Majesties Inspectorate (HMI) visit to our school looking at SEN provision across the LA. Her Majesties Inspectors are extremely influential in the setting and monitoring of policy across England. They are the most influential visitors that an English school can receive. The HMI wanted to talk to a group of pupils and suggested he could speak to the school council. We put the request to the school council, they asked what the HMI wanted to speak to them for and what was going to be the result, in essence what were the pupils going to get out of this. We explained that the HMI wanted to here their opinions about the school and the outcome would be contributing towards a report. The school council deliberated this and thanked the HMI for his invitation but they did not wish to speak to him because the pupils were not going to get anything from it! They pointed out he could speak to any pupil in any part of the school as he was going round and they would answer his questions if they wanted to, because that is what our school is like.

Rights and Responsibility

I do not want to give the impression by telling the HMI story that I believe pupil voice is concerned with giving pupils everything they ask for, but adults do need to listen, be willing to act and give an explanation as to why it may not be possible, enter into a dialogue and respect the issues communicated. Our school council communicated to the Senior Management Team (SMT) that pupils wished to have more say in the catering provision in the school. We set up various consultation exercises. Much of what the pupils wanted to say was about food choice issues, and the kitchen staff and pupils worked together on that. There were however three issues that would entail extra financial outlay: the provision of hand gel and paper towels on each table and the switch to using free range eggs. These came back to SMT for approval, we requested a proper costing of these changes which the kitchen staff helped the pupils to do. We then said we did not have enough money for all the changes, but the pupils could have either the hand gel and kitchen towels or they could have free range eggs. A vote was organised and we now have hand gel and paper towels on our dinner tables but no free range eggs.

Involvement of All

It is important to ascertain as far as possible the voice of all pupils rather than just those who shout loudest or are a particular lobby group. This may require some imagination as to using different methods of communication for those who do not readily express their opinions. This chapter goes on to explain some of the methods that I have used with difficult to reach children, however it is not a straightforward task. Two of the eight children, in my research, had profound and multiple learning difficulties (PMLD). They had no verbal or signed communication and it was difficult to assess how much receptive language they understood. Since my research was about inclusion I desperately wanted to include all eight children in the children's voice activities. I had to make the difficult decision not to include the two children with PMLD as they were not at a developmental level to be able to communicate the opinions I required. Both could indicate through facial expressions that they liked or disliked what was happening at a particular time but they could not reliably express a choice. As Kiernan (1999) has stated:

> Improved techniques have allowed people with severe learning difficulties and/or limited communication skills to express their views. However, there is still a large group of people with learning difficulties and profound or multiple impairments where it seems unlikely that they could be meaningfully involved, even as respondents in research studies. (Kiernan, 1999, p. 46)

The children's voice activities were the last part of the case studies that I carried out. This was a reasoned decision, as by that time I had contact with the children for a two-year period mostly in their school environment. The case study children needed to trust that I was interested in them and know that I truly wanted to listen to their opinions. This type of relationship needs time to be built-up.

On the surface eliciting opinions from my pupils with Autistic Spectrum Disorder/ Asperger's Syndrome would seem to be a much easier task as all the pupils speak fluently and are generally keen to express an opinion to anyone who will listen. It is however particularly important with these pupils that their understanding of the concepts involved is thoroughly checked. The use of visual cues is invaluable in this context. The methods of interview supports, use of photos and diamond ranking, as described later, are also useful in my current school context. We have used visual methods including various voting systems with symbols and using drawings to produce opinions on the 'ideal school' (Williams & Hanke, 2007).

Practice

Interviewing Pupils

I will now turn to the actual methods that were used to elicit the children's views in my research. However, 'this is a relatively young area of research methodology and there is much to learn about the processes and strategies researchers employ' (Jones, 2005, p. 61). I drew heavily on the report for the Disability Rights Commission (Lewis, Robertson, & Parsons, 2005) which studied in great detail several different methods of gaining the views of disabled children.

After some deliberation I decided to use three methods to gain children's perceptions: interviews, taking photographs and diamond ranking. All three methods elicited children's views on what they liked and disliked about school. The interviews also sought detail of the children's friends, who helped them at school and their aspirations for the future. Three methods were used to ask for the same information in order to increase the validity of the views gained, 'creating a varied repertoire of verbal and non-verbal techniques, in order to be able to adapt to the needs and preferences of individuals' (Thomas & O'Kane, 1998, p. 342).

Careful attention was paid to the way that the interviews were structured and supported to give the children maximum opportunities to respond but not to compromise the validity and reliability of the answers. I agree with Cohen et al that:

> The interview is a social encounter, not simply a site for information exchange, and researchers would be well advised to keep this at the forefront of their minds when conducting an interview. (Cohen, Manion, & Morrison, 2007, p. 350)

I took this advice when conducting the interviews with the pupils.

1. *Use of a Puppet during the Interview*

I used a puppet as a third party in the interview through which any questions asked were passed. The puppet (called Bobby) shared his own views in order to encourage the children to share theirs too.

> Children may more readily perceive the soft toy as asking a genuine question whereas the sincerity of the adult questioner may be perceived as false. (Lewis, 2004, p. 4)

I particularly wanted to use a puppet in order to try to make the interviews flow without the necessity of asking direct questions to the children.

> A range of work has suggested that making a statement to a child tends
> to elicit a fuller response than does asking a question. (Dockrell,
> Lewis, & Lindsay, 2000, p. 55)

I only used open ended question to guard against leading the children as they will tend to agree with what they think you want to hear (Lewis, 2002). Bobby was very popular with five of the six children. It was almost as if the children believed Bobby was real despite the fact that they were shown he was a puppet and they were allowed to play with him. Paul (age 5) immediately said 'Its only a toy'. Although once he got into the interview he asked Bobby two questions, one about the surname of his friends and 'Do you know what I want to be when I grow up?' His suspension of disbelief was not as complete as Steven (age 9) who gave Bobby advice on how to deal with someone who was calling him names, asked about the football team he supported, whether he had a classroom helper and how old he was. Sarah (age 6) was interested in whether Bobby liked number work, which picture he uses when he needs to go to the toilet and if he goes to assembly at his school.

I was concerned that Bobby talking about his likes and dislikes at school might lead the children to copy his responses. In fact of the 17 likes and dislikes that Bobby expressed in the interviews only 5 were also mentioned by the children. This did not mean to say that the children actually mentioned the same like/dislike straight after Bobby (this never happened) but they mentioned it at some point during the interview. Bearing in mind that there are only a limited amount of activities that pupils engage in at school and the interviewer purposely chose for Bobby to like and dislike common activities then it is reasonable to suggest that there was not any autosuggestion from using Bobby the puppet. Steven (age 9) did try to suggest otherwise, when I said 'Anything else you don't like about school', Steven replied 'Yes, when people call me names like Bobby said.' In fact it was Steven who suggested, on recognising the sad symbol, that Bobby would be sad if someone called him names.

2. *Use of Symbol Cues to Assist the Interview*

The interviews were supported by using symbol cue cards to aid the child's understanding of the spoken content of the interviews. Five of the children recognised the symbols. Paul (age 5) did not spontaneously recognise them but he was in no need of extra symbol support due to his verbal language skills. The symbols were those taken from the Widgit software package which is used extensively with special needs students in England. Symbols provide an extra permanent reminder of what the interview was focusing on at that moment in time. Words are said and then may be lost and forgotten but symbols can be constantly referred to, to remind the child of the topic of conversation (Detheridge, 2000). Visual cues are particularly important when working with ASD students: we use them extensively in many forms of communication at my current school.

3. *Taking Photographs*

Several researchers working with children with learning difficulties have used the taking of photographs in order to communicate meaning to the researcher

(Beresford, Tozer, Rabiee, & Sloper, 2004; Booth & Booth, 2003; Germain, 2004; Kaplan & Howes, 2004). I asked pupils to take a disposable camera around school and take photos of things or places they liked and disliked. I emphasised that photographs were not to be taken of people, to allay any child protection concerns. Germain (2004) also found high reliability when participants interpreted photographs as showing things they like and dislike on two occasions a week apart.

The use of photos was not without any verbal demands as the child had to indicate whether they liked or disliked the object they were photographing. Sometimes clarification was needed as to exactly what the photo was representing, as found also by Kaplan and Howes (2004) with secondary school pupils taking images of places they felt comfortable and uncomfortable and then sharing the images with other pupils. Although this method is labour intensive, in my current school the students have used digital cameras to take images of 'places I feel safe and unsafe' and 'things that encourage me to be healthy and unhealthy'. They are able to do this independently and then electronically group the images, giving a written explanation in some cases. Staff can then view the results at their leisure.

4. *Diamond Ranking*

The fourth research method I used was diamond ranking, this was again used by Lewis et al. (2005). The children were asked to participate in a diamond ranking 'game'. This involved asking the children what they liked and disliked about school, I wrote each thing down on a separate post-it note. I asked the child to pick out the thing they liked best and this was placed on the table as the top of the diamond, then the child picked out the thing they disliked most and this was placed at the bottom of the diamond, graded responses were then placed in between according to the child's views and a diamond shape was produced. In my research this was again a one to one exercise but with older or more able pupils this 'game' could be used to elicit opinions with very little staff time. Pupils themselves could be given a pack of post-it notes after having had the game explained to them. The diamond could be arranged on a piece of paper and then handed in for staff to analyse. I have also used diamond ranking as a group discussion activity to encourage negotiation of opinions and compromise, e.g. 'what helps me most to learn'.

Pupil Views on Inclusion

My research was concerned with the efficacy of inclusion and compared three variously inclusive school placements. The methods described earlier that I used to ascertain the pupil voice were used to illuminate the inclusion debate. What did the pupils communicate? The general conclusion from the children about their school placements is that their experiences are overwhelmingly positive. They particularly liked numeracy activities, creative activities, playground games (including football), playing with friends and computers. Jessica (age 10) said she liked numeracy, Emily (age 8) liked counting, Paul (age 5) liked counting money, counting in French and telling the time and Sarah (age 6) liked adding up. When asked what it was at school that the children did not like there were far fewer responses. This could be because the children were genuinely happy at school and found it difficult to come up with any aspects of school they did not like. Another point of view could be that it was more difficult for the children to express negative views, possibly because they were being interviewed in the school environment and felt an unspoken pressure to be positive (Dockrell et al., 2000). Also 'do not like' is a cognitively more complex concept than 'like' and therefore was more difficult for the children with SLD to express (Kiernan, Reid, & Goldbart, 1987). However the following dialogue was had with Adam (age 8) who used one word utterances.

> Interviewer: 'Bobby doesn't like having to count. He doesn't like having to sit in the hall. What do you not like at school?'
>
> Adam: 'Not'
>
> Interviewer: 'You like everything?'
>
> Adam: 'Yes'
>
> Interviewer: 'So you never feel sad at school?'
>
> Adam: 'No'
>
> Interviewer: 'So how do you feel at school?'
>
> Adam: 'Happy'
>
> [Adam, aged 8]

The two children with the most limited verbal abilities could not express anything they did not like, however neither could Paul (age 5) who had well-developed verbal skills. Whatever the reason may have been the children were far more willing to talk about things they liked about school than those they disliked.

The following four sub-sections describe the different opinions that were elicited from the pupils who took part in this research.

Different Methods to Express Views

Aspects of school that were liked and disliked were mentioned in all three of the means of expression: interview, diamond ranking and photos. The children did not find it easier to express positive or negative views using one medium as opposed to another. The use of the three media allowed the children to communicate a wider variety of likes and dislikes. Although the majority of responses were only mentioned in one medium there were also 42% of responses which were triangulated by being mentioned in more than one medium. This could be seen as a weakness of the research as there was not a great deal of correlation between the different research methods. Alternatively it could be seen as a strength as the children were able to use different media to express their views and using three types of media allowed more views to be expressed. I was quite pleased with the level of triangulation of responses and viewed it as significant that not one child contradicted themselves by mentioning something that they liked using one type of medium but then saying they disliked it using another or vice versa. The latter showed that the children were quite secure in their opinions and there is not a correct answer.

The photos showed the least correlation but this is not surprising as this research method was actually asking the children to look for physical objects in their environment which they liked/disliked or signified something they liked/disliked. It is not surprising that the responses were different from two methods where children were asked to express verbally things they liked. Many verbally expressed likes would not have a physical entity, which could be photographed, to represent them. This research also found that the child with the fewest verbal abilities expressed more ideas using the photos whereas the child with the most verbal abilities expressed more ideas using the interview and diamond ranking. Therefore it is important to use a variety of methods to elicit opinions as the children have different preferences and abilities.

Opinions about School

Some tentative attempts can be made at comparing the responses of the children from the different types of school placement. These comparisons must be viewed in the context of the small number of case study children and the fact that it is by no means a representative sample. There are, however, some interesting tentative patterns that seemed to emerge. The two children at mainstream school did not mention any 'academic' activities when asked what they liked at school and yet all the other children mentioned these. They were much more interested in the social aspects of school in the playground and with sport and PE. Messiou (2002) came to a similar view in her study of mainstream primary classes:

> It seems, therefore, that children give more emphasis to social aspects of
> school life, rather than its academic practices. (Messiou, 2002, p. 120)

The child in the special school mentioned numeracy, literacy and creative activities as likes at school. She liked all these classroom activities but disliked PE and playing outside. This could be viewed as a gender difference but when considering the children who attend the enhanced resource school both girls indicated they liked playing outside and the boy liked numeracy activities along with his two female peers. It could be hypothesised that the social side of school life was more important to the children in mainstream school and the academic to the child in special school with the enhanced resource school children enjoying both aspects. Further weight could be given to this argument by the fact that Steven (age 9) did not like homework which is the academic part of school encroaching on home.

Relationships

The three most interesting aspects of what the children did not like concerned relationships. Sarah (age 6) said:

> I know what makes me feel a bit sad — the teachers shouting [Sarah, aged 6]

Out of context this could be showing that Sarah saw school in a negative light, however she then went on to say:

> I don't like it when somebody goes 'Don't do that!' I don't like it when Mummy shouts as well. I don't like it when somebody says 'enough'. I don't like being told off. [Sarah, aged 6]

The girl from the special school and one of the boys from the mainstream school commented negatively about the actions of other children. Both these incidences could be viewed as bullying. Ingeniously using the photographs Jessica (age 10) was able to communicate that she did not like being hurt by a particular pupil. Steven (age 9) did not like being called names at school, however this needs to be taken in context. Steven thought of two other dislikes first before he mentioned that he did not like being called names. Steven was also clear about what he had to do when others called him names and seemed satisfied with the help the adults gave him. Steven also indicated that he had lots of friends and did not seem at all distressed when he was talking about the name calling. To put the other point of view, when shown a sad picture about Bobby, Steven immediately assumed that Bobby had been called names and this had made him sad. Name calling had obviously been part of Steven's experience at school but he seemed to think it had been well dealt with by the adults he trusted.

I think Steven showed that he had a strong self-image as he mentioned many friends and chose to take a photo of the Good Work Board, telling me that his friends often chose for his name to go on the board where children's production of work of a high standard (for that child) is celebrated. However he said, while taking a photo, that he did not like the Merit Points Board because the teacher took points away (the two types of board mentioned were used in Steven's classroom to give pupils rewards for good work, the points on the Good Work Board were given by the pupils themselves whereas the Merit Points were controlled by the teacher). Although taking a photo of the Unifix cubes (plastic counting apparatus) arranged on top of the Interactive Whiteboard, he said he did not like whole class numeracy work because he got the answers wrong. My conclusion from listening to Steven was that he derived a great deal of pleasure from his peers and the games they played together but it was the academic side of school life that he found stressful.

Important People and the Future

Friends came up at several points during the activities with the children, not just when they were specifically asked about them. Paul (age 5), Steven (age 9) and Jessica (age 10) all mentioned activities with friends when they were asked what they liked at school. Paul liked playing imaginative games:

> Paul: 'Scooby Doo and the Cyboids, and I play pirates and monsters and dragons and monster rats and princess cats'
>
> Interviewer: 'Who do you play those games with?'
>
> Paul: 'Nancy and Lisa and Mary.'
>
> [Paul, aged 5]

When specifically asked about friends all the children were quick to name a number apart from Emily (age 8) who needed some prompting. Again this painted a very positive picture which gave no indication of isolation of any of the children in any of the different settings. Bearne (2002) found in her research about transition from Key Stage 1 to Key Stage 2, 'For many of the children in the project, friendship was a key to successful learning' (p. 123).

It was also interesting and unexpected that when asked who they worked with at school the majority of children identified peers. Only Sarah (who attends the enhanced resource school) did not recognise her peers in this role and talked about support staff. One child from special school (Jessica) and one from mainstream (Steven) identified support staff when asked about who helps them in school. One child from the enhanced resource school (Paul) and one from mainstream (Adam) said they were helped by friends. It is of note however that the only real difference that Jessica identified between her time at special school and the one and a half days a week at mainstream was that staff helped her at the special school and a friend at mainstream. The children therefore identified that they mainly worked with peers at school but they felt their help came from both staff and peers with no particular pattern with reference to the type of provision they attended. Staff were only mentioned by half the children in the interviews and activities and these children only mentioned them once. It seems that their peers were far more important to them. Jones (2005) highlighted the importance of other children to allow the child to feel accepted and valued.

Steven (age 9) raised the issue of bullying again when talking about secondary placement. Bullying was obviously closely connected to his thoughts about secondary school. This was interesting because when his Mum had been interviewed (Bishton, 2006) she expressed similar concerns about secondary school. Steven seemed to be indicating concerns about bullying whichever secondary school you went to rather than at one particular school. None of the other children expressed such concerns. The children and young people that Lewis et al. (2005) interviewed identified bullying as an issue that had made inclusive experiences negative. All the children were confident about expressing an opinion about what they wanted to be when they grew up. The answers were quite typical of any primary child's responses.

Conclusion

By using a variety of research methods the research was able to build up a rich picture of the likes and dislikes of this small group of children in variously inclusive primary school placements. The variety of methods was important to the breadth and depth of opinions that were expressed. Different children seemed to prefer different research methods. This research does not indicate that children are happier or form better relationships with adults and their peers depending on the inclusivity of their school placement. The research did indicate that the children in mainstream school found the social side of school more important, whereas in special school it was the academic side, the enhanced resource school seemed to find the balance between the two. Friends were equally important and available to children in the different types of placement. More negative views on relationships were also spread equally among the children from different types of provision.

From the results of this research it does not seem that children find adults all that important with regard to their enjoyment of school. The pupils were willing to give their voice to expressing opinions on the 'adults' world' but it seemed to me that in their own sub-culture in school their peers were far more important, for example in helping them learn. Recently at my school the students spontaneously organised a strike. As a headteacher I obviously had to subvert this to stop it happening but a large part of me was really proud that the students had thought through a current issue, taken note of others reactions nationally, decide on their own reaction, gathered peers' opinions and had the organisational abilities to collectively express their views. Perhaps we ought to listen more to the views of children when we are trying to 'get it right' for the 'flexible continuum of provision for children with SEN' espoused by the Government (Department for Education and Skills, 2006, p. 25).

The research I carried out for my EdD was specifically centred on a small number of children and getting to know their opinions very well through working with them individually. That may seem to have little relevance to my everyday life of being a headteacher, because you so rarely get the opportunity for considering one child, as the whole organisation is your concern. However I would argue that the exact place to start is with the individual child. Each child needs to be confident that they will be listened to before they are willing to express their opinions. Developing a culture of being listened to takes time, particularly when working with children with SEN as they are not only likely to need more processing time, but also in terms of learning together about developing a culture of learning. When I first arrived at my present school we wanted to change the uniform so I instigated a consultation among the pupils. They chose a particular logo which was duely printed on the sweatshirts. Within a year the students were complaining about the logo. I spoke to the school council about this and they said that the students had been given a choice of 5 logos, none of which they particularly liked, but they had to choose one. What they really wanted was to be able to design their own logo but they did not think this was an option as we had presented 5 choices! I would like to think today that if the same thing happened the culture in school and level of student confidence would be that they would tell us they wanted their own design.

The research was also concerned with pupil personal opinion and development. In dealing with groups, a class or a whole school, the opinions of a number of pupils need to be taken into consideration and a consensus agreed. This is really an important process for the powerfulness of change in a school culture. Opinions need to be sought, valued, considered and an agreement reached which everyone can accept, then all can work for this change to come to fruition.

References

Ainscow, M. (2002). Using research to encourage the development of inclusive practices. In: M. Ainscow & P. Farrell (Eds), *Making special education inclusive* (pp. 25–37). London: Fulton.

Bearne, E. (2002). A good listening to: Year 3 pupils talk about learning. *Support for Learning*, *17*(3), 122–127.

Beresford, B., Tozer, R., Rabiee, P., & Sloper, P. (2004). Developing an approach to involving children with autistic spectrum disorders in a social care research project. *British Journal of Learning Disability*, *32*, 180–185.

Bishton, H. (2006). Parental views of their child's inclusive or special school placement. Unpublished EdD Special Study, Warwick University, UK.

Booth, T., & Booth, W. (2003). In the frame: Photovoice and mothers with learning difficulties. *Disability and Society*, *18*(4), 431–442.

Cohen, L., Manion, L., & Morrison, K. (2007). *Research methods in education* (6th ed.). London: Routledge.

CSIE (1997). *Inclusive education a framework for change*. Bristol: CSIE.

Department for Education and Skills (2002). *The education act 2002*. London: HMSO.

Department for Education and Skills. (2006). *Government response to the education and skills committee report on special educational needs*. London: HMSO.

Department of Health (1989). *Children act*. London: Stationary Office.

Department of Health (2001). *Valuing people: A strategy for learning disability for the 21st century*. London: DoH.

Detheridge, T. (2000). Research involving children with severe learning difficulties. In: A. Lewis & G. Lindsay (Eds), *Researching children's perspectives* (pp. 112–121). Buckingham: Open University Press.

Dockrell, J., Lewis, A., & Lindsay, G. (2000). Researching children's perspectives; a psychological dimension. In: A. Lewis & G. Lindsay (Eds), *Researching children's perspectives* (pp. 46–58). Buckingham: Open University Press.

Germain, R. (2004). An exploratory study using cameras and talking mats to access the views of young people with learning disabilities on their out-of-school activities. *British Journal of Learning Disabilities*, *32*, 170–174.

Jones, P. (2005). Inclusion: Lessons from the children. *British Journal of Special Education*, *32*(2), 60–66.

Kaplan, I., & Howes, A. (2004). Seeing through different eyes: Exploring the value of participative research using images in schools. *Cambridge Journal of Education, 34*(2), 143–155.

Kiernan, C. (1999). Participation in research by people with learning disability: Origins and issues. *British Journal of Learning Disability, 27*, 43–47.

Kiernan, C., Reid, B., & Goldbart, J. (1987). *Foundations of communication and language course manual.* Manchester: Manchester University Press.

Lewis, A. (2002). Accessing through research interviews, the views of children with difficulties. *Support for Learning, 17*(4), 110–116.

Lewis, A. (2004). 'And when did you last see your father?' Exploring the views of children with learning difficulties/disabilities. *British Journal of Special Education, 31*(1), 3–9.

Lewis, A., Robertson, C., & Parsons, S. (2005). DRC research report — Experiences of disabled students and their families: Phase 1, Stratford on Avon: Disability Rights Commission.

Lindsay, G. (2003). Inclusive education: A critical perspective. *British Journal of Special Education, 30*(1), 3–12.

Lindsay, G. (2007). Educational psychology and the effectiveness of inclusive education/ mainstreaming. *British Journal of Educational Psychology, 77*, 1–24.

Messiou, K. (2002). Marginalisation in primary schools: Listening to children's voices. *Support for Learning, 17*(3), 117–121.

Thomas, N., & O'Kane, C. (1998). The ethics of participatory research with children. *Children and Society, 12*, 336–348.

UNICEF. (2007). *Promoting the rights of children with disabilities.* Florence: Innocenti Research.

Williams, J., & Hanke, D. (2007). Do you know what sort of school I want? Optimum features of a school provision for pupils with autistic spectrum disorder. *Good Autism Practice, 8*(2), 51–61.

Chapter 15

How Might the Student Voice Affect Transformation in Higher Education?

Julie Baldry Currens

Abstract

Within the past decade, the role of the student voice in higher education within the United Kingdom has undergone significant transformation, and a new relationship between students and universities is emerging. That students themselves are best qualified to examine the quality of their university experience is axiomatic. Best practice empowers meaningful dialogue and effective partnership between universities and students if significant and transformational practice is to be achieved.

   This chapter explores a range of mechanisms from the higher education sector locates the engagement of students as co-creators and architects of their own learning experiences. Consideration will be given to the 'student voice' as a vehicle for offering feedback on the student experience and programme representation as a means of enhancing student engagement. A range of case examples will illustrate innovations that help to empower and embed both the collective student voice and personal narratives in order to affect genuine growth and change.

Keywords: Student voice; student satisfaction; student engagement; co-creation; transformation

Introduction

Within the past decade, students' public commentary on their experiences of higher education in the United Kingdom (UK) has undergone considerable transformation. Attitudes are changing, and politicians and policy makers, academics and service

The Student Voice Handbook: Bridging the Academic/Practitioner Divide
Copyright © 2011 by Emerald Group Publishing Limited
All rights of reproduction in any form reserved
ISBN: 978-1-78052-040-7

colleagues now recognise that 'the student voice' commands significantly greater attention. Today's students are informed consumers and global citizens, who 'shop' for the best university 'deals' using a range of indicators as 'price comparison' markers. The evidence base suggests a range of factors inform students' choice of university, these may include geographical location, facilities, fees, bursaries and graduate employability statistics (Soutar & Turner, 2002; Wang, 2009). The student voice is significant in this regard. It may be available through satisfaction surveys reporting student experience, or through social networking that facilitates easy access to immediate, uncensored and authentic communication between current and potential students.

This chapter seeks to explore the role of the student voice in informing and shaping learning experiences within higher education. Considerable variation exists in conceptualisation and application of the student voice in this context. Whilst students may be considered to inhabit roles of 'user' and 'consumer', these are somewhat limited conceptions, which have the tendency to detach a student from their educational experience. Nevertheless, their effective use mandates the presence of adequate opportunities for the provision of feedback, though does not necessarily guarantee subsequent action in response. I prefer a richer conception, however, achieved through location of the student within a role of 'active partner', as one who 'co-creates' a learning experience.

When viewed in comparison with the role of user and provider of feedback, a conception of the student as a co-constructive partner embodies deeper levels of student engagement. Participation in choices and decisions regarding individual learning journeys is empowered. Partnerships such as these assume as fundamental the existence of dialogic structures and processes that embed student opinion and feedback and mandate accountability for subsequent responsive action. They also require innovative and meaningful pedagogies, and flexible curricula, to offer genuine opportunities for student choice in modes of attendance, learning processes and assessment activity. Such partnerships, whether between student and academic, student and service colleague, or student and peer, have the capacity to shape learning experiences and facilitate pedagogic transformation for both current and future learners.

Current conceptions of the student voice within higher education (or more correctly, 'student voices', since there is rarely a 'single student voice') are contested and variable, and often leave much to be desired. In comparison with school and college conceptions, those from the university sector may lack conviction. Seale (2010) argues that higher education conceptions are underdeveloped, since these voices rarely demand equality, empowerment, participation or transformation. In comparison, Seale believes that school and college definitions are more substantial, as they include valuing students' views, communicating those views to those able to influence change, regarding students as equal partners in the evaluation of teaching and learning and empowering a more active role for students in creating change.

Seale's position may offer uncomfortable accusations, unpalatable truths even, yet perhaps we should consider this further? It would seem reasonable to concede that the majority of student voice work in higher education appears to coalesce around a quality enhancement agenda, emphasising student engagement and student satisfaction (Higher Education Funding Council for England [HEFCE], 2009; QAA, 2005). Such work foregrounds an intention to seek to understand and evaluate the learning experience through the perception of the student who experiences it first-hand. This is in keeping with the HEFCE's Strategic Plan (2006–2011) in which an objective is to work with students to ensure a high-quality learning experience that meets their needs (HEFCE, 2007). Nevertheless, a recent report identified that despite considerable attempts to increase student engagement through programme represen-tation, a 'to-what effect?' question remains (HEFCE, 2009). This would suggest that the student voice lobby may somehow lack confidence in itself, or in its future direction, and as a consequence is left wondering how to press home any advantages when it comes to demanding real change in policy and practice. Perhaps the student voice needs to come of age before it is ready to assume a centre-stage position as an agent for transformation?

To consider how we might support and facilitate a stronger, more effective and transformational student voice, let us first explore the extent and effectiveness of our current mechanisms for listening to, and importantly, responding to student opinion. The chapter first considers the two most common vehicles for supporting expression of the student voice, commenting on the current state of play, challenges and limitations, and future directions. These comprise the use of questionnaire surveys to assess student satisfaction and the use of student representation systems to achieve student engagement. The chapter then offers four examples of good practice that illustrate different approaches that have been used to engage the student voice and effect transformation in practice and policy. It concludes by reflecting on the benefits of such transformation to individual learners and to institutions.

The Use of Questionnaire Surveys to Assess Student Satisfaction

Whilst a review of questionnaire survey methodology is beyond the scope of this chapter, it is appropriate to consider some key issues related to their use within student voice research. Large-scale questionnaire surveys have become relatively well established within the UK higher education sector, as a means of exploring student satisfaction, of which the most familiar will be the UK's National Student Survey (NSS). Within my own institution, and I suspect this is the case more broadly across the sector, an earlier chorus of dissent is now subsiding, with most colleagues now learning to live with the NSS, warts and all. Although a key area of concern has been that its central purpose remains ambiguous (to provide information, assess satisfaction, monitor standards or improve the learning experience?), the NSS has now entered its seventh year of use. An independently administered survey, the NSS surveys third year undergraduates in England, Wales, Northern Ireland and some of Scotland.[1] Questions address the experience of teaching, assessment and feedback,

---

1. Further information on the National Student Survey may be found at http://www.thestudentsurvey.com and related data at http://unistats.direct.gov.uk

academic support, organisation and management, learning resources, and personal development. An overall assessment of satisfaction with the programme of study is included, and an invitation to offer additional positive and negative comments on the learning experience. Results are publicly available and are used by many of the national league tables for higher education in the UK.

An early report, produced as part of the NSS's development by the Open University's Centre for Higher Education Research and Information (HEFCE, 2003), acknowledged the complexity of the many significant methodological issues concerning the evaluation of teaching quality. It also recognised that although institutions were becoming better at collecting and analysing feedback, considerable inadequacies remained with regard to the manner in which information was returned to students in response to feedback. A further report (HEFCE, 2008) affirmed that NSS results carry increasing importance for HEIs and offered growing evidence of institutional initiatives arising as a consequence of results. Significantly however, the report also questioned the extent to which students are actively involved in the creation of such initiatives, and how well the results are adequately communicated back to them.

A review of three years of NSS data (2005–2007), conducted for the Higher Education Academy (HEA) by Surridge (2009) noted that institutional response rates are variable, ranging from 41% to 80% and that an increasing number of institutions choose to incentivise returns. The report acknowledged the large range of student and institutional characteristics that influence returns, and the complexity of responses according to different groups. For example black, Asian and white students have differing levels of satisfaction with assessment and feedback, yet these data are masked in reports of the overall return. Similarly, the experience of particular groups such as mature and part-time students and those engaged in blended or distance-learning approaches to study are also masked by general results. Furthermore, although variation in student experience has been demonstrated between subjects, there is little statistical difference between institutions. This indicates a need for discriminatory caution, particularly since these data are usually viewed in isolation, stripped back to overall figures that are relatively meaningless without the all-important context of student body and broader institutional performance.

In addition to the NSS, many institutions in the UK now ask its students to participate in a number of other institutional surveys, which seek to explore the views of different student cohorts. These may include, for example, use of the post graduate experience surveys for taught and research students (operated by the HEA)[2] and the international student barometer (operated by the International Graduate Insight Group or 'i-graduate', an independent benchmarking and consultancy service).[3] In addition, several institutions are choosing to develop their own internal surveys in

2. Further information on post graduate surveys operated by the HEA may be found at http://www.heacademy.ac.uk/ourwork/supportingresearch/postgraduatework
3. Further information on the international student barometer may be found at http://www.igraduate.org/services/student_insight-student_barometer.html

which the design of questions is often based on those found in external surveys and applied to a larger audience (e.g. NSS-type questions used for level one and two students). Applied at module, programme and institutional level, these surveys are used with the intention of providing a more comprehensive, annual overview of satisfaction (HEFCE, 2009).

Given the proliferation of survey use in higher education institutions, it is likely that students across the sector, are exposed to the use of several similar instruments. Students consequently become weary of providing feedback on their experience, and critical of their value in achieving change. Probably the most critical part of the process then is to ensure continuing dialogue with students in the aftermath of survey completion. Once again, it is wise to return to the earlier criticisms made in this regard:

> If students are to be willing to keep completing surveys, it is important that the HEI has rapid and effective mechanisms for deciding, and reporting, what follow-up action has been, and will be, taken to enhance quality and standards and to address areas of concern identified by students.... My experience ... suggests students are less interested in statistical interpretations of their responses ... [than] in the way valid concerns are identified and a plan of action, whether immediate or aspirational, articulated. (Cook, 2004, p. 55)

In terms of next steps, it is likely that the large-scale survey will continue to be with us for the foreseeable future, as will smaller surveys at faculty, department, programme and/or module level. It is gratifying however that many universities are also beginning to consider the use of alternative approaches to engage the student voice and explore issues that arise. In particular, targeted discussion forums, focus groups, and other consultation events utilising approaches such as 'World Cafe' and 'Open Space' techniques[4] are growing in popularity, and are often enhanced by the use of social networking technology utilising a variety of discussion facilities.

The Use of Student Representation Systems to Achieve Student Engagement

The practice of students acting as programme representatives is well established within the UK higher education sector, with regular feedback from students on their programme experience being a standard and expected feature of quality assurance and enhancement processes (QAA, 2005). Students are, by now, familiar with the practice of electing fellow students to act as their representatives, entrusted with

---

4. For more information on World Cafe and Open Space techniques see http://www.theworldcafe.com and http://www.openspaceworld.org

responsibility to consult their views and express opinions on their behalf at events such as programme committees. Student representatives will also be consulted when activities related to programme delivery require an informed student opinion, as may occur, for example, when changes to a module are proposed and related quality processes require evidence of student agreement. In addition, representatives will often provide a student perspective on university-wide committees and will be called upon to represent the student body during larger-scale activities such as academic review and institutional audit.

Significant challenges and limitations to the practice and processes involved in student representation were acknowledged by studies conducted early in the 2000s, which in some institutions have still not been fully addressed or resolved. The aforementioned report (HEFCE, 2003) identified that although systems work well at institutional level, much variability exists within and between institutions. A range of common concerns were found to exist in relation to two key issues. First, the extent to which individuals can adequately represent the views of the broader student community. Second, how the 'feedback loop' is closed, ensuring student representatives are adequately informed of how and where their views have been considered, and subsequent actions that have taken place. A further report (QAA, 2005) that drew on data from seventy institutional audit reports also reinforced the importance of 'closing the loop' and acknowledged that although operational arrangements in this regard were highly significant, they were often flawed.

A report to HEFCE on student engagement (HEFCE, 2009) explored institutional and student union processes and practices with regard to enhancing collective engagement in learning activities. The report found that most HEIs considered their student engagement systems to be effective, although student unions were less satisfied than institutions. Basic provision of student questionnaires and programme representation systems was evident, although considerable variation persisted within and between HEIs. Management of issues relating to all aspects of the representation process (including role recognition, nominations, elections, training, monitoring and evaluation of effectiveness) were recognised by institutions and student unions to be challenging and of variable quality. Issues relating to 'closing the feedback loop' identified previously (HEFCE, 2003) appear to have persisted, though many institutions were reported to be making progress in providing information to students. In some, however, responsibility for monitoring follow-up processes was acknowledged to remain problematic.

The HEFCE report (2009) acknowledged that HEIs and student unions are investing considerable effort in creating and enhancing their student engagement mechanisms. It also recognised that the effects of this investment are uncertain, since little clarity exists regarding criteria that are likely to assist in evaluating the effectiveness of these practices. Importantly, it proposed a model for systematic review of the multi-layered student engagement processes. It recommended a sector-wide commitment to working together to develop common student representation practices that embrace the needs of part-time students and the wider student body as a whole. Recommendations also included recognising the importance of learning and teaching strategies in clarifying rationales for student engagement and for staff and students to explore how development needs in this area might be met. Crucially, the 2009 report emphasised the importance of students taking action to follow up on planned actions and improvements, investigating specific issues and developing discussion papers for debate at committees. It is precisely this sort of activity that will empower and embed the student voice as 'a force to be reckoned with', requiring that issues raised by students are taken seriously.

Clearly a need exists for significantly more work to be undertaken here, requiring sector-wide clarification of purpose and sharing of good practice as it emerges. One such example may be seen from colleagues at Sheffield Hallam University who have identified the need for mentoring schemes for school representatives within the faculty, helping induct students into relevant practices and processes, and in so doing enhancing engagement and effectiveness (Flint & O'Hara, 2010).

Four Examples of Good Practice in Use of the Student Voice

This section offers four examples to illustrate how the student voice, when channelled effectively, may produce significant change in approaches to practice and pedagogy.

Example One

An example from the University of East London is of a learning and teaching funded project, led by the Quality Assurance and Enhancement team, run in collaboration with its student union (Carter, 2010). It explored perceptions of the institutional processes involved in programme representation, using extensive student feedback elicited through focus group interviews with student representatives, and interviews with programme leaders and student union staff. This successful project resulted in many improvements, including the creation of:

- a revised administrative process for registration of representatives
- a leaflet series for student representatives on managing meetings, the role of a student representative, effective communication and helping other students
- a virtual learning environment site that provides an online resource base
- online training for students who are unable to attend face-to-face training for their role as student representatives
- a handbook for programme leaders and servicing officers on managing programme committee business
- enhanced training for programme leaders in the role of programme representatives.

Example Two

In the second case example, an ESCalate-funded project involving four HEIs (Napier, Leeds Metropolitan, UCE Birmingham and Westminster) sought to use the student voice to enhance professional development in learning, teaching and assessment practice, and ultimately to improve the learning experience for students (Campbell, Beasley, Eland, & Rumpus, 2007). The 'Hearing the Student Voice' project[5] had a primary commitment to facilitating contexts in which colleagues were more able to effectively engage with students' perspectives. Through the use of eight innovative case studies, it offered a remarkable illustration of achievements gained through partnership working. Three sector-wide dissemination events were held, with guidance provided on a range of aspects related to implementation for prospective projects. These included 'how to capture and use the student voice' and issues related to 'student involvement'. The project contains good reflection on the processes involved; it underlines the importance of creating meaningful opportunities for students to speak freely and of offering professional support to colleagues as they engage with the student voice and facilitate subsequent change.

The eight studies identified within the project are as outlined below:

- Students joined staff in an accredited programme to enable masters supervisors to hear first-hand, in a non-threatening environment, how students react to supervision at various stages in the cycle;
- honest and thoughtful feedback from students on what helps or hinders their learning was sought within a whole programme review process and used to support reflective staff development at individual and departmental level;
- an interactive staff and student event was held in which staff and students shared perspectives on issues within HE and came to a fuller understanding of the views and experiences of each;
- students contributed to course development for a new pilot module in personal development planning;
- international students participated, in person and through video, in a professional development session for academic staff to strengthen cohesion in social and academic activities;
- student voices were scripted into DVD 'video diaries' to illustrate the first year experience and played at a staff conference;
- views on what helped, motivated and supported student learning, and useful teaching approaches were edited into a 20-minute DVD presentation played to staff;
- focus group data from masters level students were developed into a narrative on curriculum design and delivery of a module, used to facilitate debate and course development.

Colleagues who attended the project dissemination events offered feedback on the cases. Whilst many appeared to respond positively to the authenticity of the 'real'

---

5. Further information on this project can be obtained in this book from the contributions of Rumpus et al. (Chapter 20) and Campbell (Chapter 21).

student voice, acknowledging the impact this has for example, in comparison with reading paper-based module evaluations, some questioned the authenticity and representativeness of the views expressed. Students who participated in the project appreciated having both a platform to express their experiences, and to effect real change. The project team offered reflection on the importance of protecting the students' interests, and being loyal to the intended messages of the feedback, utilising judicious selection and careful analysis.

Example Three

Two projects from the University of Southampton illustrate harnessing the student voice through the use of participatory methods, which are claimed to more effectively deliver transformation, participation and empowerment (Seale, 2010). The first project was conducted in the context of an intention to involve students in the design and delivery of staff development materials and activities related to inclusive learning and teaching. It sought to capture student voices regarding their learning experiences and to involve them in data analysis and the creation of materials and methods that might help reduce barriers to inclusion. Students were invited to select from a range of methods by which to tell their stories (comprising writing a letter to an imaginary friend, a diary, reflective journal, piece of creative writing or art, or face-to-face interview) and to contribute to the ensuing thematic analysis. Project findings were disseminated through a website and used in teaching and development. In addition, participants created a post-project wiki in an attempt to keep the issues 'live' and encourage further engagement with issues raised by the project. Academic staff, whilst claiming to be initially unsurprised by the findings, subsequently acknowledged the stories had considerable impact, enabling them to gain a different perspective of the students' experiences.

Example Four

A second project at the University of Southampton explored the e-learning experiences of disabled learners, with the intention of understanding participation strategies, and identifying factors that enable or inhibit effective e-learning. An intended outcome was to make recommendations to aid those designing systems and developing services for disabled students (Seale, 2010). Participants were consulted through an online survey, invited to contribute their own experiences of e-learning in a manner of their own choosing, to advise on the analysis and to contribute to the design of the project website. Project findings have been integrated into a website for staff to facilitate improved practice in relation to the use of technology enhanced learning for disabled students. Participants were not a homogenous group, and particular care was taken to avoid the use of 'disability labels' in reporting the student voice. This aspect of the project was found to contribute greatly to the development of trust between project staff and students. In this project, as with the previous one, elements of choice enabled students to exert control over the sharing of their experiences, a fact that caused the resulting stories 'to have a power and authenticity that teachers responded to. This is important in the context of empowerment in that it could increase the likelihood of student voices compelling teachers into action' (Seale, 2010, p. 1010).

Conclusion

Within this chapter, three aspects of the student voice have been considered: feedback on student experience in the form of surveys, student representation as a measure of engagement and application of the student voice in an attempt to achieve change in policy and practice. The shared and consistent intention has been to engage students in meaningful dialogue about their perceptions and experiences and to create significant improvements in response to any concerns expressed. The underlying rationale for this is multifaceted (HEFCE, 2009). For some institutions this reflects a commitment to students as consumers, and a wish to offer pleasing experiences that will attract and retain satisfied customers who will speak highly of the institution. For others, there is a fundamental commitment to offering an outstanding student experience that embodies responsiveness to student concerns, whether social or academic. Still others may be committed to a vision of the institution as a learning community in which students are members, with staff and students cast as fellow learners who work together to achieve new insights, create new knowledge and develop new practices. A less often expressed rationale, though one that carries very considerable significance, contains the acknowledgement that an engaged student is likely to be a more successful and effective learner (HEFCE, 2009).

In support of a learner-centred curriculum, Cleveland-Innes and Emes (2005) consider the inter-relationship of student, environment and learning. They argue that a student, in creating their own level of engagement in social and academic activity, is simultaneously investing in their learning and achievement. Thus, creating opportunities for dialogue between students and university colleagues helps foster ownership and belonging for the individual students who offer feedback on their experience. In turn, this benefits the wider student body and academic community, and critically, it facilitates the individual's deeper engagement in their own academic study. Haywood (2009) proposed a three-tier model of student engagement, in which students might be informed (they know of the university football team), involved (they play for it) or engaged (they join the committee that organises all sporting events). Such a model may be helpful in assessing the extent to which HEIs offer opportunities for students to participate at all levels, whether in a module, or in a cross university committee role, in academic endeavour or social activity.

A particular challenge for institutions is to create environments, cultures and programmes that offer genuine opportunities for engagement. All too often students experience tokenism, in which views are requested, though seldom acknowledged or responded to. Although the days are gone when it is permissible for colleagues to dismiss critical feedback as evidence of misinformed or inadequate students, the reality may be equally devastating and far more subtle. The ubiquitous end of module questionnaire becomes a tick-box exercise, which is at best a tired and empty ritual, and at worst an activity that engenders resentment and disaffection. Similarly, programme committees and cross-institution surveys may ask important questions, but waste time if colleagues rarely engage with the real issues that students grapple with, or make empty promises that remain unfulfilled. Clearly there is a responsibility on students to try to raise issues and to follow up outcomes; however, the main responsibility must surely lie with staff to ensure that commitments are honoured, and promises kept. The real danger here is that when an institution permits a student(s) to become disaffected, then disengagement from study becomes a very real possibility. Such a situation undermines a learner's academic potential and endangers their life chances and future career. In contrast, empowered, engaged and independent learners are enthusiastic and passionate, a joy to work with and a source of considerable mutual learning and satisfaction. Clearly we must commit to transforming attitudes, environments and structures if we are to enable such positive outcomes to flourish.

References

Campbell, F., Beasley, L., Eland, J., & Rumpus, A. (2007). *Hearing the student voice: Promoting and encouraging the effective use of the student voice to enhance professional development in learning, teaching and assessment within higher education.* Edinburgh: Napier University.

Carter, R. (2010). Securing effective student representation. In: *Scholarship in learning, teaching and assessment: Enhancing the student experience through innovation, collaboration and critical enquiry.* London: University of East London. Retrieved from http://www.uel.ac.uk/apse/documents/scholarship_doc.pdf. Accessed on 18 March 2011.

Cleveland-Innes, M., & Emes, C. (2005). Principles of learner-centred curriculum: Responding to the call for change in higher education. *The Canadian Journal of Higher Education, XXXV*(4), 85–110.

Cook, E. (2004). Student feedback and its scope for enhancing learning. *Perspectives, 8*, 54–57.

Flint, A., & O'Hara, M. (2010). If you build it, they won't necessarily come: Engaging student representatives beyond the course level. Higher Education Academy Annual Conference, University of Hertfordshire, June 2010.

Haywood, W. (2009). Student engagement project. Paper presented at "Learning from Internal Change Academies" Event, Manchester Metropolitan University.

Higher Education Funding Council for England (HEFCE). (2003). Collecting and using student feedback on quality and standards of learning and teaching in HE. Report to HEFCE by the Centre for Higher Education Research and Information (Open University), NOP Research Group and SQW Ltd. Retrieved from http://www.hefce.ac.uk/pubs/rdreports/2003/rd08_03. Accessed on 18 March 2011.

Higher Education Funding Council for England (HEFCE). (2007). Strategic plan 2006–2011. HEFCE 2007/09, Bristol, HEFCE.

Higher Education Funding Council for England (HEFCE). (2008). Counting what is measured, or measuring what counts? League tables and their impact on higher education institutions in England. Report to HEFCE by the Centre for Higher Education Research and Information (Open University) and Hobsons Research. Retrieved from http://www.hefce.ac.uk/pubs/hefce/2008/08_14. Accessed on 18 March 2011.

Higher Education Funding Council for England (HEFCE). (2009). Report to HEFCE on student engagement (2009) by the Centre for Higher Education Research and Information (Open University).

Quality Assurance Agency for Higher Education. (2005). *Outcomes from institutional audit – student representation and feedback arrangements*. Gloucester: Quality Assurance Agency.

Seale, J. (2010). Doing student voice work in higher education: An exploration of the value of participatory methods. *British Educational Research Journal, 36*(6), 995–1015; December.

Soutar, G. N., & Turner, J. P. (2002). Students' preferences for university: A conjoint analysis. *International Journal of Educational Management, 16*(1), 40–45.

Surridge, P. (2009). The National Student Survey three years on: What have we learned? York: Higher Education Academy. Retrieved from http://www.heacademy.ac.uk/assets/EvidenceNet/Summaries/surridge_nss_three_years_on_summary.pdf. Accessed on 18 March 2011.

Wang, X. (2009). Factors influencing international students' choice of universities: A country-specific analysis. Paper presented at the annual meeting of the 53rd Annual Conference of the Comparative and International Education Society, Francis Marion Hotel, Charleston, South Carolina. Retrieved from http://www.allacademic.com/meta/p301661_index.html. Accessed on 11 March, 2011.

PART THREE
THE ROLE OF STUDENT VOICE IN INFORMING TEACHERS' PROFESSIONAL PRACTICE

Editors' Summary to Part Three

In this third part of the book our authors, in very different ways, explore professional and learning partnerships, investigating how Student Voice can be used in such a way that teachers learn from learners. We start Part Three with a contribution from Mick Waters exploring the ways in which pupils can influence the curriculum that they are offered. Waters considers what we mean by a curriculum and why learning works for some and not others. The chapter examines the extent to which pupils might be involved in setting the learning agenda, shaping their own experience and evaluating the quality of their learning. In Chapter 17, Gill Mullis draws on teacher and student testimonies as to why they believe Student Voice is important, and how daily encounters are challenging and changing understandings and definitions of students' roles, teaching and learning relationships, school structures and organisation. Although acknowledging the relevance of official policy, Mullis highlights principles and practice represented in schools, concluding that what is required is an educational paradigm which better reflects C21st learners. Joy Morgan (Chapter 18) explores the potential and possibilities for Student Voice initiatives to influence learning in the classroom by structuring partnerships between trainee teachers and students. Her project considers how students co-planning lessons with trainee teachers can result in higher quality learning experiences in the classroom. In Chapter 19, David Godfrey examines the nature of Student Voice activities at a Sixth Form College in Farnborough, England, and the way that the differing structures, processes and activities of the college enable the variety of Student Voices in a large organisation to be heard. And in the final contribution to this part of the book, Ann Rumpus, Jenny Eland and Rai Shacklock (Chapter 20) consider the use of 'authentic' Student Voice in ongoing professional development for lecturers in Higher Education and potentially for teacher training courses.

Chapter 16

Setting the Learning Agenda: Can Pupils Do That?

Mick Waters

Abstract

This chapter sets out to explore ways in which pupils can influence the curriculum that they are offered. It looks at what is natural in learning and considers what we mean by a curriculum and why learning works for some and not others. The chapter then considers the extent to which pupils might be involved in setting the learning agenda, shaping their own experience and evaluating the quality of their learning.

Across the globe, governments are reviewing their national curriculum offers at the start of the new millennium. From Singapore to Scandinavia, Australia to Scotland, South Africa to New Zealand each government is trying to work out how to represent the need to teach skills, knowledge and attitudes. Pupil attitude is acknowledged as vital. How pupils are encouraged to be involved in the shape of their learning will influence the outcome and will, in turn, shape their own attitudes to learning. It might be that attitudes are not only 'taught' in learning settings but grow through the experience of being a learner.

My work as a teacher, school leader, director of education and director of curriculum for England's government agency has led me to understand the importance of engaging with the learner and encouraging them to shape their learning by defining goals and by advising how it can be better. I hope you enjoy thinking through some of the issues around pupil voice on the point of value learning.

Keywords: Curriculum; professional practice; authentic learning; value learning

Introduction

Watch very young children learning. It is almost as if they cannot help it. They explore, set themselves the impossible task, keep trying the impossible, fail endlessly, delight in small discoveries, apply one idea to a new situation and test out ideas. They do all of these things without being told to though the guiding adult will sometimes offer a model or put a stepping stone in place or add a twist of confusion at just the right moment. Leap forward in age. The process gets repeated for the student at university on a masters course or doing a doctorate; the exploring, setting tasks, trying one idea in a new situation, the experimenting and discovery.

At both ends we see self-structured learning, hypotheses being tested, conjecture and discovery. What do we see in between these ages as children travel the school journey? Too often, they experience learning which is linear rather than rounded, incremental rather than expansive, and tested rather than testing. The most obvious difference though is the way the learning is set by others rather than the learners themselves. Is this because the learner cannot determine their own paths or because we, the teachers, know the best route? Is it because the learners need their experience to be channelled to save time? Is it because the learners suddenly lose ideas and imagination which return after they have passed examinations at the end of formal schooling?

The fact is that many schools feel unable to use the pupil voice in designing and building learning experiences. We listen to central government for the decisions about what and how to teach rather than believing or trusting the professionalism of teachers or the pupil voice

What is the Curriculum?

The school curriculum includes everything that pupils experience. It is the entire planned learning experience and includes lessons, routines, events and what the learner does after and beyond school. Good schools exploit all available time and include elements of the national curriculum throughout this entire planned learning experience, in the events of performances, sports fixtures, residential visits and in the routines of dining, assembly, and using the library. Other schools see curriculum as lessons and the rest is either management or extra curricula; a misnomer invented by fee paying schools to charge more for their service.

How far is it possible to have this entire planned learning experience defined by the learner and influenced and modified by the adult? Or is it defined by the adult and influenced and modified by the learner? Where would your school fit on the continuum?

Using Pupils' Views

Many schools are making the effort to harness and use pupils' views on their learning encounters. At its simplest level, pupils help and support the routines of school. They work with younger pupils, help at playtimes and lunchtimes in buddy sessions, they look after pets, property and plants as well as people. In some schools the School Council helps with the organisation of the school to differing levels ranging from the simplistic lip serving to the staff through to having a genuine influence, through their voice which proposes real action, often with a budget. In other schools pupils are advocates and ambassadors for their school in a range of events that promote their work Sometimes, pupils are asked what they want to know more about and, through devices like mind maps, they let their teachers know which situations they would like to experience and what to lie in their path.

Sometimes, though we confuse pupil voice with the roles pupils take in the learning process. We differentiate to fit learning to the individual pupil's needs or aptitudes. We see pupil attitude as an expression of their voice and sometimes respond in the way we set tasks.

If you had your time again, would you let people know that you could write? If you knew that once you could write they would make you do a lot of it every day, would you possibly pretend you could not? The chances are that if you could not write, you would get asked to do less and be given alternatives such as drawing pictures. What would you choose if you knew what lay ahead? Of course, matching to need is called differentiation, but again it is often not a case of pupil voice being in operation; more likely the teacher says what we need. More recently central governments have started to refer to this individualisation of work as 'personalisation'. Too often the person is left out of the process. They are offered prescribed treatment rather than a voice in their future.

Yet many schools do get it right. They actually ask pupils what they think, prefer, want, suggest and offer. They see them as having an active say in their learning rather than being people who, at worst, have to suffer or manipulate their own learning experience.

The 'Can Do; Can't Do' Dilemma

For many children learning is a greasy pole. You set off excited at the prospect, enjoying hanging on but after a while the pole tilts and spins to make it certain that you will fall off at some point. We meet adults who say they are no good at mathematics, languages, or spelling and many people have a mind set which says that most people will fail at most things before they leave school. Basically, they hang on until we confirm that they cannot continue to learn, whether that is history, art, music or physics. A few survive at some of these and are seen a specialists. Yet ask a group of teenagers in most countries if they will drive when they grow up. Hardly anyone expects not to, they simply do not countenance failure. Two feet and three pedals, we will get used to it. All those things for two hands; levers, brakes, indicators, steering wheel; we will manage. Trying to reverse, using mirrors to see behind when going forward, dipping lights, uphill, downhill; we will just have to cope. Stalling, grating gears' just problems to overcome.

Of course, driving might be hard and complex but other things work in the learner's favour. Mostly we watch others do it for years before we have a go. We sit and watch the various manoeuvres modelled by adults. There is no expectation that you will do it after two demonstrations. Most adults who model are also confident; indeed they blame other drivers for any problems. The learner is expected to struggle at first and allowances are made until success is achieved, even for taking several tests. The learner decides when they want the formal lessons and they comply with the syllabus because they have voiced their need to take it. It is odd that something we do not set out to teach in school is so certainly a success for many of the people who expect to fail on the programmes we offer and try to teach. Motivation and commitment are examples of pupil voice at its most powerful: the voice that speaks inside the head of the learner.

In curriculum terms, many pupils end up making choices, taking options based on what they believe they are good at; their developing specialisms. Given the challenge of trying to travel the greasy pole of learning, their selection of specialism might be tenuous. So what is specialism? Well, it is not simply more of what you are good at doing; not what is left when you have failed at everything else. Specialism is about taking control of learning, setting your own course, working in depth. It is that university higher level course running back into the school curriculum agenda. It sees pupils setting themselves problems, sharing their solutions, being part of a contributing learning community. It means writing for a wider audience of learners, reading the works of others and being a genuine part of a fraternity of learners.

Are examinations a spur or a deterrent for learning? For many they are a spur, the chance to test oneself against a set of criteria which indicate the level to which we have achieved. For others, they are tedious and simply offer hurdles to clear or hoops to jump through, regardless of understanding. The certificate is more important than the learning; the ticket to the next stage of confusion is achieved, rather than a delight in learning for its own sake.

In other aspects of public services engaging with the service users is often called 'co-design' or 'co-construction'. In education to date we often simply talk of pupil voice.

There is a good evidence base for the effectiveness of even very young children as peers and mentors for their peers. Not only do the pupils receiving support benefit but so do the mentors who gain insight into the learning process and understand its complexity. If every pupil during their school career had a responsibility for the learning of someone else we might see a change in the culture of schooling.

This book contributes to articulating ways in which pupils can shape their curriculum and help us redefine what is worth knowing and is valuable. Yes, pupils can do that.

How Do We Make Learning Authentic?

Learning cannot be real all the time but the various segments and elements can work together for real purposes. 'We are teaching you this so that you can use it and apply

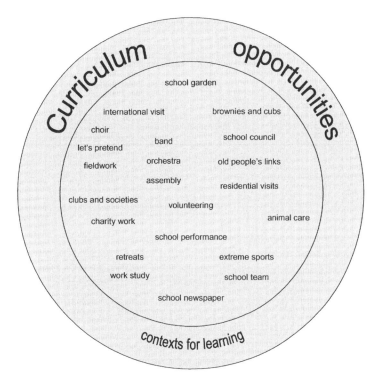

Figure 16.1: Seeing the curriculum in context.

it a set of contexts'. 'We are working in these contexts so that you can see why we learn some things in a linear and artificial way' (Figure 16.1).

Most schools use many of these contexts; some to bring learning to life, others as add-ons and some for a real benefit with pupils having a voice in their learning. The contexts provide ways into the curriculum, whether it is a national element or the planned experience of the individual school. The contexts will explore every subject discipline in an applied way. For example, a school garden is a routine activity that will have untold benefits: the maths of yield and profit as the potatoes appear in vast quantities compared with the quantity sown. The cooking of the potatoes alongside the other ingredients to explore food technology in context. The planning of a meal for residents of a local old peoples' community to offer citizenship experiences. All of these are structured experiences that offer a voice to the pupil in the learning they meet. A school newspaper is a chance to learn about purpose, process and audience in writing as well as a vehicle for meeting other languages in print. The world of make believe and let's pretend offers a vehicle for learning which surrenders to pupil voice once the situation is established. All of these contexts bring learning alive and the pupil voice will speak volumes about the worth of such activity.

Is Enjoyment Vital?

Enjoyment certainly helps. It has, though, to be authentic enjoyment. Many schools engage their pupils through versions of learning to learn, University of the First Age (UFA), Children's University or special projects that put the pupil at the centre of a different learning experience. They typically find that pupils enjoy these sessions enormously, there is little poor behaviour, considerable excitement and good engagement. They then wonder if the pupils are making enough progress compared with the normal teacher led, content dominated and outcome secure lessons. Pupils are doing mind maps, playing games with thinking hats, completing charts and posters and inventing maxims to sum up their learning. The danger is that we leave behind one set of frustrations for others that do not show in the same way with the pupils but do so, instead, with the teachers. For some pupils, the different sessions are enjoyed because they are a sort of respite from the normal lesson format. Within them, though, children do not have to extend themselves, they play games without getting the point and, in turn, feel the same frustration, though differently, that they had in the other world of the increment.

The challenge in all learning is to make the learning explicit, to exemplify progress and success and to build learners' awareness of their achievement.

Are the Pupils the Same People All the Time?

Why is it that some individuals are so different in chemistry from art, modern languages from geography? That must be that they are less good at some subjects than others. So were some individuals good at art this year and not last, or were good at science and not this? Maybe they are just growing or they have different teachers? Most likely, they are seeing some sense in the subjects for some of the time and not at others, usually due to the teacher and the level of pupil involvement offered. Clever teachers ask for insight. How do you like to learn? Shall I vary the approach? Let me show you in several ways. Shall I set the same problem in different contexts? And, most powerfully, can you tell me what you cannot understand, make sense of, or do? How would you like me to help you learn? These are the sorts of questions that good teachers ask in order to help pupils shape their learning. The best teachers listen.

So Can Pupils Influence the Way They Meet Their Learning?

Some schools have started to use surveys to better bring learning to the learner. The Pupil Online Survey Tool (POST) is used in several English Secondary Schools was developed in the Black Country to offer pupils the chance to give their views online about a set of agreed criteria for effective lessons. How does it work? Basically, the pupils identify, with help, 10 criteria which are amended and approved by the senior leadership team in the school (Figure 16.2).

1. The Point
2. Respect
3. Learn by doing
4. Work together
5. Try new things
6. Choice
7. Praise
8. Time to Think
9. Listening
10. Surroundings

Black Country See it in colour

THE BLACK
COUNTRY
CHALLENGE

Creating Futures

Figure 16.2: Dimensions of teaching quality.

Pupils then complete an online survey and the analysis shows how effective is each department on each criteria. The example below shows the results in terms of the Design and Technology department. You can see where D and T features and which are the top two departments in the school for each criterion. Each department sees only its own score and the top two; not the rest. The survey is repeated over the next three half terms (Table 16.1).

Table 16.1: Extract (1) from the POST survey.

2	Getting help – Do you receive support when stuck on a problem in class?	3	Choice – How often are you offered a choice of what to do during lessons?
	Answered 'always' or 'regularly' (in %)		Answered 'always' or 'regularly' (in %)
Design technology	66.3	PE	28.7
Modern foreign languages	65.1	Music	24.7
	64.0		17.2
	62.3		16.1
	60.6	Design technology	14.9
	59.4		13.8
	58.9		13.2
	56.6		12.1
	53.1		11.5
	52.0		9.8
	49.7		7.5
	43.4		7.5
	39.4		6.9

Table 16.1: (*Continued*)

6	Group work – How often do you work in a pair or a small group on a shared activity?	7	Being creative and active – How often are you creative or active in your lessons? e.g. making things, role play, practical work
	Answered 'always' or 'regularly' (in %)		Answered 'always' or 'regularly' (in %)
PE	75.9	Design technology	68.8
Music	61.5	Art and design	60.1
	46.0		59.5
	44.3		45.1
	40.8		35.8
	29.9		32.4
	29.3		27.7
	24.7		27.2
	19.0		27.2
	17.2		23.7
	17.2		18.5
	16.7		12.1
	12.6		11.6

What happens is that the departments towards the bottom of any list tend to go and ask those at the top what they do, how they do it and they ask if they can watch lessons. What also happens is that the gap between top and bottom shrinks and pupils get a more consistent experience across departments. There will always be a table from top to bottom but the gap between top and bottom reduces (Table 16.2).

Table 16.2: Extract (2) from the POST survey.

Overall (1)			Overall (3)		
Rank	Subject	Agree (%)	Rank	Subject	Agree (%)
1	Drama	85	1	Design & tech	89
2	Art & design	81	2	Geography	88
3	*****	75	3	*****	86
4	*****	74	4	*****	84
5	*****	73	5	*****	82
6	*****	72	5	*****	82
7	Origami	70	5	Origami	82
7	*****	70	6	*****	80
8	*****	65	7	*****	79
8	*****	65	8	*****	76
9	*****	59	9	*****	71
10	*****	57	10	*****	70
11	*****	33	11	*****	68

Within the two terms the pupils have graded the bottom department as being 21% better than at the time of the first survey and much nearer the best than previously.

This is an example of the pupil voice having a real effect because the staff want to do what they are trying to do; make learning as effective as possible. They just need to enlist the help of the people that want to be helped. Pupils take this opportunity really seriously. They see their teachers genuinely trying to respond to the 10 areas of focus agreed by the school community. They see their teachers trying new approaches, however tentatively, and try to support them in their efforts. Once staff and pupils see that they are trying to help each other in a common learning task, there is usually a better learning outcome.

Conclusion

Pupil powering a school is not easy, not least for the teaching staff as the dynamic relationship changes from control of the learning to co-operation. Real world problems motivate learners. Their own learning is something in which the majority of learners are interested and want to influence. The school needs the confidence to practice what it writes in its aims. That bit about reaching full potential, active engagement, growing responsibility. Schools which have given real responsibility to learners report changes in culture, relationships and motivation in pupils. They also report improved outcomes; more responsible citizens, more confident individuals and more successful learners.

Some schools make genuine attempts to listen to pupils. Some go further and act on the pupils' perceptions and suggestions. Other schools take things further and invite pupils to help shape their own experience. When they do this, most schools find that the pupils take the invitation seriously, they have significant perceptions and they have a willingness to make a positive difference to their own learning. Can pupils really set the learning agenda? They certainly can where schools give them the chance, the skills and the status necessary to do the job. Try it!

Acknowledgment

Figure 16.2 *Dimensions of Teaching Quality* comes courtesy of The Black Country Children and School Improvement Partnership (BCCSIP).

Reference

Pupil On line Survey Tool (POST): published by BCCSIP 2009.

Chapter 17

Student Voice: Changing Practice and Developing Partnerships

Gill Mullis

Abstract

In this chapter, I focus on opportunities schools are creating to develop "a dialogic form of engagement" (Fielding, 2001, p. 108), in and beyond the classroom. In doing so, I draw on teacher and student testimonies as to why they believe student voice is important and how daily encounters are challenging and changing understandings and definitions of students' roles, teaching and learning relationships, school structures, and organization. While acknowledging the relevance of official policy, I highlight principles and practice represented in schools, concluding that what is required is an educational paradigm that better reflects C21st learners and the C21st. This, I argue, must necessarily be informed by our understanding(s) of the needs of all young people and their capacity to actively participate in shaping our present and their futures, with teachers and students in partnership acting upon "what pupils say about teaching, learning and schooling" (Rudduck, J., Chaplain, R., & Wallace, G. (1996). Pupil voices and school improvement. In: J. Rudduck, C. Roland, & G. Wallace (Eds), *School improvement: What can pupils tell us?* (pp. 1–16). London: David Fulton Publishers).

Keywords: Partnership; inclusion; consultation; principles; student leadership; dialogue; respect and trust; curriculum; school improvement; educational paradigm

The Student Voice Handbook: Bridging the Academic/Practitioner Divide
ISBN: 978-1-78052-040-7

Introduction

The school-based case studies in this chapter, and the conclusions that arise from these, are drawn from my work as Student Voice Coordinator at the Specialist Schools and Academies Trust (SSAT)[1] from 2006 to 2010. This involved working with teachers and students in secondary schools across the country; to develop a range of student voice initiatives and to provide platforms for schools to share best practice. I have developed opportunities for students and teachers to represent their work at SSAT national student voice conferences and training events, through student-led projects, presentations, and publications. My work has been informed by 22 years' experience as a teacher and a school leader; involved in developing student voice and familiar with the challenges that arise in doing so.

Acknowledging the context provided by research literature has been significant in raising questions with schools, to encourage them to interrogate their practice. In particular, my thinking has been informed by Michael Fielding's (2001, p. 108) work and the "emphasis on dialogue and the communal," and Jean Rudduck and Donald McIntyre's (2007, p. 9) research on creating the conditions to undertake consultation with pupils:

> compared with participation, consulting pupils about teaching and learning is altogether more risky and difficult to manage: its capacity for destabilizing habitual ways of behaving and familiar patterns of expectation – about power issues in teacher-pupil relationships, for instance – is obvious.

School Contexts: What Do Teachers Tell Us?

One of the first questions I ask when facilitating training for teachers in secondary schools who are developing student voice initiatives in their schools is, why? While responses, summarized in Table 17.1, are invariably mixed, reasons and motivation varying, common themes across schools do emerge. What consistently characterizes such dialogue is teachers' willingness to reflect on and challenge existing practice to improve teaching, learning, and relationships. There is a shared recognition that listening to learners' perspectives as part of the process of curriculum review and school improvement is potentially beneficial to all, this underpinned by a belief that such activity will contribute to raising students' confidence and developing self-esteem.

---

1. The Specialist Schools and Academies Trust is an educational charity. Its stated aim is "to give practical support to the transformation of secondary education in England by building and enabling a world-class network of innovative, high performing secondary schools in partnership with business and the wider community" (www.ssatrust.org.uk).

Table 17.1: Teachers' reasons for their engagement with student voice.

Common themes	Teachers' reasons
Communication about learning	"Developing a learning language" "Dialogue" "Enriched communication"
Informing and improving classroom practice	"Improve teaching and learning" "A means of evaluating lessons" "Impact on lesson plans and schemes of work" "Honest opinions, honest feedback" "Opportunity to talk to pupils about what they enjoy and benefit from and see change" "New ideas, new perspectives" "Increased understanding of the classroom" "Improve the teaching and learning environment" "Teach you what resource students are"
Curriculum change	"Helps shape the curriculum"
Understanding the needs of all learners	"Helps teachers understand the learning needs of different groups of students" "Greater inclusion and awareness of differentiation" "Understanding of pupils' ideas and learning"
Improving relationships between teachers and students	"Mutual/greater respect" "Trust" "Empathy" "Partnership, better relationships, improve teacher–student–student relationships"
Listening to and understanding students' views and experiences of learning	"Improved focus on students' points of view" "Greater, better access to how students think and learn"
Increased student engagement	"Students are now more engaged, think about learning"
Improving students' understanding of teachers	"Improved student insight into what teachers do to teach/improve learning"
Developing students' attributes, skills, and understanding	"Develops independent thinkers" "Helps them think about learning from their own and others' perspectives" "Students develop better relationships with one another"

Table 17.1: (*Continued*)

Common themes	Teachers' reasons
	"More responsible students"
	"Develops self-esteem and self-confidence"
	"More confident learners who know how to negotiate and talk with adults"
Empowerment	"Pupils have a voice"
	"Empowerment"
	"Their opinion matters"
Teachers' professional development	"More confident practitioners"
	"Positively influence other staff's attitude to student voice"
	"Professional development"
	"Developing as a teacher"
	"Reflective practice"
	"More room for staff to work collaboratively"
	"A chance to reflect through feedback on my practice"
	"Reflect on my own teaching style"

This sample, selected from comments by teachers from six secondary schools, is representative of responses recorded by teachers at school-based training events and SSAT conferences, during a two-year period. Interestingly, teachers volunteering to be involved in student voice initiatives see such activities as helping to develop their own confidence in the classroom and their skills as teachers, this through new understanding of students and learning. They acknowledge a responsibility to meet the challenge of supporting other staff, in the hope they may become more supportive of student voice.

Student Voice: What Does It Look Like and How Is It Changing?

Innovative work on curriculum development in schools has more recently led to increased opportunities for students to contribute views and to shape ways forward in the classroom. Initiatives include student involvement in curriculum reviews, attendance and feedback at departmental meetings, junior leadership teams with subcommittees or "satellite groups" structures, and working parties with a remit to address aspects of teaching and learning, students as researchers groups (including student observation and feedback of lessons) and students as teachers and coaches.

Assessment for Learning

Such involvement had been supported by the introduction of assessment for learning, with formative assessment strategies involving students in self and peer assessment and learner/learning conversations in the classroom. Where such activity is characterized by "a classroom culture of questioning and deep thinking in which pupils will learn from shared discussions with teachers and from one another" (Black & Wiliam, 1998, p. 13), it "transfers to the student much of what has conventionally been seen to be the professional property of the teacher" (Hargreaves, 2004, p. 22). This has the potential to challenge power relationships, with peer assessment becoming "an exercise in student voice" (Hargreaves, 2004, p. 28).

Curriculum Innovation

In addition, teacher engagement with curriculum innovation — for example, enquiry-based learning, thinking skills, and cross-curricular projects (involving more flexible use of time) — has encouraged more collaborative learning activities (Watkins, Carnell, & Lodge, 2007). This is often achieved by "freeing up" space in the timetable, as more schools compress or extend particular key stages. The more flexible structures provide increased opportunities for student to create and innovate in and beyond the classroom, to explore connections across subjects, and to address "how" they learn and to apply this learning. Reshaping the curriculum can encourage teachers to view student roles differently, as students have new opportunities to take on educator roles. For example, at Byrchall High School, student "learning analysts" have worked with teachers to plan lessons and to teach students as part of collapsed timetable days. At King Edward V1 Grammar School, students have researched learning needs and taught a sequence of Information and Communication Technology (ICT) lessons to address these (Mitchell & Debere, 2010).

Leadership

Much student voice work in schools is therefore increasingly to do with learning *with* and *from* young people as "expert witnesses" (Rudduck & Flutter, 2004, p. 105) supporting them in developing the skills and qualities to enable them not only to "create opportunities for change ... but better still become instigators of it themselves" (Kestenbaum, 2008, p. 5).

In many schools, students are working and learning with staff in restructuring and redefining models of student leadership, creating new participatory and decision-making structures to meet their needs: "to develop the leadership skills of all students involved to ensure the school can further empower and engage students" (Love, 2008, p. 13). This has led to the development of new student leadership teams, as traditional school councils and their scope are redefined. New roles have emerged, such as the introduction of students as associate governors and opportunities for students to represent their views in the wider school community, for example, at local council meetings.

What Do Students Tell Us?

The following examples draw upon two student-authored publications. "Learning with students" (SSAT, 2008) is a result of an invitation by the SSAT to students, to submit articles based on student voice work in their schools. Eleven were selected for publication. "Meeting the challenge of 21st century education and a global economy" is based on a yearlong research project with the National Endowment for Science, Technology and the Arts (NESTA),[2] wherein students were invited by the SSAT to put forward proposals for school-based projects. Those selected received funding and support to develop their ideas and to present their findings.

Where only the name of a school is given, the example cited is based either on my visits to schools or on student-led presentations at SSAT national student voice training events.

Restructuring and Redefining Student Leadership

Traditional models of school councils, whose main areas of activity may have included fund-raising and events management, are now increasingly being replaced by new and more complex leadership models. At Ringwood School, where students were dissatisfied with existing structures, this has involved the creation of a Student Voice Strategy group and a Student Voice Steering Group, which help to coordinate more effective communication across four focus groups: teaching and learning, environment, student health and welfare, and citizenship/political voice. Linked to these are approximately 50 action teams. At The Voyager School, students can become "school improvement partners" (Brazier & Ferguson, 2008, p. 16). Students identify leadership training, allocation of budget, new structures and roles, and new terms to represent these. Student management of recruitment processes is a key component, as are clear consultative processes and dialogue with the school leadership team.

The remit of student leadership groups is shifting, as students become more involved in discussing aspects of teaching and learning with teachers, this reflected in the new subcommittee and satellite group structures. Interestingly, in recent years, training programs I have designed for the SSAT, in response to needs identified by schools and reflecting developing practice, have moved from more peripheral student voice activities, which may operate outside the classroom (peer listeners, peer mediators, student councils, peer mentors, and students as interviewers), to initiatives that make a difference to interactions in the classroom. Presentations by students have included, for example, as follows:

- Students as learning partners, observing an agreed learning focus in lessons and feeding back to teacher partners.

---

2. NESTA is the National Endowment for Science, Technology and the Arts. Its stated aim "is to transform the UK's capacity for innovation. We invest in early- stage companies, inform innovation policy and encourage a culture that helps innovation to flourish" (www.nesta.org.uk).

- Students as departmental advisors, attending department meetings and participating in working parties, to help shape departmental and whole school policy and practice.
- Students as researchers, investigating student views about the use of formative assessment in the classroom and making recommendation to teachers.

Responsibility and Respect

Students themselves express a sense of responsibility for improving the quality of teaching and learning in their school:

> we joined a group wanting to make a difference to school life by making learning more interesting and having the opportunity to do something about things we weren't happy about. (Preece, Brennan, Whittingham, Kelly, & Mann, 2008, p. 39)

Their particular focus is a sense of responsibility for improving the quality of learning:

> doing our part to improve the learning and communication for all our learners. (Vincent, 2010, p. 35)

> to keep the focus on students working for students to improve their learning environment. (Grace, 2010, p. 26)

Rudduck and Flutter give examples of how student involvement in a range of initiatives, such as peer mentors, researchers, mediators, and environmental designers, is instrumental to school improvement, evidence demonstrating that "young people are more likely to commit themselves to learning in organisations that recognise their capabilities" (Rudduck & Flutter, 2004, p. 16):

> getting involved was a real eye opener for me. It made me feel responsible and that I had something to contribute to the school. (Keeley & Walker, 2008, p. 33)

In addition, the creation of leadership roles that involve students in decision-making provide "opportunities to acquire the knowledge and skills necessary for taking an active role in a democratic society in later life" (Flutter & Rudduck, 2004, p. 18). This resonates with students' own perceptions:

> We recognise that every student should have the opportunity to be an active citizen in our school and in our wider community. As young people we know that our society is always changing and one of our aims was to create a student leadership model that equips young people

with the skills to be confident and informed citizens of the future. (Brazier & Ferguson, 2008, p. 14)

In undertaking student voice activities, students articulate not only a sense of all students' responsibility for improving learning, "to voice students' opinions in order to make constructive changes" (Preece et al., 2008, p. 43) but also the importance of the student body sharing "core values":

> We acknowledge every student has a key role to play in developing and in improving the quality of learning across the school. As part of our commitment, the student executive group (SEG) set out to create opportunities that develop core values and responsibility among the student body. (Brazier & Ferguson, 2008, p. 14)

In student-led presentations, workshops, and student-authored publications, students repeatedly cite the significance of mutual respect and trust, being listened to, increased responsibility (for the quality of learning and relationships), the development of confidence and self-esteem, and their involvement in practices that contribute to school improvement and sustained change. They acknowledge that such change can be slow, because increased responsibility is often dependent on teachers and students developing trust and shared understanding over time. A year into a project based on students as learning partners/observers, students at Northampton School for Girls presented their views about the project to staff at a training day, identifying key benefits. The quotations below are taken from their presentation and represent the views of students involved in the initiative:

> I got a feeling of being treated equally and with respect
>
> We got to have our views listened to and gave us a sense of responsibility
>
> Feeling that my point of view is valued in the school
>
> It improved my self-esteem and confidence.

Students and teachers shared the view that emergent relationships based on mutual respect gave them the confidence to take more risks and to be more honest and open in their views.

Changing Roles

The increasing use of new technologies in classrooms has done much to address issues of trust, confidence, and communication in support of student voice and to shift teacher perceptions of students' roles. Students have utilized and developed electronic means, from learning platforms, blogs, and web sites to create spaces for dialogue with staff and peers. These have included student-led projects to research, design, and develop interactive web sites, for example, to post and receive teaching materials on globalization (Eadsforth, Higgins, Croft, Rudge, & Gomersall, 2010). At Skipton High School for Girls, students have collaborated with teachers from specific departments to use school-based learning platforms as spaces to share co-constructed learning activities and outcomes, also contributing to their evaluation through online discussion forum. Students as researchers, increasingly with a mandate to explore teaching and learning, have designed online questionnaires, using either school- or web-based tools such as www.surveymonkey.com (West & Griffiths, 2010).

Students' own expertise in the area of new technologies defines a clear area where students can take on the role of innovators and instigators of change, leading research. For example, at Ringwood School, student researchers elicited staff and student views on the use of handheld technologies in lessons, this leading to practical trials in class to test their effectiveness in aiding learning. As a result, the student voice strategy group contributed to a new school policy on the use of mobile technology. Taking increased responsibility in working with staff to identify and address emergent issues, students recommended the use of flip videos[3] to record learning activities and to develop "a bank of student made resources to be prepared and shared" (Grace, 2010, p. 28). At Saltash.net Community School, students produced educational videos about cyber bullying (Vincent, 2010) to use in lessons with younger students.

Students involved in such projects explicitly identify improving the quality of learning and changing culture as their core purpose: "The key question is whether students felt that increasing the use of portable technology in school would have a positive impact on their learning" (West & Griffiths, 2010, p. 49). For Ringwood student researchers, a key question was "how can we use technology to enhance learning while avoiding technology for technology's sake?" (Grace, 2010, p. 26). Both faced the challenge and "the hazards of changing the culture of the school from having a no-phones policy to having one which embraces these devices" (West & Griffiths, 2010, p. 53). Students' own understanding of teacher anxieties is expressed in their tentative hope that "a sign of success for us would be when the use of portable technologies in our school is no longer prohibited but encouraged, to increase the learning capabilities of all students" (West & Griffiths, 2010, p. 53). There is an implicit recognition that power and permissions still rest with teachers, who can block changes recommended by students, however well these are researched and argued.

In acknowledging students' own expertise, students have also designed and taught ICT lessons based on their own research into what younger students would like to learn, seeing the development of a sequences of lesson on a greater range of topics than covered as part of accredited courses, their success in teaching the subject giving them the confidence to suggest that "our goal should be to produce programmes

---

3. A pocket camcorder (Flip Mino) with USB connector, to connect the camcorder directly to a computer.

across a wide range of year groups and subjects, where student teaching plays a very active role in the learning process" (Mitchell & Debere, 2010).

The Challenge of New Partnerships

If work in this area is an representative of ways in which students may creatively work in partnership with teachers to improve learning, develop curriculum, and to extend and reverse roles, it implies that teachers' understanding and aspirations for their students' learning in all subject areas may usefully be challenged, particularly when it is teachers themselves who have the power to exclude students from active participation:

> You need a teacher who is willing to incorporate new technology into the lesson. (Grace, 2010, p. 27)

Students clearly value the invitation to work with all curriculum areas and to take part in constructive change, which contributes to curriculum review:

> We decided that all curriculum areas will benefit greatly from having pupil representatives who will be able to work closely with heads of department and link governors. [Cowling, Hill, Ritchie, & Long, 2010, p. 37]

This has led to teachers reporting "on how much help it has been to have some pupil insight into their subject" (Cowling et al., 2010, p. 38), with teachers consulting student subject leaders about how to improve learning activities in different departments.

Inclusion

This by no means guarantees that all students' voices are listened to. However, there is evidence that schools are seeking to address issues of inclusion. In their submission to present at a student voice conference, students from Christleton High School explained how as part of their peer teaching initiative:

> we began by teaching algebra to other members of our year 8 top set; both ourselves and the class enjoyed the change and new ideas that came up and wanted to do more, so peer teaching has now spread to many other ability groups and into other subjects, not only Maths. [extract from student presentation]

At the RSA Academy, the Students as Learning Partners initiative that involves student observation of lessons is "a programme in which students and staff can work in partnership to improve teaching and learning." It is promoted "so that all staff, regardless of experience, and all students, regardless of ability, are able to participate."

The development of partnerships between mainstream secondary, primary, and special schools, for example, through student conferences, visits, and joint research projects, shows some schools addressing the challenge of working inclusively and learning from one another. Person-centered approaches in special schools are characterized by increased involvement of multiagency professionals in eliciting students' views, for example, speech and language therapists. This generates useful critical frameworks, where "communication is approached in its broadest sense using all modalities encompassing information which is generated verbally, through gesture, through body language, facial expression and behaviours" (Whitehurst, 2007, p. 158). The development of student voice in schools necessarily involves addressing more widely the "barriers to learning and participation" (Booth, Ainscow, Black-Hawkins, Vaughan, & Shaw, 2000, p. 13).

Strategic Approaches

Strategic approaches, calendared meetings, action planning, and identification of "leadership pathways" with linked, sustainable training opportunities (Brazier & Ferguson, 2008) have been identified by students as supporting their work. A number of schools now employ gap year students to coordinate student voice activities, this mirrored in the SSAT's annual appointment of Student Consultants since 2007. Variations of this model include the following:

- Paid employment for students in years 12 and 13, interviewed and appointed as student voice ambassadors.
- New roles and responsibilities for teaching staff, for example, "student voice coordinator," assistant head with responsibility for teaching and learning, and student voice.
- Extended roles for teaching assistants, for example, in supporting specific initiatives such as peer mediators.
- New appointments of other nonteaching staff, for example, youth workers, to coordinate student voice activities.

Curriculum Frameworks and Legislation

Such initiatives have the potential to not only contribute to school improvement but also develop in students the skills, qualities, and attributes to be active citizens. As such, many student voice activities fulfill selected national curriculum criteria and address key legislation, for example, in the promotion of Personal, Learning and Thinking Skills (PLTS), Social, Emotional Aspects of Learning (SEAL), Citizenship education, Personal Social Health and Economic Education (PSHE), and the five Every Child Matters outcomes.[4]

Furthermore, where work in schools on student voice is characterized by democratic approaches, which address young people's participative rights, it has the potential to address Articles 12 and 13 of the United Nations Convention on the Rights of the Child (UNCRC, 1989, p. 4):

> Parties shall assure to the child who is capable of forming his or her own views the right to express those views freely in all matters affecting the child, the views of the child being given due weight in accordance with the age and maturity of the child. (Article 12)

However, where this understanding is not shared or valued by the whole school community or does not inform student voice activities, these can be tokenistic and viewed by some teachers as interrupting learning, rather than being central to it. An issue often raised by students when I visit schools is that they are denied permission to miss lessons to carry out their roles and responsibilities and are not trusted to make informed judgments themselves.

What Values and Ways of Working Are Represented in Schools?

Comments from students would indicate that an ethos based on respect, characterized by positive relationships and trust, where students can take responsibility and where their views as learners are listened to, are preconditions for student voice to develop in a meaningful way. On the basis of my experience as a teacher involved in student voice projects and research and my role at the SSAT working with teachers and students in schools, it is possible to generate a list of features and underlying principles. These relate to values, training, participatory structures/roles, resources, school calendar and timetabling, communication, curriculum, teaching, and learning and characterize student voice in schools where students are engaged in school improvement.

---

4. PLTS is a National Curriculum framework identifying six groups of skills, behaviors, and personal qualities to inform curriculum planning. SEAL is a National Strategies framework for schools to develop children's social, emotional, and behavioral skills based on five social and emotional aspects of learning. Citizenship Education provides statutory programs of study to equip young people with the knowledge, skills, and understanding to play an effective role in public life. PSHE provides programs of study based on the Every Child Matters outcomes and builds on existing frameworks and guidelines in those areas. The five outcomes identified as part of the Every Child Matters consultation (2003) are represented in the five aims at the heart of the Children Act (2004) to be healthy, stay safe, enjoy and achieve, make a positive contribution, and achieve economic well-being. At the time of writing, all these frameworks were under review.

Values

The school ethos based on respect, this represented in daily interactions between teachers and students. There are opportunities for teachers and students working together to explore the school's values and determine how these are expressed/ represented in day-to-day life of school, for example, through relationships, teaching and learning, and school environment. There is a shared understanding that student voice models are based on inclusive practice, with agreement how this may be achieved.

Training

Continuous Professional Development (CPD) opportunities for staff and governors directly address aspects of student/learner voice and include contributions by students, for example, school induction programs. Equally, there is training provision for students so that they may develop the skills, understanding, and knowledge to support student voice roles/activities. There are opportunities for students to devise, organize, and lead training and conferences to take part in student induction and transfer/transition programs, for example, new intake events, which acknowledge students' capacity to initiate and lead change.

Participatory Structures and Roles

The emergence of new leadership, participatory and consultative structures, roles and activities, is evident. These may come about as a result of students and teachers working together or are student generated, for example, students as researchers, student department representatives, student associate governors, and gap year student consultants. Students choose and manage recruitment processes relating to student voice roles, with clear job descriptions, and, in taking inclusion seriously, the means to evaluate who is represented, and to adapt procedures as needed.

Resources

There is the provision of spaces (Fielding, 2001) to meet to discuss teaching and learning: this may involve invitations from students to staff to participate in student forum or from staff to students to participate in staff forum, for example, departmental meeting, INSED days, departmental meeting, staff training, and assemblies, with the potential to develop and embed more "joint forum."

Resources are allocated to student voice groups, for example, a budget or matched funding, an office or direct access to rooms for meeting/training (e.g., though agreed booking systems) and access to a computer/laptop and to reprographics.

School Calendar and Timetable

Student voice meetings and training are agreed with students involved and identified in the school calendar, with understanding that students will miss lessons as indicated/relevant. Selected events may be timetabled across the year, for example, student-led conferences, curriculum evaluation, and review.

Communication

Means of communicating and sharing student voice work with teachers, students, the whole school, and its wider community, for example, through school web site, newsletters, notice boards, school TV and radio, learning platforms, mobile phones, e-mails, presentations in assemblies, and lessons, are developed and agreed.

Curriculum, Teaching, and Learning

Students are involved in school improvement planning, for example, generating or contributing to action plans as part of the School Improvement Plan (SIP), and in school evaluation, for example, departmental reviews, students as researcher/ coresearchers' activities, and school satisfaction surveys. There is consultation with students when generating whole school/departmental policies, for example, healthy schools, assessment for learning, and use of new technologies in learning.

The school provides structured opportunities for students to provide feedback on and contribute to schemes of work, lesson planning, and lesson materials, with regular opportunities for students to co-teach or lead lessons/parts of lessons. Student's self-assessment and peer assessment are regular features of classroom practice, and there are daily opportunities for students to engage in learning conversations. Students take a lead role in their annual review meeting with parents/ carers and related agencies.

A Framework for Auditing Student Voice Activity

In training activities with schools, this framework has been a useful tool for teachers and students to examine how student voice is represented in their school, teachers from different departments and with different responsibilities, working with students of different ages to share their understandings, and to identify next steps.[5] The extent of teacher readiness and senior management support can strongly

---

5. Sample materials, in the form of principle statement cards for discussion and a student voice audit, can be viewed at http://www.ssatrust.org.uk/innovation/studentvoicenetworks/documents/publications/module3_13.pdf and module3_5pdf and form part of training materials I produced for the SSAT in "Introducing Student Voice: training pack 1."

influence whether change then comes about as the result of small groups of volunteers working together on specific initiatives or whether a whole school approach is adopted.

Conclusion

The reasons for teacher and student commitment to student voice appear to remain independent of changes in official educational policy, relating more to the sort of learning community they aspire to create, the values that may inform it, and how these are represented in daily interactions.

Student voice may be represented in schools by a discrete set of initiatives, which can promote increased student participation in some aspects of school life. Case studies suggest that there has been a shift in recent years, from activities that are removed from the business of the classroom to initiatives that enable teachers and students to raise and explore questions about learning and about how student voice is defined. Student and teacher testimonies illustrate the benefits of such partnerships.

If schools are to develop democratic and participatory practices that make a difference to teaching, learning, and relationships and that better reflect the needs of learners, future curriculum models need to be informed by the views, experiences, understandings, and aspirations of all young people. In considering the principles and values that may underpin such forms of engagement, student voice may be represented and developed more widely as an integral part of an inclusive curriculum and ways of learning in schools. What is needed is coherent use of emergent principles to inform an educational paradigm that better reflects learning for C21st learners and the C21st and that results from consultation and dialogue between students and teachers. Such dialogue, if it is to contribute to school improvement, must involve making accessible to students the issues raised in academic research and listening to the solutions students suggest.

References

Black, P., & Wiliam, D. (1998). *Inside the black box*. London: nferNelson.

Booth, T., Ainscow, M., Black-Hawkins, K., Vaughan, M., & Shaw, L. (2000). *The index of inclusion: Developing learning and participation in schools*. London: CSIE.

Brazier, O., & Ferguson, C. (2008). Developing a student leadership model: For students, by students. In: P. Chambers (Ed.), *Learning with students* (pp. 14–18). London: Specialist Schools and Academies Trust.

Cowling, E., Hill, L., Ritchie, R., & Long, H. (2010). Creating a global village college. *Meeting the challenge of C21st century education and a global economy* (pp. 36–41). London: NESTA & SSAT. Retrieved from http://www.nesta.org.uk/library/documents/meeting-the-challenge-v6.pdf.

Eadsforth, D., Higgins, C., Croft, A., Rudge, R., & Gomersall, H. (2010). Globalisation: A shared teaching resource. *Meeting the challenge of C21st century education and a global economy* (pp. 54–55). London: NESTA & SSAT. Retrieved from http://www.nesta.org.uk/library/documents/meeting-the-challenge-v6.pdf.

Fielding, M. (2001). Beyond the rhetoric of student voice: New departures or new constraints in the transformation of 21st century schooling? *Forum, 43*(2), Retrieved from www.triangle.co.uk.

Flutter, J., & Rudduck, J. (2004). *Consulting pupils: What's in it for schools?*. London: RoutledgeFalmer.

Grace, A. (2010). Technology on trial. *Meeting the challenge of C21st century education and a global economy* (pp. 26–31). London: NESTA & SSAT. Retrieved from http://www.nesta.org.uk/library/documents/meeting-the-challenge-v6.pdf.

Hargreaves, D. (2004). *Personalising learning 2: Student voice and assessment for learning.* London: Specialist Schools and Academies Trust.

Keely, A., & Walker, P. (2008). Student voice at Veralum School: Participation in observation and feedback. In: P. Chambers (Ed.), *Learning with students* (pp. 35–38). London: Specialist Schools and Academies Trust.

Kestenbaum, J. (2008). Introduction. In: E. Levenson (Ed.), *Learning for the future* (p. 5). London: NESTA.

Love, M. (2008). Engaging students and developing student leadership. In: P. Chambers (Ed.), *Learning with students* (pp. 10–13). London: Specialist Schools and Academies Trust.

Mitchell, D., & Debere, S. (2010). Project 9: ICT curriculum co-construction. *Meeting the challenge of C21st century education and a global economy* (pp. 22–25). London: NESTA & SSAT. Retrieved from http://www.nesta.org.uk/library/documents/meeting-the-challenge-v6.pdf.

Preece, R., Brennan, H., Whittingham, H., Kelly, J., & Mann, L. (2008). Developing a student leadership model: For students, by students. In: P. Chambers (Ed.), *Learning with students* (pp. 39–44). London: Specialist Schools and Academies Trust.

Rudduck, J., & Flutter, J. (2004). *How to improve your school.* London: Continuum.

Rudduck, J., & McIntyre, D. (2007). *Improving learning through consulting pupils.* London: Routledge.

SSAT. (2008). *Learning with students.* In P. Chambers (Ed.). London: Specialist Schools and Academies Trust.

United Nations Convention on the Rights of the Child. (1989). Convention on the rights of the child. Retrieved from http://www2.ohchr.org/english/law/crc.htm.

Vincent, Z. (2010). Next Generation Kernow. *Meeting the challenge of C21st century education and a global economy* (pp. 32–35). London: NESTA & SSAT. Retrieved from http://www.nesta.org.uk/library/documents/meeting-the-challenge-v6.pdf.

Watkins, C., Carnell, E., & Lodge, L. (2007). *Effective learning in classrooms.* London: Paul Chapman Publishing.

West, S., & Griffiths, H. (2010). Developing the use of new technology in a specialist technology college. *Meeting the challenge of C21st century education and a global economy* (pp. 46–53). London: NESTA & SSAT, London. Retrieved from http://www.nesta.org.uk/library/documents/meeting-the-challenge-v6.pdf.

Whitehurst, T. (2007). Changing perspectives on disability and inclusion. In: C. Carpenter & J. Egerton (Eds), *New horizons in special education: Evidence-based practice in action* (pp. 155–169). Sunfield: Sunfield Publications.

Chapter 18

Students Training Teachers

Joy Morgan

Abstract

This chapter explores the potential and possibilities for Student Voice
initiatives to influence learning in the classroom by structuring partnerships
between trainee teachers and students. It offers practical advice on selecting
and developing students to excel in this role as well as providing tried and tested
suggestions for quality assurance and measuring impact. The project considers
how students co-planning lessons with trainee teachers can result in higher
quality learning experiences in the classroom. Students support the trainee in
constructing lessons which are interactive, personalised and engaging whilst
providing opportunities for collaborative learning, differentiation and assessing
students' learning needs. Building on this partnership, students observe the
trainee teacher in the classroom before having a constructive conversation
about the learning taking place and how this might be extended and refined.
The combination of co-planning and observing creates a powerful resource for
teacher training. Student leadership offers both confidence building and
challenge to students and trainee teachers alike.

The project began in 2003 in a girls' school of approximately 1400 students in
Tower Hamlets, a deprived area of east London. Over 80% of students spoke
English as a second language, the majority being Bengali speakers. In addition
there were significant numbers of refugees from Somalia and Afghanistan with
increasing numbers of Eastern European students. Since its introduction, the
project has been set up in over 50 schools including selective, mixed, boys and
inner city schools.

Keywords: Teacher training; partnership; co-planning; observation; dialogue;
impact

The Student Voice Handbook: Bridging the Academic/Practitioner Divide
Copyright © 2011 by Emerald Group Publishing Limited
All rights of reproduction in any form reserved
ISBN: 978-1-78052-040-7

Introduction

Developing a Student Voice initiative aimed at ensuring students are able to have a genuine, measurable and effective input into teacher training proved to be surprisingly rewarding and powerful. Until early 2003, my understanding of Student Voice had been confined to seeking students' opinions about issues affecting them at school but limited to experiences outside the classroom. Although this was extremely useful and undeniably important, students' potential for positively influencing their learning experiences in a structured, ethical manner was conspicuously absent.

I was aware that Fielding (2001) had raised questions about schools' motives for initiating student voice activity. Fielding asked, 'Are we witnessing the emergence of something genuinely new, exciting and emancipatory that builds on rich traditions of democratic renewal and transformation?' This became a useful reference point; this encouraged me to ensure students work was of real value, resulting in changes to teachers' practice that were not simply tokenistic.

My role as professional development leader based in a large inner-city, multicultural girls' school included overseeing trainee teachers who needed to spend two periods of 12–15 weeks developing their classroom practice in schools. The school would host approximately 12 trainee teachers at any one time. The school was situated in one of the most deprived areas of London so aspiring teachers were presented with exciting, challenging and varied experiences. This was a perfect forum to create opportunities for students and trainee teachers to work in partnership. Although trainees already had a wealth of opportunities to develop their classroom practice and to push the boundaries of their potential, there was no input from students. I became increasingly aware that trainees were so focussed on their own performance in the classroom — what they would be doing, saying and asking — that they often forget that what really matters is students' learning.

The project described below involved a group of carefully selected students who would observe trainees in the classroom before having a constructive dialogue about the learning taking place. They would go on to suggest how to develop the learning further, following this with written feedback. Later on, students began to work in partnership with trainee teachers to plan lessons, using their wealth of knowledge about effective learning to devise lessons which challenged and included all learners through a wide range of learning opportunities. The first stage was to pilot the project with a small number of students. After the pilot stage, the project was refined and expanded so more students were able to take on this leadership role. Over time, the project grew to include experienced as well as trainee teachers, in a wide range of schools. The chapter outlines: suggestions for recruiting students for the roles of Student Observers and Student Co-planners; a format for training students; key points for the contract; details of the observation form developed by students; protocols to build teachers' confidence in the value of the project; the processes involved building partnerships between trainee teachers and students; ideas for measuring the impact; and the benefits for participants.

Recruitment Processes

During the pilot phase, I decided to limit the number of students to eight. This enabled me to work very closely with them, building their confidence and ensuring teachers received a high-quality experience when being observed or having a dialogue with students about learning. Once this first group of Student Observers became more independent, I planned to use them to recruit and train the next cohort of Student Observers — a plan that worked well in practice. To ensure the success of the project, students were taken through a variety of recruitment stages. Initially, the Head of Year was asked to recommend students who were reliable, trustworthy and reflective as well as individuals with excellent empathy skills. The second stage was to explain the project and expectations in full so students could decide if they were interested in taking on the role of Student Observer. A small number of students decided not to take part at this point, either because they felt they could not commit the time necessary or they felt uncomfortable about talking to teachers about their classroom practice.

Those who were enthusiastic and felt able to devote time to the project were invited to a formal interview. The interview covered reasons for wanting to take part, the skills a Student Observer would need and how they would handle feeding back to a teacher whose lesson had not gone well. To be offered a place, students had to demonstrate an understanding that this project would be supportive and developmental, not judgemental.

> I was really excited when I was chosen because I realised that I could make a difference; I could give my point of view to teachers and help them with problems. [Syeda, aged 14]

This recruitment process meant that students saw acceptance onto the project as an achievement and a privilege. A student reinforced this when she said:

> I was so proud to be chosen. It felt like I had to get through a lot of stages so if you get picked you feel happy and proud of yourself. It's like a privilege. I couldn't believe that someone thought I was good enough to do it. [Jamilla, aged 14]

Training for the Role of Student Observer

Successful students then started a comprehensive training programme in preparation for starting the dialogue about learning with trainee teachers. Key elements of the training included: building trust in the team; identifying what makes a good lesson and a good teacher; teaching a mini-lesson; receiving feedback; a trial observation using a recorded lesson; getting the language right and capturing students' thoughts about the project. I examine these elements below:

1. *Building trust in the team.* Students needed to get to know each other and feel confident about asking for support when necessary. In addition, I needed to get to

know them and build trust. With this in mind, the session started with a team activity (building a bridge with tape and newspaper to support the weight of a shoe) followed by identifying the skills needed to work successfully in a team.

2. *What makes a good lesson and a good teacher?* Half the students brainstormed, 'What makes a good teacher' and the other half considered, 'What makes a good lesson?' As the students presented their decisions, they were challenged to explain what you would actually see and hear in a classroom to indicate each point they made.

3. *Teaching a mini-lesson.* Using the factors they identified, students planned and delivered a 15 minute lesson. Students repeatedly commented on this being the most useful part of the training process:

> It was really good because, once we got the opportunity to teach people and see the other side of what we were doing, we actually realised how hard that was and how much teachers have to do. When you are sitting in the class, you don't realise how much teachers have to prepare to teach a lesson. It made us believe in what we were trying to do and that it was going to help. [Lauren, aged 13]

4. *Receiving feedback.* After the mini-lesson, students fed back to each other on what had gone well and what would have improved the mini-lesson. The purpose of this was to enable students to experience feedback to so they would understand that teachers may be anxious about the students' feedback.

5. *A trial observation using a recorded lesson.* Students practised using the observation form and identified what would help the teacher to improve the learning experience for students. The Student Observers needed to understand that their suggestions should be limited to one or two and be focused on what would have the biggest impact on learning. In addition, written comments needed to be constructive, not critical.

6. *A demonstration of how not to run a feedback session.* Students used this poor demonstration to identify good practice and effective communication skills, resulting in their own guidelines for effective feedback.

7. *Getting the language right.* Feedback needed to be depersonalised and constructive so that trainees were both encouraged and challenged to improve learning for students. A student explained this to visiting teachers who were planning to use the model in their own school:

> I always say, 'Have you considered trying ...' I never tell the teacher they must do something or should do it in a particular way. It's important not to criticise so I might say, 'The writing on the whiteboard was hard to read'. I'd never say, 'Your writing is really messy'. When I find it hard, I try to explain how to make it better for students so I say, 'Students need more variety in a lesson to keep them motivated for the whole hour' and then give them some ideas of how they could have different activities. I wouldn't say, 'The lesson was really boring. [Francesca, aged 12]

8. *Capturing students' thoughts about the project.* Students' thoughts, hopes and concerns were recorded. This proved useful later as baseline data when considering the impact of the project on the Student Observers.

During the training, the first group of 13–14 year old students decided their aim would be: 'To leave the teacher feeling confident, competent and valued, yet clear how to develop'. I have used this aim ever since with teachers who are preparing to observe colleagues and with Student Observers.

Contract

To ensure trainee teachers felt comfortable working with students in this way, each student signed a contract emphasising:

- the importance of confidentiality;
- the aim of supporting, encouraging and challenging teachers to provide high-quality learning experiences from a student perspective;
- the need to consider how their feedback would impact on teachers' confidence, development and self-esteem;
- the agreement to represent the school's core values by behaving responsibly and professionally and
- the requirement to keep in close contact with the project leader for quality assurance.

Practice Observation

The next step was to practise, in pairs, on willing volunteers. A number of teachers were not comfortable about being observed by students so this had to be completely voluntary. Members of the Senior Leadership Team as well as teachers in their first year of teaching and Heads of Faculty were involved. This range helped the credibility of the project, especially as it was such a positive experience for everyone. The teachers were keen to talk about the observation and feedback in the staffroom:

> I was blown away by the quality of their feedback. [Marufa, Maths teacher in her third year of teaching]

> I don't think I've ever felt this good … they even talked about my body language. What was most amazing is what they said about getting the class to think. They said that I really make them think. I'd never thought about that before. They were quite assertive though! They felt my starter was a bit long and suggested another way of doing it so it relates more to the next part of the lesson. I'm definitely going to do the things they said. [Anne, Head of English]

The teachers' enthusiasm helped allay fears and generate interest. In addition, a recently qualified Drama teacher and a Student Observer explained the project at a staff meeting. The former enthused about how valuable the experience had been and the latter won everyone over when she announced:

> I had no idea that teaching was so difficult and complex. I take my hat off to every one of you. [Nilima, aged fourteen]

Students' Observation Form

The first cohort to become Student Observers used the observation forms provided by the trainees' universities but they quickly decided to design their own form. Each new cohort of Student Observers chose to adapt the form and yet the content never failed to impress.

For example, students consider:

- *Role modelling*: speaking to students with respect, body language, avoiding confrontation, punctuality and organisation, high expectations, humour and voice (tone, volume and pace).
- *Lesson planning:* inspiring learning objectives, how does the lesson meet the needs of the most able/students with special needs including dyslexia/the least able/students whose first language is not English? How does the teacher promote inclusion?
- *Assessment*: opportunities for reflection, self-evaluation, peer marking and peer assessment, use of higher order questions, monitoring progress and understanding during the lesson, quality of marking.
- *Classroom management*: layout of furniture to support activities, tidiness, attractiveness of displays, students' access to resources, grouping and seating arrangements.
- *Behaviour management*: relationships, keeping students on task, school rules, handling difficult behaviours, communication, dealing with latecomers.
- *Resources*: how appropriate are resources for meeting the learning objectives and students' needs? Use of technology, quality of resources, layout and content.

These sections are followed by:

- a summary of the lesson;
- key points for feedback;
- suggestions and
- comments by the teacher observed (optional).

Protocols to Build Teachers' Confidence in the Value of the Project

I was aware that the project was dependent on building trust between students and teachers. As Rudduck and Flutter (2002) note:

it takes time and very careful preparation to build a climate in which both teachers and pupils feel comfortable working together on a constructive view of aspects of teaching, learning and schooling.

In light of this, students devised guidelines for themselves (this became important for each cohort of students). I was aware that students needed to be highly professional; failure to turn up or poor quality feedback would have been seized upon by those who felt that students should not have been given this task.

The students decided to:

- work in pairs, observing and feeding back together;
- set up a communication system so they could cover for each other if absent or not allowed to miss their own lesson;
- feedback in the teaching room at the start of lunchtime on the same day as the observation or the following day for afternoon observations;
- arrive 5 min before the start of the lesson, whenever possible. This enabled the students to greet the teacher, collect the lesson plan and organise somewhere to sit before the class arrived;
- take all the paperwork with them at the end of a lesson observation so there was no possibility of other students in the class reading their comments and
- hand all copies of the lesson observation forms to the trainee teacher at the end of the feedback and to keep no record of the observation.

In addition, the students felt it would be better not to observe someone who taught them. Later in the project, students did observe their own teachers and this has worked well. However, I would always check with the teacher first to make sure she/he is comfortable with this arrangement.

Partnerships with Trainee Teachers

When the next group of trainee teachers arrived, the Student Observers greeted them and took them on a tour of the school to start building working relationships. Students also ran a session on 'Lesson Planning: a Student Perspective' which enabled trainees to see just how much students had to offer. A pair of Student Observers was assigned to each trainee for the duration of the school placement (a three to four month period). Students organised the observations themselves as this had proven difficult and time consuming for me to do for them during the practice stage.

I kept in regular contact with both the students and trainees to monitor the impact of the project and extent of the interactions. In addition, I quality assured the observation forms and feedback, meeting the students when I felt they would benefit from discussing any aspect of the observation. I was careful to ask the trainee teachers about their experience, although on most occasions trainees would seek me out directly after their feedback to let me know how "amazing" or "incredible" it had been. The following quotations illustrate typical reactions during this pilot phase:

> I found the whole process very useful. I think new teachers often worry so much about teaching, they forget what students are doing. This made me really think about what the lesson is like for students. They gave me so much praise - it was wonderful. [Trainee Science teacher]

> I am extremely impressed by the way the students conducted themselves and displayed a very professional attitude. Their feedback was very valuable, concise and valid. They were clearly concerned to boost my confidence and were very positive in their feedback, while providing realistic and well judged targets. Well done to the students. [Trainee Drama teacher]

Student Co-Planners

After about a year, the second project, Student Co-planners, emerged. This resulted from a Student Observer who had been part of a class (not observing) where the trainee had had a very difficult lesson. At the end, the student lingered until everyone had left and asked the trainee if he would like help planning his next lesson. The trainee was delighted, the lesson was planned jointly and the next encounter with the class was far more successful. The logical thing to do was to build in opportunities for the Student Observers to co-plan lessons as part of their remit with trainee teachers.

The Student Observers had demonstrated their extensive knowledge about good learning strategies so a short training session was all that was required to prepare them. In fact, I decided the aim of the training would be, 'To remind students of their wealth of knowledge about what makes a good lesson and good learning'. The half-day training session focussed on the importance of collaborative learning followed by deconstructing an exemplary lesson into its component parts. For this, students considered collaborative, visual, auditory and kinaesthetic learning as well as perseverance and assessing students' understanding and learning needs using three key questions:

- What examples of each did you see in the lesson?
- How did this impact on the learning?
- What other ideas do you have to extend this aspect of the learning?

By the end of this activity, conducted as a carousel where students worked in pairs or threes to add to each others' ideas, students could see that they had a myriad of suggestions for learning activities.

The next step was to practise on volunteers who had been briefed to challenge the students to explain suggestions in detail, provide alternative ideas if the teacher was unsure of the first idea and to ask their advice about a wide range of learning issues. The result was a group of teachers who left the practice planning session surprised by the wealth of ideas and expertise that students offered and keen to be involved in the project further:

> I am being observed by the Head Teacher on Thursday. I'm going to use this plan! [John, Head of Science]

> That was amazing. I gave them a map and a question and they have produced a brilliant lesson. It's a great Geography lesson. It's much better than I would have managed on my own. I will use it next week. Why haven't we done this with students before? [Louise, Deputy Head Teacher]

Co-Planning Process

Once the training was completed, students worked in pairs to co-plan a lesson with a trainee, observe the lesson and provide feedback before setting a time to plan another lesson and restart the cycle. This enabled real and meaningful partnerships to develop. Students were able to see that their advice and suggestions were implemented and that classroom practice changed as a direct result of the intervention.

> I couldn't believe that a teacher actually did what I suggested. I thought he'd just go 'Yeah, yeah' but he actually did everything I suggested. I'm so proud. [Shahida, aged 12]

In addition, a number of experienced teachers requested a pair of students to work with, sometimes re-writing complete schemes of work. They were astute at handling sensitive topics such as sex education and teaching about the holocaust:

> The students save me time. I can just take a learning objective to our meeting and they transform it into a really interesting lesson in no time at all. I asked them about differentiation and they didn't seem to know what I meant but once I explained it, they just said, 'Oh yes, you just need to …' And they differentiated the whole thing. Chrissie and Isobel have become my benchmark now. Even when I'm not with them, I think to myself, 'What would Chrissie and Isobel think of this?' and I know if I've got it right or not. [Jenny, Religious Education teacher]

Students proved helpful in revising seating plans, often providing insights into relationships between students that teachers are unaware of. They were surprisingly open about the most effective groupings in a variety of different contexts and were able to support struggling and new teachers with managing behaviour. On many occasions, trainee teachers commented that they felt they could ask students questions they felt unwilling or embarrassed to ask other teachers:

> I was really struggling with the long lessons but I didn't want to ask my mentor. I take up so much of his time already. It's great to have the students there. They don't judge you but they do tell you straight. [Trainee French teacher]

Measuring the Impact of the Intervention by Student Observers and Co-Planners

Formal evaluation of the project indicates a significant positive impact. For example:

- Comparisons of lesson plans before and after student input demonstrated that the students' role resulted in a wider variety of collaborative learning activities and increased opportunities for higher order thinking.
- Formal observations of trainee teachers by Subject Mentors or University Tutors showed positive changes to behaviour management and learning opportunities for all abilities which, when explored during the feedback, could be traced back to students' advice and suggestions.
- Interviews with the trainees before and after their involvement in the project chronicled their developing understanding of how students learn, how to differentiate, manage group work and the ability to see students as individuals rather than as a mass to be controlled!
- Interviewing students indicated that they believed the project had enabled them to gain a variety of skills, for example, communication skills and the ability to lead constructive dialogue around difficult issues. They often identified increased self-confidence and a new found belief in their ability to impact positively on their classroom experiences and more widely in their community.

> At the beginning of the project, I didn't feel as confident as I am now to speak in public to other people but now I really like having the chance to talk to teachers. I feel I can put my point of view across and it will be listened to. It's like I can have a say in the school and how the teachers teach. I think it will help me in my future. [Thomas, aged 15]

Benefits for the Trainee Teachers

Initially, I believed that students would have the most to gain in terms of confidence. I did not anticipate the enormous impact the students would have on the self-confidence of the trainee teachers involved and how effective their insights would be. Although being observed by students was initially more daunting for trainees (and experienced teachers) than being observed by colleagues or University Tutors, the feedback repeatedly provided the trainees with increased confidence. This encouraged teachers to try a wider range of behaviour management and learning activities in the classroom.

> This was a very positive experience. I was anxious beforehand but I have come away with much more confidence and a couple of very important changes I will be making to my teaching. [Mary, Trainee English teacher]

Occasionally, students enabled trainees to persevere when they were close to giving up their teacher training programme.

> It's been really good for my self-confidence. I try to make it interesting for students but when you hear them say it, it's really encouraging. I sort of feel I can do the job now. I was having doubts about it all — it's so hard. When I heard them say they liked my lesson, it meant so much. [Alan, Trainee Maths teacher]

Conclusion

Having established the success of the Student Observers and Co-planners at the pilot stage, the project was expanded within the school and introduced to schools throughout South East England and North West England. Students played a key role in presenting their project at conferences and to visiting students and teachers. Each cohort of Student Co-planners and Student Observers participated in the recruitment and training of the next cohort. At their suggestion, an additional question was added to the interview to find out if students were prepared to catch up on any work they missed and how they would manage the extra workload. Similarly, more time was given to assessment strategies in the classroom as a result of their feedback on the training programme.

I now train 11–12 year old students for the role of Student Observers and Co-planners. This enables students to develop their expertise and empathy before the demands of external examinations make it difficult for them to be out of class for observations. The project has been trialled with 10-year olds who were insightful and adept. However, the low number of trainee teachers in smaller primary schools meant that the initial investment in time was only worthwhile if experienced teachers were interested in working with children in this way. This was also the case in schools that worked with fewer trainee teachers.

It continues to be an enormous pleasure and privilege to work with students in this way and the experience has significantly changed my views of their capabilities. As a Subject Mentor told me after watching a student feedback to a trainee who was having enormous difficulties in class:

> I have learned so much from watching Halima. She handled this difficult situation so well and wasn't swayed by any excuses he made. I wish I was half as good as her. [Tim, Head of Psychology]

Feedback from schools running similar projects shows that Student Voice in Teacher Training worked well wherever it was carefully set up and monitored. Student Co-planners worked successfully as a stand-alone project and was often an excellent first step in a school which may not have been ready to embrace student observers. Over the years, trainee and experienced teachers, even those who were sceptical at first, have acknowledged the value of co-planning or being observed by students:

> It's definitely worth doing. I was sceptical when you introduced it but I'm converted! They had so many great ideas. [Adam, History Teacher]

Students are our richest resource. They have the time to work alongside teachers in a way that other teachers can only dream of. They have the experience of being taught and taking part in an enormous variety of learning activities which provides them with a wealth of ideas to share and they do this generously, professionally and skilfully. The final words from Neepa, a student from the pilot group of Student Observers, encapsulate the essence of the project:

> I hope my advice and work are valuable to the teachers. For me, it's helped my personal development and communication skills with teachers and students. It's helped me understand the way I learn. I assumed that everyone was the same as me and they all learnt the same way but now I understand about different learning styles, I can use this to help when I get stuck. I've learnt so much about students as well as about teachers. I think everyone should just try it; it can't hurt and you'll gain a lot from it. The students are just there to help. [Neepa, aged 17]

References

Fielding, M. (2001). *Forum for Providing 13-19 Comprehensive Education*, *4.3*(2), 100.
Rudduck, J., & Flutter, J. (2002). *Cambridge Journal of Education*, *30*(1), 53.

Chapter 19

Enabling Students' Right to Participate in a Large Sixth Form College: Different Voices, Mechanisms and Agendas

David Godfrey

Abstract

The Sixth Form College Farnborough is a large, thriving Beacon College in North East Hampshire, England, with over 3000 full-time 16- to 18-year-old students in post-compulsory education. The college has an active Student Association (SA), whose committee members have contributed their perceptions through a student-led series of interviews on issues of 'student voice'. These interviews, conducted by a member of the SA, reveal their views regarding the impact they have had on decision-making and college life in general. As the author of this chapter, and at the time a member of staff at the college, I write this chapter drawing upon my own insider's knowledge. In this way, my views are expressed alongside some student comments, informed by some of the literature on students-as-researchers and student voice. These observations are framed by Lundy's model (2007) for applying Article 12 of the UN Convention on the Rights of the Child in relation to student's rights to be consulted over decisions in schools and colleges.

Keywords: Research-engagement; action research; young researchers; student voice; student council; students-as-researchers

Introduction

This chapter seeks to outline the characteristics of The Sixth Form College Farnborough in relation to student voice, specifically, the extent to which it is

The Student Voice Handbook: Bridging the Academic/Practitioner Divide
Copyright © 2011 by Emerald Group Publishing Limited
All rights of reproduction in any form reserved
ISBN: 978-1-78052-040-7

successful at involving its students in decision-making through the Student Association (SA) and within an environment of research-engagement. The Sixth Form College Farnborough is the UK's largest Sixth Form College, with well over 3000 full-time students, the vast majority of whom take two-year, advanced-level courses. Its position in the country (North East Hampshire) means that it has an intake from mainly (relatively) affluent areas around Hampshire, from bordering Surrey and some from Berkshire and beyond. Sixth Form Colleges are state-funded institutions, characterised by their provision of mainly academic rather than vocational qualifications and act as 'the sixth form' for linked 11-16 schools or as an alternative to continuing into years 12 and 13 at the student's own secondary school. Heavily oversubscribed, it has an excellent local reputation due to its glowing inspection reports from Ofsted[1] (the Office for Standards in Education) and its value-added results data. The college operates a non-selective admission process, taking students from a broad spectrum of abilities, unlike many other state or private schools providing the same advanced (A level) qualifications. (Thus, ranks in school league tables based on final examination results, rather than 'value-added', provide an unfair comparison.) The majority of students at Farnborough go on to universities and colleges of Higher Education in the United Kingdom, the most popular destinations being Portsmouth, Bournemouth, Southampton and London.

The author is an assistant director of Personalised Learning, whose specific remit is to build the college's research-engagement, mainly through a series of small-scale action research projects carried out by teachers each year. This approach has been cited by Ofsted, who, in addition to their role as a schools' inspectorate, put together examples of good practice for the Learning Skills and Improvement Service (LSIS) Excellence Gateway.[2] The college's research-engagement has also been formally recognised by the National Foundation for Educational Research (NFER).[3] Farnborough's teachers are well motivated, and its senior management has introduced many innovative and progressive teaching and learning initiatives. Taking a look at the contents page of the termly publication 'Voice',[4] with articles from teachers on Assessment for Learning, action researchers, the 'young researchers' group, learner voice and experiential learning', can give the reader a glimpse into the life of a dynamic workplace, relentlessly focused on continuous

---

1. Ofsted carry out inspections of a wide range of educational establishments in England, including schools, colleges and centres of initial teacher education in England. Its inspection reports are visible to parents, teachers, policy makers and all who might be interested. In The Sixth Form College Farnborough's last Ofsted inspection in 2007, provision was rated as 'outstanding' (grade 1) in each of the report's five categories.
2. The Learning and Skills Improvement Service works in England's 'Learning and Skills Sector' (schools and colleges in the 16 to adult phase); for a fuller description of its role, see http://www.lsis.org.uk/AboutLSIS/Pages/default.aspx. One function of LSIS is to collect and publish examples of good practice in the sector on their good practice pages (http://www.excellencegateway.org.uk/page.aspx?o=167263).
3. http://www.nfer.ac.uk/schools/research-engaged-award/past-recipients.cfm.
4. Internal college publication that aims to 'share, focus and collaborate', Issue 1, December 2010.

improvement and its mantra of 'Improving Students' Achievements', the principal's one overriding mission statement.

Since 2004, the author has led a well-known programme of teacher action research, with links to the NFER[5] and, more recently, the Centre for the Use of Research and Evidence in Education (CUREE[6]). Over the present academic year, the college has also become involved in the NFER's 'young researchers' project,[7] aimed at developing guidance for staff on how to work with young people engaged in research projects. The potential for opening up a new voice in the college, that is, where staff and students are engaged in a dialogic co-construction of pedagogical understanding, is explored later.

It is in this context we turn to the broader setting in which to place Farnborough's 'student voice' practices and realities.

The National Context and the Rights of the Child

Student voice has been promoted through three broad movements in the United Kingdom — Human Rights, School Improvement and Citizenship Education — and can thus be seen as an enshrined right of all 'children' (and in this context, young adults), an invaluable tool for the promotion of school improvement and, as a way of embodying the principles of a democratic society within citizenship education (Rudduck & Flutter, 2004, p. 100).

Student councils are a well-known way of responding to the various top-down initiatives, legislative frameworks and traditions for pupil, student or learner voice, consultation or participation. Although there has been considerable focus within the college on the previous UK government's 'Every Child Matters' framework (DfES, 2006), the issue of young people's indisputable legal right to consultation has, from my professional perspective, not been strongly highlighted. However, as Roberts and Nash (2009, p. 175) state,

> Article 12 of the 1989 United Nations Convention on the Rights of the Child placed in law the rights of young people to be consulted about matters which affect their lives. (UN, 1989)

Given that Article 12 of the UN Convention of the Rights of the Child (CRC) states that 'the views of the child (be) given due weight in accordance with the age and maturity of the child' (Osler, 2010, p. 21), young adult students (16–18), who are

---

5. The NFER is a not-for-profit organisation that provides research, assessment and information for the education and children services sectors (http://www.nfer.ac.uk/about-nfer/about-nfer_home.cfm).

6. CUREE is an independent company with a particular focus on improving the connections between knowledge and practice in education (http://www.curee-paccts.com/about-us).

7. See http://www.nfer.ac.uk/nfer/research/projects/developing-young-researchers/developing-young-researchers_home.cfm.

moving towards voting age in their second year at college, might therefore reasonably expect their views to be taken pretty seriously.

Experience at some schools shows that student councils are often tokenistic and not valued by teachers or senior management (e.g. Klein, 2003, p. 40). Students sometimes complain that these councils are only involved in trivial matters, hence one Midland schoolboy's comment in Osler's book, about the need for more than just a 'poxy little council which discusses how much the price of chips are' (Osler, 2010, p. 110). It seems clear then that the mere establishment of a student council or procedures for consulting pupils is not enough to guarantee compliance with the spirit of the CRC. Laura Lundy's (2007) four-pronged model for applying the principles of Article 12 in practice proves a useful one to use as a test in the Farnborough context. Lundy suggests how children's rights should be enacted within the context of all of the rights set out in the CRC, but with a central focus on Article 12:

> Space: Children must be given the opportunity to express a view
>
> Voice: Children must be facilitated to express their views
>
> Audience: The view must be listened to
>
> Influence: The view must be acted upon, as appropriate. (Lundy, 2007, p. 933)

Later, I present some observations and comments about Farnborough's SA, in relation to Lundy's model:

Space

The SA committee is an elected body of 12 students, voted every year after the Easter holidays, by the whole student population. 'Turnout' for the elections is very high, helped by the convenience of the electronic voting system. The roles represent a wide range of interests and activities: president, vice-president, treasurer, charities, events, personalised learning, publications, community links, performing arts, sports, environment and communications. The SA committee has its own office and each member its own subcommittees that work on relevant activities during the year. The student quotes (later) are taken from a series of interviews conducted by Amy Grandvoinet (Personalised Learning Officer) on fellow members of the SA committee as well as from Amy herself.

Given the large student population, gaining representation from all students is a particular challenge, and this is to some extent achieved by having a tutor representative from each tutorial group.[8] These students can then pass on the views of students from each group in assembly meetings, to which all tutor reps are invited.

---

8. Each student is assigned to a 'personal tutor'. These are specialist pastoral tutors, paid on a management scale, with responsibility for 120 students. All personal tutors also teach their specialist curriculum subjects on a reduced timetable. This is sometimes referred to as the 'super tutor' system.

These provide a mechanism for a dialogue between, in theory, all students and their elected SA committee:

> The tutor rep system gives more people an opportunity to communicate with us. Because it's such a big institution, it's difficult for us, in a position of representatives, to make sure that we are actually reflecting in what we do what people want. [Richard, 18 years old]

Direct feedback to and from the SA has also been recently facilitated by the emergence of college Virtual Learning Environment's (VLE) (MOODLE) discussion forum feature.

Voice

Simply having the opportunity to vote and to express a view does not guarantee the wholehearted involvement of the entire student body. In one large Northern Ireland[9] study, a common observation was that teachers did not encourage students enough to express their views (Lundy, 2007, p. 935). Chris Eustace, Lead Tutor for Student Liaison at the college states,

> In my opinion the student voice in college could be strong but isn't always. There is a lot of apathy around and it is our job to promote "Student Voice" and prove to students that we do listen to them and it works. [Chris, Lead tutor for student liaison]

Helen, 18 years old (SA communications officer), adds a related view:

> By using the tutor rep system, everyone has a **chance** (her emphasis) to voice their opinion.

However, some personal tutors may assume that 'young adult' students should not need much encouragement or may be wary of interfering with the process of tutor reps consulting their fellow tutees. In practice, the tutor group benefits if they have a tutor rep who is reliable at turning up to meetings, confident at taking students' views and articulate in feeding back discussions from assembly meetings.

The recent introduction of the college's VLE for SA communications was also mentioned:

> There may be rather shy students that are just a bit scared about talking to people, so maybe a forum would be good for those people who are a bit nervous about talking to individuals. [Charlie, 17 years old]

---

9. Northern Ireland Committee on the Rights of the Child.

It would also be naive to have a picture of universal enthusiasm among the student population to be involved in the college's decision-making. Although first-year tutorial groups often have keenly fought 'mini-elections' for the tutor rep role, in the upper sixth tutorials, the personal tutor will sometimes have to cajole a 'suitable' student into representing their group.

Audience

Having one senior member of the tutorial team whose job is to liaise closely with the SA sends out a strong signal that student voice is valued. The principal also shows willingness to listen to students' views, helping to create a culture of listening that is borne out in some of SA members' comments:

> There's a freedom to say what you'd like to in a respectful and communicative way; you're working with the staff and working with each other. There's a really healthy relationship. [Maddy, 17 years old]

> The Students' Association has got close links with the Principalship and a lot of the senior management. The fact that the college has a dedicated member of staff to liaise with us is important. [Richard, 18 years old]

There is also a constitutional structure that allows for full participation of the SA president and vice-president in decision-making:

> The fact that myself (sic) and Josie are full voting members of the governor's committee gives us considerable involvement in long term and strategic decisions for the college. We can have our input to that, which is important. [Richard, 18 years old]

It is clear that the SA members value regular, open conversations with staff in both formal and informal settings. Having these 'audiences' is as much a matter of attitude and the approachability of staff as it is about the existence of structures to allow such meetings to take place.

Influence

Whether the SA, in practice, has influenced important decisions taken at the college is a moot point. The views of the present committee — whose views may be biased in this respect — are very positive:

> I think we have a big impact. Because of the system in place with the Students' Association, whereby we've got Richard and Josie who are both governors, our voice is taken seriously. [Maddy, 17 years old]

Such a comment, however, may reflect more the feeling that students are happy to be listened to and consulted, rather than having a deeply held desire to affect important decisions. Nevertheless, the benefits to the learning environment of consulting students should not be underestimated:

> If pupils feel that they matter in school and that they are respected, then they are more likely to commit themselves to the school's purposes. (Rudduck & Flutter, 2004, p. 133)

The views of Amy (17 years old), the SA Personalised Learning Officer, the Sixth Form College, reflects the apparent surplus of 'good will' among students:

> I think there is a limit to how much students can have an impact on decisions within college. Of course, 'decisions' is a very broad term: in terms of day-to-day college life, I think students most definitely have a big impact on making decisions. Though these may be small, they are hugely important in creating a positive academic and social environment in college, for example organising charity days and putting on 'live lunches'.

The SA participates in a wide range of college events, including college open days, sporting, theatre and community link events, thus taking it upon themselves to exemplify a spirit of helping and promoting the college to outsiders visiting the site. The excellent impression this creates for parents, dignitaries and, occasionally, to Ofsted inspectors should not be underestimated.

Whose Voice Is Being Heard?

Amy's view (earlier), while very encouraging in terms of the climate of altruism and energetic volunteering activities of the committee members, may also reflect a (until now) fairly 'apolitical', non-pedagogical and rather conservative view about the remit of the SA. A more pessimistic reading of this would be along the line that Osler (2010, p. 1) states,

> Even when schools have active student councils or school councils, these may operate with very limited power and authority, and those students who are not members of the student council may feel their voices are not heard.

I suspect that many of the activities of the SA reflect the priorities of the wider student population, which are geared towards high-profile social and charitable events more than the less 'sexy' matters of teaching and learning. Nevertheless, the latter point in the preceding quote may resonate with Farnborough when we look at the characteristics of the members of the SA committee. Of the 12 members on this elected body, half come from independent (private) schools, compared to the overall college proportion of roughly 16% independent to over 80% state schools (college own data). More than half has an average GCSE score of an A grade or above, and none has an average of less than a B grade. These are very high achieving students in the context of a non-selective state Sixth Form College. These characteristics may reflect, at least in part, the skills and assurance needed to stand for election to the SA:

> the problem is that consultation assumes a degree of social confidence and linguistic competence that not all students have. (Rudduck & Fielding, 2006)

The annual college SA elections do indeed require of candidates a high level of competencies and skills in the art of public speaking, presentation, Information and Communication Technology (ICT) and networking. Prospective committee members have to speak at 'Hustings' in front of hundreds of peers in a noisy, crowded cafeteria in the lead up to the voting. They will benefit from having a network of friends and allies to help distribute leaflets, posters and provide moral support. Successful candidates may also have liaised with incumbent SA members or teachers to get some informal advice on which issues to put forward in their 'manifesto'. In addition to these skills and dispositions, the young person also needs to demonstrate great courage in placing themselves into the firing line and risk a 'humiliating defeat', in a process that may be viewed by some as a popularity contest.

Given such a process, perhaps, it is unsurprising to find 'atypical' students being elected to these posts. In terms of social class and educational background, the demographic of the SA closely parallels the unrepresentative make-up of MPs in our national parliament (Garner, 2010).

Student Voice in a Research-Engaged College

The college sponsors about half a dozen teacher-led research projects each year. These interventions are supported by the author, and also, since 2010 by CUREE, as one of their designated lab sites.[10] Following a yearly cycle from proposal to completed report[11] and annual conference, these are now firmly embedded in the culture of the college. These projects, by taking action research as their methodology, tend to involve students fairly strongly in the conception of whether the intervention has proved successful.

---

10. CUREE lab sites are designated schools and colleges in which research staff at CUREE help support teachers to carry out and write up their own research (http://www.curee-paccts.com/our-products-and-services).

11. http://actionresearch.farnborough.ac.uk/Home/Index.

One project on the use of 'audience-response technology' (McGuinness, 2010) showed how students studying GCSE psychology — often low-achieving, under-motivated youngsters — were able to comment on the benefits of using 'Optivote' in their classes; with one student commenting as follows:

> it encourages me to answer all the questions. [Anonymous student, in McGuinness, 2010, p. 7]

and another, requesting,

> Could we have more questions on statistics, as they are hard to remember? [Anonymous student, in McGuinness, 2010, p. 7]

One of the principal advantages of this system appeared to be the way that it encouraged participation in learning by this group. This teacher was able to make changes to her usual approach and to make recommendations to her colleagues as a result of this enquiry. The students no doubt benefited from reflecting on their own learning process while commenting on the usefulness of this technique. This chimes with a view given by a Greek study, which used action research in lessons in Ancient Greek literature:

> Of course, the very fact that they participated in an action research project helped them (the students) considerably in terms of expressing their views. [Tsafos, 2009]

These projects can help provide very direct feedback on the teaching process, through which students can be helped to articulate to their teacher. Such feedback can be challenging and requires an openness and willingness by the teacher to have their conceptions about pedagogy overturned. A diary entry from a teacher involved in a formative assessment project in her media and communications course reveals how her own values are challenged:

> It feels like we're on this relentless line to keep churning work out, constantly refining, improving – feels like there's something of a gap developing between those who are secure with this and those for whom it is overwhelming. [Brennan, 2006, p. 8]

And, in the same project, a student notes (in a video diary) how she felt about getting some feedback on her coursework:

> Rubbish because we thought we had the wrong idea. [Anonymous student, in Brennan, 2006, p. 6]

One conception of student voice is a 'transformative' one whereby, through the joint venture into research by students alongside teachers, there can be space for a dialogue about teaching and learning (e.g. Fielding, 2004). Students-as-researchers programmes may provide a way forward in this respect. Farnborough has, this year, set up such a group, in conjunction with the NFER's 'young researchers' project.[12] Ten students have volunteered for this research project along with about the same number of teachers (also volunteers). The students attend lunchtime research sessions once every week and will be interviewing, observing and feeding back to teachers in the scheme. It is interesting to compare the composition of this group with that of the SA (see earlier): of the 10 students who have volunteered to take part, only one has a GCSE average of more than an A grade, 3 with averages between A and B grade averages, 6 with averages between C and B and 1 with a GCSE average of less than a C grade. All of these students attended state schools.

The student researchers' project is a welcome new development in my view, addressing a need to engage more students in the teaching and learning process. This echoes the feelings of some of the SA committee too, who have recognised the need for students to have a more direct input into how their subjects are taught. Current mechanisms for feeding back on teaching and learning methods may not generate the kind of flexible exchange of ideas about which strategies work the best and are most valued, for students and their teachers to

> meet one another as equals, as genuine partners in the shared understanding of making meaning of their work together. (Fielding, 2004, p. 309)

Framing the discourse in the language of 'research', rather than 'feedback' or 'evaluation', may elicit connotations more conducive to such a dialogue.

Conclusion

This chapter has examined the nature of student voice activities at The Sixth Form College Farnborough. We have looked at the inalienable rights of students to be consulted as stated in the UN Convention for the Rights of the Child and the way that the differing structures, processes and activities of the college enable the various student voices in a large organisation to be heard. In particular, the characteristics of students in the SA have been contrasted to the volunteer participants in the new students-as-researchers project at the college. It is the author's contention that the latter activity can build on the existing pattern of teacher action research and enable the voice of more 'typical' students to be heard in relation to decisions regarding teaching and learning practices.

---

12. http://www.nfer.ac.uk/nfer/research/projects/developing-young-researchers/developing-young-research-ers_home.cfm.

Acknowledgements

I would particularly like to thank Amy Grandvoinet, the Student Association's Personalised Learning Officer, for finding the time to conduct and transcribe a number of interviews with members of the SA committee. I would also like to thank the interviewees, whose full names and SA role titles are given here: Rob Vaughan — environmental officer; Charlie Fooks — publications officer; Maddy Sakakini — charities; Richard Acton — president; Helen Lafferty — communications; Chloe East — performing arts. Finally, thank you to Christine Eustace — lead tutor (student liaison) — for her own comments and whose hard work enables students to participate so strongly in the life of the college.

References

Brennan, C. (2006). Formative assessment: Getting back into the box. *The 6th Journal*, (1), The Sixth Form College Farnborough. Retrieved from http://actionresearch.farnborough.ac.uk/files/ARP/File/Collette%20Brennan%201.pdf. Accessed on March 2011.

DfES. (2006). Every Child Matters: Change for children. Retrieved from http://education.gov.uk/publications/standard/publicationDetail/Page1/DFES-0012-2006. Accessed on 10 March, 2011.

Garner, R. (2010, May). The independent. Retrieved from http://www.independent.co.uk/news/education/education-news/increase-in-number%20of-mps-from-private-schools-1970414.html. Accessed on March 2011.

Fielding, M. (2004). Transformative approaches to student voice: Theoretical underpinnings, recalcitrant realities. *British Educational Research Journal*, *30*(2), 295–311.

Klein, R. (2003). *We want our say*. Stoke-on-Trent: Trentham books.

Lundy, L. (2007). Voice' is not enough: Conceptualising Article 12 of the United Nations convention on the rights of the Child. *British Educational Research Journal*, *33*(6), 927–942.

McGuinness. (2010). Ask the audience: Just a bit of fun or a valuable learning tool? *The 6th Journal* (5), The Sixth Form College Farnborough. Retrieved from http://actionresearch.-farnborough.ac.uk/files/ARP/file/final%20Action%20research%20project_steph.pdf. Accessed on March 2011.

Osler, A. (2010). *Students' perspectives on schooling*. London: Open University Press.

Roberts, A., & Nash, J. (2009). Enabling students to participate in school improvement through a students as researchers programme. *Improving Schools*, *12*(2), 174–187.

Rudduck, J., & Fielding, M. (2006). Student voice and the perils of popularity. *Educational Review*, *58*(2), 219–231.

Rudduck, J., & Flutter, J. (2004). *How to improve your school: Giving pupils a voice*. London: Continuum.

Tsafos, V. (2009). Teacher-student negotiation in an action research project. *Educational Action Research*, *17*(2), 197–211.

UN. (1989). Convention on the rights of the child. Geneva: UN. Retrieved from http://www.unicef.org/crc/files/Participation.pdf. Accessed on March 2011.

Chapter 20

The Student Voice in Teacher Training and Professional Development

Ann Rumpus, Jenny Eland, and Rai Shacklock

Abstract

This chapter considers using the authentic student voice in ongoing professional development for lecturers in Higher Education and potentially for teacher training courses. It is based on projects undertaken within Higher Education and highlights the importance of finding authentic ways of gaining student opinion for use in professional development. It considers the impact this has on the lecturers, as an addition to more traditional forms of feedback from students. Useful input may be generic, the University students' views on their wider experiences or specific input relating to defined courses, modules or sessions. Such specific feedback, which is positive as well as critical, can enhance staff's enthusiasm and motivation. It is recognised that the development sessions both provide student input which influences lecturers' teaching practice and model ways in which staff can engage with their own students' voice through a variety of different approaches.

Keywords: Student voice; professional development; teacher training; student feedback

Introduction

The current climate in Higher Education is characterised by large class sizes and a range of other commitments for lecturers (Nicholls, 2005) such that time talking to students is limited. Indeed it is possible that the lack of direct dialogue between students and staff may contribute to low morale in University lecturers. Currently

The Student Voice Handbook: Bridging the Academic/Practitioner Divide
Copyright © 2011 by Emerald Group Publishing Limited
All rights of reproduction in any form reserved
ISBN: 978-1-78052-040-7

there is a strong emphasis on ensuring that the views of students are fully listened to (Campbell, Beasley, Eland, & Rumpus, 2007); this chapter considers the value of this in continuing professional development and teacher training.

The use of the student voice as evidence in continuing professional development in Higher Education was explored by Campbell (2007). This demonstrated that to date the extent of using student input into staff development was very limited, although academic staff professed enthusiasm for the idea. This was further investigated through the project 'Hearing the Student Voice in professional development in learning, teaching and assessment within Higher Education' (Campbell et al., 2007). This project used case studies, in a number of Higher Education institutions, in which input from students studying on a range of degree courses was collected through a variety of means. The students' comments were then used in staff development sessions for lecturers, provided by educational development colleagues within the institution where the case study was implemented. Ways of capturing the student voice included a student-generated video of students describing their learning experiences; video diaries where actors relayed students' reflections on their first months at University; audio-tapes of conversations between students and an independent lecturer; focus groups held by independent staff who then transcribed the comments for the course team; and a range of facilitated conversations between staff and students. Further details of these approaches can be found in Chapter 21 of this volume, by Fiona Campbell. Towards the end of the project, wider views were sought through regional dissemination seminars where the case studies were presented to a range of staff from Universities and Colleges.

Impact on lecturers

An important purpose of the project was to evaluate the impact that the use of the student voice in staff development had on the Higher Education lecturers. At the end of the staff development sessions the staff participating evaluated the extent to which they had found the student input helpful. Their feedback identified that the use of an authentic student voice in professional development was powerful, prompting ideas for the enhancement of the lecturers' teaching practice. For some lecturers this provided a new perspective on student attitudes and expanded their knowledge. A lecturer participating in a facilitated discussion with students included as part of a course review commented:

> A benefit is that we have a richer picture of the student experience and how teachers affect this [HE lecturer]

A lecturer participating in a facilitated discussion between research supervisors and their students reflected:

> I was not aware of the extent to which they expected their supervisor to "motivate" them, I found this very revealing [HE lecturer]

For other staff it was a reminder of aspects that they already acknowledged but which benefited from the student perspective. The following comments are from lecturers viewing a student-made DVD in which students from across the University reflect on their experiences of learning and teaching:

> Useful to hear student feedback and reassuring that their comments reinforce my own ideas of what is needed for effective teaching and learning [HE lecturer]

> It has confirmed to me the centrality of the student/tutor relationship. I will quote it as evidence of the importance of this and the importance of students being known [HE lecturer]

The content of the student input had not only an impact, but also the direct presentation of the student voice carried greater authority. A lecturer viewing video diaries recording students' reflections on their first year experiences said:

> More immediate and effective in getting the message over than having a member of staff presenting anecdotal evidence [HE lecturer]

Colleagues also indicated that the use of the student voice would prompt them to further development of their practice. A lecturer participating in the discussion between research supervisors and their students commented:

> The 'student voice' segment of the course was invaluable and will certainly lead me to change and modify certain aspects of my supervisory style. Fab. [HE lecturer]

and a lecturer after viewing the video diaries recording students' reflections on their first year experiences said:

> I will try and be more aware that small comments/actions of mine can be very important. [HE lecturer]

Perhaps inevitably some staff were sceptical of the value of the approach and more negative in their responses, but these were a minority of the staff involved. A lecturer viewing the student-made DVD on their experiences of learning and teaching commented:

> Nothing new that I was aware of. I think most staff are aware of student views [HE lecturer]

Feedback from the University students who made their views known through participating in the case studies demonstrated that they also found this engagement valuable. Comments from students participating in a discussion between lecturers and students whom they taught, facilitated by a Higher Education Academy Subject Centre, included:

> I gained a fuller appreciation of the responsibilities and commitments of lecturers [HE student]

> Lecturers can't guess how students feel and this activity gave both sides an opportunity to voice concerns and beliefs of what is important to each other [HE student]

Nature and Use of the Student Voice

Through the project it became clear that the nature of the input from the students had an effect on its value to lecturers. This applied to the means by which the input was conveyed to staff and to the specificity of the comments to the lecturer's own work. Importantly the work demonstrated that the reflections students made, and their opinions and suggestions, were more powerful when given directly in narrative form in the students' own words (whether through direct, recorded or reported speech). These methods carried greater credibility with staff than previously used methods of information gathering such as the fairly standard module/course questionnaires. A lecturer viewing the student-made DVD on their experiences of learning and teaching said:

> Actually seeing and hearing responses carries a veracity that reading through piles of module feedback comments never can [HE lecturer]

and a lecturer receiving feedback from an independently facilitated focus group with students on an MA course on which the lecturer taught commented:

> More useful to have this narrative than the limited feedback provided by the module feedback questionnaire forms [HE lecturer]

Some of the value of the information related to its specificity to the lecturers' interests. More generic data on the students' perception of their overall learning experience can be useful in improving broad aspects of the context of study and of the course delivery. In particular this is helpful in relation to resources to support teaching and to the general curriculum approach. These insights are valuable to those with responsibility for managing the provision. However, academic staff are often more interested in precise student perceptions of the content and delivery methods of their own particular course units and modules. The commonly used anonymous questionnaire data is often aggregated; the comments are therefore generic and hence less useful to lecturers, who may be unsure as to how much of the comment relates to their own practice. However, it was noted (Campbell, Eland, Rumpus, & Shacklock, 2009) that the use of electronic questionnaires rather than paper-based ones, elicited a greater number and variety of qualitative comments; generally perceived as more useful to the lecturers.

The way in which some questionnaire data is used, for instance in quality assurance for an institution as whole or in the National Student Survey (www.thestudentsurvey.com) may seem less relevant to lecturers who cannot relate the outcomes directly to their own work. The project findings reinforced the value of direct specific student comment relating to lecturers' own practice. In the project different methods of gaining student input were used in the case studies. Some methods generated comment which applied to the University as a whole, whereas others were targeted on a specific course, and in one case on a particular module. For instance the use of the DVD in which students from across the University described how they preferred to be taught not only raised a lot of positive comments but also demonstrated that some colleagues felt they could not relate this to their own teaching, one lecturer commenting:

> I'm not sure how relevant the feedback is to the courses for which I am responsible [HE lecturer]

The case study in which a selected range of students commented on their first year experiences, conveyed through video diaries, elicited a similar response; many staff found the general input informative but others expressed reservations as to how useful it was. One comment was:

> We need to find ways of judging how typical these personal accounts may be [HE lecturer]

However where a facilitated staff–student discussion was organised for research students and supervisors, which focused directly on supervisory practice, comments from staff suggested that they could identify specific further enhancements:

> As I have limited experience in supervising, [...] I feel this experience will help me in managing expectations and communicating appropriate information [HE lecturer]

> Excellent — this will enable me to review and reflect on current practices and conventions within the department with a view to improving the experience for all [HE lecturer]

Playing audio tapes of students giving feedback on a particular Personal Development Planning module to the module team also led to an action plan for change and comments from lecturers teaching on the module included:

> Very positive – the more student involvement the better in respect of a student centred approach [HE lecturer]

> Take on board some of the comments and influencing the delivery next time [HE lecturer]

Similarly the outcomes of independently facilitated student focus groups were conveyed to an MA course team who were preparing for a course review. The team recognised specific outcomes which could be addressed. They identified needs such as providing more guidance on the assessments, developing improved ways of encouraging students to ask questions and reviewing a particular module to resolve issues about depth versus breadth. One colleague from the course team commented that the sessions and student input was helpful because:

> [It was a] chance to get data pertinent to my department and discuss these with colleagues [HE lecturer]

It may well be that the combination of direct student comment and the opportunity to discuss this with close colleagues (often commented on as a positive element of staff development sessions) provides a very potent tool for personal development. On the whole staff welcomed this approach, finding it stimulating, challenging and positive.

Using the Student Voice to Inform Teaching

Selecting appropriate approaches enabled colleagues to receive students' comments which they could directly relate to their own teaching and related activities. The different relevance of generic and specific comment suggests that where student input is used in professional development it is important to match the methods of gaining and using the student voice to the target group of staff carefully. Additionally any differences generated by disciplinary cultures should be taken into account (Nicholls, 2005).This was supported by comments from Higher Education lecturers participating in the regional project dissemination seminars:

> The voice is an important part of the student identity therefore we need multiple ways of voicing and listening [HE lecturer]

> Different methods of using the student voice might be appropriate for different disciplines [HE lecturer]

It was acknowledged through the work that there are constraints to the level of individuality and specificity of comment given the need to ensure that students' interests are protected, and that a range of views are collected. Throughout the project staff expressed concern as to whether the views of the participating students were representative, the following comment coming from a lecturer who viewed the student-made DVD on their experiences of learning and teaching:

> Entirely anecdotal. No idea whether views are representative of general opinion [HE lecturer]

   This issue of whether the student input was representative was considered within the project. In most case studies the student group was a subset of the appropriate student population, which had volunteered; hence this could not be seen as fully representative. One of the project findings was that it could be difficult to recruit the students to the project due to other demands on their time. This proved to be difficult to resolve, although providing some incentive or collecting the input in scheduled classroom sessions were helpful. It was also recognised constructing a fully 'representative' group is difficult as students can be classified in many different ways. However, this caution would apply to many forms of student feedback. Questionnaire data may not be representative either, as students completing them may not have attended many classes, and may be heavily influenced by immediate dissatisfactions relating to other aspects of the course as a whole. It was concluded that when asking students to participate it would be best to draw on as wide a range of students as possible and to recognise that full representation cannot be achieved. It is essential to be clear to staff using the data what limitations applied and how the students were recruited. This, and a range of other issues relating to the participation of the students in the project, is discussed in more detail in chapter 21 of this volume, by Fiona Campbell.

   Nevertheless, in spite of some of the unavoidable limitations of the methods applied, it was concluded that using the student voice in professional development was of high value due to its impact on staff. However, this should not be seen as the only source of evidence for the enhancement of the curriculum design and delivery. Student input must be mediated by other forms of evidence, such as student achievement, external examiners' comments, information gathered though standard mechanisms of feedback and, importantly, lecturers' own reflections. In collecting students' views on their courses it has to be recognised that this does not represent some fundamental 'truth' which must be adhered to. The students' views and suggestions should not wholly dictate what they should be learning, or how, but are one source of evidence as to what might be beneficial. Ideally their input would be the basis for further negotiation of the curriculum, as described later in relation to students studying on a Foundation Degree.

'Authentic' Student Voice

The project team concluded that using the student voice in professional development for Higher Education staff is a valuable strategy which impacts on both the staff and students involved. However, the voice must be authentic, students being willing to contribute and saying what they genuinely feel, not what they think they are expected to say (by staff or peers). This also requires that a range of students' views are put forward and that the input is not dominated by the views of a few dominant individuals, or those with very individual concerns. Meaningful opportunities have to be provided which enable students to reflect on their experiences and speak freely, with a caution over protecting the students' interests; the nature of the autonomous and authentic student voice is discussed by Barnett (2007).

Care should also be exercised to ensure that any data collected from students and used in staff development is current. It emerged from the project that some of the processes of gathering the student voice can be resource intensive, in particular demanding of staff time. Hence there needs to be a balance between the effort put in and the benefit gained. Appropriate professional development interventions must be provided which are relevant to the staff groups involved and which enable those staff to be engaged by hearing the student voice and then by being motivated to make changes to academic practice as a result.

Learning from Students in a Professional Context; Case Studies

The initial project examining the impact of hearing the student voice in professional development covered various aspects of the student experience (case studies included insights into learning and teaching, international students' experience, induction and project supervision). The second project (Campbell et al., 2009) examined the use of the student voice particularly in influencing curriculum design and delivery. In contrast to the first project which was managed by colleagues from educational development units, this project intended to involve academic staff directly. These staff would gather the student voice from their own student groups and use this to inform their own course or module design and delivery; the input would be specific to these staff. This approach was intended to encourage the use of the student voice to be a more routine and sustainable activity rather than a centrally driven initiative. The project used a range of case studies across a number of Higher Education institutions. Again this proved a powerful developmental tool for staff involved. A lecturer participating in a case study where assessment on a module with high student numbers was adapted in light of student comment gathered through tutorial input commented:

> It pushed the module team into thinking "outside the box" in assessment terms. Yes, there were risks but overall this has taken a step in a good direction which will inform teaching across the whole course [HE lecturer]

In the current climate the Higher Education staff can feel de-motivated by the large class sizes, pressure of assessment and marking and level of administrative tasks (Nicholls, 2005). The time available for individual and informal discussion with students about their learning is diminished. We suggest that staff may feel rather removed from the students, hence the impact of approaches which staff perceive as restoring elements of more personal interaction and dialogue. Throughout the work of the projects it also became evident that some lecturers are extremely enthusiastic to engage with their students' views. It was notable that staff were very motivated by positive comments from students which were specific and attributable directly to the staff's work. These direct comments had a great impact on the lecturer's morale and their enthusiasm for their role than the more aggregated questionnaire-type feedback (which may emphasise numerical scores, on a wide range of processes). A lecturer's comment after viewing the student-made DVD on their experiences of learning and teaching was:

> Good to see students involved in the production of the DVD. I found it inspirational. It reminded me what we are here for! [HE lecturer]

When discussing the use of reflective video diaries by first year students, a lecturer commented:

> Gave me confidence to continue to refine my teaching [HE lecturer]

In the second project, the benefits of gaining specific feedback from a precise student group was addressed through three case studies focussed on specific modules (Campbell et al., 2009). Here the process of eliciting the student voice was embedded in the teaching, during the normal teaching time, rather than being an added-on activity. Although this approach might not involve all students on the module (due to absences from the class), it provided more reassurance that the views would be representative. Time was generated within these modules for students to discuss aspects of the learning and teaching, as part the module delivery; it was not flagged up as in any way as a 'different' activity or 'feedback' device, it was simply integral to the teaching. This method of hearing the student voice also demanded less resource, although it does depend on a good level of trust between the staff and students.

Case Study 1

Two Art and Design modules used what was termed as 'think tank' where the students, in small groups, were encouraged to reflect on their learning and assessment processes. The students selected the topics, with only gentle guidance from the lecturer, and the students perceived the session as an integrated part of their learning. The Module Leader found these sessions very helpful, the students had constructive and informative things to say and she felt that she gained a much better insight into their motivation for studying. She realised that there was a gulf between her and the students in understanding the assessment criteria, which she was able to amend immediately along with some aspects of feedback on assessment. She noted that this approach would be helpful in managing the different needs of different cohorts and might also help with issue of student socialisation in very diverse groups. The Module Leader is intending to continue this approach as part of the standard module teaching provision as she found it so beneficial. This case study was integrated into a larger Higher Education Academy funded National Teaching Fellowship Scheme project on supporting students with Specific Learning Difficulties (InCurriculum, 2011).

Case Study 2

Two Biological Sciences modules incorporated hearing the student voice directly within the modules. In one small postgraduate module reflection on learning activities was encouraged throughout the sessions through discussion, questions, Post-it® notes and use of a flip camera. The Module Leader received some valuable constructive criticism and suggestions on both the content and the delivery of the module which led to him making changes. He also noted that it made the entire group more interactive in discussions throughout the module, and he felt this was helpful for the integration of the international students. In the second module, a large first year module, the opportunity to comment was built into the Virtual Learning Environment, which was used significantly in the module delivery. One discussion board, called 'Let's Talk Science', was widely used by the students who made some very constructive input on the curriculum content, suggested guest speakers and supplied a wider range of literature sources. This dialogue ultimately led to the establishment of a student Biological Society to continue their learning beyond the formal teaching elements. Again both Module Leaders found this input invaluable and continued the approach. They noted that it helped them to know their students better and to understand their motivation and interests more fully. On the whole the resources involved were small although some time had gone into the website design.

The project concluded that this approach, where 'capturing' the students' voice was embedded in the module delivery, was valuable in helping staff gain a real appreciation of student's views and needs. The outcomes were specific to their interests and the process reasonably cost effective. The students' input was more spontaneous and therefore likely to be more authentic. The approach had the added benefit of supporting the development of a dialogue between staff and students which enhanced all the learning processes in the modules. Such interactions are also recognised as increasing students' and pupils' self-confidence (Barnett, 2007; Pollard et al., 2005). This particular way of using the student voice to inform lecturer's practice more informally would be included in Nicholls's (2001) definition of 'professional development' and is clearly an important way of contributing to the staff's reflective practice and enhancement activities.

Case Study 3

In a further case study in which the student voice was embedded into a module, a group of Foundation Degree Early Years students voiced their views on assessment. This led to the negotiation, on an individual basis, of the assessment method used by each of them. This initiative was taken in response to feedback from the student group that they found the current assessment inappropriate. The students found choosing their own assessment to be a challenging, valuable and motivating activity, which led to increased levels of both confidence and performance. The Module Leader has continued this approach as she valued the constructive dialogue on assessment and other aspects of learning which was established.

Conclusion

Both projects provided evidence that the direct use of the student voice is valuable in offering lecturers insights into their individual teaching and learning support activities, facilitating them in enhancing their practice. Hearing the depth and clarity of the student voice engaged and motivated staff. Staff found this a positive experience and identified, and committed to, changes in academic practice as a result: the two criteria identified as measures of the impact of professional development interventions by Rust (1998). The case for professional development in a changing context in Higher Education is well argued by Nicholls (2001) and would also apply to other educational sectors.

It became evident throughout the projects that the value of using the student voice in staff development sessions could apply to a potentially very wide range of continuing professional development opportunities, for example in induction for new staff, staff meetings, formal professional development sessions, project work, course review meetings and formal courses for inexperienced staff.

Another insight was that not only can the student voice provide evidence for any staff development provision (giving perceptions on various curriculum aspects) but also that the use of such approaches can encourage staff to embed mechanisms for engaging with their students' views into their own teaching provision. The professional development session can in itself be used as a means of modelling the ways in which lecturers can gather their own students' reflections. Additionally staff providing professional development programmes can themselves use information gathered from the participants (their students) to develop this provision. They can use the range of techniques described in the project case studies to gather feedback, beyond the characteristic feedback sheets ('happy sheets') which are used at the end of many staff development sessions.

A logical development of this perceived value of the student voice in professional development, and as a tool for staff in re-shaping their own curriculum content and delivery, is that these aspects should be included in a more systematic way in teacher training courses. The engagement of staff with professional development is often haphazard and dependent on the lecturers' or teacher's enthusiasms and specific interests, often to meet their immediate needs at any particular point in time. However, the majority of staff teaching in all sectors of education will now go through some initial form of teacher training, whether pre- or in-service.

In professional development sessions using the student voice can demonstrate the value and means by which participants could gain insights from their students to use in enhancing their own teaching practice. Equally teacher training provision can model the use of the student voice within curriculum design and delivery. The function of gathering the student voice in teacher training is thus twofold. It is as important for staff teaching on teacher training programmes (for all sectors) to gather the trainees' input (their students) as for any other HE course. This should be a standard inclusion in the curriculum of teacher training courses. Additionally it is a way of educating the trainees to pay attention to using the student voice in their own teaching practice. The majority of teacher training provision supports the use of student-centred approaches; students being actively engaged in a range of learning interactions with the lecturer/teacher and other students (Biggs & Tang, 2007; Lowe, 2003; Moore, 2000). However we would suggest that this is largely focused on helping students engage with the concepts and information relating to the subjects being taught (although we acknowledge the current emphasis on student engagement in a wider sense across all sectors). For instance, the Lifelong Learning UK Units of Assessment for Generic Qualifications for Teachers in the Further Education sector (Lifelong Learning UK, 2007) specify teaching and assessment approaches which engage and motivate learners, which meet the needs of individual learners and which use feedback from learners, but are not specific about the role of the student voice in this. Many teacher training curricula are very intensive, with heavy content requirements covering many topics. Bringing out the value of interactive delivery methods as a means of gaining helpful feedback to the teacher/lecturer, as well as to deliver the subject content, may be overlooked.

However, the use of the student voice in teacher training may in itself contain a dilemma. One of the outcomes of the second project (Campbell et al., 2009) was the value of embedding the capture of the student voice into the module such that students perceived this as integral to the course design. The students were unaware that this was anything other than a 'normal' delivery. This will have increased the authenticity of the input as it involves the majority of the students in an unself-conscious way. Individual students are less likely to rehearse particular ongoing issues of concern which may not reflect the views of the majority, and they are more likely to respond in spontaneous ways; a constructive dialogue is developed.

However, if a completely embedded approach is used in teacher training the impact of it could be lost for the trainees. They would be unaware that techniques are being modelled which they could use with their student groups in future; hence it would be imperative to make this approach explicit. Teacher training courses (in any sector) with their emphasis on reflection and the use of mentors are suitable for this embedded approach, but its dual purpose needs to be elucidated. A solution lies in initially using techniques to engender and collect the trainees' insights and reflections on the curriculum and delivery such that they are unconscious of this purpose. This could then be followed by a reflective session which uncovers the value of the approach and the way it can be utilised within the trainees' future practice. The role of the lecturer then is to maintain a degree of vigilance throughout the course to ensure that this attention to feedback is sustained within the pressures of the breadth of the curriculum.

From this work it can be concluded that a major aspect of teaching, at any level, is to engage the students and teachers as partners in a dialogue, both to provide support for learning a subject, and to ensure that the context of the learning and mode of delivery are influenced by the students' views so as to enhance their effectiveness. Professional development and teacher training courses are just as much taught programmes as any other Higher Education course so the same principles of engaging in dialogue with the students should apply on these courses. They also have the added dimension that they can model good practice in engaging the student voice.

References

Barnett, R. (2007). *A will to learn. Being a student in an age of uncertainty.* Maidenhead: McGraw-Hill/Society for Research into Higher Education & Open University Press.

Biggs, J., & Tang, C. (2007). *Teaching for quality learning at university: What the student does.* Maidenhead: McGraw-Hill/Society for Research into Higher Education & Open University Press.

Campbell, F. (2007). Hearing the student voice: Enhancing academic professional development through the involvement of students. *Educational Developments, 8*(1), 4–8.

Campbell, F., Beasley, L., Eland, J., & Rumpus, A. (2007). Hearing the student voice. Promoting and encouraging the effective use of the student voice to enhance professional development in learning, teaching and assessment within higher education. An ESCalate-funded project involving Napier University, Leeds Metropolitan University, UCE Birmingham and the University of Westminster, Edinburgh, Edinburgh Napier University. Available at www2.napier.ac.uk/studentvoices/curriculum/index.htm. Accessed on 14.03.2011.

Campbell, F., Eland, J., Rumpus, A., & Shacklock, R. (2009). Hearing the student voice. Involving students in curriculum design and delivery. An ESCalate-funded project involving Edinburgh Napier University, Leeds Metropolitan University, Birmingham City University and the University of Westminster. Available at www2.napier.ac.uk/studentvoices/curriculum/index.htm. Accessed on 14.03.2011.

InCurriculum. (2011). Developing the achieveability of an inclusive curriculum in higher education drawn from learning and teaching strategies for students with specific learning differences. Available at www.incurriculum.org.uk. Accessed on 14.03.2011.

Lifelong Learning UK. (2007). Mandatory units of assessment — Generic qualifications, teachers, tutors and trainers in the further education (FE) sector in England. Available at http://www.lluk.org/standards-and-qualificationswww.lluk.org/standards-and-qualifications. Accessed on 14.03.2011.

Lowe, K. (2003). Developing and using a range of teaching and learning techniques. In: F. Fawbert (Ed.), *Teaching in post-compulsory education* (pp. 107–146). London: Continuum.

Moore, A. (2000). *Teaching and learning: pedagogy, curriculum and culture.* London: Routledge Farmer.

Nicholls, G. (2001). *Professional development in higher education.* London: Kogan Page.

Nicholls, G. (2005). *The challenge to scholarship. Re-thinking learning, teaching and research.* London: Routledge.

Pollard, A., Collins, J., Maddock, M., Simco, N., Swaffield, S., Warin, J., & Warwick, P. (2005). *Reflective teaching* (2nd ed.). London: Continuum.

Rust, C. (1998). The impact of educational development workshops on teachers' practice. *International Journal for Academic Development, 3*(1), 72–80.

PART FOUR
CAPTURING STUDENT VOICE

Editors' Summary to Part Four

As we can see by the contributions collected together in this fourth part of the book, the intentionality behind how and why student voices might be used, shape research agendas and frame research problematics in the very first place. In Chapter 21, Fiona Cambell discusses methodological issues and nuances involved in student voice research and in doing so provides practical advice to all colleagues undertaking this work in their own institutions. In Chapter 22, Gerry Czerniawski along with his colleague Su Garlick offer a case study examining the importance of contextual sensitivity when young student researchers embark on work in the field. Joanne Waterhouse (Chapter 23) and Tina Cook (Chapter 24) in their separate contributions explore pupil engagement and 'authenticity' in Student Voice research, whereas Warren Kidd in Chapter 25 discusses the use of student voice research to inform teacher education. Kidd's articulation of the learner voice through the use of audio recordings (podcasts) is used pedagogically as a means to inform trainee teachers, supporting them to co-construct meanings of 'what teaching means' at the very start of their professional education. There are many links between student voice research conducted by practitioners and the methodological and epistemological practices and frameworks offered within 'action research'; it is often the case that practitioners researching in their own local settings, adopt the spirit and practices of action research, using their own learners (and their 'voices') as data. These links between student voice and action research practices are explored by Rita Cheminais' second contribution to this book in Chapter 26. Finally, in this fourth part, the contribution from Raymonde Sneddon making up Chapter 27 explores the use of 'voice' in a slightly different way — looking at how young learners can capture and narrate stories of bilingual learning and 'speaking' across diverse cultures.

Chapter 21

How to Hear and to Heed the Student Voice

Fiona Campbell

Abstract

The student voice can make a significant and powerful impact leading to enhancements in academic practice and course provision. But by what means can we enable students to contribute their voices meaningfully, safely and confidently? And by what mechanisms can we best capture and harness those voices to enable them to be heard and heeded? If you are a researcher or a practitioner keen to employ the student voice in your own investigations or to inform your professional practice, this chapter will be of value to you by providing you with practical and pragmatic advice. Through staged guidance, you will learn how to conceive, conduct and conclude action research or other investigative work involving the student voice. The guidance draws on the experiences and outcomes of two UK-based, inter-university initiatives — the Hearing the Student Voice projects (2007 and 2009) — which employed the student voice to inform academic practice and curriculum development within degree programmes in the contributing universities. The chapter is informed by the voices of some of the staff and students who contributed to the projects.

Keywords: Academic practice; staff development; guidance; recording; feedback; action research

Introduction

This chapter aims to help you to achieve what Mann (2006) has described — paraphrasing George Eliot (1874, p. 194) — as 'getting close to the roar that lies on the other side of the silence of the classroom, for it is only in that roar that we can begin to develop an understanding of the lived experience of individuals within classroom contexts'. This chapter seeks to support you use the student voice to help hear that roar.

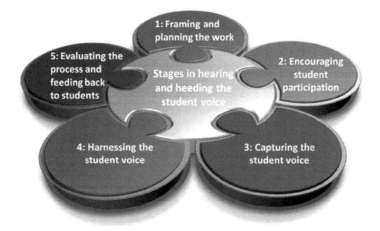

Figure 21.1: Stages in hearing and heeding the student voice.

Through the five stages represented in Figure 21.1, this chapter aims to provide you with practical guidance on how to develop and progress your student voice work.

Stage 1 will help you to consider how to frame your student voice work and the relevance of action research methodology to it. Effective early framing will help guide your decisions as to what approaches to adopt. Student participation will be discussed in stage 2: how you can communicate the value of their views to students and how to encourage students to contribute and be confident that they can do so freely. Stage 3 will guide you in how to provide meaningful opportunities to enable students' views to be effectively captured. Next, in stage 4, we will explore how the captured student voice can be harnessed for you to use in a range of contexts to engage staff in making a difference to the learning experience. In stage 5, you will consider how your work involving student voices can be effectively evaluated with all the participants involved so that lessons learnt by you and others in the process can inform future activity. This stage will also emphasise the importance of you feeding back to students on changes in practice and provision made as a result of their contributions to assure students that their voices have been both heard and heeded.

Much of the chapter draws on the work and experiences of the Hearing the Student Voice projects — two UK-based, inter-university projects that were funded through the Higher Education Academy's education subject centre, ESCalate. The projects were primarily focused on the experiences of undergraduate and postgraduate students undertaking courses of studies within British universities. The two projects, respectively, investigated how the student voice could be used to enhance academic professional development (Hearing the Student Voice, 2007) and to inform curriculum development and design (Hearing the Student Voice, 2009).

The project team concluded that using the student voice was a powerful strategy and it had impacted on both the staff and the students involved in the two projects. Students appreciated the opportunity to contribute their perspectives on issues that impacted on their learning. They valued doing this in meaningful ways — often in collaboration with their peers — which encouraged reflection. Through the provision of a safe environment, students felt free to contribute constructive, valuable and fresh perspectives that had clear implications for academic practice. Students felt more engaged when they perceived that their views were valued by their institution and, particularly, when they could see a direct benefit of their contribution. Staff were often surprised and motivated by hearing the depth and clarity of the student voice. They were engaged not only by *what* was said but also *how* it was said underlining the importance of actually hearing the spoken word. When the student voice was employed within appropriate professional development contexts, staff usually found this a very positive experience and identified changes they planned to make to their academic practice as a result.

To investigate the stages detailed in this chapter further, you are encouraged to visit the projects' websites (Hearing the Student Voice, 2007, 2009) that contain detailed case studies, reflections on key issues (such as student representation), practical advice and downloadable document templates together with staff and (of course!) student views. Further information about the two projects can also be found in their final reports by Campbell, Beasley, Eland, and Rumpus (2007) and Campbell, Eland, Rumpus, and Shacklock (2009) and in Chapter 20 of this book by Rumpus, Eland and Shacklock.

Stage 1: Framing and Planning the Work

How can you frame your investigation to enable it to have impact? What are you trying to do? How do you intend to employ the student voice that Verrill and Worden (2006) have described as 'the motor which drives reflective staff development'?

Adopt Action Research Methodology

Consider action research as the framework for undertaking your student voice work. The action research process in itself helps to bridge the divide between practitioners and academics as, within this investigative methodology, 'no distinction is made between who is a researcher and who is a practitioner. Practitioners are potential researchers, and researchers are practitioners' (McNiff & Whitehead, 2002, p. 15). From a practical perspective, you will also find that the different steps of the action research process mirror the stages outlined within this chapter.

Action research is particularly relevant where you are investigating aspects of your own practice as its focus is on enquiry *into* self *by* self: in our context, it provides a means to assess your academic practice, generate information to improve it and make changes — and communicate them — as a result. In action research investigations, the context is therefore usually local, the setting specific and the scope focused. Action research can also assist your student voice work by helping you define your overall research questions — and beyond that — the specific questions you want to ask students. Creating these questions so that they generate valuable and specific information while also enabling unexpected contributions is essential to effective student voice work.

McNiff and Whitehead (2002, 2006, 2009) have written a series of books focused on action research and providing practical guidelines that can assist you in planning and conducting your work, engaging in sound ethical practice and analysing outputs to inform your practice. They also provide specific guidance in defining effective research questions.

Decide on Intended Purpose

Significantly, at this initial stage, it is essential to consider the context in which the student voices will eventually be used as this will inform and dictate the form, scale and nature in which they are collected. Does your work relate to issues at class or module level? If so, small-scale approaches that are not expensive or time-consuming to implement could be adopted. You could ask for views written on Post-it® notes, ideas for a suggestion box or involve students in focus group discussions. Or do you intend that the student voice will be used at an institutional level or beyond? If so, you will need to adopt more complex approaches that will have impact with a wider audience. This could include the production of an audio or video recording or the commissioning of a dramatic production. These issues are also raised in stage 4.

To guide you in making informed decisions, investigate the 19 case studies within the Hearing the Student Voice (2007, 2009) projects. These case studies were mainly developed by university teachers to enable the voices of their undergraduate and postgraduate students to inform learning, teaching and assessment practice and curriculum design and development within their universities. Each had different aims and adopted different approaches, and the reflections of their developers and the participants are provided on the projects' websites. Examples are also discussed in Chapter 20 by Rumpus, Eland and Shacklock.

Plan Process to Protect Students' Interests

Many students are rightly concerned about contributing their voices, and therefore, they must be sure that their views, once expressed, will not impact on themselves or on their progress. When designing your investigation, seek out and comply with any institutional ethical protocols. You can also ensure that the work is carried out practically to best protect students' interests: discussions can be facilitated by a member of staff who is distant from the project or course team, contributions from students can be anonymised and any identifying information deleted.

> We must be aware that there is a power relationship between staff and students and so important for the student voice to be collected – and used – ethically. (Participant in Hearing the Student Voice Project, London seminar, 2007; Campbell et al., 2007)

Obtain Student Permissions

Take time at the start of the work to formalise student agreement to their contributions being used. This will be time well spent as students will be encouraged to speak freely (see stage 3 later), and difficulties that could prevent valuable contributions from being employed as you intended will be pre-empted. Obtain prior student permission through forms that clearly specify the purpose of the activity, the approach, any recording and the ways in which student identities will be protected. An example of a student permission form is provided on the Hearing the Student Voice project website from where it can be downloaded and adapted (Hearing the Student Voice, 2007). The signed forms should be retained to ensure that they are available should concerns arise later.

Stage 2: Encouraging Student Participation

How can you encourage students to participate and best enable their contribution? Although students have fresh and perceptive views, persuading them to part with these can be difficult. This is usually for reasons of time, but they may also have concerns over later repercussions that you can allay as discussed in stage 1.

Different methods call for different approaches to students. Is your activity relatively small-scale and with one particular purpose? If so, engaging students may be fairly straightforward as you can approach a specific group — a class or cohort — for contributions and arrange for the activity to be carried out during normal contact time. Is your activity wider and does it need to involve a cross-section of the student population? If so, you will need to consider other approaches as discussed later.

Investigate the Procedure within Your Own Institution

How can your investigation avoid contributing to the feedback fatigue and survey saturation that some students complain of? Of course, they are likely to be keener to contribute to the meaningful opportunities you devise rather than the form-filling that characterises so much of the feedback that is requested of them. But how will they know this and how can you reach them? Many institutions are adopting methods so that students can choose to participate in such activity. For instance, at matriculation, students may be asked to indicate if they are prepared to contribute their views, and a register of those that respond affirmatively is then compiled. Valuable though this is, proceed here with some caution as those that agree are a self-selecting group that does not necessarily reflect the make-up or the views of the majority of the student body. Also, consider targeting already established groups of students. For instance, class representatives may already feel they have this role and will be experienced in articulating opinions.

Consider Appropriate Ways to Advertise

An alternative strategy is to advertise for student participation. Could you involve the Students Association in this? Could posters be displayed in visible places frequented by students? Could you send an all-student email? All of these mechanisms require the request to be as clear and informative as possible regarding purpose, mechanism and outputs so that students can be assured that they are not subscribing to an open-ended commitment. This information should enable students to know exactly what is expected of them, help them consider the issues in advance and be sure of the benefits.

Enable Student Participation

Most students, although keen, just find it too difficult to schedule the time to participate. To get over this, what ways could you facilitate their contribution? Could you go to *them* rather than the other way round? Perhaps, timetable a session to take place immediately after a class or instead of a class? Can the session be held on their home campus? Can you provide them with lunch so that you are saving time during their day as well as providing them with an incentive to attend? Not only does this mean that students are fed, but the relaxed situation can also encourage students to be candid in their views. Do funds permit you to take students out for an evening meal? This may prove a worthwhile investment as the resulting conversation is likely to show that the conviviality of the occasion enabled students to engage in meaningful dialogue, rich in valuable insights.

What other incentives could you offer? Students are not mercenary, but, with many other calls on their time, an incentive that offers something extra may just make the difference. Can you pay them for their time, provide the expenses to cover their attendance and offer print credits, tokens or vouchers? Could they be entered into a prize draw for a more significant item? Where some form of incentive is offered, make this explicit. Mention of the incentive in large letters on a poster or in the subject line of an email may be enough to encourage students to read on.

But students are, in the main, altruistic and there is plenty of evidence to show that they are willing to contribute their views if they believe it will make a difference to the learning experience of themselves or those that come after and are pleased to have some responsibility for changes:

> I would like to give and share my experience to help following fellow students. (Student participant in Hearing the Student Voice Project case study: Social Integration of overseas students, Campbell et al., 2007)

> Next year tell the year twos that we made the changes. (Student participant in Hearing the Student Voice Project case study: Using the student voice in staff development to progress a pilot Personal Development Planning module, Campbell et al., 2007)

So a commitment to feeding back to students on the impact of their contribution is an essential part of student voice investigations and is discussed in stage 5.

Stage 3: Capturing the Student Voice

Enable Meaningful Opportunities

Students will provide valuable views and perspectives if they are given the appropriate conditions to do so. How can you create a positive environment in which they feel confident, safe and valued? Can you arrange for the session to be neutrally facilitated? If recording the proceedings (following agreement from the students participating — see stage 1), how can you make this unobtrusive to avoid changing the dynamic and charging the atmosphere?

Depending on your eventual purpose, any recording should be of a commensurate quality. Do you just need to generate a record to enable student views to be used in a different format? If so, an audible recording made on a handheld device with a good microphone should be sufficient. Do you need to create a more permanent or high-quality output for later playback? This could involve more extensive resource implications such as professional equipment and operators. If you have media students, they may well welcome opportunities to work to an assignment brief and carry out production roles and may also be willing to contribute their voices!

Could you also adopt online methods such as discussion boards or conferencing? These provide a means to include the voices of students such as international or remote students or those with pressing domestic or employment commitments who, for logistical reason, are often not represented. Online questionnaires can reach a large number of students but, as they are completed individually, can lose the benefit of the evolving conversation characteristic of a group discussion. A way to safeguard this is to enable online contributions in addition to face-to-face dialogue. The benefit of this two-pronged approach is to generate valuable quotes through discussions with a small number of students but to ensure the views are representative by using quantitative instruments with a larger number of students to verify and triangulate the qualitative results.

Give Students Their Voice

> I feel you are listening more to our feelings and queries. (Student participant in Hearing the Student Voice Project case study: Voices off? Using student voice for reflective staff development, Campbell et al., 2007)

How can you be sure that you are truly giving students an opportunity to contribute their views on the things that matter to them? In framing questions, take care that they are open and that you do not have preset ideas about outcomes;

otherwise, there is a danger of losing unanticipated contributions. Often it is these insights and perspectives that can give us a much clearer idea as to student concerns. Therefore, to hear what the students want to say, consider how you will enable them to enter into a dialogue rather than just react to your questions. By providing the opportunity for more collegiate conversation, you demonstrate to students that their views are valued and they will engage in the process thoughtfully and enthusiastically.

Take care also to ensure that the conversation itself is conducted democratically to include all participants and not just the most confident or articulate:

> We need to compensate for the reticent by giving them more time and listening harder. (Participant in Hearing the Student Voice Project, Glasgow seminar, 2007; Campbell et al., 2007)

Stage 4: Harnessing the Student Voice

Once captured, how can the student voice be heard to make a difference? 'Heard' is a key word here as a significant finding of the Hearing the Student Voice projects was that the physicality of actually hearing what the students said that made a difference to staff:

> Powerful stuff! Rang true. Brings issues to life. (Staff participant in Hearing the Student Voice Project case study: 'My first year experience': constructing student video diaries, Campbell et al., 2007)

> The impact of a 'live' student beats the books anytime. (Staff participant in Hearing the Student Voice Project case study: 'My first year experience': constructing student video diaries, Campbell et al., 2007)

Hearing the spoken word builds an emotional connection between speaker and listener, and the gap between what is said and what is heard is closed. This resonates with Alterio's (2006) assertion that

> Listening to student stories can have a transformative impact for the hearer enabling a shift in values and valences. It enables empathy by awakening what is ordinarily not heard, enabling staff to wear another's shoes and see things from their perspective.

Find the Appropriate Forum and Context

In framing your investigation (stage 1), you will have already considered the fora for hearing the student voice. For small-scale activities, perhaps you will be using the student voice to stimulate individual reflection or discussions in class or course team meetings? For larger-scale investigations, you may be using the student voice to stimulate key strategic discussions in themed staff conferences, student senate meetings or developmental workshops. Depending on the context, the student voice could be replayed through audio or video recordings or through a video diary with the student words acted out. You may also be considering the many print options in which student quotes are used as prompts within structured conversations. Preprinted dialogue sheets as described by Flint and Oxley (2008) are a particularly effective tool for this, and they also encourage contributions from all participants and enable outcomes to be logged.

Stage 5: Evaluating the Process and Feeding Back to Students

How can you evaluate your use of the student voice to ensure that you and others benefit in future from the lessons learnt in the process? How can you ensure that the students involved are informed as to the worth and impact of their contribution?

Request Evaluative Feedback from Students and Staff Involved

To ensure you and others learn from the experience and the process informs future work, collect responses from both staff and students involved as soon as possible after the intervention to benefit from spontaneous reflections. Examples of evaluation forms that have been developed are available from the Hearing the Student Voice (2007) website from where you can download them and adapt them to meet your needs.

Feedback to Students

In stage 3, the incentive of 'making a difference' was raised as a means to encourage students to contribute their views. So how can you find appropriate mechanisms to enable students to see what changes have resulted from their intervention?

If there have been direct changes, can these be shared with students in class, student senate meetings or other suitable fora? Can they be listed in 'You said, we did' posters or in other communications to students? Not all of their suggestions will be realisable, but we must also feed this back and explain why not.

This action is significant as evidence (Quality Assurance Agency [QAA], 2005) shows that where students perceive their views are valued by their institution and, particularly, when they see direct benefits of their contributions, there is a virtuous circle of increased engagement with their courses of study (Figure 21.2).

Closing the loop through feedback enables an essential element of student voice work: if we fail to respond to what our students have told us, then we have merely been listening. Smith (1989) discusses how only listening to the student voice is

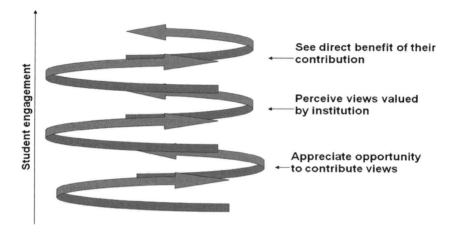

Figure 21.2: Impact of student voice activities on student engagement.

sometimes seen as sufficient: 'a celebration after which we return to the everyday'. Show your students you value their contribution by both listening and responding. Build feeding back to students into your work and actually do it: our student contributors deserve no less.

Conclusion

This chapter has provided you with staged guidance to support you in undertaking action research or other investigations involving the student voice to research the student experience or to inform your professional practice as a practitioner. The focus has primarily been on students undertaking degree programmes within universities but could be adapted for use within other educational contexts.

By following the guidance outlined in the stages within this chapter, you should be able to ensure, through the provision of meaningful opportunities that have enabled enough students to contribute their views confidently and effectively, that you have generated sufficient and reliable evidence. You will also be assured that you have carried out your work with students ethically and thoughtfully and mindful of their expectations and aspirations for their involvement in your investigation. Above all, you will be able to guarantee to those students who have entrusted their voices to you, that they have been both heard and heeded.

References

Alterio, M. (2006). Using story to enhance learning and teaching practices. A keynote address presented at the assessment, learning and teaching conference, Leeds Metropolitan University, UK.

Campbell, F., Beasley, L., Eland, J., & Rumpus, A. (2007). Hearing the student voice: Promoting and encouraging the effective use of the student voice to enhance professional development in learning, teaching and assessment within higher education. Napier University, Edinburgh, UK. Retrieved from http://www2.napier.ac.uk/studentvoices/profdev/publications.htm.

Campbell, F., Eland, J., Rumpus, A., & Shacklock, R. (2009). Hearing the student voice: Involving students in curriculum design and development. Edinburgh Napier University, Edinburgh, UK. Retrieved from http://www2.napier.ac.uk/studentvoices/curriculum/publications.htm.

Eliot, G. (1874). *Middlemarch* (Rev. ed. 2003). London, UK: Penguin Classics.

Flint, A., & Oxley, A. (2008). Placing student voices at the Heart of Institutional Dialogue Staff and Educational Development Association Spring Conference, London, UK.

Hearing the Student Voice. (2007). Hearing the student voice project website: Promoting and encouraging the effective use of the student voice to enhance professional development in learning, teaching and assessment within higher education. Retrieved from http://www2.napier.ac.uk/studentvoices/.

Hearing the Student Voice. (2009). Hearing the student voice project website: Involving students in curriculum design and development. Retrieved from http://www2.napier.ac.uk/studentvoices/curriculum/index.htm.

Mann, S. (2006). The advance of evidence-informed practice. Staff and Educational Development Association Conference, Liverpool, UK.

McNiff, J., & Whitehead, J. (2002). *Action research principles and practice*. Abingdon, UK: Routledge.

McNiff, J., & Whitehead, J. (2006). *All you need to know about action research*. Abingdon, UK: Routledge.

McNiff, J., & Whitehead, J. (2009). *You and your action research project*. Abingdon, UK: Routledge.

Quality Assurance Agency. (2005). Outcomes from institutional audit: Student representation and feedback arrangements, QAA, Gloucester, UK.

Smith, P. (1989). Pedagogy and the popular-cultural-commodity-text. In: H. A. Giroux & R. Simon (Eds), *Popular culture: Schooling and everyday life*. New York, NY: Bergin & Garvey.

Verrill, P., & Worden, I. (2006). International Consortium of Educational Development Conference, Sheffield, UK.

Chapter 22

Trust, Contextual Sensitivity and Student Voice

Gerry Czerniawski and Su Garlick

Abstract

This ongoing case study examines the collaboration between a secondary school in a London borough and a local university — the University of East London. The original focus of the case study was to look at students as informants/respondents and their journey in becoming student researchers within the context of student voice. In this chapter, we examine data from interviews with six student researchers from the school who received research training from the university and spent four days as researchers at a school in Finland. Their remit, from the school's 92 strong student voice body, was to carry out research at the Finnish school and report their findings with a view to implementing change within that school through various student voice initiatives. The data in this chapter are taken from interviews carried out by researchers from the university, involved in the project.

Keywords: Trust; contextual sensitivity; community; Finland; students as researchers

Introduction

Student voice has been the subject of considerable academic debate over the past 20 years (e.g. Ashworth, 1995; Fielding, Chapter 1, this volume; Giroux, 1986). Some driving forces for this renewed attention include the United Nations Convention on the Rights of the Child, the UK Healthy Schools Initiative, Building Schools for the Future (BSF) and increasingly School Self-Evaluation (SEF). Many studies have explored the role of student voice in educational change and reform (e.g. Fielding, 2001; Mitra, 2001), while others have stressed the importance of not only listening to

The Student Voice Handbook: Bridging the Academic/Practitioner Divide
Copyright © 2011 by Emerald Group Publishing Limited
All rights of reproduction in any form reserved
ISBN: 978-1-78052-040-7

voices, but engaging in dialogue (e.g. Lodge, 2005). Over the past few years, dialogue and consultation have been major themes emerging from the student voice agenda (e.g. Arnot, McIntyre, Pedder, & Reay, 2003; Flutter & Rudduck, 2004). We have moved from the notions of dialogue, 'shared responsibility' and consultation (Huddleston, 2007) to students becoming researchers in their own right (cf. Fielding & Bragg, 2003), which is, according to Thomson and Gunter (2006, p. 839), potentially a more 'transformative/disruptive process'. This chapter explores some of these debates further by focussing on the issue of 'trust' and in particular how its contextual specificity can be explored by young researchers when carrying out research within another national education system. This chapter initially examines competing narratives associated with student voice before introducing the reader to the importance of contextual sensitivity when carrying out research in different educational settings. After familiarising the reader with the Finnish educational context and case study, a brief overview of the research design is explained before finally discussing the issue of 'trust' through an examination of extracts taken from the interviews with these young researchers.

Student Voice — Conflicting Narratives

Fielding (2009) describes 'student voice' as 'a portmanteau term', and as 'student voice', 'pupil voice' and 'learner voice' are concepts often used synonymously, we have reluctantly done likewise in this chapter when reviewing some of the literature. However, the term 'voice' should be used cautiously. As Robinson and Taylor note, not only are "monolingual assumptions illusory" (Robinson & Taylor, 2007, p. 6), but as we shall see in this chapter 'voice' encompasses much more than the speech of the speaker. Halsey, Murfield, Harland, and Lord (2008) argue that there are considerable benefits to some educational stakeholders when the voices of young people are listened:

- Improvements in student services (e.g. changes in school dinners; improving toilet facilities etc.).
- Improvements in decision making (e.g. giving learners more of a say in the financial decisions taken by schools).
- Greater democracy for learners (e.g. allowing pupils a say in which teachers are employed; how long lessons run for; influencing subjects offered).
- Fulfilling legal requirements within schools (e.g. in terms of 'citizenship' and Every Child Matters legislation).
- Enhancing children's skills (e.g. allowing learners to run meetings with staff; including learners on interview panels).
- Empowering child self-esteem (e.g. increasing self-confidence and status when learners are consulted by their peers and teachers).

In addition to these advantages, many teachers, heads, administrators and policy makers can gain access to the specialist (and largely untapped) knowledge that learners have about their schools. This leads Fielding (2001) to argue that many student voice projects can act as a catalyst for change in schools including improvements in teaching, the curriculum and most importantly, student–teacher relationships. However, Fielding is also highly critical of some of the ways that Student Voice is articulated:

> Are we witnessing the emergence of something genuinely new, exciting and emancipatory that builds on rich traditions of democratic renewal and transformation? ... or are we presiding over the further entrench-ment of existing assumptions and intentions using student or pupil voice as an additional mechanism of control. (Fielding, 2001, p. 100)

We therefore use 'voice' as 'strategic shorthand' recognising its limitations (Robinson & Taylor, 2007, p. 6) and its multiple contestations. Broadly speaking these contestations fit comfortably within two competing narratives. The first situates student voice within discourses that relate to empowerment, democratic education, transformation and radical pedagogy (Fielding & Bragg, 2003; Giroux, 1986; Lodge, 2005; Taylor & Robinson, 2009). The second narrative positions student voice as a policy technology (Ball, 2001) embodying tokenism, regimes of audit and instrumentalism leading to greater organisational efficiency and the enhanced competitive positioning of the school (Fielding & Bragg, 2003; Gunter & Thomson, 2007; Reay, 2006).

Context Sensitivity and Student Voice

Contextual sensitivity is central to the repertoire of any student researcher visiting educational contexts they are unfamiliar with. By 'contextual sensitivity' we mean the sensitivity to actions, symbols and relationships that may carry different meanings in different societies or cultures. The problem of meaning and significance of actions is particularly important when considering the views of the young learners in this study and the preparation they received for their research trip to Finland. This is because much of the work that teachers and pupils do is conducted in terms of signals, symbols, coded language and symbolic behaviour.

Crossley and Jarvis (2001) highlight the significance of differing world views, forms of knowledge and frames of reference when embarking on cross-national research:

> In a world marked by the rapid intensification of globalisation, tensions between global and local agendas and developments clearly demand ever more specialist knowledge, insight and understanding. This is of vital importance; but the very same global factors heighten the significance of the contextual sensitivities that comparative researchers have a particular responsibility to identify. (p. 407)

Questions related to any cross-societal and intra-societal equivalence between concepts are prominent in the literature on comparative education and are crucial factors when considering how the student researchers in this study comprehend and explain the phenomena and relationships they encounter. For example the meaning of a teacher's action in one location can depend on the conventions, norms and values of not only the country concerned but also the particular type and location of the school in which that teacher's action takes place. The word 'inclusion', for example, within the diversity of school institutions that typify English schools might cause confusion to a Finnish teacher working within an education system that is by its nature 'inclusive' and 'comprehensive'. Carey-Wood (1991) argues that equivalence in meaning and concepts is not necessarily obtainable by 'correct' linguistic translations because of the semantic, cultural and societal differences inherent in words and concepts. Nevertheless:

> concepts are necessary as common points of reference for grouping phenomena that are differentiated geographically and often linguistically. (Rose, 1991, p. 447).

Without utilizing concepts, information collected about different countries provides no basis for relating one country to another.

Student Voice at 'East Valley' School in London

'East Valley' Comprehensive Secondary School consists of approximately 860 learners and is located in a London Borough on the outskirts of the city in a predominantly white working-class semi-industrial catchment area. The school has been described as 'outstandingly effective' in a recent government inspection report (reference retained for ethical purposes), and many of its teachers and students have represented the school at high profile national events showcasing good practice including its work on Student Voice. The Student Voice project that this chapter explores was launched in January 2007 at the school by members of the Senior Management Team (SMT). The aim of the project, from the school's point of view, was to provide a method of encouraging students to become actively involved in decisions about their own learning and empowering them with appropriate ways to do so. The school set out to:

- Ensure that all learners, irrespective of their class, gender, ethnicity, and ability, were involved in decisions about how, what and when they learn, with whom and the type of environment in which this occurs.
- Ensure that students were involved in school improvement strategies and the co-construction of policy making with teachers. (Czerniawski, Garlick, Hudson, & Peters, 2010).

Under clear direction from the school each form group elected three student voice representatives making a total of 92 learners directly involved in the Student Voice initiative. Each of the three students were chosen to represent the form on one of the following 'voices' instigated by the school's SMT:

'Blue Voice':   Focussing on teaching and learning.
'Red Voice':   Focussing on behaviour, independent learning and individual
                progress.
'Green Voice': Focussing on the environment of the school.

Each 'voice' had an executive group to represent them at meetings (pupil representatives in each form group and a member of teaching staff from the SMT). The 92 students were voted onto the scheme by their peers with the intention that they represented the student population of the school. In the early stages of the project all 92 students received school and university based training at UEL's docklands campus in London. A team of academics (including the authors of this paper) ran a series of short lectures and workshops at the university designed to help them: run productive meetings; gain confidence in various ways they can voice an opinion; listen to one another's point of view; have a rudimentary understanding of research skills and have a rudimentary understanding of research ethics. Visits to the university raised the Student Voice initiative profile in the eyes of the students as well as 'tick' boxes for the school's SMT in terms of raising aspirations for university applications.

Following training the students returned to school where they carried out research on their focus group 'voice' using various methods including questionnaires, lesson observations and interviews with young learners and staff at the school. This culminated at the end of the year in the production of three charters the school was to use that reflected the concerns of the three 'voices' as directed initially from the school's SMT. The second year of the project involved reflection and dissemination of the work carried out. The success of the first year, as interpreted by the school SMT was evident because students were asked to talk at conferences and were invited to national and regional award ceremonies. This second year was crucial in moving forward the project, maintaining moment and enabling different students to become involved. Further training took place at the University of East London (UEL) to enable the 'new' representatives to understand their role as researchers and to recognise some of the issues in relation to respect and ethical working on such a project. We have written elsewhere (Czerniawski et al., 2010) about the degree to which learners in this project were able to determine the direction of enquiry behind the three Voices along with the degree to which the three strands represented the interests of the school student body as a whole. Similarly we discussed issues related to those included, empowered, marginalised and alienated from the student voice experience at the school.

In the third year of the project a variety of initiatives have taken place under the 'Student Voice' banner. This chapter reports on one particular outcome, namely, the training of six students from the 'Global Voice' body at the school, to become researchers and their experiences at a school in Finland. In the words of these student researchers — the aim of their visit to Finland was to: 'To take on board any beneficial ideas from the Finish School System that we could try to introduce here at [East Valley]' (quotation taken from the presentation by students to their school governors). The volunteering students, aged between 15 and 16 years were members of the executive student voice body at the school and were allowed to take part in the research based on various criteria including attendance, behaviour, affordability and the degree to which they are up-to-date with school assignments. Research training was given by university staff (the authors of this article) on frequent visits to the school covering: an introduction to the Scandinavian education system; the relationship between methodology and methods; ethics; tools of analysis and the significance of contextual sensitivity. The sessions varied in nature from quite didactic (e.g. the briefings about the Finnish education system) to ones that involved the six students discussing, choosing and designing their research tools with the authors taking a 'back seat' offering support/clarification as and when this was requested by the students. These sessions were then backed up with further preparatory sessions by the head of modern foreign languages, himself a champion of global initiatives at the school, with further in-depth briefings on Finnish education, cultural norms/values and the specificities associated with the school trip regulations. One student in particular, recognised by the school for his linguistic abilities, embarked on Finnish language instruction in the months leading up to the trip to Finland.

Two staff members of the school accompanied the six students on a six-day visit to Finland in which four days were spent at 'Quiet haven School'. During the visit students carried out lesson observations, interviews with young learners and members of staff at the school, and gathered photographic documentary evidence of their trip.

Contrasting Educational Contexts — 'Quiet Haven School' in Finland

Given the restrictions of space for an article of this nature, it will have to be sufficient to state that both England and Finland fall into Esping-Anderson and Myles's (2009) welfare state types: namely, the free market liberal approach to social welfare characterised as typical to the English welfare state (2009) and the more social democratic approach to welfare policy found in Finland. Broadhead (2001) notes that English education policy locates national standards, rather than pupil autonomy, at the heart of school effectiveness. We characterise the English system of schooling as one containing a philosophy embracing a competitive, individual and standards based system of education and one typified by 'East Valley'. In contrast to most schools in England, Nordic countries have a longer and more firmly embedded tradition of democratic participatory education than does England (Moos, 2004; Czerniawski, 2010). Unlike various school types that exist in England, in general Finnish schools are 'schools for all' that is there is little or no differentiation or selection. A number of features characterise Finnish schooling that include:

- Professional trust in teachers.
- Small class sizes.
- Cultural and social homogeneity.
- Children starting compulsory education at the age of seven.
- Teachers trained in academic universities to Master's level.
- No mandatory tests or exams.
- Regional Support Networks help schools and teachers to incorporate technology into the classroom.
- Stakeholders from local businesses, parent bodies and universities working in close consultation with schools in the delivery of new educational initiatives.
- Educational decisions made by a collaboration of all political parties and organisations.
- The development of 'Professional Learning Communities', where school leaders enable teachers to share good practice, enrich ideas and match the needs of the learners to the local economic development (Maes, 2010; Ofsted, 2010).

'Quiet Haven School' in Western Finland was established in the past decade and came about following the merger of the town's primary and secondary schools. Most primary and secondary schooling in Finland is combined avoiding a potentially disruptive transition from one school to another (Burridge, 2010). 616 learners attend 'Quiet Haven school', with over 70 staff in what is a relatively ethnically mono-cultural catchment area. The school works with parents and the local community to maintain a sustainable ethos, and it prides itself on the work carried out promoting sustainable development and community engagement.

Research Design

Our work has been theoretically and methodologically framed by questions related to student voice at societal, cultural and institutional levels. The approach to data analysis adopted for this study owes much to the grounded theory tradition associated with Glaser and Strauss (1967). This tradition is not a consistent single methodology but has a number of interpretations (Charmaz, 2000; Layder, 1993). Using Layder's (1993) sensitising categories of 'context' and 'setting', the transcripts of the interview texts were coded. 'Context' has been used to refer to the wider socio and economic environments situating English and Finnish schools. 'Setting' has been used to focus on organizational cultures and communities of practice (Wenger, 1998), patterns of social activity and some of the power and authority structures within the two educational contexts. In this small-scale exploratory study the data collection that this chapter concerns itself with took the form of guided/semi-structured interviews (Kvale, 1996) carried out with students before and shortly after the trip to Finland took place. This was in addition to extensive field notes taken during the many training sessions that both authors offered in the months and weeks leading up to the Finland trip. Initial open coding (Glaser & Strauss, 1967) forced the authors to make analytic decisions about the data while selective/focused coding highlighted more frequently appearing initial codes to sort and conceptualise the data sets (Charmaz, 2000). A number of codes emerged that included: culture; teaching and learning; relationships with parents, family and teachers; community; exam systems; uniform; behaviour; trust and respect. In this chapter we focus on the issue of 'trust' and how this was interpreted differently by students once they had visited their school in Finland.

The Significance of 'Trust'

Like student voice, trust is a problematic, complex and contested concept. Hosmer (1995), for example, states that 'there appears to be wide-spread agreement on the importance of trust in human conduct, but unfortunately there also appears to be an equally widespread lack of agreement on a suitable definition of the construct' (p. 380). Empirical studies have, for example, focussed on trusting relationships between individuals (Frost & Moussavi, 1992); between individuals and organisations (Hoy & Kupersmith, 1985); and in events and processes (Hoffman, Sabo, Bliss, & Hoy, 1994). Different forms of professional trust are said to range from relatively high degrees in social democratic countries such as Finland to extremely low in more free-market liberal countries such as England (Elliot, 2004; Patulny, 2004). Trust has been strongly identified with a sense of community, belonging, civic virtue and social capital (Bourdieu, 1983; Coleman, 1988; Fukuyama, 1995). Putnam for example argues that:

> social capital refers to connections among individuals – social networks and the norms of reciprocity and trustworthiness that arise from them. In that sense social capital is closely related to what some have called "civic virtue." (Putnam, 2000, p. 19)

This would imply that certain types of social interaction based on trust and mutual tolerance can enable people to build communities, forge stronger links with each other and strengthen social cohesion. In relation to Student Voice, by 'trust' the authors refer to a young person's readiness to be exposed to significant others (e.g. parents and teachers) (Mead, 1934) in the belief that such exposure will be treated with compassion, capability, honesty and transparency. The six students interviewed in this article highlight their perceived differences in the ways that trust permeate teacher–student and student–student relationships as noted from their research trip to a Finnish school.

Results

Before their visit to Finland, there was a clear sense from all six student researchers that they felt trusted members of their school in England and this was backed up by discussions held between the authors and members of staff at the school. The positions of these young learners as members of the executive body of the schools SV initiative, their role as 'ambassadors' of the school to Finland, and the fact that they were predicted to do well in their final exams contributed to these feelings. This was conveyed in different ways with James (16 years old) acknowledging that it felt 'good to be able to observe and comment on things that teachers were doing knowing that our views are trusted'. Alanna (16 years old) believed that the school 'takes seriously most of our views that are put to them and we've seen some real changes and it's nice to feel that level of respect'. Martin (15 years old), reflecting on the fact that they were part of the student voice executive, felt that 'it's cool – although some [learners] are cynical and see us as the "good" kids but I think they trust us and they tell us what they want'. Rita (15 years old) spoke enthusiastically about attending meetings with other staff members and how 'it felt really strange and very grown-up at first to be around a table with my teachers but they listened to what I had to say and it felt really good'. In the build up to their trip to Finland these young people, who admittedly represented students considered by members of staff to be 'gifted and talented' and 'good students', felt that they were trusted and valued members of their school embarking on research as 'ambassadors' from their school.

Despite the intensive preparatory sessions they received in England before their departure to Finland, all six participants expressed surprise on arrival in Finland at what they saw as 'fundamental differences' permeating the school with one participant stating that he 'never considered that education could be so different'. One of the first things they noticed was the fact that most of the schools they drove past and the one they carried out their research at did not have fences, as Rhianna notes below:

> Over the past few years, we've had a fence put up, its kind of, I don't know if we should call it a prison, I dunno if I would go that far, it is definitely separate, 'you can't come here, you can't go there ... whereas there it is open ... there a lot of trust. You see mums and dads using the playground in the evenings for their kids. That would never happen at our school. [Rhianna, 15 years old]

In-depth coding of the interview data revealed that trust was also inextricably linked, by five of the six students, with a sense of 'community' and 'closeness' they felt existed within and beyond the school borders. It was widely felt, for example, that students at the school shared a 'similar demeanour', how everybody seemed to 'trust each other' and how students 'feel more part of the community'. Rita believed that it:

> seemed like a closer community. I still don't think we're anywhere near the closeness that they have in their community. We talk about the [name of English School] community, but it's nowhere near. [Rita, 15 years old]

'Respect' and 'trust' were often used interchangeably by participants with James, saying on his return from Finland that 'our school [East Valley] talks a lot about trust' but whether they actually have it is another matter'. A combination of what these young researchers felt as 'cultural' and 'institutional' differences, accounted for an overwhelming sense of 'mutual respect' between learners and teachers, said to exist by all six student researchers and explained by the following student:

> I think the key word is respect ... teachers trust them [Finish learners] in ways that they don't us, they are given responsibility in the idea that there isn't such a strict regime of sanctions and rewards and such. They're given the responsibility ... but not to the teachers as such, but to each other and themselves. And I think a lot of students there really respected that. That was one of the reasons why they think, 'we actually won't do that [behave badly] because we've been given the responsibility now not to' in effect. [Joe, 16 years old]

Most students believed that the mutual respect they witnessed in Finland created a very different learning environment from the ones they were used to in their school in England. Joe explains further:

> there was an informality in class so the teacher and pupil bonded I think because of the respect and freedom and the pupil would call the teacher by their first name, so I think its those little things between them – the teacher-pupil relationship. It made it much more easy-a much more easy ambience in class.

Almost all students contrasted the more egalitarian relationships between Finnish teachers and learners with those of their British counterparts. For example all six students compared the contrived distance (e.g. the English use 'sir'/'miss', the wearing of uniforms etc.) they experience in their English school with the comparatively 'trusting' 'informal' 'friendly' and 'first named'-based relationships that they said Finnish teachers cultivated with their learners. Three students referred to how 'homely' Finnish classrooms felt with one student explaining that this was because:

> with uniform when you're coming into school you just wear it you think 'okay I'm coming here, I don't really have to take care of it'. In Finland, when I took my shoes off I thought right, because you feel so much more homely, you think 'I'm gonna treat this like my house ... it felt good ... weird at first but good. Wish our school was like that. [Martin, 15 years old]

Olssen et al. (2004) have discussed the ways in which professional trust has been eroded with neo-liberal accountability practices of monitoring, reporting, recording and surveillance associated with aspects of economic globalisation and particularly pervasive in the English educational context. Four students contrasted a 'happier' and 'trusting' environment with what they saw as a more 'pressurised', 'competitive' and 'exam-based' culture in England. While one student believed that 'maybe the pressure is good for life, like when you have a job' another, despite her loyalty to her own institution contrasted her experience at her own school with her perception of the school she visited in Finland:

> I don't think people enjoy school here [England], I don't think people want to come to school-they're forced to come to school. I think its all to do with this relaxed happy atmosphere that have in Finland, they enjoy coming to school coz they haven't got the rules, they haven't got the regulation, they haven't got exams, they haven't got the pressure, they enjoy their time at school. Whereas here, we got pressure thing to adhere to, we got criteria to meet, I think sometimes we're just seen as a set of statistics, which isn't really a nice thing to be. [Rhianna, 15 years old]

While all six student researchers endorsed and enthused about their four days experience of the Finnish education system, there was far less agreement over the ways in which Finnish school policies could be implemented in England. Most felt that seeing one Finnish school was 'not enough' and that 'more time' was needed there. Two participants believed that it would also have helped to have 'experienced another school' in England to add authority to their inquiry. All were 'surprised' and 'amazed' at how much, in addition to the interviews they carried out they had learnt about schooling in Finland and how much as 'researchers' they had understood from 'non verbal communication', 'just watching' and 'body language'.

Almost all agreed that the system was better with one student saying 'why can't we have something like that over here?' and another stating that in England 'the school system is monotonous whereas over there every day is different, over there every day is a new surprise'. It was much harder, however, for participants to perceive how a similar environment could be created in England despite a clear desire for this to happen. One student felt 'we can't really incorporate it over here because were just so much more stricter' while another questioned 'how can we make it work here in a way that fits our own current system but also is reflective of their system?'. Joe, a passionate student voice advocate is clearly in two minds about what sorts of ideas, gleamed from the Finnish trip, could successfully be initiated at his own school:

> I think if the government tried hard enough, if they got their act together and produced a report that absolutely pushed this system, then perhaps it could work if you built it up from primary school to secondary, perhaps it could work, but it would also mean a different attitude from the parenting community, so in that respect perhaps it couldn't, because I suppose it's the way our parents have been brought up that influences children growing up. [Joe, 16 years old]

We finish this data section with a quotation from Rita, clearly moved by her research trip to a Finnish school:

> I'm quite mixed up about it ... I loved it and loved being in that environment. Thought I loved this [her school in England] school but this trip has done my head in. They really trust and care about people there, and our school can learn from this. Teachers seem to let kids do what they want but here is the weird thing – they seem to really learn out there and get excited about it where all I can think of right now is if I'm going to pass my exams – its rubbish really. [Rita, 15 years old]

Discussion

In an article of this size the authors have had to make some over-simplifications in a small-scale exploratory case study that is framed within the broader context of student voice. We therefore acknowledge that these findings are not generalisable to contexts beyond this particular case study. We also fully appreciate the limitations of a six-day trip to Finland with four days spent in a school and its ability equip these young researchers with sufficient information to make fully informed judgements about the merits and disadvantages of a very different educational system. However this qualitative small-scale study does serve useful and illuminative purposes that accommodate some level of generalisation, while recognising the specificity of context and setting when discussing young people becoming researchers in their own right.

At the start of this chapter, we drew attention to the fact that Fielding (2001) has argued that many student voice projects can act as a catalyst for change in schools including improvements to student–teacher relationships. These student researchers believed they possessed trusting relationships with many of their teachers in 'East Valley' before their departure to Finland. But then again, why would they question 'trust' as constructed, positioned and situated within an institutional setting and context they have been socialised into. Their perceptions of trust, we argue, are partially grounded within school-based structures, procedures and cultural values that obscure a 'gulf in trust' (Leitch & Mitchell, 2007) between learners and teachers despite the rhetoric of student voice participation. In fact, it is only by taking student researchers *out* of their own institutions to research and interpret a world elsewhere that young learners can possibly hope to bring back critically informed perspectives of benefit to them and their schools and avoid interpreting the already interpreted world of education they know. Strikingly apparent from these interviews is the perception by these student researchers of fundamentally different sets of relationships between teachers and learners cultivated in the Finnish school they visited and the impact that these relationships had on the learning environments they observed. While some might attribute this to a different type of culture, one that is less populated, more rural, more ethnically mono-cultural and so on, a lot more, in the eyes of these student researchers is to do with institutional arrangements and trusting relationships forged in the school they visited.

Of course, any cross-national comparison and qualitative analysis presents both conceptual and methodological challenges to the researcher be they young/old, experienced or novice. The provision of education is deeply influenced by the cultural context in which it is located, as well as by the economy and the political system responsible for educational policies (Hayhoe, 2007). Alexander (2005) notes that 'the language of education contains few universals and educational conversation across cultures is laced with pitfalls for the unwary' (Alexander, 2005, p. 5). We were, however, surprised by the apparent ease in which these student researchers honed in on substantial differences between, what they perceived as two very different education systems. However they also expressed doubt at the extent to which they believed that what they observed in Finland could exist in schools in England. While they firmly believed that things could 'be done differently' in English schools they also felt that there was a closer alignment in Finland between the sorts of values and relationships that circulate schools and the immediate community and a de-alignment between those that exist in schools in England and the community in which those schools are located.

Lodge (2008) notes that there has been a shift in the 19th and 20th century 'children-should-be-seen-and-not-heard' perceptions of childhood compared to more child-centred discourses that exist in many private and public spheres. That said, in many schools in England, expectations about children are still shaped by an 'ideology of immaturity' (Grace, 1995) that characterised both centuries. This ideology is based on an outdated view of childhood in which school exclusion of young people from the processes of dialogue and decision making fails to acknowledge young learners' capacity for resourcefulness, ingenuity, enterprise and an ability to reflect on issues affecting their education. Tensions exist between this ideology and more marketised, consumer-based ideologies in schools in which the student voice agenda can fit albeit for more instrumentalist purposes.

Although schools in England have made significant changes to the ways in which they assess and teach young learners, they have been largely unsuccessful in recognising societal expectations that young people mature at an increasingly younger age. The danger of not recognising this mismatch in expectations has been identified by Rudduck (2002):

> Schools in their deep structures and patterns of relationship have changed less in the last fifteen years or so than young people have changed ... we know that from an early age young people are capable of insightful and constructive analysis of social situations and if their insights are not harnessed in support of their own learning then they may use them strategically to avoid learning in school and conspire unwittingly in the process of their own underachievement. (Rudduck, 2002, pp. 123-124)

The question still remains, how can schools become more able to embrace student voice and work towards a better future for all? The key seems, from these interviews, to be in the feeling of being trusted, respected – both by staff and fellow students.

Conclusion

At a time when it has been acknowledged that British Children represent some of the unhappiest within the industrialised world (UNICEF, 2007), recognising and acting on the pervasiveness of the 'ideology of immaturity' (Grace, 1995) that exists in many schools in England can increase hope in an increasingly convoluted world. Often couched in terms of inevitability, such an ideology can drain energy and commitment from both learners and teachers. This case study illustrates how contextually sensitive young researchers identified 'trust' as a culturally situated and embedded value within an educational environment radically different from the one they were used to. The voices, sensitivities, and expertise of these young researchers in this study and their concerns give rise to complex hope in exceedingly complex times. The escalation of market forces in education means that both learners and teachers are 'now working within a new value context in which image and impression management ... are becoming as important as the educational process' (Ball, 2001, p. 13). It would therefore be a tragedy if the zeitgeist devotion to student voice gets reduced to a 'rhetoric of agency' (Gunter & Thomson, 2007) associated with the second of the two narratives we discussed at the start of this chapter, namely those that embody tokenism, instrumentalism and the enhanced competitive positioning of the school.

It is true that student voice initiatives are performed, grappled with, mediated in, hectic institutions where learners and teachers have, for the very best of intentions, competing commitments, priorities and values. It is also true that, taking an historical perspective, the student voice movement is contested, tentative, embryonic and culturally situated. But most student voice initiatives are also collaborative and comprise the integrity and passion that young learners and teachers bring to their work. One starting point then is to trust young people in the ways that these student researchers clearly believe their counterparts are trusted in Finland. In essence then, if schooling is to be effective according to these six young researchers, we need to rethink what we mean by 'efficacy' in institutions of learning. The socially re-produced sites we know as schools need to be ones where all forms of symbolic communication used is non-threatening, where learners and teachers feel valued and comfortable in their learning environments and are equally comfortable to change, experiment and take risks. Schools are sites in which trust and respect should form the cornerstones of all teacher/student interactions. Without this, any claim that formal education is in some way, a preparation, enactment and rehearsal for democratic citizenship is disingenuous.

References

Alexander, R. (2005). Culture, dialogue and learning: Notes on an emerging pedagogy. Paper given at *Education, Culture and Cognition: Intervening for Growth* International Association for Cognitive Education and Psychology (IACEP), 10th International Conference, University of Durham, UK, July 10–14, 2005.

Arnot, M., McIntyre, D., Pedder, D., & Reay, D. (2003). *Consultation in the classroom: Pupil perspectives on teaching and learning*. Cambridge: Pearson.

Ashworth, L. (1995). *Children's voices in school matters*. London: Advisory Centre for Education.

Ball, S. J. (2001). Better read! Theorising the teacher. In: M. Maguire & J. Dillon (Eds), *Becoming a teacher*. Buckingham: Open University Press.

Bourdieu, P. (1983). Forms of capital. In: J. C. Richards (Ed.), *Handbook of theory and research for the sociology of education*. New York: Greenwood Press.

Broadhead, P. (2001). Curriculum change in Norway: Thematic approaches, active learning and pupil cooperation – from curriculum design to classroom implementation. *Scandinavian Journal of Educational Research*, *45*(1), 27–42.

Burridge, T. (2010). *Why do Finland's schools get the best results?* http://news.bbc.co.uk/1/hi/programmes/world_news_america/8601207.stm?ls

Carey-Wood, J. (1991). Leaving home: Housing for young people in England and France. Unpublished book – University of Bristol – cited in: Kennet P, 2001. *Comparative Social Policy*, Buckingham: Open University Press.

Charmaz, K. (2000). Qualitative interviewing and grounded theory analysis. In: J. F. Gubrium & J. A. Holstein (Eds), *Handbook of interviewing*. Thousand Oaks, CA: Sage.

Coleman, J. C. (1988). Social capital in the creation of human capital. *American Journal of Sociology*, *94*, S95–S120.

Crossley, M., & Jarvis, P. (2001). Context matters. *Comparative Education*, *37*(4), 405–408.

Czerniawski, G., Garlick, S., Hudson, T., & Peters, P. (2010). *Listening to learners*, Report for the Higher Education Acadamy/Escalate.

Czerniawski, G. (2010). *Emerging teachers and globalisation*. London: Routledge.

Elliot, J. (2004). Making teachers more accountable: Models, methods and processes. *Research Papers in Education*, *19*(1), 7–14.

Esping-Anderson, G., & Myles, J. (2009). *The welfare state and redistribution*. Unpublished paper. Retrieved from http://www.esping-anderson.com/?a201ce18.

Fielding, M. (2001). Students as radical agents of change. *Journal of Educational Change*, *2*(2), 123–141.

Fielding, M. (2009). Interrogating student voice: pre-occupations, purposes and possibilities. In: H. Daniels, H. Lauder, & J. Porter (Eds.), *Educational Theories, Cultures and Learning: A Critical Perspective* (pp. 101–116). London: Routledge.

Fielding, M. (2009). Listening to learners: Partnerships in action conference, *Student voice, democracy and the necessity of radical education*. [Key note presentation] April 22, London: University of East London.

Fielding, M., & Bragg, S. (2003). *Students as researchers; making a difference*. London: Routledge.

Flutter, J., & Rudduck, J. (2004). *Consulting pupils: What's in it for schools?*. London: RoutledgeFalmer.

Frost, T., & Moussavi, F. (1992). The relationship between leader power base and influence: The moderating role of trust. *Journal of Applied Business Research*, *8*(4), 9–14.

Fukuyama, F. (1995). *Trust: Social virtues and the creation of prosperity*. New York, NY: Free Press.

Glaser, B. G., & Strauss, A. L. (1967). *The discovery of grounded theory*. Chicago, IL: Aldine.

Giroux, H. A. (1986). Radical pedagogy and the politics of student voice. *Interchange – A Quarterly Review of Education*, *17*(1), 48–69.

Grace, G. R. (1995). *School leadership: beyond education management: An essay in policy scholarship*. London: Falmer.

Gunter, H., & Thomson, T. (2007). Learning about student voice. *Support for Learning*, *22*(4), 181–188.

Halsey, K., Murfield, J., Harland, J., & Lord, P. (2008). *The voice of young people: An Engine for improvement? Scoping the evidence*. London: National Foundation for Educational Research.

Hayhoe, R. (2007). The use of ideal types in comparative education: A personal reflection. *Comparative Education*, *43*(2), 189–205.

Hoffman, J., Sabo, D., Bliss, J., & Hoy, W. K. (1994). Building a culture of trust. *Journal of School Leadership*, *4*(9), 484–501.

Hosmer, L. T. (1995). Trust: The connecting link between organizational theory and philosophical ethics. *Academy of Management Review*, *20*, 379–403.

Hoy, W. K., & Kupersmith, W. J. (1985). The meaning and measure of faculty trust. *Educational and Psychological Research*, *5*, 1–10.

Huddleston, T. (2007). *From student voice to shared responsibility. Effective practice in democratic school governance in European schools*. Strasbourg: Council of Europe/Network of European Foundations.

Kvale, S. (1996). *Interviews – An introduction to qualitative research interviewing*. London: Sage.

Layder, D. (1993). *New strategies in social research*. Cambridge: Blackwell.

Leitch, R., & Mitchell, S. (2007). Caged birds and cloning machines: how student imagery 'speaks' to use about cultures of schooling and student participation. *Improving Schools*, *10*(1), 53–71.

Lodge, C. (2005). From hearing voices to engaging in dialogue: Problematising student participation in school improvement. *Journal of Educational Change*, *6*(2), 125–146.

Lodge, C. (2008). *Student voice and learning-focused school improvement*. Research Matters No. 32, INSI, London.

Maes, B. (2010). Retrieved from http://bertmaes.worldpress.com/2010/02/24/why-is-education-in-finland-that-good-10-reform-principles-behind-the-success/

Mead, G. H. (1934). *Mind, self and society*. Chicago, IL: Chicago University Press.

Mitra, D. (2001). Opening the floodgates: Giving students a voice in school reform. *Forum*, *43*(2), 91–94.

Moos, L. (2004). Introduction. In: J. MacBeath & L. Moos (Eds), *Democratic learning: The challenge to school effectiveness*. London: RoutledgeFalmer.

Ofsted (2010). *Finnish pupil's success in mathematics – Factors that contribute to Finnish pupils' success in mathematics*. Report no 100105, Ofsted, London.

Olssen, M., Codd, J., & O'Neil, A. (2004). *Education policy, globalisation, citizenship and democracy*. London: Sage.

Patulny, R. (2004). *Social capital, norms, networks and practices – A critical evaluation*. SPRC Discussion Paper. The Social Policy Research Centre. University of South Wales, Sydney.

Putnam, R. (2000). Interview with Ken Newton, *ECPR News* (2000) Leaders of the Profession: *ECPR News* 11, p. 2.

Reay, D. (2006). 'I'm not seen as one of the clever children': Consulting primary pupils about the social conditions of learning. *Educational Review*, *58*, 171–181.

Robinson, C., & Taylor, C. (2007). Theorising student voice: Values and perspectives. *Improving Schools*, *10*(1), 5–17.

Rose, R. (1991). Comparing forms of comparative analysis. *Political Studies*, *39*, 446–462.

Rudduck, J. (2002). The transformative potential of consulting young people about teaching, learning and schooling. *Scottish Educational Review*, *34*(2), 123–137.

Taylor, C., & Robinson, C. (2009). Student voice: Theorising power and participation. *Pedagogy, Culture and Society, 17,* 161–175.

Thomson, P., & Gunter, H. (2006). From 'consulting pupils' to 'pupils as researchers': A situated case narrative. *British Educational Research Journal, 32*(6), 839–856.

UNICEF. (2007). *Child poverty in perspective: An overview of child well-being in rich countries, Innocenti Research Centre Report Card 7.* London: The United Nations Children's Fund.

Wenger, R. (1998). *Communities of practice: Learning, meaning and identity.* Cambridge: Cambridge University Press.

Chapter 23

Research Methods for Pupil Engagement: Hearing Student Voice

Joanne Waterhouse

Abstract

This is an account of the methodology and methods used in a current project aimed at learning about pupil engagement. The project is a collaborative research initiative between university and school colleagues within an enduring partnership. The main data-gathering method used with pupils was a focus group interview, but this was embedded in a series of activities involving the class teacher and the whole class and which included informal observations and video recording. In this chapter, first-hand testimony from the pupils is incorporated to illustrate the depth of understanding and breadth of individuality among the pupils listened to. The main argument within the chapter is that research methods for capturing student voice need to be contextualised for the students in a way that is predicated on positive, trustful relationships and the inherent value of their perspectives and opinions and of explicit purpose to them.

Keywords: Engagement; collaboration; purpose; relationships; trust

Introduction

The research featured in this chapter took place in the context of a school–university partnership in the United Kingdom whose defining function is the practice and study of collaborative research. The eight participant schools are all serving the secondary sector, with some designated as Upper Schools, comprising students aged 13–19 and others taking students at age 11 until 16. The particular research activity with pupils cited later was focus group interviews conducted in all the schools by university colleagues and facilitated by class teachers. The author of this work is a member of the university team working as a critical friend and researcher alongside two of the partnership schools. The research was intended to generate data about pupil engagement. All the pupils were in year 10 and aged between 14 and 15 years.

The oft-used metaphor of peeling away the layers of an onion serves well here to imagine the embedded nature of the research activity nested within a multilayered research collaboration bound by extensive and enduring relationships resulting from years of shared experiences. Each layer of the endeavour is contextualised by a shared commitment to the purpose of the research and to the research being purposeful. In a similar vein, the activity with pupils is contextualised by the trusting relationships they have with the teacher facilitating their participation, and, in turn, their participation reinforces that trust and sense of value. I will return to this in the conclusion. Purposeful, explicit and contextual engagement with key players in any endeavour has the potential to increase engagement. When the issue under investigation is engagement itself, then a symbiosis takes place in which one is inspired to argue for the formal realignment of pupils as key collaborators in planning for teaching and learning.

In this chapter, I begin by explaining the purpose and composition of the partnership and outlining the methodology and methods for the research with schools and pupils in particular. I then report on encounters with three focus groups in two schools, describing the forms of participation and providing examples of their contributions. This section is organised under the key themes of *Learning and Teaching* and *Relationships and Trust*. I conclude by discussing the significance of the nature and form of their participation in such groups for their ongoing engagement in school in the final concluding section.

The Research Design: Multilayered and in Context

This research is embedded in the collaborative work of a School–University Partnership for Educational Research (SUPER) located in the east of England (McLaughlin, Black-Hawkins, Brindley, McIntyre, & Taber, 2006; McLaughlin, Black-Hawkins, & McIntyre, 2007). This partnership was initiated over a dozen years previously and is composed of eight member schools and university staff from a faculty of education. Partnership activities have included school-based action research projects and collaborative learning about research processes and practices. The partnership has endured in part due to the forging of resilient relationships characterised by trust and commitment. The current project focusing on pupil engagement began three years ago and was decided upon through an extended consultation between schools, within schools and between schools and the university. A key priority was to establish a focus that was of interest to all schools and that could be pursued autonomously as well as collaboratively. We were interested to learn about teachers' and pupils' views of engagement and what engagement looks like in classrooms. Our research questions were framed by the analysis of an initial large-scale pupil survey conducted across the schools and informed by a literature review. In addition to views of engagement, we wanted to learn what influences and shapes that understanding. Crucially, we designed a project that included a study of teaching and learning in classrooms so that we could answer the question: 'What happens when you look at engagement in action?' The process in each school was similar and included teacher focus group interviews, pupil focus group interviews and a series of interviews with a single class teacher. This teacher facilitated the work with pupils and framed the discussions about their beliefs and practices with the aid of edited video footage of lessons. The focus group interviews were informed by responses to activities and included discussions between members of the group. In this way, the research developed incrementally in each site, and the school coordinator worked closely with the university colleague and the participants to ensure the research remained purposeful, contextualised and meaningful. As a member of the faculty staff, I was partnered with two schools, and in both sites, the individual class teacher proved a significant collaborator in the arrangements of purposeful and dynamic pupil focus group interviews.

At Shaftesbury School, the class teacher was Tim, the head of English with over 10 years of teaching experience. He arranged for me to meet with a group of six students from year 10. He talked with the whole class about the research in general and asked for volunteers. Then, when I arrived in the class, he showed them all the video he had edited of their recent lesson and narrated for them what he thought was happening, focusing on his behaviour and decision-making. This helped to contextualise the ensuing group interview and provided the pupils with a powerful stimulus for discussion. It also emphasised the inclusive, collaborative nature of the relationship between Tim and the class when he took time to demonstrate how footage of them was to be used to illuminate his practice and how his plans for teaching them were influenced by his knowledge and interactions with them. In Archdeacon College, Sara was a young history teacher in her second year who displayed a fierce commitment to providing the richest learning environment for her pupils. She arranged for me to meet with two groups' representative of the diversity of her classes and thus including some who were predictably lively and egocentric.

Hearing Students' Voices

In this section, I describe the attitudes and responses within the groups and share extracts and quotes from the transcripts. The aim is to illuminate the enthusiasm and engagement of the students with the activity and to offer a glimpse of some of the key commentaries that emerged. I recognise that the context for these conversations was atypical. The pressures on teachers in busy classrooms with large groups of disparate students will create environments in which some young people behave in ways distinct from how they can respond in small, quiet groups. No criticism of teachers or school leaders is implied. This data and discussion is situated in a discourse about how such reflections might routinely be heard and appreciated to incorporate the perspectives of the other key players in the classroom.

Learning and Teaching — Making the Links

Each group of students I interviewed had significant things to say. Some groups needed encouragement to begin with in response to an unfamiliar adult, but once we had established clearly what the discussion was about, the comments came tumbling out with children finishing one another's sentences, sometimes interrupting one another and occasionally talking at the same time as one another. In Shaftesbury School, it was as if a cork had been removed from the metaphorical bottle that had been containing their knowledge and experiences of being in school. Even in a setting with proud traditions of listening to student voice and fresh from a classroom in which they were respected members, these young people were expressing opinions they claimed had never been sought before. One child commented that 'I've never been asked questions like this in fifteen years I've been at this school' (Gary). He was reflecting his time in the system rather than at a single school, but his heartfelt comment was met with agreement around the table. The phenomenon of 'group speak' in which they anticipated the content of one another's contributions and finished one another's sentences evoked a sense of familiar conversations and shared understandings. In one exchange, at an interview in Archdeacon College, three boys reflected together about learning with the stimulus of a film:

Jason: I generally find I learn something if I watch a film about it.
Paul: Yeah, I do too.
Will: You feel like you're there.
Paul: You write notes too.
Jason: I remember a lot more.
Paul: When you're reading about it ....
Will: It goes in one ear and out of the other.
Jason: When the teacher writes something on the board, talks about it and then rubs it off, I've forgotten everything that was on that board. But say I've watched it on a film, and it's been acted out in the film, I will know it then, if you know what I mean.

Each of the groups demonstrated an appreciation of the efforts that teachers go to to help them achieve success. A student at Archdeacon College was thoughtful about how a teacher helped him remember things: 'I have one teacher and he helps us to remember. We have one lesson and he'll tell us what to do, ask us questions, then adapt on it, make another set of questions. Then it stays in' (Dan). Another responded to a discussion about latitude and humour in lessons by considering how it could be balanced and supportive of her studies:

Carol: In some lessons, like History, you can have a laugh and a joke but we always get the work done as well. So we know that even if we do spend half the lesson laughing and joking we know that by the end of the year when we're doing the exam, we've still got all the work that we need.

When discussing how Tim engages them, the students at Shaftesbury School were clear and enthusiastic:

Tom: The way Mr Jones teaches, his teaching methods are fun compared to any other teacher we have.
Susan: It's his enthusiasm and his sense of humour. And the way he relates to you. He doesn't talk down to you. He talks at your level, the same level.
Matt: Most of what he does, he talks to us and gets our contributions back and we can make notes. We get quite detailed notes.
Helen: It's not as if he talks to us as just one group. He talks to us as individuals.
Tom: He doesn't talk to us from a teacher's view. He talks to us as one of us.
Elena: He says it in a way that quite easy for us to understand. And he goes over it quite a lot and if anyone has any questions he's like answers them quite detailed.
Susan: It's easy to draw, he draws things out of us, that you normally wouldn't think of. He encourages it and people think 'oh yeah!' He says it in a way that's easy for you to write down. He's put these packs together about the essays we have to do. We've got a pack for each one. He analyses the scenes from each play.
Tom: We did Educating Rita and he put all the references in it.
Susan: We have them on our table.
Tom: He sticks key scenes and acts in it.
Susan: The scenes we need to work on. And we highlight them. And they're really good references for when we go back and actually write the essay.

Throughout the interview, this group gave numerous examples of how Mr Jones helped them and managed them. They made explicit links between his actions and behaviour and their achievements in their work. They demonstrated a sophisticated level of awareness of the dynamics within the classroom and of the different strategies deployed by Mr Jones to work with individuals and the larger group. They recognised that the seating arrangements allowed for disparate groups to colonise the room and maintain a balance to proceedings. For example, some rows contained the 'talkers and those who will ask questions', another row was filled with 'quiet ones, who will put their heads down and get on' and the front row was populated by those who perhaps need closer attention to maintain their efforts. The students know the teacher's strategies and appreciate the control:

Susan: He balances it out. So there's questioning people, then quieter people then a mixed row at the front. I think he didn't put the two lots of louder people together so that there wasn't as much disruption. Little things like that really work for us because if I was sat near Ella I wouldn't concentrate as much because obviously we're friends outside of lessons and I don't think I would engage as much as I do if I wasn't where I'm sitting.

They were equally aware of how he facilitated their learning. When they discussed this, they showed awareness of their own dispositions for paying attention. One young lad insisted that he needed talk in the classroom to concentrate. He required an atmosphere that allowed him to relax:

Howard: If I'm in a classroom where it's a relaxed environment I seem to do better than if it's just sitting and just writing in silence. So if there's background chat, I find that a lot more easy to work with than a silent room.

This was a theme across all three focus groups. The students had thoughts and knowledge about how they learned and what the conditions needed to be for them to retain and make sense of new information. Some discussed the importance of being allowed to ask questions. One young girl in Archdeacon College was frustrated that she sometimes struggled to have sufficient opportunities to ask on an individual basis so that she could understand something for herself:

Becca: I always find that when the teacher explains to the whole class I don't understand it so I have to ask one of my friends and they have to explain it just to me. Then if they explain it, or a teacher explains it just to me I always find I understand it more because I can ask questions as well. When I put my hand up in class, sometimes I feel like I don't want to get it wrong.

Another discussion that took place among each group was the idea of body language and the possibilities for misunderstanding based on presumption. Sometimes this can be straightforward, such as the problems for Lydia and her notes: 'I get told off a lot for drawing in my margins and they think 'Lydia you're not listening'. No, I'm just doodling.' Sometimes, it is the result of a misalignment between a teacher offering help and a student trying to think. Peter expresses frustration at being disturbed by a well-meaning teacher:

Peter: I'm sitting there and I'm trying to work through a question in my head and the teacher thinks I'm not doing any work and comes to see what I'm doing. And I'm sitting there going 'I'm trying to figure this out'. And he just butts in and I've lost it completely.

For another student, it is an issue about eye contact. She is often challenged to pay attention by looking at the teacher and being seen to pay attention, but that does not always work for her. Being seen to pay attention is itself a distraction: 'If I look at them I might get distracted by something else. So I can be concentrating on them by not looking at them' (Milly). There is a sense in these discussions of other pressures in the classroom disabling opportunities for meaningful talk about learning and sharing perspectives. Will comments almost as an aside that 'I always get misunderstood and stuff. It's really annoying.' The students all demonstrated knowledge of various behaviours that signify engagement and back in Shaftesbury

School Emily refers again to the classroom arrangements and reflects on the need to know the individuals concerned:

Emily: I think it depends on the person as well, because we have – you know the middle row of people in the video, at the back of us, they're quieter than other people in the class so I think their engagement is kind of sitting there watching and writing and then they understand. But for people like me I have to ask questions in order to understand and engage in it. I think it depends on the people who you're watching.

So 'reading' engagement is understood by the students as a complex business in which assumptions based on body language are often mistaken and a result of a misreading. It would seem imperative to have a range of cues and sources of information. Good relationships and knowledge of one another's feelings and motivation are important.

Relationships and Trust — Key Features for Engagement

Relationships with the teachers are paramount and students talked variously of being listened to, being understood and knowing the boundaries. This was linked to the extent to which a teacher was focused on the responsibilities of student achievement. It was summed up for one group as a matter of trust:

Tom: With Mr Jones you feel you can trust him and what he says is how it is. And how it's going to happen. So if he says he's going to get something for the next lesson, he gets it. You have that trust in him.

This brings to mind a sense of professionalism and thoroughness in the teacher's approach. The focus on success was absolutely measured by formal examinations by all the groups. The students tended to have a functional approach to their time in class and judged teacher effectiveness in terms of how they facilitated useful note-taking that could be turned into currency for exam success. There was seriousness and determination about summative assessments, which is perhaps belied by the casual insouciance of youths as observed in passing. They knew clearly how important exam success was and demonstrated a focus on the means to obtain it. For one student, her awareness of the pressures upon them in the system went beyond the immediacy of the classroom and was the source of her motivation and concentration:

Helen: I think I work well with pretty much any teacher because I have a lot of determination in myself to do well so it's not always about the teacher it's about the subject I think as well. Most of the time I'm really engaged in all of my lessons because I know it's really important, especially with all the competition with universities now. It's so important to do well. I think a lot of us are engaged in lessons because you know how important it is get good notes and everything.

A common protocol for talking to students about their schooling is to prohibit naming teachers or becoming in any way personal. It is important not to invoke criticism fuelled by particular encounters or based on individual animosities. However, my experience with two of the student groups was that they were able to discuss difficulties in their classrooms and describe particular events in ways that seemed fair and reasonable. They talked about particular teachers in terms of their behaviour and how it sometimes frustrated them without making personal or derogatory remarks. Indeed, it could be argued that it is only in the depiction of the actual event or circumstance that young people can articulate what works and what does not. In the extract below, the students are discussing their reaction to the work of a teacher whom they judged to be less effective than another:

Holly: If I hadn't done homework for Miss West, I'd never just go up to her and say I'd never done it.
Elena: Because we only have her once a fortnight it's hard to build a relationship with her.
Tom: I don't think she's angry, I think it's because she doesn't know us very well so she doesn't know how to control us very well.
Holly: I just don't get a lot out of her lessons.
Jenny: Her lessons are not stressful, but I can't concentrate in her lessons as well as I can in Mr Jones'.
Will: Adults don't pick up that children pick up on under-confidence and low self esteem within teaching.
Emily: Like, in yesterday's lesson, I listened to my Ipod all lesson. Ok, I shouldn't have and I know that. Mr Jones would have said 'Em, put that away' – in a polite way. But she didn't even tell me off.
Holly: She just sat at the computer all lesson. I'm pretty sure no one worked.

There is evidence of empathy and a consideration of circumstances beyond their immediate experience, such as the appreciation of the low incidence of their encounters leading to a lack of mutual knowledge. There is also an interesting comment about disengaged behaviour that shows a lack of personal accountability on behalf of the student. She needs the imposition of control from the teacher to conform. This was echoed in another group when the students talked extensively about the importance of the teachers always displaying generosity, forgiveness and reasonableness and then they would, in turn, behave:

Lydia: If teachers are friendly to you as soon as you walk in, then you're going to be nice back to them and get on with the work. Treat people as you want to be treated. If they come in and they're like shouting then you're going to shout back.

Indeed, for one young man, it was very straightforward that the reciprocal relationship was fundamental to his willingness to conform. He displayed a sensitivity to tone and attitude that rendered fragility to his capacity to concentrate:

Mark: If they're going to be nice to us and give us a bit more freedom in what we do, we would be a lot more willing to learn. We would do what they asked. If they said to me 'don't talk' or something the chances are, if they'd been nice to me earlier in that lesson, I wouldn't argue with them, I'd go 'oh, alright then.'

One of the most interesting aspects of the discussions with all three student groups was their reflections on teachers who learn or who do not. One young man had learned about criticism in his English lessons and understood it as an important creative and analytical tool. He used this knowledge to comment on the effective practice of his teacher who demonstrated a readiness to ask for feedback and change his resources:

Will: He's the only teacher who understands criticism as a positive thing. He'll be showing us something, in our packs say, and maybe the whole group hasn't done as well as he thought we would on a piece. And then he really would, he'd spend a whole lesson asking us what went well, what he could improve on, not just for us, but also for future classes.

Similarly, such behaviour was high on another student's list of ways for her teachers to improve. In the context of the focus group interview, the student makes the point reasonably and thoughtfully and it seems hard to argue against the eminent sense to be made. Why would you not ask such questions?

Lynn: If they listen to suggestions. Because sometimes, every other lesson will be like 'write a newspaper article'. And the whole class will be moaning about doing it. I think the teacher needs to take that into consideration and ask us what we want to do instead. 'If you don't want to do that, what do you want to do instead? You need to get this information down, but how do you want to do it?'

Such comments give an impression of a dearth of positive, constructive conversations in the classroom focused on ways for the learning to be improved. The experience of listening to these student groups reinforced a sense that these young people were mindful of their learning situations and were capable of astute commentary about teachers that was fair and reasonable. For some, their maturity and personalities required explicit control and direction, but they all displayed a capacity to be collaborators in planning for effective teaching and learning encounters. What left the most indelible mark on me was the enthusiasm they demonstrated to express opinions and the insight that they showed to the processes of their own learning.

Conclusion

Learning about pupil engagement through engaging with pupils seems self-evidently appropriate. It certainly proved rewarding and informative. Unsurprisingly, pupils know a great deal about the business of teaching and the work of their teachers. Perhaps, more surprising was their awareness of the complex dynamics within the classroom and their tolerance of difficulties. We have a lot to learn from the observations and understanding of pupils in how to make lessons more effective. Our research with pupils also generated data that was suggestive of the inherent merits of engaging with pupils about their learning and school experiences to enhance their engagement. The pupil focus group interviews in both schools were facilitated by the class teacher to contextualise the event and in ways that emphasised the value we were placing on their opinions and perspectives. It became clear in their responses that their relationships with their teachers were paramount in promoting their engagement. Being valued, trusted and cared for mattered. The significance of trust as an element of relationships is crucial. Founded in ideas of social capital as a quality of interpersonal ties across a community, trustworthiness has been identified as 'a property of the relational ties among individuals within a social system through sustained social interactions' (Bryk & Schneider, 2002, p. 12). The consequential organisational property has been defined as 'relational trust' and is to be found in the 'nature of the interpersonal exchanges among members who comprise that community' (Bryk & Schneider, 2002, p. 14). Schooling is identified as a social enterprise, and the social exchanges that take place are deemed to have intrinsic value. They 'shape participant's lives in powerful ways, and provide opportunities for self-identification and affiliation' (Bryk & Schneider, 2002, p. 19). The young people featured in our research demonstrated relational trust between themselves and between them and their teachers. High levels of trust were directly associated for them with more positive levels of engagement. This trust was founded on mutual knowledge and regard and fostered by humour and care.

Participating in this research and being asked questions about what engaged them emphasised the degree to which the students were indeed valued and trusted. It is my contention that our research with pupils in focus group interviews demonstrates the inherent value for enhanced engagement of seeking the opinions and perspectives of pupils about their learning and experience of school. High levels of relational trust secure their attention and results in constructive, informed commentary. This is one way in which student voice can be heard in the most active sense, as an integral part of the teaching and learning process and with pupils as key collaborators.

References

Bryk, A. S., & Schneider, B. (2002). *Trust in schools: A core resource for improvement.* New York, NY: Russell Sage Foundation.

McLaughlin, C., Black-Hawkins, K., Brindley, S., McIntyre, D., & Taber, K. (2006). *Researching schools: Stories from a School-University Partnership for Educational Research.* Abingdon, Oxon: Routledge.

McLaughlin, C., Black-Hawkins, K., & McIntyre, D. (2007). *Networking practitioner research.* London: Routledge.

Chapter 24

Authentic Voice: The Role of Methodology and Method in Transformational Research

Tina Cook

Abstract

For historical, cultural and organisational reasons, the voice of students, especially young students, or those with special educational needs, have been marginalised in qualitative research. To exclude the voice of those with lived experience, or to include their voice without careful attention to how that voice is heard and interpreted, raises questions in relation to the effectiveness of research, its validity and its moral and ethical standpoint.

This chapter forefronts issues relating to how voice is offered, heard and developed and how it is afforded meaningful and affective space within the research process. Drawing on the practice of action research, particularly collaborative action research, this chapter explores and develops the notion of authentic voice as an integral part of knowledge production in transformational research. It highlights the power of research processes and procedures to enable or silence voice and illuminates issues researchers might need to consider when designing research processes for mutual sense making about practice.

Keywords: Authentic voice; collaborative action research; marginalised; transformational; methodology

Introduction

Having worked as a teacher for many years, predominately with pupils with special educational needs and/or behavioural problems, I now work within a university

The Student Voice Handbook: Bridging the Academic/Practitioner Divide
Copyright © 2011 by Emerald Group Publishing Limited
All rights of reproduction in any form reserved
ISBN: 978-1-78052-040-7

setting as an educator and qualitative researcher. My research approach is participatory and practical. My understandings of effective research are embedded in purposeful systematic inquiry where notions of practice are challenged, (re)conceptualised and developed through the voices of those who have insight, experience, expertise and practical wisdom fundamental to the practice being researched. It is a dynamic approach that seeks to hold authentic voice at the heart of research in practice.

Much has been written about the power of dominant populations to silence, wittingly and unwittingly, the voices of people who find themselves marginalised (see e.g. Cruddas, 2007; Foucault 1980; March, Steingold, Justice, & Mitchell, 1997; Northway, 2000). This chapter considers the power of research design and how it too can unwittingly eclipse the voices of people at the core of its work.

Authentic Voice

> authentic voice, a voice with which to speak one's experience and one's ability to learn from that experience. (Winter, 1998, p. 54)

Authentic voice as characterised in this chapter, draws on Winter's description as one that includes speaking about your own experiences and learning from that articulation. It also borrows from the notion of authentic participation, defined by McTaggart (1997) as:

> responsible agency in the production of knowledge and improvement in practice. ... Mere involvement implies none of this and creates the risk of cooption and exploitation in the realisation of the plans of others. (McTaggart, 1997, p. 28)

Authentic voice goes beyond mere articulation. Whilst this is the starting point, whether through speech or other formalised systems of non-verbal communication,[1] the two key characteristics of authentic voice are, first, meaningful articulation and, second, the capacity to have an impact on (transform) both what we know about practice and that practice itself.

Meaningful Articulation

Speech is mediated through a range of intellectual and emotional functions, personal history and experience, hierarchy and power, culture and community. It is not necessarily related to personal knowing or personal truths. This is not because

---

1. This chapter does not engage with the vast array of technical forms of supporting articulation for those who are unable to verbalise or sign, rather it highlights the conceptual underpinnings of the need to directly link purpose and methods for research with the notion of authentic voice, however articulated.

we wish to tell untruths (although obviously this can be the case) but because it is often hard to marshal thoughts to articulate what we know. We have thoughts and ideas that as yet have not crystallised, knowings that are yet to be known and useful. These knowings reside just beneath the surface of our conscious recognition awaiting the right conditions to become explicit. Polanyi (1958) called this 'tacit' knowledge. It is what we nearly know but have not, as yet, surfaced and recognised.

Authentic voice also goes beyond mythopesis "the act of mythmaking in which people tell certain stories to justify their preferred interpretation of the world" (Stoll, 1998, p. 9). Mining the tacit underpinnings that frame perceptions of reality, the interface between the known and the nearly known, takes us beyond the articulation of current culturally and contextually driven perceptions to clarifications of personal knowledge. It steps outside everyday presuppositions and working beliefs we use uncritically in our daily lives and incorporates deeper knowing yet to be understood:

> Words themselves are doors; Janus is to a certain extent their deity, looking back to a ramification of roots and associations and forward to a clarification of sense and meaning. (Heaney, 1991, Preoccupations 52)

The Impact of Meaningful Articulation

Authentic voice is more than meaningful articulation. It is a communication with the potential to have an impact on what is known and the way that knowledge is used in practice. It is a change mechanism. That change may be personal, across groups or organisations, but it is instigated through meaningful articulation following critical reflection, or praxis. Praxis is a term used in research, and derived from the work of Aristotle, to convey the art of acting on the conditions one faces and following due critical reflection, to change them (see Lather, 1986). Enabling speech but not embedding its message leaves it impotent in the process of knowledge development; its place in research mere tokenism.

Lincoln and Guba (2000, p. 183) suggest that voice is a major issue confronting qualitative researchers today.

Finding Spaces for Authentic Voice in Research

What follows is an exploration of three aspects of research in practice that have a pivotal effect on the facilitation of authentic voice.

1. Who we allow to speak: sample
2. How we enable people to speak: methodology and method
3. How what is said is interpreted: data analysis

Who We Allow to Speak: Sample

Once research is initiated the 'sample', that is who we invite to participate, acts as gatekeeper to voice. Qualitative research offers, through the use of multi-method research frameworks, opportunities to engage with those who may not speak the language of researchers, of policy makers and officialdom. Listening to many voices provides opportunities to take into account the multi-perspectives of many actors in a situation. Over the years, however, qualitative researchers could be accused of having been somewhat circumspect about the application of this in practice. Certain sectors of society, whilst central to the substantive research topic, have been denied their own voice in research. The perspective of people who have been marginalised from mainstream society for reasons of age, cognitive ability or communication skills, for example, have been at best under-represented, more generally ignored and at worst exploited and manipulated (Oliver, 1992; Priestley, Waddington, & Bessozi, 2010). As Nutbrown and Hannon (2003) point out, this includes the perspective of children:

> until recently there has been relatively little interest in understanding the perspectives of children on what we might call the 'ordinary, everyday aspects' of their own lives (Dyer, 2002; Filippini & Vecci, 2000 cited in Nutbrown & Hannon, 2003, p. 118)

Historically, if researchers wanted to know about the lives of people considered harder to involve or engage in the research process they would ask those around them (proxy respondents). It was common to only ask doctors about patients, teachers about students, parents about children. Yet, who amongst us would wish to have our thoughts, feelings, ideas and expectations articulated by our mother, our partner, our friend or our doctor? The use of such approaches raises questions about why one set of people might feel competent to speak for others.

It has been suggested that as all adults have been children they can put themselves into a child's position. Kellett (2005) argues, however, that if we want to understand the lived experiences of children of today, applying the principles of a childhood from a generation ago lacks relevance (Kellett, 2005, p. 8). Adults cannot discard experiences they have acquired since being children. Their 'adult filters' affect their perceptions of a situation. There is a large gulf between adult observations about a child's understandings of a situation and perceptions of children (Scott, 2000). Approaches that explore children's lives from the standpoint of adult caretakers are now challenged by:

> a perspective which sees children as possessing distinctive cognitive and social developmental characteristics with which researchers, wishing to use child informants, must consider in their research design. (Christensen & James, 2000, p. 2)

Children are now more readily acknowledged as competent respondents about their own lives, as experts on their own childhood (Dahlberg & Moss, 2005; Greene & Hogan, 2005). This is leading to "the gradual acceptance that children could be more than participants in research; they could be co-researchers" (Kellett, 2005, p. 5). At present research led by children is exceptional rather than commonplace, particularly for children in the middle childhood years and younger (Kellett, 2005). There is, however, a small but growing amount of research carried out by children. The recently established Children's Research Centre at the Open University in the United Kingdom (http://childrens-research-centre.open.ac.uk) publishes a range of research led by children as young as 7 years of age. The research agendas children prioritise, the research questions they frame and the ways in which they collect data are substantially different from the ways of adults.

Involving children in research, either as participants or as researchers, has associated procedures that can act as a deterrent to their inclusion. Procedures such as criminal record bureau checks (UK) and extra ethical scrutiny necessary before research with children can be approved that extends the time frame for the development of research and can be a disincentive to work with children (Abbott & Langston, 2005; Conroy & Harcourt, 2009; Dalli & Stephenson, 2010; Lewis, 2010). Issues of informed consent are not always clear and well understood in relation to when children can make their own decisions. This leaves researchers apprehensive about making the right decisions. If children are included the time necessary to ensure that they are truly aware of the notion of informed consent (especially when working with young children and those with learning difficulties) can be lengthy (Conroy & Harcourt, 2009; Cook & Inglis, 2009; Lewis, 2010). Short time scales determined by research funding and other external imperatives can, therefore, have the effect of excluding children's voice. The perceived complexity of the research, in forms of both organisation and conceptualisation, can be off-putting for would be researchers, including young people themselves.

Whose voice is being heard when 'student voice' is invoked, and whose voices are absent or marginalised raises issues of representation and the authenticity of claims we make for knowing.

How We Enable People to Speak: Methodology and Method

When authentic voice is central to the legitimisation or our practice, we must choose carefully from places the vast array of methodological approaches to identify the opportunities within those approaches for empowering voice. The term methodology is used here to denote:

> the whole system of principles, rules, theories and values that underpin a particular approach to research. (Somekh & Lewin, 2005, pp. 346–347)

Methods are the tools we use to carry out our research in line with those principles.

Methodology: An Action Research Approach

Methodologies articulate the inter-twining of the philosophies, principles and practice that shape our research design. When seeking to forefront authentic voice, it is necessary to consider an approach that facilitates meaningful articulation alongside a commitment to transform thinking and practice. My own methodological approach draws on the principles and practices of action research. What is vital to action research is:

> the way groups of people can organise the conditions under which they can learn from their own experience, and make this experience accessible to others.... (McTaggart, 1994, p. 317)

I choose action research (or more precisely collaborative action research (CAR)) because it emphasises a joint enterprise and struggle that takes place, the co-labouring (Sumara & Luce-Kapler, 1993). Through working together we attempt to:

- facilitate spaces for disciplined, public conversations in which reasons for action are scrutinised, critiqued and modified
- pull apart rhetoric and general consensus to forefront and discuss the plurality of perceptions and allow new understandings to emerge
- break down the binary between researcher and the researched to develop a shared understanding for praxis
- embed action and change as an integral part of the research process.

Action Research in the UK emerged in the 1970s with Lawrence Stenhouse's Ford Curriculum Project (Stenhouse, 1975). Stenhouse engaged teachers as researchers as a way of working alongside their students to find their own voices and develop their own practice. Action research is rooted in people's in-depth, critical and practical experience of the situation to be understood and acted in and on.

The origins of action research date back to the early 20th century and the questioning of positivist, modernist thinking. The fore fronting of complexity led to changes in theories for research that accepted diversity as a positive and vital element of the research process. A number of social reformists began to use approaches to enquiry that addressed the complexity of inequality is society. Using social justice as the driver, they began to engage the voices of the marginalised and oppressed in critical debate (McKernan, 1991, p. 8). One such researcher, Kurt Lewin in the USA, was concerned with raising the self-esteem of minority groups to help them seek for themselves 'independence, equality, and co-operation' (Adelman, 1993, p. 7). Lewin is widely recognised as key to establish firm foundations for action research.

What is essential to action research is that it is:

> a form of self-reflective enquiry undertaken by participants in social situations in order to improve the rationality and justice of their own practices, their understanding of these practices, and the situations in which the practices are carried out. (Carr & Kemmis, 1986, p. 162)

The diversity and plurality of meaning and the collaboration between those who hold different perspectives, whatever the foundation for those perspectives, is fundamental to knowing. What is important in action research is not existing 'hierarchies of credibility' (Winter, 1998, p. 57) but mutual learning and emergent knowledge. It is 'a series of commitments to observe and problematise' (McTaggart, 1994, p. 315). The purpose of this series of observations and problematising, which although classically depicted as 'proceeding in a spiral of steps, each of which is composed of planning, action and the evaluation of the result of action' (Kemmis & McTaggart, 1990, p. 8) often take unexpected and complex twists and turns, is clarified by Alf.[2] Alf was part of a collaborative research project based in a medium secure (forensic) unit for men with learning disability in the North East of England.

> Research is like finding pieces of the jigsaw.... It's looking over and over again because sometimes if you look at something once you don't get to see the full picture but when you come back and look at it again you'll see something different. And the more times you go backward and forward to it, the more you see. So that's good [Alf]. (Cook & Inglis, 2008, p. 49)

This project used a CAR approach to investigate, with the men and staff of the unit, what people with learning a disability understand about research, consent and ethics and how that understanding could be enhanced. A number of men became very interested in the collaborative nature of the research process and its importance for learning. At first, when someone had a different idea during discussion, this was seen by other men as 'wrong', or that their own idea was being criticised. As the work progressed, the men recognised the importance of their own contribution as a springboard for discussion and learning and made full use of it as a way of developing understandings. Working together was identified by this man as the key element in supporting understanding.

> The more things just got blown into the air, the more fun it was ... When we were discussing and debating stuff, during some of the discussion that we had, your mind slipped a few times before it settled. It's like you started it off and someone would say something and it would be like, 'Erm, I'm not quite sure of...' And then it started a bit of a debate up. And then by the time you finished the debate you had most of the answers and then it was like, 'Erh..., you know, we've just answered it [David]'. (Cook & Inglis, 2009, p. 62)

The men recognised that the many interruptions, revisits and re-conceptualisations that occurred when working together made the process messy, but this mess was key

---

2. The names of all the men used in the chapter are all pseudonyms.

to moving our thinking forward. Here mess is characterised, not as undesirable, but as Mellor (1999) suggested:

> a complex process of inquiry, involving a wide range of techniques, where messy is taken to mean difficult, not careless. (Mellor, 1999, Abstract, PhD thesis)

The purpose of mess is to facilitate a 'turn towards new constructions of knowing that lead to transformation in practice' (Cook, 2009, p. 277). The messy area is where people publically articulate their thoughts as part of ongoing debate. Where surfacing tacit knowledge through purposeful, positive, critical enquiry takes place. It is in this messy area that people forge shared understandings and new knowledge. It is the pivotal point of action research in practice.

Method: Choosing the Tools for the Job

Once we are clear about the methodological underpinnings for our research, method must match its aspirations. Each method must be critically analysed in relation to the purpose of getting beyond mere words and rhetoric and towards authentic voice. Traditionally qualitative researchers have used a form of inquiry based on interviews and focus groups as their main tools. Whilst these are valid methods in a wide variety of circumstances, including action research, they are not a universal key to hearing what is at the heart of people's experience. In particular, the use of a questionnaire styled, fully structured, one-off interview, where the framework for discussion is pre-set by the interviewer, restricts opportunities for participants to move beyond what is known. They cannot revisit and reflect upon what they have said in the light of their own articulations, reframe, reconstruct and redevelop their responses as their understandings develop. In its strictest form, therefore, a formulaic interview can be incompatible with research that places authentic voice at the forefront of its legitimisation. If the purpose of method is to open up spaces for voice rather than provide a rigid box for articulation determined by those without lived experience of the practice being researched, then other ways of engagement need to be considered.

Researchers have become increasingly creative in their ways and means to hear children. (Clark, 2004, 2007; Dahlberg & Moss, 2005; Dahlberg, Moss, & Pence, 2007). This example from my own work on a project in an Early Excellence Centre[3] in the North East of England provides an example of how the use of 'roving cameras' enabled us to get closer to the voice of young children (Cook & Hess, 2007). The aim of the project was to improve the interface between young children and education. We spent time talking with the children on both a one-to-one basis and in groups, but also armed them with cameras. The purpose of the cameras was to allow the

---

3. Early Excellence Centres were a facet of New Labour policy for integrated childcare and education in the UK.

children to take photographs of what was important to them about their school. One day, when out on an educational visit, a young boy aged 5 was spotted taking a picture of what looked like an empty space. Struggling to understand why he was taking this photograph an adult researcher asked him to explain. His reply 'I'm taking this picture because no-body asked me to look at it' (Cook & Hess, 2007, p. 38) revealed more about why he might be struggling in the classroom environment than any one-to-one conversation with adults could hope to elicit.

How What is Said is Interpreted: Data Analysis

My own experience as researcher, reviewer of research proposals and of journal articles, is that the practice of analysing data is least likely to be participatory. It is here, however, that decisions are made about what constitutes new knowledge. In more traditional forms of research, where the researcher is distanced from those who are researched, the process of data analysis tends to be governed by the notion of objectification and adherence to strict, formulaic processes. Following the same procedures is construed as evidence of rigour, getting the same outcome as a form of validity and asking research subjects about the findings is likely to be construed as bias.

How decisions are made and who makes them is one of the major issues of the researchers' art and craft. An approach to data analysis, where the researcher is treated as culturally neutral to the research, and participants are excluded from making sense of their own data, would appear inappropriate when seeking to use authentic voice as an indicator of legitimation. Leaving external authorial voice to translate research narratives (Tierney & Lincoln, 1997) runs counter to the philosophical underpinnings for such research; it has the potential to limit what is recognised as key data to the researchers' (and/or funders) original perceptions of the issues (or future policy needs). There is, as Somekh (2002) suggests, more than one way of deciding on what 'counts' as knowledge' (p. 89).

In CAR knowledge production is an integral part of the collaborative process. Meanings and understandings are forged together as a key element of research practice. This provides an insight into the nature of knowing that involves the 'privileging of transparency over idealization in reconstructed logic' (Carter, Jordens, McGrath, & Little, 2008; p. 1265). In a recent research project, funded through the Department of Health in the UK, over 100 participants, many of whom have neurological impairments, were involved in a case study looking at the impact of inclusive practice in neuro-rehabilitation/neuro-psychiatry services (Cook, 2008–2011). The approach to the project was founded on the dual premise that:

- actions are driven by meanings people derive from social interaction and modified through interpretation (symbolic interactionism, see Blumer, 1969)
- a way of allowing new meanings to emerge is to subject the divergent views people hold to critical dialogue (hermeneutic dialecticism, see Guba & Lincoln, 1989).

Much of the data in the project consisted of pictures and stories from practice that had been discussed, critiqued and re-visited through a number of cycles in the research process. We struggled, however, with how to engage people in the final decision making (data analysis). As we did not want to lose their voice in the final stage of the project, we developed a range of processes to enable people to revisit some of their own data and the understandings that had emerged through that data. The aim of revisiting the data was to critique the meanings being drawn from the data as opposed to the stories themselves. This was a complex notion to convey to people. One of the ways in which we attempted this was to take some of the stories from the raw data relating to key themes currently being surfaced and script them into scenarios. These scenarios, directly constructed from the words of the research participants, were then acted out and filmed. Everyone who had taken part in the project was invited to view the filmed scenarios and discuss what they took to be the meaning of those stories. This way of revisiting their own data through a new lens, as an external watcher, in the company of others who had participated in the project, led to much interested and animated discussion. Some themes were confirmed and new ways of seeing were offered to further develop our combined knowledge. This way of analysing the data was in keeping with a research approach that had, as one of its key aims, the facilitation of authentic voice.

Conclusion

It is important to find ways of supporting authentic voice, particularly when externally imposed systems and curricula sit beside continued inequalities within societies. If marginalised, less powerful voices are eclipsed by historical and cultural dominant voices, then the course of community action will be based on partial knowledge. To reset the balance we need to use our energies to find effective means of giving audience to all voices. The rationale for doing this is ethical, political and methodological.

Ethical: because to exclude the voices of those with lived experience in relation to the issue or practice being researched challenges our notions of the moral, the fair and the just. If authentic voice is not afforded to the currently marginalised, issues relating to their lives are over-shadowed by the voices of others who may have different experiences, needs and interests.

Political: because even when the project is not political in itself, asserting a right to be heard is a form of social justice. Who decides on the meaning drawn from research, and how it is disseminated, distributes power. Being excluded from knowledge production reduces opportunities, and power, to inform, shape and transform practice for improving lives.

Methodological: because the way we hear what is said decide on what it means in a given situation, and how what is heard is acted upon, is dependent on the way in which we choose to do research, its conceptual and theoretical underpinnings. Knowledge can only ever be partial if it is constructed without the authentic voice of those with lived experience.

References

Abbott, L., & Langston, A. (2005). Ethical research with very young children. In: A. Farrell (Ed.), *Ethical research with children* (pp. 37–48). Maidenhead: Open University Press.

Adelman, C. (1993). Kurt Lewin and the origins of action research. *Educational Action Research, 1*(1), 7–24.

Blumer, H. (1969). *Symbolic interactionism: Perspective and method.* Berkeley: University of California Press.

Carr, W., & Kemmis, S. (1986). *Becoming critical: Education, knowledge and action research.* Lewes: Falmer.

Carter, S. M., Jordens, C. F., McGrath, C., & Little, M. (2008). You have to make something of all that rubbish, do you? An empirical investigation of the social process of qualitative research. *Qualitative Health Research, 18*(9), 1264–1276.

Christensen, P., & James, A. (Eds). (2000). *Research with children: Perspectives and practices.* London: Falmer Press.

Clark, A. (2004). The mosaic approach and research with young children. In: V. Lewis, M. Kellett, C. Robinson, S. Fraser & S. Ding (Eds), *The reality of research with children and young people* (pp. 157–180). London: Sage.

Clark, A. (2007). A hundred ways of listening: Gathering children's perspectives of their early childhood environment. *Young Children, 62*(3), 76–81.

Conroy, H., & Harcourt, D. (2009). Informed agreement to participate: Beginning the partnership with children in research. *Early Child Development and Care, 179*(2), 157–165.

Cook, T. (2009). The purpose of mess in action research: Building rigour through a messy turn. *Educational Action Research, 17*(2), 277–291.

Cook, T. (2008–2011). A case study of the impact of inclusive practice in neuro-rehabilitation/neuro-psychiatry services. Retrieved from http://www.ltnc.org.uk/research_files/impact_inclusive.html

Cook, T., & Hess, E. (2007). What the camera sees and from whose perspective? Fun methodologies for engaging children in enlightening adults. *Childhood, 14*(1), 29–46.

Cook, T., & Inglis, P. (2008). Understanding research, consent and ethics: a participatory research methodology in a medium secure unit for men with a learning disability. Retrieved from http://northumbria.openrepository.com/northumbria/browse?type=author&order=ASC&value=Cook%2C+Tina

Cook, T., & Inglis, P. (2009). Making our own decisions: Researching the process of 'being informed' with people with learning difficulties. *Research Ethics Review, 5*(2), 49–55.

Cruddas, L. (2007). Engaged voices — Dialogic interaction and the construction of shared social meanings. *Educational Action Research, 15*(3), 479–488.

Dahlberg, G., & Moss, P. (2005). *Ethics and politics in early childhood education.* London: Routledge.

Dahlberg, G., Moss, P., & Pence, A. (2007). *Beyond quality in early childhood education and care: Languages of evaluation* (2nd ed.). London: Falmer Press.

Dalli, C., & Stephenson, A. (2010). Involving children in research in early childhood education settings: Opening up the issues. In: J. Loveridge (Ed.), *Involving children and young people in research in educational settings*, Report to the Ministry of Education Victoria University of Wellington, Jessie Hetherington Centre for Educational Research, pp. 11–41.

Foucault, M. (1980). In: C. Gordon (Ed.), *Power/knowledge: Selected interviews and other writings 1972–1977*. Brighton, Sussex: Harvester Press.

Greene, S., & Hogan, D. (Eds). (2005). *Researching children's experience: Methods and methodological issues*. London: Sage Publications.

Guba, E. G., & Lincoln, Y. S. (1989). *Fourth generation evaluation*. Newbury Park, CA: Sage Publications.

Heaney, S. (1991). *Door into the dark*. London: Faber and Faber.

Kellett, M. (2005). Children as active researchers: A new research paradigm for the 21st century? ESRC National Centre for Research Methods, Methods Review Papers.

Kemmis, S., & McTaggart, R. (1990). *The action research planner*. Geelong: Deakin University Press.

Lather, P. (1986). Research as praxis. *Harvard Educational Review*, *56*(3), 257–277.

Lewis, A. (2010). Silence in the context of 'child voice'. *Children and Society*, *24*(1), 14–23.

Lincoln, Y. S., & Guba, E. G. (2000). Paradigmatic controversies, contradictions, and emerging confluences. In: N. K. Denzin & Y. S. Lincoln (Eds), *Handbook of qualitative research*. (2nd ed., pp. 163–188). London: Sage.

March, J., Steingold, B., Justice, S., & Mitchell, P. (1997). Follow the yellow brick road! People with learning disabilities as co-researchers. *British Journal of Learning Disabilities*, *33*(2), 77–80.

McKernan, J. (1991). *Curriculum action research: A handbook of methods and resources for the reflective practitioner*. London: Kogan Page.

McTaggart, R. (1994). Participatory action research: Issues in theory and practice. *Educational Action Research*, *2*(3), 313–338.

McTaggart, R. (Ed.) (1997). *Participatory action research*. New York: Albany.

Mellor, N. (1999). *From exploring practice to exploring inquiry: A practitioner researcher's experience*. PhD thesis, University of Northumbria at Newcastle.

Northway, R. (2000). Finding out together: Lessons in participatory research for the learning disability nurse. *Mental Health Care*, *3*(7), 229–232.

Nutbrown, C., & Hannon, P. (2003). Children's perspectives on family literacy: Methodological issues, findings and implications for practice. *Journal of Early Childhood Literacy*, *3*(2), 115–145.

Oliver, M. (1992). Changing the social relations of research production. *Disability, Handicap and Society*, *7*(2), 101–114.

Polanyi, M. (1958). *Personal knowledge: Towards a post critical philosophy*. London: Routledge.

Priestley, M., Waddington, L., & Bessozi, C. (2010). Towards an agenda for disability research in Europe: Learning from disabled people's organizations. *Disability and Society*, *25*(6), 731–746.

Scott, J. (2000). Children as respondents. In: A. James & P. Christensen (Eds), *Research with children: Perspectives and practices* (pp. 98–119). London; New York: Falmer Press.

Somekh, B. (2002). Inhabiting each other's castles: Towards knowledge and mutual growth through collaboration. In: C. Day, J. Elliott, B. Somekh & R. Winter (Eds), *Theory and practice in action research: Some international perspectives* (pp. 79–104). UK: Symposium Books.

Somekh, B., & Lewin, K. (2005). *Research methods in the social sciences*. London: Sage.

Stenhouse, L. (1975). *An introduction to curriculum research and development*. London: Heinemann Press.

Stoll, D. (1998). Life history as mythopoesis. *Anthropology Newsletter*, pp. 9–11. In: W. G. Tierney, Undaunted courage: Life history and the postmodern challenge (p. 546). In: N. K. Denzin & Y. S. Lincoln (Eds.), *Handbook of qualitative research* (2nd ed., pp. 537–553). London: Sage.

Sumara, D. J., & Luce-Kapler, R. (1993). Action research as a Writerly text: Locating co-labouring in collaboration. *Education Action Research*, *1*(3), 387–396.

Tierney, W., & Lincoln, Y. (Eds). (1997). *Representation and the text: Re-framing the narrative voice*. Albany: State University of New York Press.

Winter, R. (1998). Finding a voice –Thinking with others: A conception of action research. *Educational Action Research* (1), 53–68.

Chapter 25

uSpeak, iPod, iTrain: Adopting Emergent Technologies to Inform Trainee Teachers of Young Learners' Views of Teaching and Learning

Warren Kidd

Abstract

This chapter explores a piece of small-scale student voice research conducted by the author as part of the provision on an initial teacher education programme for the post-compulsory education sector at the University of East London, United Kingdom. As a means to better inform pre-service trainee teachers regarding teaching and learning, a variety of audio recordings (podcasts) were produced, through semi-structured interviews of 16- to 19-year-old learners in the London/South East Area, United Kingdom. The interviews have been conducted in a diverse variety of locally situated contexts in schools and colleges seeking to explore young learners' views on teaching and teachers. These recordings have then been used as part of a blended delivery to aid the reflective practice of trainee teachers. The articulation of the learner voice through the recordings enables trainee teachers to (re)contextualise their assumptions (and ultimately their biographies) regarding expectations of learners and teaching and learning before starting teaching placement. In this way, the discursive and reflective practices supported by these learner voice audios enable the reformation of (un)situated learning and better informs trainees' initial boundary-crossing practices from 'outsider' to 'novice teacher'.

This enquiry captures student voice in two, related contexts. Firstly, the trainee teachers who are being supported are '(professional) learners'. Their voice has been captured through the adoption of reflective journals on their teacher education programme. Secondly, young learners' voices have been captured through interviews leading to the creation of an audio archive. The audio resource is used pedagogically as a means to inform the trainee teachers, supporting them to co-construct meanings of 'what teaching means' at the very start of their professional education. I write this account as both researcher and teacher educator — seeking to support the professional learning of my own trainee teachers and in doing so to demonstrate to them the pedagogic and democratic value that 'listening to learners' brings: both listening to trainee teachers and their anxieties and concerns and providing a reflective and reflexive context through which these can be expressed; and the value to be had for (new) teachers to listen to their own learners.

Keywords: Teacher education; podcasts; lifelong learning sector; audio; situated learning; reflective practice

Introduction

In an attempt to build a digital teaching resource making use of podcasting emergent technologies, this project[1] has captured audio recordings through semi-structured interviews of young people aged 16–19 in Essex, Kent and London talking about 'good teaching' and 'good teachers'. These recordings provide an insight into what young learners in various situated contexts — schools and colleges — think about teaching and teachers. As noted by Salisbury, Martin, and Roberts (2009, p. 421), teacher learning and teaching and learning itself:

> is shaped by the nature of the social contexts in which interaction occurs and the ways in which teachers and students construct their roles within it ... teachers' conceptualisations of their students' learning can be related not only to their own and students' backgrounds and learning biographies, but also to the wider structural context within which learning in FE is currently located.

In this chapter, I explore the nature of reflective learning undertaken by trainee teachers and argue that reflecting on the student voice can support novices' boundary-crossing and legitimate peripheral participation (Heggen, 2008; Lave & Wenger, 1991). I have located discussions of this use of student voice within the postmodern and post-

1. This chapter and the research described herein has been previously presented as a paper at the 6th annual symposium of the *Learning Development in Higher Education Network* (LDHEN) — *The Challenge of Learning Development* — held on 6 Monday and 7 Tuesday, April, 2009, at Bournemouth University. The title of the paper was 'iLearn, iTrain, iTeach: What do young people think about good teaching and successful learning? Capturing learners' voice with a view to using podcast recordings to better inform trainee teachers on initial teacher education programmes'.

Fordist structural context of the lifelong learning sector in the United Kingdom (Avis, 1999, 2002) where the specific teaching and learning behaviours that are the focus of this enquiry are acted out (Salisbury et al., 2009). Student voice — and its role in trainee teacher learning — are linked to arguments around teacher identity formation (Beauchamp & Thomas, 2009; Day & Gu, 2010) and the role of situated context and community membership in this process (Lave & Wenger, 1991). Throughout this chapter, while aware of the contested nature of notions of 'voice' (Bragg, 2001; Fielding, 2000, 2004), I use student voice and learner voice interchangeably.

The audio recordings this enquiry generated are being used as part of a blended delivery during trainee teacher induction to aid reflection and discursive practices. The trainees themselves are all learning to teach in the lifelong learning or 'Further Education' (FE) sector in the United Kingdom and are all on voluntary 'placement' in ethnically diverse areas of East London. The recordings represent for the institutions taking part an attempt to capture the learner voice and to generate stimulus materials designed to support staff training, self-evaluation and action research. This chapter discusses the following three key themes:

- It illustrates how audio teaching tools can be used with trainee teachers within a higher education context and to reflect upon and evaluate the creation and development of this e-learning resource.
- To develop a commentary on the fears and anxieties of teachers-in-the-making regarding their own learners and regarding the boundary-crossing practices they undertake while starting their training programme as a (new) 'professional learner'.
- To give a voice to the thoughts that young learners (aged 16–19) have about 'good teaching'.

This enquiry is interested in exploring two key questions:

- What do young learners in the United Kingdom lifelong learning sector think about good teaching and successful learning and how do they articulate these views?
- How can audio of these views be captured to enable capacity building and e-learning on post-16 teacher training programs?

Unsituated Voices

My own recent experience of supporting professional learners — 'trainee teachers' — would indicate that many trainee teachers in initial teacher education arrive at the start of their programmes without much contact with younger learners. Thus, they are often surprised by the degrees of confidence, reflection and articulation with which many younger learners are able to engage with their own learning. They are surprised at how learners are able to talk confidently about what they think is good teaching and to be able to describe in some depth and with sophistication styles of teaching and teaching tools and techniques. At the same time, many trainees are understandably cautious and concerned about the teaching role — in particular, over issues of classroom and behaviour management, often clouded by their perceptions of what learners (aged 14–19) are like. This chapter, and the enquiry it critically outlines, starts with the explicit value proposition so deeply embedded in many notions of student voice (Fielding, 2004; Ruddock & Flutter, 2000; Ruddock & McIntyre, 2007), that teachers and learners can be, are and must be co-constructors of their own practice and social endeavours. As Salisbury et al. (2009, p. 421) suggest, 'it is important to locate teachers and learners as active participants in at least some of the processes of learning'.

Until trainee teachers visit colleges and meet learners, the 'location' and groundedness of their initial professional learning is highly 'unsituated'. In other words, learning is not rooted or grounded in a context of lived experience as a *professional-in-the-making*, but perceptions are drawn upon autobiographical histories of the self, which are limited by the individuals' experience. Often, trainee teachers are learning how to teach (and how to learn) in contexts radically different from their own educational biographies and in socio-economic geographical locations different from their own upbringing. This is both a pedagogic issue and a professional issue — how do trainees as *professionals-in-the-making* come to develop sensitivity towards their learners and towards the mechanics and craft of teaching and learning itself? How can we, as teacher educators, model best practice in supporting trainees in this crucial initial development? It is by adopting the student voice — and using this to inform professional learning — that we might hope to achieve the 'democratic schooling' spoken of by Giroux (2005). As Giroux (2005, p. 454) notes,

> The concept of voice constitutes the focal point for a theory of teaching and learning that generates new forms of sociality as well as new and challenging ways of confronting and engaging everyday life.

Contested Voices

In characterising the student voice movement, Taylor and Robinson (2009, p. 163) comment that 'As a field of educational endeavour student voice has been largely seen as oriented to action, participation and change'. However, not all voices are heard, or at least, not all voices are heard the same way. Literature suggests that learners most likely to be involved in student voice initiatives are those learners who would mostly likely have a 'stake' or investment in education due to the accumulation of cultural capital (Bragg, 2001; McIntyre, Pedder, & Ruddock, 2005; Taylor & Robinson, 2009). In some school and colleges, the 'zeitgeist commitment to student voice' (Rudduck, 2006, p. 133) is little more than an attempt to engage in 'surface compliance with a notionally transformational agenda but which fail to take account of the intransigencies of power or disrupt its operations at a deeper level' (Taylor & Robinson, 2009, p. 166). When student voice is linked to 'school improvement' agendas, it often reproduces 'surface compliance' (Taylor & Robinson, 2009, p. 163) rather than more authentic and meaningful attempts to develop democratic processes (Fielding, 2000).

The agenda of some student voice work is to capture voices to give 'privileging' to the learner as the author of their voice (Solorzano & Yosso, 2002) — a claim seen by some authors informed by post-structural theories to be a 'romanticisation' of an 'authentic' voice (Jackson, 2003; Mazzei, 2009; St. Pierre, 2000). For Fielding (2004, 2009) and Rudduck (2006), an authentic voice is possible and can operate as an alternative to performance cultures and 'managerialism'.

Reflective Voices

In this enquiry, I seek to use student voice to support the learning and development of trainee teachers. As professional learners, these trainee teachers also have a 'learner voice' that we can explore. Extracts from trainee teacher's reflective journals[2] (quoted here with permission of the trainees themselves) express clearly ambiguous locations and tensions in the initial development of a professional self (Czerniawski, 2011; Day & Gu, 2010; Layder, 1993) and a 'professional identity' — what Beauchamp and Thomas (2009) describe as 'how to be', 'how to act' and 'how to understand'. In this way, 'becoming a teacher' is a *learning process* and based on socialisation from within groups and interactional encounters (Hobson et al., 2004). In forming the initial stages of this professional identity, the trainee teachers in this enquiry express a range of emotions when thinking about the learners they are likely to meet in their training year:

> When I arrived at a local sixth form to have a look around I felt a little intimidated, as my experiences of sixth form were very different studying in middle class York. However, during our tour I saw nothing but eager, hardworking students who were all focussed and seemingly interested in what they were learning. I had half expected to walk past classrooms and see students running around, shouting, fighting and generally getting out of hand ... [Trainee teacher reflection]

> in light of some of the early discussions on my PGCE I was worried that I had been too naïve about the challenges of teaching in FE colleges, particularly in Newham, and was left wondering if this was the right path for me after all ... [Trainee teacher reflection]

---

2. The trainee teachers who are supported by me and colleagues undertake an extensive 'induction' programme to help build more firmly the 'bridge' between professional learner and novice practitioner. This induction concentrates upon issues of professional identity, reflection as a professional learning tool and the socio-economic context within which colleges local to the university work. This practice also adopts the use of a *Reflective Journal* to allow and encourage trainees to formally express their ongoing and changing professional identity and to encourage the recording of critical incidents and lesson self-reflections and evaluations. Some of this content is formally assessed because it makes up part of marked assignments, but a great deal is there for the self-reflection and professional learning of the individual involved.

As my choice to come to UEL was mainly based on the fact that I would be studying and working in east London, the introduction to the socio-economic "peculiars" of the local area was of no surprise or shock. As I looked around the room I wondered how many in the group had a similar point of view (I'm guessing and hoping the majority) and how many might end up struggling to deal with East End's "deprived youth". One of course does not negate the other, and I suspect I too will find it rather challenging at times – despite all my good intentions and genuine interest in giving my students the best possible opportunities. [Trainee teacher reflection]

This reflection, as discussed above, is initially unsituated — it is uncontextualised by practice at this early stage. Tensions exist between excitement and fear; between wanting to 'change lives' and being worried about the 'nature' of the lives of their younger learners; tensions between wanting to patronise learners and being willing to learn from them. Once they have started their teaching placement, this hope for young learners can sometimes all too quickly become frustration:

I have an issue with student's complete inability to work independently or for themselves. In many lessons it feels as through students would prefer me to just give them definitions of keywords and tell them to memorise. The idea of building skills for themselves seems beyond them. [Trainee teacher reflection]

On recalling the group's induction walk along the East London 'Docklands' area of the Thames, one trainee reflects as follows:

The walk from Canary Wharf along the river to just east of Tower Bridge was a good addition, as it said plenty about what the area used to be like (warehouses etc) and what it is like now (posh flats, gated communities). It is in stark contrast to most of the rest of east London – as a walk to Shadwell station reminded us later – but the gated communities and riverside apartments could have as much an effect on the lives of East London's young people as the council estates and tower blocks of Bow and Poplar. I can only try and guess what that effect might be at this point (anger? resentment? feeling of worthlessness? Who knows …) but I suspect I might find out once I start my placement! [Trainee teacher reflection]

Many of trainees (as indeed do many 'established' teachers) find themselves occupying highly contested and ambiguous relationships with their learners:

I feel that I need to challenge them, and help broaden their horizons and their aspirations. Even if it needs to be done while they are kicking and screaming … [Trainee teacher reflection]

> My opinion varies-They are sweet and lovely, smart and enthusiastic, frustrating and hard work, stubborn and disrespectful. They can reduce you to tears in one lesson, but amaze you with their creativity and enthusiasm two days later. They are given a hard time by the media and the police-twice in the last four days I witnessed the police stop and search my students, once at the tube station and once outside the theatre. Their lives are not easy, or fair, and yet they sometimes seem resigned to their fate. I think they are scared of what they don't know, so choose to dismiss it and stick to their small (and safe) known worlds. I find teaching them hard work, but also extremely rewarding when they 'get it'. I feel it's a greater duty to do the absolute best I can and give it my all … [Trainee teacher reflection]

> Students do have the ability to surprise you. Some students appear quite unmotivated until you get to know them and they turn out to be amongst the best students. [Trainee teacher reflection]

Within all these hopes, fears, insecurities and frustrations, the importance of the induction period into the initial teacher education programme becomes paramount for supporting teachers' learning and development. The importance of using student voice to inform the professional learning of teachers-in-the-making also becomes apparent. Induction into a professional learning programme needs to be supported through recognition on behalf of the trainee that the construction of their professional identity and self is about to undergo rapid transformation. The induction period becomes an attempt to turn this reflection into more *situated learning* — to contextualise first visits to placements and first contacts with learners within broader brush strokes. It is this research problematic that has lead to the construction of the learner voice audio resource that this chapter addresses.

Post-Fordist Voices

To support teacher education and professional learning, we also need to consider the situatedness of where and how professionals in the lifelong learning sector, in the United Kingdom, 'learn' once they move from university training to 'novice' and eventually legitimate practice in the educational institutions that make up the sector in question. It is this very context that informs the need to encourage trainee teachers moving into the lifelong learning sector to listen to learners. It is also this context that informs the 'voice' of trainee teachers' reflective accounts, as presented earlier, of their learning and boundary-crossing (Heggen, 2008; Van Oers, 1998).

Much of the literature commenting on the past decade of 'workplace reform' within the UK lifelong learning sector adopts the language of a postmodern (and at times a post-structural) pessimism: it speaks of a late-modern and reflexive modern ennui characterised by anxiety, uncertainty, de-professionalism and surveillance (Ainley & Bailey, 1997; Avis, 2002; Wallace, 2002). Such is the prevalence of managerialism within the sector; Reeves (1995) described this sector in the United Kingdom as being 'totalitarian' in outlook and in working conditions and relationships.

However, there is another interpretation. This second narrative does recognise the realities of problematic conditions in the UK lifelong learning sector. However, while not negating the application of post-structural analytical tools, neo-Fordist working regimes and anxious, unconstructed, fragmented postmodern identities, it is possible to offer another framework. It is possible to see change within lifelong learning as a space for *possibility*, not pessimism. To see the possibility of identity change and also the possibility for newly formed identities for teachers in this sector. The fluidity of FE, as characterised in the writings of Avis (1999, 2002), points to *shifting (teacher) identities* as global policy agendas shape the reality of the FE sector but, more importantly, are in turn adopted, managed, maintained and subverted by the lived experience of trainees, teachers and teacher educators in the FE sector.

Avis (1999) offers an interpretation of the FE sector where previous notions of 'proletarianisation' or 'de-skilling' are seen as lacking and limited. For Avis (as for Bathmaker & Avis, 2007), FE is witnessing a transformation process — of both teaching and learning and of identity. The transformation of teaching and learning itself opens up a space within which it is possible for Vocational Education and Training (VET) professionals to explore new professional knowledge, re-evaluate practice and construct new identities. This is a positive interpretation of the workplace reforms undertaken by the sector over the past decade, but one that owes as much to post-structuralism as do the more nihilistic interpretations of 'risk' and the onset of control and compliance. For example, education as a site for 'policy technologies' (Ball, 2001) is a space where teachers are 'accountable and constantly recorded' (Ball, 2004, p. 144).

Both these interpretations recognise that discourses produce subjects under their gaze, but the interpretation placed upon this subjectification process by Avis suggests that agents within policy settlements and ideologies are able to carve out and negotiate futures and identities for themselves (Avis, 2002; Avis, Bathmaker, & Parsons, 2002). As trainee teachers 'boundary-cross' from the university to the training placement (Heggen, 2008), we might recognise that their identities are even more fluid than the identities being worked on by established teachers already working in a fluid and moving workplace. As such, trainee teachers' identities are being worked-*up* rather than worked-*on*.

Theorising Voices

My argument here is that adopting student voice work — talking with learners and making this dialogue transparent to trainee teachers — allows teachers to develop their theorising. As Carr and Kemmis (1986, p. 113) note,

> Theories are not bodies of knowledge that can be generated out of a vacuum and teaching is not some kind of robot-like mechanical performance that is devoid of any theoretical reflection.

Many teachers — and certainly many trainee teachers — find both reflection and the application of theoretical insights difficult and find theory somehow distanced and separated from their experiences of their own practice (Griffin, 2003). While most trainees value and see the importance of their 'field experience' (Avis et al., 2002; Heggen, 2008), the other side of the coin, the teaching theory, is usually ignored and at best used in a clinical and cynical fashion for the writing of essays and assignments (Elliott, 1991). Field experience is invaluable, being in the classroom as a practical exercise is clearly essential, but practice without reflection and without critical thinking is ultimately of surface value only for teacher learning. The 'craft knowledge' of teachers as spoken about by Hagger and McIntyre (2006) is not atheoretical — far from it: it is situated in practice but also straddles the workplace and the academy by linking theory to practical know-how. Adopting Bourdieu's (1977) sociocultural theory, Heggen (2008), writing within the Norwegian context, has made the claim that there is a gap between professional practice and what professionals are taught about this practice. For Haggen, this makes teachers 'boundary crossers' — they are members of different horizontally segregated communities of practice (Wenger, 1998). This polycontextuality informs their identity and professional socialisation, but the 'realities' of the field constitute the stronger pull. Following the Norwegian example once more, Van Oers (1998) offers a social-constructivist approach to notions of professional formation arguing that knowledge learned on training programmes needs to be recontextualised before it can become of practical use in the field. Student voice work — and positive and democratic relationships with learners — can have the potential to transform the contextuality of trainee teachers as they begin this process of identity formation.

Pedagogic Voices

It is important that we recognise that notwithstanding the 'unsettling boundaries' in and around the lifelong learning sector itself (R. Edwards & Fowler, 2007), teacher education in general and teacher education and learning within the lifelong learning sector in particular are contested and enacted by the professionals who 'profess' to practice them. Teacher education is equally constructed as a 'subject' in policy narratives and discourses. The shifting field of teacher education makes many claims: It is seen by some as the means by which teachers better know their 'craft' (Hagger & McIntyre, 2006) and to better know their 'selves' (Atkinson, 2004). While a new field, or at least, a marginal contribution to a larger and more established field, teacher education literature points to the need for teacher educators to articulate their pedagogies as a meaningful and collegiate way forward within a professional research community (Murray, Jones, McNamara, & Stanley, 2009). There is also recognition that within the ambiguity that surrounds the teacher education field, it is impossible to make certain knowledge claims about teacher's own practices as a professional body — let alone teacher educator's own practice. The particular location for teacher educators — the double hermeneutical location of being both teacher and a teacher of teachers — seems to sit easily with notions of a pedagogy built upon 'modelling' (Hagger & McIntyre, 2006; Loughran, 1996; Malderez & Wedell, 2007), although the modelling of *what* is unsure. Through the enquiry, which is the subject of the research-informed practice identified in this chapter, I seek to demonstrate to trainee teachers, modelling in my practice, the importance of a 'democratic education' (Giroux, 2005, p. 454) and the value to be had in 'listening to learners':

> Voice, quite simply, refers to the various measures by which students and teachers actively participate in dialogue. It is related to the discursive means whereby teachers and students attempt to make themselves 'heard' and to define themselves as active authors of their own worlds.

I do this essentially through 'story-telling' practices bound up with the adoption of learner voice. Thus, trainee teacher are not just listening to learners — but are encouraged to speak with (not to) learners as a means to develop their professional identities. The voices of the young learners captured in this enquiry speak of their enjoyment, anxiety and at times frustration with the teaching they all too often 'receive' rather than *participate* in:

> You can tell those poor teachers ... they just seem like they turn up and don't care; nothing planned and it's just, like, do these exercises out of the book. [Female student, aged 17]

Digital Voices

To develop the learner voice audio resource, the recordings themselves were edited audio files drawn from a series of semi-structured interviews with 16- to 19-year-old learners. On the basis of a 'something-for-something' contractual relationship to participant participation, the learners themselves were drawn from students currently studying sociology. It was hoped that the experience of taking part in a research interview would be a learning experience for them and one that they could apply to their own sociological studies. As an elicitation technique, considerable time was taken before and after each private individual interview to speak to each student about their studies, their coursework and in doing so to answer any questions about the research methodology and techniques of this research. Full openness was established at every point in the process:

1. All learners received a copy of the same proposal sent to the institutions when seeking permission for access.
2. Learners were chosen by the institution and a private and quiet room was set aside for the interviews (necessary for the audio quality of the recordings that would eventually form the individual podcasts).

3. Learners were initially briefed together along with a member of staff where possible — full disclosure and full entitlement to withdraw were made clear at each stage.
4. Learners were asked to sign a consent/release form before taking part.
5. Participants took part with full understanding that the recordings would be taken and turned into audio files to be podcast to trainees and at conferences — and that their institution would also receive a copy of the files for potential staff training purposes.

A central feature of the research interviews was the emphasis at all times upon 'good teaching'; all institutions and all learners were briefed on the importance to speak about positive experiences (and that those listening to the audio resource afterwards would infer from the research that 'bad teaching' would be the opposite of 'good teaching'). In this way, the institutions themselves were comfortable with the recordings taking place, and the learners themselves were comfortable with the idea that others would get to hear the files. All learners who took part spoke candidly, positively and enthusiastically about the experience and expressed interest and pleasure in the idea that their institutions and teachers new to the profession might develop their practice because of the creation of their participation.

Each interview lasted between 25 and 40 minutes long and was recorded digitally using MP3 recorders and microphones. Each interview started with the question 'What makes a good teacher?' and ended with the question 'What advice do you have for trainee teachers about to start to teach for the first time?'. Nineteen interviews were recorded in total, generating over nine hours of audio. Audio files were uploaded into sound editing freeware programmes and then edited down into a series of smaller chunks — each lasting between 45 seconds and up to 3 minutes. These chunks of data were recoded with a file name that best summarised the content of the recording, often where possible drawing upon the exact words of the participants themselves (see Table 25.1 for a selection of file names).

File names coded in this way start to develop a sense of the authentic voice of the participant and yet at the same time help to establish anonymity. Each set of files — later to become part of the audio teaching tool — was then burned onto a CD-ROM and sent back to each institution for internal staff training. This part of the research is still ongoing with two out of the three institutions having made, to date, a strong

Table 25.1: (Selected) file names and coding of learner voice audios.

What makes a good teacher?	Talking helps thinking	Repetition is important
They shouldn't be too removed	My advice is …	It's all about trust
I wonder if they understand	It's best when we are engaged	Always be involved with the class
I like it when my class is a community	It's important to get good feedback	I hate it when they are unprepared

indication that they are interested in developing an action research project/resource coming out of the data. Final data was coded using tools and a sensibility indebted to the 'Grounded Theory' approach as (re)versioned by Charmaz (2006, p. 14), whereby the audios (as data) are brought closer into frame:

> Like a camera with many lenses, first you view a broad sweep of the landscape. Subsequently, you change your lens several times to bring scenes closer and closer into view.

Theoretical sensitivity and frames have been constructed as the audios have been further coded down — a process replicating and mirroring the twin 'archiving' process of the audio for the learning resource. The individual pieces of audio — 247 in all — were merged into a digital archive and grouped according to theme. The audios are then used extensively during induction and early teaching sessions on the teacher education programme as a means to prompt and stimulate debate — allowing stories to come through. Learners spoke about what teaching methods, techniques and assessment strategies they found most helpful and what qualities and characteristics 'good teachers' displayed:

> He was really freaky. You went into his lesson and thought 'What's he on?' Every lesson different materials and they were all games and things. But the lessons were so interesting – so many things to do. I really felt like I was learning and no one had the time to be disruptive or anything like that. [Female student, aged 16]

Disembodied Voices?

Most striking about the 19 interviews conducted for this enquiry is the common themes learners identified about 'good teaching' — within the three institutions taking part (as might be expected), but also across all participants. Key findings are presented and summarised in Table 25.2.

It is possible to identify five domains (Figure 25.1) representing the sum of the learners' stock-of-knowledge at hand regarding how they saw the nature of the teaching and learning process. These domains — *relational, dialogic, reactional, reflective* and *pedagogic* — allow us to conceive of learners as active agents, critical and self-aware.

> it gets you really involved and interested. Lots of activities and it really whizzes by. Before you know it the lesson has ended and you think 'I've really learned a lot this lesson'. [Male student, aged 16]

Learners interviewed were able to speak with both clarity and authority of what they felt 'works' in the classroom. For many trainee teachers, the socio-economic and geographical location of these voices — their accents and (sub) cultural languages — provided a stark contrast to the depth and authority with which their voices and

Table 25.2: Summary of the learner voice audio archive.

Domain	Characteristic
Relational	Good teachers are spoken about by learners more in terms of their relational qualities than in terms of the teaching techniques and methods they might employ
Dialogic	Almost all learners spoke of the need for their own talk to be used within classes as a means through which they come to understand the materials being learnt. Unsuccessful learning was seen to take place in quiet classes where learner talk was at a minimum
Reactional	Learners felt that personal and individual feedback was perhaps more important for their learning than the actual classroom experience itself. Teachers respond and react to learners in different ways and learners are able to identify that teachers' attention and support are essential
Reflective	Learners recognised that while 'good teachers' often 'got things wrong' or had lessons that 'did not quite work', they were open in seeking learner evaluation and would engage in a process of self-reflection with their students in a positive and open manner. This made learners feel valued and included
Pedagogic	Finally, learners spoke positively of pace and variety in classes as the key factor in capturing their own interest and motivation in the lesson itself

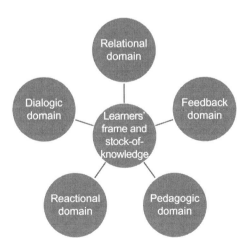

Figure 25.1: The Stock-of-Knowledge at Hand of Learners.

stories were received by the trainees. The unpacking of judgements and assumptions in this way was also useful in demonstrating to trainee teachers the importance of locating learners as authoritative and 'expert' in their own right. However, the audios and voices were not 'received' by the trainee teachers in a straightforward way. Presenting the audios in a deconstructed form has the problem of making, at times, the learners and the learner's voice disembodied. Along with this, disembodied voices are themselves unsituated. The audio teaching and learning resource requires great orchestration on behalf of teacher educators to allow the stories and voices to become more fully formed as they become more context-sensitive. The 'fully-realised', context-dependent voices are themselves reflective — learners are articulating their stories, their voice, through reflection and in doing so are demonstrating the significant degree of reflective pedagogic work they have already added to the frame through which they see the classrooms and institutions they inhabit. Thus, we have a relationship between the reflective practitioner (Schön, 1983) and the reflective learner.

Hermeneutical Voices

For Brookfield (1995), we have four 'lenses' through which reflective practice for professional learners can be developed: the autobiographical, fellow professionals, research literature and our students. The student voice movement and this enquiry seek to demonstrate the value to be had in adopting this fourth lens. In this enquiry, and the research-informed practice it supports, I seek to demonstrate to trainee teachers that their learners are 'reflective learners' too and that what such learners bring to the classroom and interactional encounters is an often detailed and well-articulated understandings of pedagogy — more so, perhaps, than many trainee teachers when they start their professional learning. For Charmaz (2006, p. 15),

> Neither observer nor observed come to a scene untouched by the world. Researchers and research participants make assumptions about what is real, possess stocks of knowledge ... Nevertheless, researchers, not participants, are obligated to be reflexive about what we bring to the scene, what we see, and how we do it.

The enquiry herein, and the wider student voice movement, conceives participants (in both learning partnerships and research enquiry) to also be 'reflexive' (and reflective) about what they 'bring' — about their stock-of-knowledge and its value in forming the world as seen around them. This image of the learner-participant as having a reflective self (of being articulate, opinionated and grounded) is embedded in some of the literature around student voice (see Fielding, 2004) and action research (see Grant, 2007) — itself often employed by student voice practitioner-researchers. The cultivation of this reflective self is also what is both asked and required of trainee teachers as they move from *teacher-in-the-making* to 'novice outsiders', ready to legitimately participate (Lave & Wenger, 1991) in first employments and new sociocultural surroundings. Contrary to the 'dangerous' and 'therapeutic education' heavily critiqued by Ecclestone and Hayes (2009), this enquiry is an attempt to place learners at both the heart of teaching and the training of teachers — seeking to capture and be sensitive to their voice, development and emotional and relational qualities and encounters. In this process, I seek to demonstrate to trainee teachers the legitimate value of what learners know and the stock-of-knowledge they bring to interactional encounters in the classroom. However, this is far from uncontested. Post-structural readings of power show us that knowledge is constructed by the 'knower' and about the 'known' through the objectification of the known in the interplay of discourses (Derrida, 1977, 1978; Foucault, 1984). Indeed, as Fielding (2004, p. 302) notes,

> In working with students, whether we are teachers, teacher-researchers, or researchers, we will inevitably find ourselves talking about them and, perhaps less frequently, on behalf of them or for them.

For Fielding, student voice research, not uncontested by any means, raises three key problematics for the power dynamic embedded in research. We have

(1) 'Problems of speaking *about* others',
(2) 'problems of speaking *for* others',
(3) problems of 'Getting heard'. (Fielding, 2004, p. 296)

In this enquiry, I have sought to speak 'with' rather than 'for' learners — although at times the distinction is tenuous. In using student voice for the training of teachers and to develop their reflective (and reflexive) practices, I seek to encourage teachers to relate to learners with the 'radical collegiality' (Fielding, 1999) needed to demonstrate that learners and what they have to say are both valued and can inform the professional learning of the teacher. This approach can be characterised as

> a critical pedagogy takes into account the various ways in which the voices that teachers use to communicate with students can either silence or legitimate them. (Giroux, 2005, p. 454)

Conclusion

This enquiry, like a great deal of small-scale, qualitative student voice work, can only hope to begin to support transformation and democratic education on a local level. But, perhaps this is enough? As Les Back (2007, p. 1) notes,

> While the scale and complexity of global society may escape our total understanding, the sociologists can still pay attention to the fragments, the voices and stories that are otherwise passed over or ignored.

It has been important for this enquiry to frame trainee teachers as able to learn from the authority of authentic student voice and to conceptualise learners as having useful and meaningful insights and stories to share. I have attempted to talk *with* learners, although at times I have had no choice but to allow them to talk *through*, my teacher education pedagogy. But in this small way, we attempt to ensure that trainee teachers as they become novice and then legitimate participants understand the democratic value in the co-construction of meanings of teaching and learning with learners. We need to encourage trainee teachers to understand that these voices should command our attention. Again, as Back (2007, p. 1) suggests, 'the task of sociology is to admit these voices and pay them the courtesy of serious attention'. To do this is, though, a highly modernist approach to the problems of the managerial, marketized and post-Fordist (Avis, 1999, 2002; Salisbury et al., 2009), changes sweeping across the lifelong learning sector in the United Kingdom, as elsewhere in other Northern European societies. As Savage and Warde (1993) have noted, modernity is itself 'double-edged': on the one hand, it promises the 'self' ripe for active development — a personal identity project, and yet, on the other, the need to shape and mould self-identity comes with it risk and anxiety. For Savage and Warde (1993, p. 150), modernity is thus 'disorderly' because it 'obliges individuals to experiment, to hope, to gamble and to be ambitious'. This means that the project of the self, of becoming who one is, for teachers and other professional learners, is fundamentally a risky proposition. Notwithstanding post-structural insights into the way teachers and learners are formed as objects through power relations, I have argued here that teachers and trainee teachers are best conceptualised as active agents — that the rapid and hyper-intensive ebb and flow of structural and discourse changes, which characterise the UK lifelong learning sector in turn creates places and spaces for identity work, and for the learning from learners as much as from other sources. In this sense, I argue here that it is better not just to conceive trainee teachers as 'boundary-crossers' (Heggen, 2008) but also as in need of (successful) 'relational agency':

> Relational agency involves a capacity to offer support and to ask for support from others. One's ability to engage with the world is enhanced by doing so alongside others. (A. Edwards & Mackenzie, 2005, p. 282)

As A. Edwards (2005) notes, the problems and social change associated with late capitalism 'create paradoxical tensions for those who inhabit them and put strain on a sense of self' (A. Edwards, 2005, p. 169). This is true for teachers and for trainee teachers — they need to locate themselves within a world that is redefining around them what it means to be a teacher. To do so, locating professional practice in authentic student voice might offer a counterpoint to more market-driven educational sensibilities. As A. Edwards (2005, p. 169) also contends,

> strong forms of agency are required to help people, such as practitioners who need to collaborate across organisational

boundaries, to find moments of stability as they move in and out of different settings without the protection of what Sennett (1999) describes as 'institutional shelters'.

With relational agency comes the need for relational *intimacy*: for those who engage in collective social encounters to better understand one another so that mutual support can be established. A mutual support that might fend off the risks and tensions of the project of the self in the late capitalist and postmodern age. Teachers need to work with one another, but they need to work with learners too. Only by capturing and utilising student voice can we hope to redefine what it means to teach — and to learn how to teach.

References

Ainley, P., & Bailey, B. (1997). *The business of learning: Staff and student experiences of FE in the 1990s*. London: Cassell.

Atkinson, D. (2004). Theorising how student teachers form their identities in initial teacher education. *British Educational Research Journal, 30*(3), 379–394.

Avis, J. (1999). Shifting identity: New conditions and the transformation of practice-teaching within post-compulsory education. *Journal of Vocational Education and Training, 51*(2), 245–264.

Avis, J. (2002). Imaginary friends: Managerialism, globalization and post-compulsory education and training in England. *Discourse Studies in the Cultural Politics of Education, 23*(1), 75–90.

Avis, J., Bathmaker, A-M., & Parsons, J. (2002). 'I think a lot of staff are dinosaurs': Further education trainee teachers' understandings of pedagogic relations'. *Journal of Education and Work, 15*(2), 181–200.

Back, L. (2007). *The art of listening*. Oxford: Berg.

Ball, S. J. (2001). Better read! Theorising the teacher. In: M. Maguire & J. Dillon (Eds), *Becoming a teacher*. Buckingham: Open University Press.

Ball, S. J. (2004). *The RoutledgeFalmer reader in sociology of education*. London: RoutledgeFalmer.

Bathmaker, A., & Avis, J. (2007). How do I cope with that?' The challenge of 'schooling' cultures in further education for trainee FE lecturers. *British Educational Research Journal, 33*(4), 509–532.

Beauchamp, C., & Thomas, L. (2009). Understanding teacher identity: An overview of issues in the literature and implications for teacher education. *Cambridge Journal of Education, 39*(2), 175–189.

Bourdieu, P. (1977). *Outline of a theory of practice*. Cambridge: Cambridge University Press.

Bragg, S. (2001). Taking a joke: Learning from the voices we don't want to hear. *Forum, 43*(2), 70–73.

Brookfield, S. (1995). *Becoming a critically reflective teacher*. San Francisco, CA: Jossey-Bass.

Carr, W., & Kemmis, S. (1986). *Becoming critical: Education, knowledge and action research*. Lewes: Falmer Press.

Charmaz, C. (2006). *Constructing grounded theory: A practical guide through qualitative analysis*. London: Sage.

Czerniawski, G. (2011). *Emerging teachers and globalisation*. London: Routledge.

Day, C., & Gu, Q. (2010). *The new lives of teachers*. London: Routledge.

Derrida, J. (1977). *Of grammatology*. Baltimore, MD: John Hopkins University Press.

Derrida, J. (1978). *Writing and difference*. Chicago, IL: University of Chicago Press.

Ecclestone, K., & Hayes, D. (2009). *The dangerous rise of therapeutic education*. London: Routledge.

Edwards, A. (2005). Relational agency: Learning to be a resourceful practitioner. *International Journal of Educational Research, 43*, 168–182.

Edwards, R., & Fowler, Z. (2007). Unsettling boundaries in making a space for research. *British Educational Research Journal, 33*(1), 107–123.

Edwards, A., & Mackenzie, L. (2005). Steps towards participation: The social support of learning trajectories. *International Journal of Lifelong Education, 24*(4), 282–302.

Elliott, J. (1991). *Action research for educational change*. Buckingham: Open University Press.

Fielding, M. (1999). Radical collegiality: Affirming teaching as an inclusive professional practice. *Australian Educational Researcher, 26*(2), 1–34.

Fielding, M. (2000). Education and the challenge of living philosophy. *Journal of Education Policy, 15*, 377–381.

Fielding, M. (2004). Transformative approaches to student voice: Theoretical underpinnings, recalcitrant realities. *British Educational Research Journal, 30*(2), 295–311.

Fielding, M. (2009). Listening to learners: Partnerships in action conference, student voice, democracy and the necessity of radical education. [Key note presentation], April 22. London: University of East London.

Foucault, M. (1984). *The Foucault reader*. London: Penguin.

Giroux, H. (2005). *Schooling and the struggle for public life: Democracy's promise and education's failure*. Boulder, CO: Paradigm Publishers.

Grant, S. (2007). Learning through 'being' and 'doing'. *Action Research, 5*(3), 265–274.

Griffin, M. L. (2003). Using critical incidents to promote and assess reflective thinking in preservice teachers. *Reflective Practice, 4*(2).

Hagger, H., & McIntyre, D. (2006). *Learning teaching from teachers: Realising the potential of school-based teacher education*. Maidenhead: Open University Press.

Heggen, K. (2008). Social workers, teachers and nurses — From college to professional work. *Journal of Education and Work, 21*(3), 217–231.

Hobson, A., Tracey, L., Kerr, K., Malderaz, A., Pell, G., Simm, C., & Johnson, F. (2004). Why people choose to become teachers and the factors influencing their choice of initial teacher training route: Early findings from the Becoming a Teacher (BaT) Project. DfES Brief RBX08-04.

Jackson, A. Y. (2003). Rhizovocality. *Qualitative Studies in Education, 16*(5), 693–710.

Lave, J., & Wenger, E. (1991). *Situated learning: Legitimate peripheral participation*. Cambridge: Cambridge University Press.

Layder, D. (1993). *New strategies in social research*. Cambridge: Blackwell.

Loughran, J. (1996). *Developing reflective practice: Learning about teaching and learning through modelling*. London: RoutledgeFalmer.

Malderez, A., & Wedell, M. (2007). *Teaching teachers: Processes and practices*. London: Continuum.

Mazzei, L. A. (2009). An impossibly full voice. In: Jackson & Mazzei (Eds), *Voice in qualitative inquiry: Challenging conventional, interpretive and critical conceptions in qualitative research*. Abingdon; New York, NY: Routledge.

McIntyre, D., Pedder, D., & Rudduck, J. (2005). Pupil voice: Comfortable and uncomfortable learnings for teachers. *Research Papers in Education, 20*, 149–168.

Murray, J., Jones, M., McNamara, O., & Stanley, G. (2009). *Evaluation of the Teacher Education Research Network (TERN): Final report to the ESRC.* ESRC/TLRP, October.

Reeves, F. (1995). *The modernity of further education.* Bilston and Ticknall.

Ruddock, J., & Flutter, J. (2000). Pupil participation and the pupil perspective: Carving a new order of experience. *Cambridge Journal of Education, 30*(1), 75–89.

Ruddock, J., & McIntyre, D. (Eds). (2007). *Improving learning through consulting pupils. Teaching and learning research programme (TLRP) consulting pupils project team.* London: Routledge.

Rudduck, J. (2006). The past, the papers and the project. *Educational Review, 58,* 131–143.

Salisbury, J., Martin, J., & Roberts, J. (2009). FE teachers talking about students' learning. *Research Papers in Education, 24*(4), 421–438.

Savage, M., & Warde, A. (1993). *Urban sociology, capitalism and modernity.* London: Macmillan.

Schön, D. A. (1983). *The reflective practitioner: How professionals think in action.* New York, NY: Basic Books.

Solorzano, D. G., & Yosso, T. J. (2002). Critical race methodology: Counter-storytelling as an analytical framework for educational research. *Qualitative Inquiry, 8*(1), 23–44.

St. Pierre, E. A. (2000). Poststructural feminism in education: An overview. *International Journal of Qualitative Studies in Education, 13*(5), 477–515.

Taylor, C., & Robinson, C. (2009). Student voice: Theorising power and participation. *Pedagogy, Culture & Society, 17*(2), 161–175.

Van Oers, B. (1998). The fallacy of decontextualization. *Mind, Culture, and Activity, 5*(2), 135–142.

Wallace, S. (2002). No good surprises: Intending lecturers' preconceptions and initial experiences of further education. *British Educational Research Journal, 28*(1), 79–93.

Wenger, E. (1998). *Communities of practice: Learning, meaning, and identity.* Cambridge: Cambridge University Press.

Chapter 26

Pupil Voice and Action Research

Rita Cheminais

Abstract

This chapter describes how pupils as action researchers[1] can make a positive contribution to improve the five Every Child Matters (ECM) outcomes.[2] Four school-based action research projects, initiated and led by pupils, are included in the chapter as cameos of good practice. Two cameos are taken from two contrasting primary schools, one of which is located in an urban area and the other in a rural area. The urban primary school involved pupils as members of the learning council, researching the features that make learning active, challenging and engaging for pupils in the school. The rural primary school, engaged children as members of one of five ECM outcome pupil teams, in researching what economic well-being topics and activities should be included in the primary school curriculum. The two secondary school action research projects were undertaken and led by pupils in two large secondary schools, both of which were located in pleasant suburban areas, catering for the full diversity of learners. The first project focused on members of the school

---

1. Action research entails a group of pupils finding out, establishing the truth and gaining a better understanding about a concern, issue or problem raised by their peers in school, to bring about a change or improvement.
2. ECM was a Labour government initiative introduced in 2003 through a Green Paper, with the key aim of protecting, nurturing and improving the Life chances and well-being outcomes (be healthy, stay safe, enjoy and achieve, make a positive contribution, and achieve economic well-being) of all children and young people from birth to 19, particularly those of the most vulnerable. Since August 2010, the coalition government has replaced the term ECM outcomes with 'Help children achieve more' placing greater importance on achievement and academic standards.

---

council[3] exploring how the school dining experience could be improved for pupils aged from 11 to 18. The second project in the other school focused on pupils identifying what would improve the delivery of the English curriculum in school, for those taking the subject at examination level. In each school, the head teacher gave the pupil action researchers' total ownership and the freedom to explore the pupil issue of concern. Key messages for best practice emerging from the cameos stress the need for equal importance being given to pupil well-being[4] and pupil attainment; a visible, dynamic and approachable head teacher who promotes and encourages pupil voice and participation in school decision-making; an inclusive school, where pupil diversity and voice are respected, valued and listened to; a high level of trust existing among teachers pupils; and, teachers acting as facilitators rather than directors of pupil-led action research. Lessons learned from the good practice pupil-led action research projects indicate that pupils are more receptive to engaging in action research when the topics being explored are of interest to them, and relevant to their school life and work. Pupils as action researchers thrive best in a school culture that promotes and acknowledges the rights of children in accordance with the United Nations Convention on the Rights of the Child. Pre-tutoring in basic research methods and how to analyse research data are essential to prepare pupils as action researchers for their role.

Keywords: Action research; school council; Every Child Matters; well-being; pupil voice

Introduction

Pupil voice and action research are discussed and illustrated in the context of the previous Labour Government's Every Child Matters (ECM) change for children initiative,[5] which was the Prime Minister Tony Blair's response to the tragic death of Victoria Climbié, which could have been prevented had the agencies working with Victoria shared the intelligence gathered and acted early on the information about the family circumstances in which the child was living. The ECM change for children programme was influenced by the United States of America initiative 'No Child Left

---

3. A school council is a democratically elected body of pupils who represent the views of their peers. They provide an active forum for constructive pupil input and positive contributions to inform head teacher decision making in relation to improving aspects of school life and work relevant to pupils.
4. Well-being refers to children and young people having the basic essentials needed to enable them to live, be healthy, safe and happy. It also refers to the five ECM outcomes.
5. The ECM change for children programme, as a 10-year strategy (2003–2013), adopts a holistic approach to identifying and removing barriers to children and young people's learning, which may be the result of poor teaching, an inappropriate curriculum, inflexible timetabling, or external factors such as family circumstances, poverty, or negative community influences.

Behind', which aimed to close the pupil achievement gap between white, black and Hispanic groups of children and young people. Since the Conservative and Liberal Democrat coalition government came into power on the 11 May 2010, the ECM agenda has not featured in any subsequent government education policies, as the focus has been on teaching in relation to pupils achievement and attainment.

The fourth ECM outcome: 'Make a positive contribution' stated as one of its aims that: 'Children and young people should engage in decision making... .' In relation to pupil voice in schools in England, this entails children and young people expressing their views, opinions and ideas and sharing their experience and knowledge in a range of ways, with fellow peers and adults. This helps to inform school policy development and practice relevant to them, for example, in respect of teaching and learning, the curriculum, the school environment and school organisation.

Hadfield and Haw (2004) refer to three types of pupil voice: authoritative, critical and therapeutic, all of which are relevant in the pupil-led action research context. Authoritative pupil voice represents the views of a particular group of children and young people, for example, gifted and talented pupils in a school.[6] The pupil-led action research may investigate and explore how far learning in a school really does extend and enrich gifted and talented pupils learning. Critical pupil voice refers to pupils as researchers presenting the views of a marginal group of children in the school, for example, of those with special educational needs, to teachers and other professionals, to better inform policy and provision to meet their needs. Therapeutic pupil voice relates to pupils sharing their own experiences and ways of coping in a particular situation with other peers in the school, to help them deal with a similar situation or problem. Peer mentoring is a good example of this type of pupil voice in practice, and in the action research context, is likely to involve more experienced pupil researchers mentoring other peers who are new to undertaking action research.

Pupil voice has been central to the ECM agenda, a 10-year Labour Government strategy, first introduced by a Green Paper in 2003 in England. The voice and rights of children and young people were equally promoted, honoured and recognised by the government in their document *Youth Matters* (2005). Both acknowledged the importance of children and young people having a say in developing policies that affect them, particularly in relation to improving and promoting the five ECM well-being outcomes: be healthy, stay safe, enjoy and achieve, make a positive contribution, and achieve economic well-being. Their views informed the Labour Government's Children's Plan in 2007.

ECM renewed interest in consulting with children and young people inspired many forward thinking schools, academies[7] and pupil referral units (PRUs) across

---

6. Gifted refers to those pupils who are capable of excelling academically in one or more subjects. Talented refers to those pupils who may excel in practical skills such as sport, leadership, artistic performance. Gifted and talented pupils work at a level beyond that expected for their chronological age.

7. An academy is a publicly funded school that works in partnership with a poor performing school in order to disseminate and share their good practice and expertise. They are free from local authority control, having greater autonomy to make decisions about how they use their resources.

the United Kingdom to undertake pupil-led action research in the primary and secondary education phase, as illustrated by the good practice cameos featured in this chapter.

The first Children's Commissioner in England, Professor Albert Aynsley Green expressed the view that while it was good practice for the government and other national organisations to consult children and young people on a regular basis to seek their views and opinions on issues relating to the ECM outcomes, they were not being proactively involved enough in the actual decision-making process. Pupil-led action research is the ideal process to ensure children and young people have a voice, as active participants, in bringing about change.

Action research from the cameos of good practice featured in this chapter have entailed pupils finding out, establishing the truth and gaining a better understanding about a concern, issue or problem raised by a group of pupils. The meaningful and authentic pupil-led action research in the cameos empowered the children and young people to consult with their peers to decide on the issue, concern, problem or topic to research in school, requiring improvement. The pupils were able to decide which research methods they wished to utilise and to carry out the research with confidence. A senior member of staff, acting as a facilitator and mentor to the pupil researchers, supported the analysis of the evidence gathered. Pupil researchers in each instance were able to take responsibility for making recommendations and disseminating their research findings and results to a range of different stakeholders. In addition, they engaged in purposeful discussion on the outcomes and findings from their research, with the head teacher, the governing body, and the senior leadership team in school. This significantly helped to influence, persuade and convince adult decision makers in the schools, to ensure the right change or improvement occurred, as soon as possible, for the benefit of fellow pupils. If pupils don't get involved in the decision-making process in school through the action research process, then they are likely to only get what the teachers think the pupils want.

There was a noticeable difference in the type and nature of action research pupils undertook in the primary and secondary school cameos. For example, there was a greater level of teacher guidance, support and supervision provided to primary pupils undertaking action research in their own school. In addition, the primary school pupil action research methods adopted a more child-friendly fun approach. For example, the economic well-being action research pupil team were able to put into practice the practical activities they suggested, that is, the millionaire's club with its fantasy Stock Exchange, to help young children understand the importance and value of becoming financially literate (Table 26.1).

Primary school pupil-led action research may take the form of investigative journalism or photo journalism and include gathering evidence on the views of young children through the use of puppets, toys, art, drawing, role play, storytelling and circle time. The Children's Research Centre at the Open University provides examples of these methods being used in primary schools (http://childrens-research-centre.open.ac.uk/).

Table 26.1: Cameo of good practice — enhancing the economic well-being of pupils.

School: A Community Primary School in Tadley, Hampshire

ECM outcome: Achieve economic well-being

Focus of the pupil research: How to ensure economic well-being topics are areas that pupils throughout the school wanted to learn about

Who was involved: The members of the pupil Economic Well-Being Team, with pupil representatives from each year group throughout the school. This team also had a governor and parent representative on it. A class teacher, who acted as a facilitator, oversaw the pupil-initiated activities

What the pupil researchers did: The pupil Economic Well-Being Team devised and distributed a questionnaire to children in the school, which asked them to identify what areas relating to economic well-being they wanted to learn about and to seek their views on pocket money and saving money

Outcomes from the research:
- A millionaire's Club was formed which entailed a fantasy Stock Exchange for pupils
- A Dragons Den0Apprentice Competition ran, with each class making a new product to sell and to make a profit, from the £50 funding provided by the PTA
- A Fantasy Football initiative that involved pupils developing skills in budgeting and pricing to buy and sell players.
- A pupil Journalism Club with a team of pupils producing the 'Writers Block' Magazine
- Information about different careers provided to children in the school

(The school had formed five teams, one for each of the five ECM outcomes. The economic well-being team had undertaken the most innovative work)

Key Features that Promote Pupil Voice and Pupil-Led Action Research

The following essential features and key drivers promoting pupil voice and pupil-led action research were identified in some schools that were working towards achieving the international ECM Standards Award.[8]

- Pupil well-being is given equal importance as pupil attainment.
- Visible, dynamic school leaders with a passion for removing pupils barriers to learning promote their vision on pupil voice, choice and participation across the entire school, as part of everyday practice.

8. The Every Child Matters Standards Award was developed by ECM Solutions, which enables schools to audit their current ECM policy and practice, to develop an action plan to address any gaps, build a portfolio of good practice evidence, and an external validation on-site of policy and practice in action.

- The school has a very strong pastoral ethos where pupils come first, and every child really does matter. Pupil exclusions don't occur or are very rare.
- A culture of 'risk taking' learning enquiry exists among staff and pupils, where teachers and pupils, as co-partners and co-learners explore issues together to inform school improvement and school self-review processes.
- The views, opinions and ideas of pupils are valued, respected and listened to by other pupils and adults in the school.
- The school has an active listening culture existing equally among pupils and staff.
- The schools are inclusive, valuing diversity and difference highly for the enrichment both bring to the learning community.
- A good level of trust and openness exists among staff, governors, pupils, parents, carers, the wider family and members of the community.
- Pupils are empowered and given the opportunity to take responsibility; for example, they participate in the appointment of new staff; they undertake paired lesson observations with the head teacher or deputy head teacher.
- Teachers are willing to 'let go' acting as facilitators of pupils learning, allowing them to take greater ownership for their own learning, and for reviewing their own progress.
- The school has a well-established effective pupil peer mentoring or pupil buddy system operating.
- Pupils are pre-tutored in research methods, and have ongoing mentoring and coaching while they are undertaking pupil-led action research in school.

The list of key features is by no means definitive, and it does offer a useful checklist of success criteria to senior leaders and managers in other schools, academies and PRUs, who wish to introduce and increase pupil-led action research.

Good Practice Examples of Pupil-Led Action Research

The following three good practice cameos have also been gathered from some of the schools, who have been participating in working towards achieving the international ECM Standards Award (rebranded the Achievement through Well-Being Award in 2011, to better reflect the coalition government's educational focus on the achievement of children and young people as opposed to their overall well-being).

The good practice cameos of pupil-led action research provide a valuable insight into what the pupils chose to research; the research approaches they selected; and the outcomes arising from their research findings. All the research projects were manageable within the context of each school setting. Pupils were given the time and permission to undertake their research by visionary head teachers and deputy head teachers. A senior member of staff in each school and class teachers in the primary sector oversaw but did not control the work of the pupil-led action research teams. Having a governor taking an interest, and in some instances being a member of the pupil team, had a very positive impact in giving added importance to the research being undertaken by the pupils in school. Equally, parental representation on the pupil ECM teams in one school, not only provided a valuable external 'critical friend' perspective, as an ambassador for pupil participation and pupil-led research, but also strengthened links between the school council and the parent council in school (Tables 26.2–26.4).

Table 26.2: Cameo of good practice — researching pupils' learning in school.

School: Primary phase Academy, in Walthamstow, Waltham Forest

ECM outcome: Enjoy and achieve

Focus of the pupil research: The pupil learning council researched how children learn and which learning activities promote pupil engagement, challenge and enjoyment in learning. The research focused on five aspects of learning: fun, challenge, joining in, equipment, and using ICT

Who was involved: Pupils from the school Learning Council

What the pupil researchers did: The Learning Council devised and distributed a pupil questionnaire on learning. They undertook paired lesson observations using an observation schedule with the senior leadership team, and they undertook some pupil interviews

Outcomes from the research:
- The Learning Council wrote a formal letter to the head teacher that highlighted the outcomes from their research findings on learning with suggested recommendations, along with other general school improvements
- For each of the five aspects of learning, they identified useful activities and approaches that would enable pupils to find learning enjoyable, challenging and more engaging
- The head teacher has subsequently enabled the pupils suggested changes in learning to take place. This has resulted in the recommendations made by the pupils regarding learning having been implemented consistently across the entire school
- Children throughout the school enjoy their learning even more and feel far more empowered as learners

---

Table 26.3: Cameo of good practice — school council action research on the school cafeteria.

School: A large secondary school, which is a Specialist Science College, in Liverpool

ECM outcome: Be healthy

Focus of the pupil research: Improving the school cafeteria and the pupils dining experience

Who was involved: The members of the school council

Table 26.3: (*Continued*)

What the pupil researchers did: The school council devised and distributed a survey to 250 pupils throughout KS3 & KS4 and to 40 sixth form students, which asked a series of questions relating to food choice and service; the hygiene and cleanliness of the dining area; and any improvements pupils would like to see being made in the cafeteria. The school council interpreted and analysed their research findings, and presented the results and outcomes to the head teacher, the senior leadership team and the governing body. The survey results were also publicised on the school's virtual learning environment (VLE) the 'Frog' platform, for pupils and parents to view the findings

Outcomes from the research:
The catering manager took on board the findings from the school council research and made the following improvements:
• A healthy salad bar was introduced to the cafeteria
• Chips were only served once a week and they were oven cooked not fried
• Meals became healthier and more nutritious
• Menus were published on the school's VLE 'Frog' platform
• The quality of food improved that resulted in meals tasting more like home cooked meals

The school council also devised and distributed a pupil survey that focused on pupil satisfaction with the five ECM outcomes in the school. The outcomes from this survey were fed into the school's self-evaluation form
The school council share their good practice in pupil voice and empowerment with other local school councils, by providing advice and consultancy

---

Table 26.4: Cameo of good practice — seeking pupil views on a curriculum subject.

School: A Community High School in Gee Cross, Tameside, Greater Manchester

ECM outcome: Enjoy and achieve

Focus of the pupil research: Seeking students views on the English Curriculum in KS4

Who was involved: Year 10 students

What the pupil researchers did: Year 10 students participated in student interviews and undertook a student survey. The findings from both methods of research were fed back to the Subject Curriculum Leader for English in the school. The survey focused on seeking students views on what aspects they most enjoyed and which they least enjoyed in the subject; it asked students what they would wish to see improved in English, as well as what students would like to see more of in the subject.

Outcomes from the research:
The Subject Curriculum Leader for English took on board the feedback from the students and the following improvements happened:

Table 26.4: (*Continued*)

- More films and moving images are used in English lessons
- The after-school English coursework club has extended its hours from 1 hour to 2 hours
- The subject department has enhanced its stock of digital and video cameras
- The English department has invested in more inspirational English curriculum software for student and teacher use in lessons
- A wider range of up-to-date reading texts have been purchased for students
- English teachers seek more regular student feedback at the end of lessons and at the end of a unit of work
- Extra-curricular opportunities have been further enhanced for students, e.g. students have worked with a professional actor from The Royal Exchange Theatre in Manchester; students participated in an external Public Speaking Competition

The English Department at the school is a 'Lead Department' in Tameside, in recognition of their hard work and good practice in assessing pupil progress

Lessons Learned from the Pupil-Led Action Research

Evaluation, as a reflective process, clearly engages pupil researchers in the systematic collection of information to make judgements about effectiveness, and to inform future decisions and future research activities. Pupil researchers, by undertaking frequent ongoing small evaluations throughout the action research process, as in the case of the cameos of good practice, were able to make valid judgements about the research experience. This was achieved through pupils keeping a reflective research journal, diary or log. Summative evaluation judges an action research project's overall impact and effectiveness, as well as checking if the original aims and objectives set at the beginning of the pupil-led action research project have been achieved.

Evaluation, undertaken throughout the entire action research journey, needs to find out from the pupil researchers how they identified and agreed upon the topic, concern, issue or problem to research on behalf of their fellow peers. It also needs to identify if there were any problems in selecting the research methods, undertaking the research fieldwork or in collecting and analysing the research data for the pupil researchers. If any problems or difficulties were encountered, then pupil researchers need to indicate how these were overcome, and what lessons have been learned for future pupil-led action research within the educational setting.

Reporting on, and presenting the research findings and results from the pupil-led action research project to different audiences, should also be evaluated by the pupil researchers. This enables them to discover if there are more effective, time-saving ways of getting the main findings and key message across to the head teacher, governors, senior leadership team, staff, pupils, parents and carers.

Pupil evaluation needs to utilise a range of different formats to ensure the full diversity of pupils can participate. For example, using comment boxes, email, text messaging, blogs, podcasting, electronic forum on the school website, photographs, video clips, drawings, symbols, graffiti walls or mind maps.

It is essential that the head teacher listens to and takes note of the pupil researchers' feedback from their evaluation, in relation to what went well, what didn't go as well, and what could be improved next time, when any future pupil-led action research projects take place. The head teacher by acknowledging how much he/she values pupil voice and guaranteeing to make any necessary adjustments or modifications for future pupil action research activities within the school will earn the respect of the pupil researchers.

Conclusion

The pupil-led action research good practice cameos featured in this chapter have enabled head teachers and senior leaders in school to give teachers the confidence to seek pupils' views and engage them in learning enquiry. All four head teachers, and the senior member of staff overseeing the work of the pupil-led action research team were open to risk-taking, being willing to trust pupils to make valid judgements and realistic recommendations, as a result of their research findings. All schools were judged to be good or outstanding in their school inspections by OFSTED, and particularly in relation to pupils making a positive contribution.

Pupils are more receptive to expressing their views and participating in action research, when the topic being researched interests them is relevant to their life and work in the school, and the head teacher and senior leadership team demonstrate they are authentic listeners to pupils concerns, by taking what the pupils tell them seriously.

Pupils respond best to pupil-led action research when they learn in a school school culture that promotes and acknowledges the rights of children and young people. They also thrive as action researchers within an inclusive environment, which promotes equality of opportunity, where the contributions of every pupil matter. Utilising inclusive research approaches enables the full diversity of pupils to give their views and to participate meaningfully in the research process and project.

Pupils as action researchers will feel truly empowered when teachers and senior managers step back from directly controlling their research activities. The teacher acting as a facilitator, mentor and coach to pupil researchers is a core role in the primary and secondary phase of education. Pupils in either phase of education do need pre-tutoring in the basic research methods and in how best to analyse the research data collected.

References

DfES (2005). *Youth matters*. London: Department for Education and Skills.
Hadfield, M., & Haw, K. (2004). 'Aspects of voice', *NEXUS*, 7, pp. 24–25, National College of School Leadership, Nottingham.

Chapter 27

Two Languages — Two Voices: Magda and Albana Become Authors

Raymonde Sneddon

Abstract

Children who live their daily lives in two languages may develop many ways of expressing their identities. As they explore their identity, they develop and experiment with their voice. How much opportunity they have to be heard in different cultural and linguistic contexts will depend on their social, economic, educational, and political environment and the status accorded to their languages within that.

The present chapter follows two girls from age 6 to age 10, born and educated in East London, as they talk about their developing identity as Albanian/English bilinguals at home, in their primary school, and in their complementary school and how they found their voice as writers. As the girls reflect on their experiences, they reveal how the close collaboration between their parents and their teachers in both their mainstream and their complementary school supported them in developing confident Albanian and English identities and voices.

Keywords: Bilingualism; biliteracy; creative writing; complementary school; primary school

Introduction

The present chapter follows two girls from age 6 to age 10 as they talk about their developing identity as Albanian/English bilinguals at home, in their primary and their complementary school, and how they found their voice as writers. The area of

East London into which they were born has been a site of immigration for centuries. The area has traditionally offered unskilled and semiskilled employment and cheap housing to those seeking work or fleeing persecution. Since the 1990s, political changes, war and ecological disasters, as well as the expansion of the European Union have greatly increased the ethnic and linguistic diversity of the area. Magda's and Albana's families arrived in England in the 1990s as refugees from Albania. The case study developed from a research project I initiated into young children becoming biliterate (Sneddon, 2008, 2009a). At the time of writing, the girls were in their final year of primary school. Interviewed both separately and jointly, they were invited to comment on the transcripts of observation sessions and to reflect on their journey into language and culture.

In the first section, the chapter outlines briefly the social and educational context in which the girls are discovering their personal identities. This context exposes them to the risk of becoming "subtractive bilinguals" (Cummins, 2000), losing the active use of the language of the home, as they acquire the language of education. The second section describes strategies and experiences that helped to maintain and develop their language skills and their personal voice. It highlights the crucial role played by schools and teachers in collaboration with determined parents. The third section introduces the role of the voluntary complementary school sector. The fourth section and the conclusion document the girls' development of two strong and confident voices and their emergence as independent writers. It also highlights the role research itself played in validating the process.

The text is structured to follow the girls' recollections and reflections in their own words, on how they developed their two voices from the time, aged 6, when they first took part in the research project into biliteracy, until they developed a confident writing voice and published their second dual-language book at the age of 10.

Losing a Language — Losing a Voice

Children whose families have moved to a new country and who live their daily lives in two languages (or more) develop many ways of using their languages and expressing their identities. The experience of different cultures and languages impacts on individuals in different ways (Hall, 1992) as they develop "cultures of hybridity" that change according to time, place, and environment alongside patterns of language use.

How much opportunity children have to be heard in different cultural and linguistic contexts depends on their social, economic, educational, and political environment and the status accorded to their languages within that. In societies that are officially monolingual, power differentials between the official and the minority languages impact on personal identity. Identities can be assumed, imposed by a dominant culture, challenged, and resisted or created symbolically and imaginatively (Pavlenko & Blackledge, 2004).

Although the Convention on the Rights of the Child (Office of the UN Commissioner for Human Rights, 1989) recognizes, under Articles 29 and 30, as a fundamental right of childhood, the right for children who are members of linguistic minorities to have access to appropriate cultural resources and to use their own language, the educational system in England takes little official note of linguistic and cultural diversity. The English National Curriculum (Department of Education and Employment [DEE], 2000) covers all main subjects and is compulsory in all publicly maintained schools in England. It is resolutely monolingual and monocultural and makes only passing reference to the value of bilingualism. Bilingual education is not available in mainstream schools in the United Kingdom. More recent UK government documents have suggested that community languages can be a valuable resource and that bilingualism is beneficial to both the individual and the society (CILT, 2008; Department for Education and Skills [DfES], 2002, 2003). They acknowledge the research that demonstrates that bilingual pupils benefit from schools engaging with their families and communities (Cummins, 1986, 2000; Department for Education and Skills [DfES], 2006). However, these more positive messages have made little impact on day-to-day practice in schools. Community languages are still only marginally available to study as foreign languages (CILT, 2005).

Children understand the little value afforded to the language of their home: they see the invisible sign on the classroom wall that reads "English only" (Cummins, 2008). It is rare to hear children speak a language other than English on school premises and many rapidly lose a voice as their use of the family language declines.

The following section documents a journey, initiated by a teacher, pursued by parents and studied and supported by myself as researcher, which set Magda and Albana on a course from the early stages of language loss to recovery and the full development of their two spoken and written voices.

Magda's and Albana's Journey through Biliteracy

At Primary School

Magda and Albana became close friends in their first year in school. The great majority of the children who attend their large primary school in East London are bilingual and speak many different languages between them. The school is familiar with the research on how to empower bilingual pupils (Cummins, 2000) and have a tradition of respecting and valuing children's home languages. Magda's and Albana's teacher, a bilingual herself, makes extensive use of dual-language story books in the languages spoken by the children in her classroom. She knows about the transfer of reading skills from one language to another (Cummins, op. cit.) and uses the books to teach reading in English as well as very actively supporting parents to read with and teach their children to read in the language of the home.

When I interviewed her in year 1, Magda recalled her early time at nursery and starting school "I didn't speak very well English ... people were helpful"; this help included small group work with a teaching assistant who supported the girls in learning to read English with understanding. They grew to enjoy reading in English.

Learning with Their Mothers

Four years on, in their final year at primary school, Magda and Albana talk to me in separate interviews about that first year. Magda recalls her mother's concern at her declining use of Albanian, her initial reluctance, the impact of her teacher's language practice and of the books made available to her, as well as her mother's dedication to reversing her loss of Albanian:

> my Mum really wanted me to learn the Albanian language, so Ms P. would give us books and, I didn't really want to read them but my Mum would make me and … I would read them every day, and I could say them properly and I got confident.

She goes on to explain "in the shop you can't really find kids' books in Albanian" and why the dual-language format was important to her:

> Ms P. gave us books in Albanian and English but my Mum didn't have any Albanian and English … in a book that's only Albanian, she would try to explain but I wouldn't, wouldn't, like, get it, because my Mum wasn't that good at English in those times.

My research notes from the original study showed both girls and their mothers engaged in complex negotiations of meaning across languages, supported by the two texts in the books they used. It also revealed the women using a range of strategies to support their daughters' decoding of text, as Albana recalls,

> I remember I used to know the main words but I used to have to sometimes like, go over the words again. And if I said it wrong my Mum would be, like, 'it's this'. Or if I struggled she would slowly say the word to me and she would sound it out. And I remember I felt, not nervous, but I felt like it was a bit hard and that my Mum always helped me and I got more better at it because it's, like, she helped me a lot, like with the sounds and the words.

As their reading skills developed in Albanian, these were legitimized and celebrated by the school: Magda and Albana were invited to read in assembly. Subsequently, friends overheard them speak to each other occasionally in Albanian in school.

Learning to Read with Dual-Language Books: The Research Project

Both girls remember their teacher approaching them and their mothers, half way through that first year at school, about being observed reading by a researcher. By the time I got involved, it was obvious to me that both girls were motivated and were steadily working their way through the school library's considerable stock of Albanian/English books.

After a series of six observations and a number of interviews over several months, I concluded that the intensive reading work across both languages seemed to have had a positive impact on the girls' language and cultural development: they read and understood simple stories in Albanian, they were proud and confident to talk about their skills, and they had developed a stronger voice in Albanian within the family. Albana's mother commented proudly "she knows words in Albanian I don't know!" The girls' teacher reported that, from needing some assistance with reading with understanding at the start of year 1, both Magda and Albana had moved into her top reading group by the end of the year and had developed a confident voice in English (Sneddon, 2009a).

By the end of the summer term, both families were planning independently to visit relatives in Albania during the holiday, and the girls were very excited at the prospect. Both the girls and their mothers indicated that they would like to keep in touch with me and meet after the holidays, although the project had formally come to an end. At that point, I moved into a more active role and suggested that, as the girls had made so much progress in learning to read in Albanian, they might like to experiment with writing and keep diaries, with their mothers' help, during the summer.

Recalling that summer in an interview four years later, Magda talks to me about the impact that learning more Albanian had on her relationship with her family in Albania and her personal voice:

> it helped me a lot because my family in Albania, the first time I went, that was before I started Year 1, before you came, and I didn't know Albanian a lot and I didn't know any books or anything, so my grandparents found it very hard to communicate, because they don't know English, and it was just like, I ... I ... I didn't want to come again because I thought, what can I do here? Just talk to my Mum and Dad in English and do nothing else, except going to the beach. That was fun but I couldn't communicate with anyone. So, then ... next year when I went it was just like I was a completely different person ... They were just proud of me and they were, like, now you know how to speak, it's good for you and now you're much more, you're fluent and ... I'm more confident and I think it's going to help me in my life as well.

The First Book

When the diaries came back in the autumn term, I suggested, with the support of the Ethnic Minority Achievement (EMA) teacher who specializes in supporting children who are learning English as an additional language, that they both be turned into illustrated dual-language books. Throughout the spring term, the girls worked with their mothers to produce text in both languages. Progress with drafts, design, and illustrations was discussed with both the teacher and me. Albana explains the process:

> At home I just wrote in English because I've always liked English and I've always been able to do it, so I did it in English and then I showed my Mum and then me and her together we just slowly translated it in Albanian. Bit by bit. And we checked over it, like.

While they wrote independently at home, Magda and Albana conferred and produced books in the same format, A4 landscape, with an illustration and two boxes of text, in English and in Albanian on each page. Their photograph and a brief biography featured on the back cover of each. Both books had similar titles: *Pushimet et mia verore ne shquiperi/My holiday in Albania*. Seven copies of each were produced in full color, accompanied by a CD with the girls' reading in both languages. Copies were included in the school library.

The interviews reveal how the girls' improved fluency in Albanian opened up close relationships with their extended family and connected them with Albanian life. The text in the books shows how they made friends, participated in local events, and enjoyed the freedom that children have in a rural environment. Magda writes about her grandparents and the large group of cousins who made her welcome, her participation in a wedding and family events, and ends.

> I never thought we will go to England that quick. I felt upset because in Albania I was very happy between my relatives and my cousins.

Albana writes movingly about her relationship with her grandparents and also leaves with regret.

> Day after day just when we were most enjoying our holiday, just when we got closer to our relatives and grandparents and cousins, just when we started speaking our language better, our holiday had finished.

While both girls regretted the end of their holiday in Albania, a new experience was about to enable them to build on their newly developed language skills.

Finding Two Voices

The Role of Shpresa

For children like Magda and Albana, in a potentially subtractive bilingual situation, complementary schools offer one of the few opportunities to learn the language of their community. Also known as Mother Tongue Schools and Saturday Schools, they are voluntary classes run by communities themselves and have existed in England for many years (Department of Education and Science [DES], 1985;

Linguistic Minorities Project [LMP], 1985). Recent research into the schools has revealed the important role they play in the development of multiple and dynamic personal and learner identities (Creese, Bhatt, Bhojani, & Martin, 2006). As they explore these multidimensional identities, children develop and experiment with their voice and the impact it may have on their environment and their future.

No one meeting Magda and Albana in their second year would guess they were bilingual: their appearance, their speech, and even their first names identify them as articulate and confident English girls. However, the researcher noted with interest that, in the final stages of the original research project, when the girls and their mothers were invited to discuss the findings, both Magda and Albana chose traditional Albanian names as their pseudonyms for publication.

At this point, a new opportunity to develop their Albanian voice became available. Magda explains how the EMA teacher at the school, who had helped with the first book, started an Albanian lunchtime club attended by Albanian children and their friends:

> She got an Albanian teacher. She's in Shpresa Programme. She came to teach us Albanian. And there was a dancing teacher. We would play lots of Albanian games and we would do dancing and I would always see Albanian dancing, and I think it was like, very cool, and, when I tried it out myself, I really enjoyed it.

So cool and popular was the dancing in school that the lunch club group were invited to perform in full traditional Albanian costumes, provided by Shpresa, at refugee week events and at a conference of EMA teachers.

The Shpresa teachers who came to the lunchtime club invited Magda and Albana to visit. The Shpresa ("hope" in Albanian) Programme organization, based in East London, was founded in 2003 by a refugee from Albania to support fellow refugees in all key areas of their lives in England. Their complementary school programme offers a wide range of activities for 350 young people in North and East London (Sneddon, 2009b). Magda joined first:

> F. told my Mum and so my Mum went and, the first day I went I enjoyed myself. There was lots of children that were, like, my culture, and from my country and I felt quite well because I never, I would never in school, there's barely any Albanians, but there it was just full and you have more friends and you only speak Albanian. So now I'm still here and it helped me a lot and it's very fun as well.

Some weeks later, Albana joined her friend:

> After a few weeks, she was probably there 4 or 5 weeks ... she and her Mum told my Mum that it was really good, it really helped and I should come to. Then I came along and ... I think it was a bit easier for me to make friends than Magda, because she introduced me to everyone.

Performance

As well as teaching the Albanian language, Shpresa develops young people's skills for public performance. These include dancing, both traditional and contemporary, drama, and poetry. Performance became important to both girls, but especially to Magda. She describes her initial reactions,

> I wasn't confident at all. I used to, like, first time I was scared and I thought look, I'm never going to do this again. But now I am very confident, although I'm still scared. So if I ever go on stage, it will help me.

About a year after she joined Shpresa classes, I sat in the audience of a theatre packed with 350 people and witnessed Magda, then aged 8, alone on stage with a microphone, reciting Albanian poetry in a powerful voice that moved the audience to tears.

Albana was a less ambitious performer but was quite confident about her skills:

> when the shows came along, I actually didn't feel very bad, I felt quite confident. I just went up there and did what I thought I could do and ... it all came out good.

Participation, Civic Engagement, and Public Voice

Magda and Albana gained confidence in expressing their views in the Shpresa environment. I observed them at the annual children's forum, an event attended by around 250 children and young people, which offers a showcase for the special activities and campaigns they have been involved in in the course of the year. Children evaluate the year's activities, draw up plans for the coming year, and elect representatives to the forum. Both Magda and Albana took an active part in the event, representing their group in a feedback session. In the course of this, Magda expressed strong views about the fairness of the selection of representatives to take a petition to Downing Street and argued confidently with the director of Shpresa on this issue.

Albana describes how they learned to make their voices heard in Albanian:

> we would all get into a circle and we would, like, she (the director) would bring up a subject and we would say opinions about it. In the first few weeks I felt a bit, like, shy, ashamed because there was so many people older than me. But after, I didn't really mind what they thought and I just said my opinion ... we were actually talking in Albanian and once I got used to it, even if I made mistakes, I didn't feel really bad. Because I knew I wasn't the only one. I felt more confident and I don't feel bad any more.

She recalls regular discussions on issues like,

> poverty and injustice and these things are in the world, these things
> usually happen

and a campaign to end child detention,

> it was about when people come from other countries, and they need to
> be sent back, families get put in ... a bit like a prison, something like
> that. And we all campaigned about that ... And 3 or 4 people from
> Shpresa, the big people, they went to London and gave it to the
> Government, to look at it ... The Government said they would try and
> do something, but we haven't been told anything else.

Albana goes on to explain her new role as a mentor,

> they call it a mentoring course. They chose a group of people and then
> instead of going to class, Albanian class, they do mentoring. They go in
> the classroom and they talk about how to help people with their
> problems and different problems, how to sort them out. How not to
> get too involved. I finished my training last year. I have a mentee, so
> I'm a mentor of someone else. A younger person. ... If anything ...
> like, she can't do something or she doesn't know something that's
> going on, she asks me. And I ... I just help her with things like that.
> I sometimes help her improve, like dancing and acting, because she's in
> drama with me. Yeah. Like that.

It was Magda's passion for performance that initially led her to assert herself,

> I wasn't really picked for like, lots of performance but then ... I was very
> truthful and I told them it's unfair ... I thought maybe they are going to
> pick me, but then, I was just like, what can I do? I'm just left out. But
> I thought I'm going to tell them what I really want and if it's possible. So
> then I told them, like, and they're OK, OK, OK, we're going to pick
> different children this time. But ... um ... it's actually good, because how
> do they know if you really want to be in a performance? So you do have to
> stand up and tell them ... So then, at home, I started learning poems ...

Becoming Authors, Developing a Writing Voice

Response to the First Book

At the time of writing, Magda and Albana were articulate and literate, handling the
language of books as well as that of everyday communication. They are self-assured

and their current teachers expect a strong performance from them in their forthcoming end-of-primary school tests. As a result of the active support of the school, their mothers' commitment, and their experiences at complementary school, they are developing as confident speakers and writers of Albanian. Although English is still clearly their dominant language, the girls are closer to being balanced bilinguals and having two strong voices than is common in their situation in England.

The previous sections have tracked the girls' perceptions and feelings about reclaiming and developing their Albanian voice. The initial response to their writing made them feel very special. Albana explains that she was originally nervous when the book about her Albanian holiday was published in school:

> At first I felt a little bit nervous thinking that it, that the book wouldn't come out right or it wouldn't be very good.

But the reaction from school friends indicated that Albana's writing skills as well as her culture and language were acknowledged in a very positive way.

> Then I found out that lots of people liked it and I felt special. My teacher told the whole class and it was mentioned in assembly. And I felt really special because loads of people in my class and in my year group would come up and say, oh, look, I got your book and it's really good.

Magda feels that the first book was a milestone,

> I felt quite, like, grown up and like, I was thinking, look, I have a book and everything! And when my class knew and everything, they were all 'oh! How did you make a book?' And I felt quite good.

and began to think of herself as an author.

> I never imagined that I would actually make a book, and, reading all those English and Albanian books, and now when I think, when I read an English book, I'm always, like, 'I've made a book as well'.

Both girls had very positive reactions from their families and felt they had made their parents proud, as Albana reports,

> My family in Albania ... my Mum told them and they seemed pretty amazed because they didn't think I'd actually publish a book in Albanian. They knew I was good at speaking, but they would never imagine ... And my actual family, they thought it was really good. My Mum was so proud and my Dad was too. And my brother got a little bit jealous.

As the girls became confident and revealed their pleasure in performance and in poetry, yet another opportunity became available to build on their love of stories.

Becoming Independent Writers, Collaborative Writing, and Collaborative Voices

Following on the success of their first personal books, Magda and Albana were invited by the school to write a book together on a topic of their choice. I observed several sessions in which the girls initially composed the English text together and then worked to translate it into Albanian. Those sessions were recorded and transcribed. A few months later, I invited Magda and Albana to comment together on the transcripts and on the process of writing together.

The girls' close friendship and collaboration is apparent in the transcript of this joint interview. As they describe how they first thought of topics in their own home and then met in school to discuss ideas and start drafting, they finish each other's sentences, make the same comment, and build on each other's suggestions. Their story of a computer geek who gets lost in a terrifying adventure inside his laptop is action-packed and full of twists and turns.

Magda describes the process,

> I would think of an idea and Albana would think of one and Albana would be like, I've got a good idea! And I would be like ... we wouldn't fight but we would see which one was the best one and ...

Albana adds,

> Some of the ideas ... I sort of mixed them a little bit with some of my ideas, but I added, like, a little twist.

As experienced writers in English, they wrote the first version of the story in that language and edited their own text before publication. However, writing in Albanian without parental assistance presented a challenge. They explained that the very close relationship between sound and spelling greatly facilitated this, but that they still made a lot of mistakes that their parents corrected. Translation presented considerable challenges that they addressed together. When I asked "So, why were you arguing about that word (*serjoze*)?" I was firmly corrected by Albana,

> We weren't arguing, we were discussing which one was right.

Magda and Albana enjoyed the challenge of working independently on their story, outlining, planning, arranging sequences, layout, and illustrations. Magda explains the feeling of ownership, "This time, because we published it ourselves ... I'm just like, proud of myself."

And Albana adds,

> I feel really proud of that book, actually. I like both of the books. Because the first one is like, about me, real life. That one is, like, special because it's about fiction and imagination and we made it up in English and Albanian.

Conclusion

As economic migration, humanitarian crises and globalization increase the mobility of populations around the world, societies become super-diverse, and many children, like Magda and Albana, find themselves, as speakers of minority languages, having to find a voice in a new society that does not greatly value their heritage and may question their allegiance. But the phenomenon of super-diversity, developing since the 1990s, is also characterized by the Internet, cheap international communications, and travel. Families that have crossed borders can keep in touch much more readily, both virtually and physically, with the languages and cultures of origin than previous generations of migrants (Vertovec, 2007). Magda and Albana have been able to travel to Albania several times. They use the Internet and the telephone to keep in touch with their extended families.

While much capital has occasionally been made in the British press about the need for communities of immigrant origin to assimilate and adopt a "British identity" (Blunkett, 2002; Martin, Bhatt, Bhojani, & Creese, 2007), evidence suggests that those who maintain close ties with their country of origin are also most likely to integrate successfully into British mainstream society (Vertovec, op. cit.).

At age 6, as they became increasingly fluent in English and integrated successfully into the life of the school, Magda's and Albana's recollections reveal how they began to lose the active use of Albanian and felt divorced from their extended family and unable to engage with life in Albania. The proactive approach of their school and their teachers to language development, the commitment of their mothers, and the complementary school's commitment to empowering their students provided an environment in which they could confidently find their voice as British Albanians.

> I feel happy now, because everyone in my school knows that I'm Albanian and all my teachers, especially Ms P. and also Ms J., they used to help, they used to always be proud and used to tell all the other teachers how good we were in Albanian and English. I always feel proud to think that I have been good in my language and I've made a book. [Albana]

Although I played a role in introducing book-making as a means of learning to write, it was the girls' enthusiasm for the task and their strong bond of friendship that enabled them, not only to develop two strong voices but also to bring them together in a creative endeavor.

Magda acknowledges this and thinks of the impact it may have on her future:

> Well I was going to say thank you very much because you've, like, helped us publish actually two books and I actually think that I would be in this club but not have published two books and like, yeah ... It might help me in my life if I become an author. Well I think I'm confident about my future seeing as I'm really confident and been in

loads of shows and made two books and I think when I grow up and I can be able to be even more things.

And Albana concludes,

I think my future will carry on good.

References

Blunkett, D. (2002). Integration with diversity: Globalisation and the renewal of democracy and civil society. In: P. Griffith & M. Leonard (Eds), *Reclaiming Britishness*. London: The Foreign Policy Centre.

CILT (National Centre for Languages). (2005). *Language trends 2005: Community language learning in England, Wales and Scotland*. London: CILT.

CILT (National Centre for Languages). (2008). Our languages. Retrieved from www.ourlanguages.org. Accessed January 2011.

Creese, A., Bhatt, A., Bhojani, N., & Martin, P. (2006). Multicultural, heritage and learner identities in complementary schools. *Language and Education*, *20*(1), 23–43.

Cummins, J. (1986). Empowering minority students: A framework for intervention. *Harvard Educational Review*, *56*(1), 18–36.

Cummins, J. (2000). *Language, power and pedagogy: Bilingual children in the crossfire*. Clevedon: Multilingual Matters.

Cummins, J. (2008). Evidence-based literacy strategies: Bilingualism as a resource within the classroom. *Bilingualism, learning and achievement*. Conference at London Metropolitan University, 3 March, 2007.

Department of Education and Employment. (2000). *The National Curriculum KS1 and KS2 Handbook for primary teachers in England*. London: DfEE/QCA.

Department of Education and Science. (1985). *Education for all (The Swann Report)*. London: HMSO.

Department for Education and Skills. (2002). *Languages for all, languages for life*. Annesley, Notts: DfES.

Department for Education and Skills. (2003). *Aiming high. Raising attainment for minority ethnic pupils*. Annesley, Notts: DfES.

Department for Education and Skills. (2006). *Learning and teaching for bilingual children in the primary years*. Annesley, Notts: DfES.

Hall, S. (1992). New ethnicities. In: A. Rattansi & J. Donald (Eds), *Culture and difference*. London: Sage.

Linguistic Minorities Project. (1985). *The other languages of England: The linguistic minorities report*. London: Routledge and Kegan Paul.

Martin, P., Bhatt, A., Bhojani, N., & Creese, A. (2007). Multilingual learning stories in two Gujarati complementary schools in Leicester. In: J. Conteh, P. Martin & L. H. Robertson (Eds), *Multilingual learning stories from schools and communities in Britain*. Stoke-on-Trent: Trentham Books.

Office of the United Nations Commissioner for Human Rights. (1989). Convention on the rights of the child. Retrieved from http://www2.ohchr.org/english/law/crc.htm. Accessed January 2011.

Pavlenko, A., & Blackledge, A. (2004). New theoretical approaches to the study of negotiation of identities in multilingual contexts. In: A. Pavlenko & A. Blackledge (Eds), *Negotiation of identities in multilingual contexts*. Clevedon: Multilingual Matters.

Sneddon, R. (2008). Magda and Albana: Learning to read using dual language books. *Language and Education*, *22*(2), 137–154.

Sneddon, R. (2009a). *Bilingual books — Biliterate children*. Stoke-on-Trent: Trentham Books.

Sneddon, R. (2009b). Hope, literacy and dancing. Paper presented at the British Educational Research Association conference. University of Manchester, 2/5 September 2009. Retrieved from http://www.uel.ac.uk/education/staff/documents/HOPELITERACYANDDANCING140809.doc. Accessed January 2011.

Vertovec, S. (2007). *New complexities of cohesion in Britain: Super-diversity, transnationalism and civil-integration*. Commission on Integration and Cohesion. Wetherby: Communities and Local Government Publications.

PART FIVE
STUDENT VOICES AROUND THE WORLD

Editors' Summary to Part Five

In this final part of the book international and global perspectives on Student Voice are presented by authors writing about initiatives taking place in the United States, Kenya, Tanzania, South Africa, Australia, Sweden, China and Brazil. In Chapter 28, Dana L. Mitra, William C. Frick and Emily R. Crawford, writing about the American context, explore how Student Voice efforts fit with — and perhaps enhance — intentions to act in the 'best interest of the student'. Their chapter examines the ways in which student voice activities intersect with the multiple ethics that scaffold the 'Ethic of Profession' — the ethics of justice, care and critique. Colleen McLaughlin and Susan Kiragu (Chapter 29) explore notions of student consultation and involvement in curricula for HIV-related education. Their chapter draws on a research project in Kenya, Tanzania and South Africa in 2009–2010 where primary school students in three schools in each country were consulted. In Chapter 30, Derek Bland, examines the ways in which participants in an Australian 'students-as-researchers' (SaR) project were able to raise knowledge of and address, to some extent, long-standing issues of racism in their schools. Ulrika Bergmark and Catrine Kostenius (Chapter 31) focus on Student Voice within the context of educational research in Sweden. The authors explore the issues researchers need to consider when researching the idea of student voice from a Swedish perspective, arguing for a *tact of researching* when adhering to student voice research: the development of ethical research practice which affirms participants. In Chapter 32, Wei Kan reports on a qualitative study, conducted in 2008, which explored 15 pupils who were mostly aged between 15 and 16 and their views of the pedagogy change in Beijing. His study enlisted the students as 'co-researchers', who were both the subjects of the enquiry and partners in its processes. The students' voices indicated that, in the context of Chinese schools, there is a powerful pedagogical culture that is so ingrained that it is resistant to change. Latin America has been the site of a number of experiments in participatory democracy in recent years, involving social movements, progressive local governments and community organisations. In Chapter 33, the final contribution to this section of the book, Tristan McCowan explores one of these experiences, the Landless Movement of Brazil, which works for agrarian reform and has established a large number of rural communities based on principles of co-operativism and egalitarianism. McCowan's chapter provides a significant illustration of radical transformations that can be achieved within formal education.

Chapter 28

The Ethical Dimensions of Student Voice Activities in the United States

Dana L. Mitra, William C. Frick and Emily R. Crawford

Abstract

The 'Ethic of the Profession' recognizes moral aspects unique to educational leadership and is based on a concept that all decisions should be based on serving the best interests of the student. Student voice research suggests that part of this ethical process would, at best, include students themselves in decision-making processes and, at least, access the meanings students have about going to school. This chapter explores how do student voice efforts fit with — and perhaps enhance — intentions to act in the 'best interest of the student'. It examines the ways in which student voice activities intersect with the multiple ethics that scaffold the Ethic of Profession — the ethics of justice, care, and critique. We present a brief consideration of each of the theoretical standpoints and explain ways in which student voice efforts can enhance moral purposes of schooling.

Keywords: Student voice; ethics; best interest; leadership

Introduction

'Student voice' in the United States has examined the many ways in which young people can and sometimes do, have opportunities to share in the school decisions that will shape their lives and the lives of their peers (Fielding, 2001; Mitra, 2008b). The notion of working to increase student voice is not new to education. Research has described similar processes in schools as democratic participation, pupil participation, active citizenship, youth leadership, and youth empowerment. While research has often

The Student Voice Handbook: Bridging the Academic/Practitioner Divide
Copyright © 2011 by Emerald Group Publishing Limited
All rights of reproduction in any form reserved
ISBN: 978-1-78052-040-7

focused on student rights and activism, recent initiatives focus more on the connection between student voice combined with the notion of democratic practice as well as efforts to actively engage young people in their classrooms, schools and communities.

Student voice and participation efforts can also serve as a catalyst for school reform efforts. These reforms include improvements in instruction and curriculum (Rudduck and McIntyre, 2007), teacher–student relationships (Mitra, 2008a; Rudduck, 2007), teacher preparation (Cook-Sather, 2002), assessment systems (Colatos & Morrell, 2003; Fielding, 2001), and visioning and strategic planning (Eccles & Gootman, 2002; Holdsworth & Thomson, 2002; Lee & Zimmerman, 1999; Zeldin, 2004). Additionally, involving young people can improve the quality of implementation of reform efforts. Students can serve as important sources of information that are otherwise unavailable as schools seek to implement educational changes (Kushman, 1997; Rudduck, Day, & Wallace, 1997). Since effective implementation of reform benefits from participation by and acceptance from those most affected, efforts to actively involve students can lead to better student understanding of the educational changes in their schools (Mitra, 2004).

Despite the promising ways in which student voice can influence students, classrooms, schools, and broader change, such efforts occur only in small pockets rather than an integrated activity of basic education. In result, the deeper integration of student voice efforts into daily educational practice can enhance the influence and scale of change resulting from these initiatives. In particular, one area of long-term concern within and outside the field of education is students' knowledge of and participation in civic engagement opportunities, which are critical to sustaining the foundation of any democratic nation. Since the U.S. democracy is built on the assumption of participation, participation should be the standard upon which a democracy is measured (Hart, 1992). Yet the tone set by U.S. educational policy limits opportunities for young people to participate in the public sphere. Although over 100 nations have ratified the Convention on the Rights of the Child (CRC), the United States has yet to sign (United Nations, 1989). Additionally, mandatory testing of all students in the No Child Left Behind Act (a reauthorization of the Elementary and Secondary Education Act of 1965) has caused a narrowing of the curriculum that has led to a reduction in civic engagement opportunities (Rose, 2009). Therefore, careful thought is needed as to how such hurdles can be overcome. We posit that the root for such thought lies in the ethics used to guide educational practice. We believe three key principles — ethics of justice, care and critique — all of which structure an overarching Ethic of the Profession, provide one practical way to think through these issues. In this chapter, we discuss how this ethical framework provides a solid basis from which educational leaders can integrate student voice efforts with students' best interests and the moral purposes of schooling.

Ethical Approaches to U.S. Education

In part due to the need to reconceptualize democratic practice and to improve civic engagement opportunities for young people, U.S. educational circles are increasingly concentrating on the development, articulation and empirical basis for an emerging 'Ethic of the Profession'(Shapiro & Stefkovich, 2011; Stefkovich, 2006). An Ethic of the Profession has evolved for over a decade in the thinking of scholars, researchers, and higher education teaching faculty focusing on educational leadership and ethics. This ethic posits that as educational leaders become cognizant of discrepancies between professional codes and their personal codes of ethics, they are enabled to approach ethical dilemmas with increase in conscientiousness of the reasoning behind their decisions. Furthermore, this professional ethical framework recognizes moral aspects unique to educational leadership and grounds the moral dimension of the profession on the nomothetic injunction, 'serve the best interests of the student' (Shapiro & Stefkovich, 2011) thereby 'promoting the success of all students' (ISLLC, 2008) by focusing on the needs of children (Walker, 1998).

As an eclectic framework incorporating established ethical viewpoints within the field of educational leadership specifically, professional ethics are commonly viewed 'as an extension of [other] paradigms [typically justice-oriented perspectives] and not thought to stand alone' (Shapiro & Stefkovich, 2011, p. 7). The Ethic of the Profession highlights the moral dissonance, or a 'clashing of codes' that can occur when educators seek to integrate *professional codes* meant to inform decision making and conduct, the *personal moral values* of administrators and *professional and/or community standards* and expectations for professional practice.

The Ethic of the Profession is grounded in a reasoned consideration of the educational 'shibboleth' (Walker, 1995, pp. 3–4) of 'the best interests of the [student]' — a concept that influences the daily decisions of school administrators and teachers. It is structured by the three Rs — a robust adherence to the essential nature of a child's individual *rights*, the child's duty of mutual *responsibility* to others for a common interest and the school leader's role in encouraging that responsibility and mutual *respect* as reciprocal acknowledgement of the other as having worth, value and dignity unto him/herself (Stefkovich, 2006; Stefkovich & O'Brien, 2004).

The framework recognizes that adults possess a great deal of power in determining students' best interests and that it is 'incumbent upon school leaders to make ethical decisions that truly reflect the needs of students and not their own self-interest' (Stefkovich, 2006, p. 21). The framework is a 'free standing' ethical orientation on its own terms, which emphasizes the contemporary characteristics of a pluralistic approach to ethical reasoning and moral action (Hinman, 2008). It seeks to assist educational leaders with understanding that self-reflection, open-mindedness, and sensitivity are important aspects of moral choice when 'ethically-sound decisions profoundly influence others' lives' (p. 21). Student voice research suggests that part of this ethical process would, at best, include students themselves in decision making processes and, at least, access the meanings students have about going to school. The practice of including students in a wide range of decisions that directly affect their lived experience could be a check against the adult-driven and interpreted reality of young people who often have different views and proposed solutions to what might really be in their best interests.

Integrating Student Voice Efforts with the 'Best Interests of the Student'

How do student voice efforts fit with and perhaps enhance intentions to decide and act for the 'best interest of the student'? The remainder of this chapter explores this question by examining the ways in which student voice activities intersect with the multiple ethics that scaffold the Ethic of Profession — the ethics of justice, care and critique (Starratt, 1994). We present a brief consideration of each of the three theoretical standpoints identified above and explain ways in which student voice efforts can enhance moral purposes of schooling. For each section, we provide an illustrative example of a student voice effort that fits within this ethical frame. The examples are drawn from a study that examined the conditions that enabled and constrained the development of student voice initiatives in Northern California. The 13 secondary schools in this study were situated within an urban environment. They all consisted of an ethnically diverse population comprised of students of Asian, Latin, African and European descent; a public school system that lacked sufficient resources to prepare its children; and high concentrations of poverty. All but three of the schools were very large — 2000 students or more; of the remaining three schools, one was a charter school and the remaining two were 'last chance' schools offering students an opportunity to finish their degrees when they had been expelled or otherwise removed from traditional district schools. All names of the schools and projects have been changed to preserve the anonymity of the cases, as have the names of individuals.[1]

Justice

A justice perspective focuses on ethical concepts that constitute the foundational principles of liberal democracies. Fundamental human rights and the protection of those rights by means of justice are central concepts of postindustrial, liberally democratic, constitutional nation states such as the United States (Rawls, 1971; Strike, Haller, & Soltis, 1998). Taken as a whole, they can be described as a 'civic ethic', in which all persons irrespective of culture, race or other defining categories possess the capacity for a sense of fairness and the ability to conceptualize their own good. Principles such as individual rights, due process, freedom, equality and responsibility for the common good are central to this orientation.

Student voice efforts provide ways to discuss issues of justice and to show young people ways they can seek to address wrongs they see and experience. Indeed, when examining student voice research in the United States, the most compelling examples are often instances of young people challenging injustice in their schools and communities. Previous research shows that being authentic to group members within student voice efforts and youth–adult partnerships is an essential part of youth

---

1. For more information on data collection, analysis processes and findings from this study, see Mitra (2006, 2008b, 2009a, 2009b, 2009c).

culture — also known as being 'real' (Mitra, 2008b; Denner, Meyer, & Bean, 2005; Perkins & Borden, 2003). For example, youth members of Sierra High School in Northern California believed that students would remain committed to their video project documenting racial injustice in their community because, according to one student, 'It reaches us teens. It reaches issues that we're going through'. Such instances tend to closely align with student visions of right and wrong, including drawing attention to inequities.

The reasons for schools to choose student voice initiatives in the Northern California study highlighted a common focus on justice-oriented goals of inequity and injustices experienced in their lives, schools, communities and broader society. For example, College Center High School focused its efforts on creating a Student Unity Council. The youth leader explained (Mitra, 2006a):

> [The school had] a huge problem for the last 30-plus years of African Americans and Latinos getting two or more F's. Last year, two-thirds of the freshman class got two or more F's, meaning they really wouldn't go on to being juniors, or sophomore.

Through dialogue and a common meeting place, the intention was to increase the voice of students to try to help to address the achievement gap problem in the school, to reduce racial tensions through a source of dialogue and to provide a focus point for community celebrations.

Care

Interpersonal in nature, a moral perspective that focuses on care emphasizes the demands of relationship from a position of unconditional positive regard, or described elsewhere as a deep awareness of 'the other' as persons in community with ourselves as subjects (Gilkey, 1993). This position asserts that human beings have the capacity to feel deep respect or love for other people, especially people different from ourselves. Attitudes toward others 'are determined in part by an understanding of who and what they are: in this case, that they are human beings, persons, and that as persons they possess an inner integrity, a self-determination, a capacity for free and spiritual activity that we also sense in ourselves' (Gilkey, 1993, p. 79). This level of empathy and self-understanding applied to the other can become the foundation for treating persons as ends and not as means and can, in large part, provide the inner basis of an outward social order through 'motivational displacement toward the projects of the cared-for' (Noddings, 1984, p. 176; Beck, 1994).

For student voice efforts, the type of relationships among the group members proves to be as important, if not more important, than the content of the work itself. The successful youth–adult partnerships in the Northern California study revealed how mutual respect and responsibility are two values contributing to the formation of successful partnerships. Young people identified mutual respect and responsibility as the key differences in the relationships within their youth–adult partnerships as compared to most of their other interactions with adults. In nearly every interview, young people spoke of needing 'respect' in connection with establishing a greater connection with adults and other young people in the group. They connected this concept of creating respect with establishing trust, caring for one another, creating safe spaces, and getting to know adults and young people in ways fundamentally different than traditional teacher and student roles.

Research consistently indicates the importance of *establishing respect and trust among group members* (Mitra, 2009b; Zeldin, Camino, & Mook, 2005). Often in student voice initiatives, groups are so anxious to make change that little time is devoted to build the capacity of members to work together as partners, including taking on responsibilities and forming the group's identity. In such cases, adults and young people may successfully complete a specific project, but without a broader vision and collective purpose, the group disbands and even the accomplished activities often disappear as well (Mitra, 2009c).

The most successful adult advisors possessed not only compassion but also a solid understanding of youth development theory and cultural trends affecting young people. Strong adult advisors intentionally cultivated a sense of respect and caring with young people, because they understood the developmental need for young people to build close connections with adults and with peers (Mitra, 2004). Sierra High School was a 'last chance' high school of 200 students who were expelled or otherwise unable to succeed in the district's traditional schools. The school had been partnering for over 20 years with a non-profit, Imagine Change, and its founder, Irene Montague — a dedicated, licensed family therapist. Montague created a successful program that started out as traditional social work support and evolved to include youth activism and leadership projects. Their current project, according to the words of one youth, sought 'to let everybody know that there's other ways to deal with situations than with violence. Speech is powerful too' (Mitra, 2009b). The group worked toward this goal by creating a documentary called 'Take a Look Around' that explored three critical issues in their community — the abundance of drugs and alcohol, the high rates of domestic violence and the lack of grocery and retail stores.

Because Sierra was a 'last chance' school and the student population comes in large part from very disadvantaged backgrounds, the students at the school tended to have little faith in school-sanctioned activities with few opportunities in their lives for trusting others. Developing a youth–adult partnership in such an environment proved challenging but invaluable (Mitra, 2008a). Montague explained:

> I want them to do a youth-led program. And they're doing it. But teaching them leadership [is tough] when their skills are so bad. Some days I'm just ready to pull my hair out! They need a safe place that they know that they're…respected. They need…the skills modeled to them. What we, the adults, are trying to do is to show them all how to funnel their best skills into the work of their project.

The students at Sierra also expressed great appreciation for the ability of Montague to give them respect and to trust their ability to work as partners on the project. Montague's extended experience working with young people also served to bring out the best in even the most challenging of individuals, including a young woman, Hallie, who had great difficulty working with others. Hallie explained:

> She tries to have me [lead activities so [that] I can have the skills to do it. But if I find I'm struggling she'll help me out. Like if I'm starting to get a little angry ... she'll redirect it so that I don't say it wrong and offend people. (Mitra, 2009b)

Critique[2]

The critique perspective serves as a moral posture and examination of larger social and institutional dimensions of human life. The focus of critical concern highlights competing interests, power, the structure of bureaucracy, the influence of language, and redress for institutionalized injustice as they relate to the legitimacy of social arrangements. The disproportionate benefit of some groups over others as a result of political, economic and judicial hegemony are moral concerns that transcend the naïve perspective that societal structures and properties are simply 'the way things are'. Reasoning and acting ethically also entails the inherent paradoxes of school leadership that must support institutional position on the one hand and stand up for broader values of freedom and social justice on the other (see Apple, 1982; Giroux, 1992).

A perspective of critique is especially important to teach to youth who faced oppression due to the structure and power of U.S. institutions. Youth of colour growing up in under-resourced urban neighbourhoods, including those who are not attending college or who were born outside of the United States, especially face significant barriers to civic integration and political power. They tend to experience fewer civic learning opportunities in their schools (Kahne & Middaugh, 2008) and fewer civic institutions in their neighbourhoods (Hart & Atkins, 2002), and therefore fewer student voice opportunities overall.

Often called *youth activism*, we define this type of student voice as civic engagement in which young people identify common interests, mobilize their peers and work collectively to alter power relations in ways that lead to meaningful institutional change (Oakes & Rogers, 2006). These types of initiatives question inequities in the broader system of schooling and often participate in broader community organizing efforts beyond the school setting (Colatos & Morrell, 2003; Fine, Burns, & Payne, 2004). Westheimer & Kahne (2004) and describe this type of citizenship as a 'justice oriented approach'. Instead of only preparing meals at a soup kitchen for example, a justice-oriented perspective would examine the causes of hunger, draw attention to the injustices that create the inequities and seek to effect larger scale changes that could help to lessen these inequities.

---

2. This section draws heavily on Mitra and Kirshner (forthcoming).

Activist student voice initiatives often maintain a separation from school administration and work outside of school auspices. This independence helps student voice initiatives heighten awareness of problems in the school system. Activist strategies are sometimes confrontational and have flourished in regions of the country with a strong tradition of social protest, including major cities such as New York, Chicago, Los Angeles, San Francisco and Oakland. The language in such organizations focuses on 'acting on' organizations, including schools, to raise awareness of injustice (Mitra & Kirshner, forthcoming). Youth organizing groups based outside of schools have sometimes shown their ability to hold political decision-makers accountable to constituents and thereby promote equitable reforms (Oakes & Rogers, 2006; Warren, Mira, & Nikundiwe, 2008).

Two of the schools in the Northern California study, Midland's Campaigns for Justice and Hillside's Unity of Youth approached their focus on social injustice through a traditional form of organizing, sharing information and, at times, protest. A student leader at Unity of Youth explained, 'We've joined the campaign to help stop the high school exit exam. We're [also] trying to help some teachers who are getting transferred out of [our school]. And we are trying to get them [the district and state] to stop the budget cuts' (Mitra, 2006). Such actions included marches to the state capitol building in Sacramento and local protests at district offices. These initiatives were usually coordinated with groups from other schools. Community-based organizations often took the lead in facilitating communication and planning for such events. Campaigns for Justice also took the importance of student voice and empowerment literally through creating a series of campaigns aimed at education youth about their rights as citizens, lobbying for a student position on the district's school board, and fighting a community effort to impose a daytime curfew on youth between the times of 8:30 a.m. and 1:30 p.m.

Applying the Ethic of the Profession to Student Voice Initiatives

In the examples of successful student voice initiatives provided earlier, we see how the multi-paradigmatic basis for ethical decision making in education, comprised of the ethics of *justice*, *care* and *critique*, serve to scaffold an Ethic of the Profession (Shapiro & Stefkovich, 2011; Stefkovich, 2006). The ethic of justice corresponds best to the first of the three Rs: the notion that students have individual rights within the context of their educational experiences. Specifically, educators should be mindful of those rights and students' own sense of fairness when they make decisions that affecting students.

Student voice research has demonstrated that students' enactment of their rights can have positive outcomes in terms of increasing students' sense of agency, orientation toward social justice issues addressing inequity and intolerance, as well as closer collaboration with peers and teachers to find peaceful resolution to conflict among others. Despite the promising outcomes of student voice initiatives, more could be done to seize the advantages these efforts have proved they can offer. As previously stated, student voice initiatives remain limited in scope and are also isolated in small pockets instead of being well integrated into educational practice. Yet, with increased latitude to express their rights, youth become more invested to bring positive change to their communities and believe their efforts have power to make an impact. Additionally, the more invested youth become in issues of justice, the more sophisticated their understanding of those issues becomes. Students' interests expand to include issues affecting broader society. Student conversations about issues of inequity and imbalance in power structures simultaneously gain greater authenticity the more they engage in those types of conversations.

Care, another component of the three paradigms forming the ethic of the profession, is closely connected to the concept of respect and trust. Closer interpersonal connections prove beneficial as students and adults work toward common goals. Successful student voice initiatives that emphasize the reciprocal nature of relationships have resulted in youths and adults getting to know each other in ways fundamentally different than in traditional teacher and student roles. Students also often acquire an increased sense of shared ownership in their projects.

The ethic of critique takes a moral stance by questioning the larger social and institutional aspects of human life and experience, identifying what is problematic about them, and taking responsibility at some level. Student voice opportunities demonstrate the ethic of critique by questioning current power structures and using public tactics such as protests and boycott to draw public attention to inequity. Student voice initiatives acting within the realm of critique remind power structures of their responsibilities to others by holding them accountable for their actions and to the common interest. Fitting with 'the personal is political' paradigm, youth activists also understand how power and privilege operate in their own lives and discover the agency that they possess to address power imbalances in their own sphere of influence.

Conclusion

Exploring how research might better integrate knowledge of educational ethics with student voice efforts has potentially powerful implications for strengthening the analytical abilities of educational practitioners and students alike. Such opportunities can result in subsequent improvements to classroom practice in particular and schooling in general. Strengthening the ties between research on student voice and the application of educational ethics could provide educators with a deeper, richer knowledge of students' school experiences as well as their life experiences outside of school. More research is needed to explore exactly how educators make ethical decisions and respond to the outcomes of those decisions. However, this chapter has shown how giving voice to students and attending seriously to their voices within the school context has the power to improve the lives of all students in a school — but oftentimes the lives of society members as well.

The conjoining of student voice activity and research with various ethical perspectives common to the field of education is synergistic. This chapter highlighted ways in which student voice research aligns with ethical paradigms. The findings in this chapter are echoed in emerging research on ethical frameworks for educational leaders. For example, when attempting to articulate what is in a student's or students' 'best interests', school leaders resonate with these very notions of connectedness and respect noted as important in the that student voice research (Frick, in press). This research indicates that responsive relationships are central to the notion of what 'best interests' might mean for school leaders. Such a relationships are grounded in respect — a fundamental conviction about one's view and treatment of students as persons.

   In this chapter we have attempted to describe the symbiotic ways in which student voice initiatives can enhance civic efficacy and the moral purposes of schooling if program goals align with concepts from ethical vantage points common to the field of education. In doing so, we hope to have articulated a fuller appreciation of both and contributed to the 'images of possibility' (Rose, 2009, p. 152) that public schools can become. Indeed, a new language of public schooling is desperately needed. We hope that we have added to an important and desperately needed change in discourse.

References

Apple, M. (1982). *Education and power*. Boston, MA: Routledge & Kegan Paul.

Beck, L. G. (1994). *Reclaiming educational administration as a caring profession*. New York, NY: Teachers College Press.

Colatos, A. M., & Morrell, E. (2003). Apprenticing urban youth as critical researchers: Implications for increasing equity and access in diverse urban schools. In: B. Rubin & E. Silva (Eds), *Critical voices in school reform: Students living through change* (pp. 113–131). London: Routledge Farmer.

Cook-Sather, A. (2002). Authorizing students' perspectives: Toward trust, dialogue, and change in education. *Educational Researcher*, *31*(4), 3–14.

Denner, J., Meyer, B., & Bean, S. (2005). Young women's leadership alliance: Youth–adult partnerships in an all-female after-school program. *Journal of Community Psychology*, *33*, 87–100.

Eccles, J., & Gootman, J. A. (Eds). (2002). *Community programs to promote youth development*. Washington, DC: National Academy Press.

Fielding, M. (2001). Students as radical agents of change. *Journal of Educational Change*, *2*(2), 123–141.

Fine, M., Burns, A., & Payne, Y. (2004). Civics lessons: The color and class of betrayal. *Teachers College Record*, *106*(11), 2193–2223.

Frick, W. C. (in press). Practicing a professional ethic: Leading for students' best interests. *American Journal of Education*, *117*(4). Available online 13 June 2011.

Gilkey, L. (1993). *Nature, reality, and the sacred*. Minneapolis, MN: Augsburg-Fortress Press.

Giroux, H. (1992). Educational leadership and the crisis of democratic government. *Educational Researcher*, *21*(4), 4–11.

Hart, R. (1992). Children's participation: From tokenism to citizenship. UNICEF Innocenti Essays, Vol 4.

Hart, D., & Atkins, R. (2002). Civic competence in urban youth. *Applied Developmental Science*, *6*(4), 227–236.

Hinman, L. M. (2008). *Ethics: A pluralistic approach to moral theory* (4th ed). Belmont, CA: Wadsworth.

Holdsworth, R., & Thomson, P. (2002). Options within the regulation and containment of student voice and/or Students researching and acting for change: Australian experiences. Annual Meeting of the American Educational Research Association, 2002 New Orleans, LA.

Interstate School Leaders Licensure Consortium (ISLLC). (2008). Educational leadership and policy standards, Council of Chief State School Officers, Washington, DC.

Kahne, J., & Middaugh, E. (2008). High quality civic education: What is it and who gets it?. *Social Education, 72*(1), 34–39.

Kushman, J. W. (Ed.). (1997). Look who's talking now: Student views of learning in restructuring schools (Vol. ED028257). Office of Educational Research and Improvement, Washington, DC.

Lee, L., & Zimmerman, M. (1999). Passion, action and a new vision for student voice: Learnings from the Manitoba School Improvement Program. *Education Canada*, pp. 34–35.

Mitra, D. L. (2004). The significance of students: Can increasing "student voice" in schools lead to gains in youth development? *Teachers College Record, 106*, 651–688.

Mitra, D. L. (2006). Student voice or empowerment? Examining the role of school-based youth-adult partnerships as an avenue toward focusing on social justice. *International Electronic Journal for Leadership in Learning*, 10(22). Retrieved from http://www.acs. ucalgary.ca/~iejll/.

Mitra, D. L. (2008a). Balancing power in communities of practice: An examination of increasing student voice through school-based youth-adult partnerships. *Journal of Educational Change, 9*(3), 221–324.

Mitra, D. L. (2008b). *Student voice in school reform: Building youth-adult partnerships that strengthen schools and empower youth*. Albany, NY: State University of New York Press.

Mitra, D. L. (2009a). Strengthening student voice initiatives in high schools: An examination of the supports needed for school-based youth-adult partnerships. *Youth and Society, 40*(3), 311–335.

Mitra, D. L. (2009b). Collaborating with students: Building youth-adult partnerships in schools. *American Journal of Education, 15*(3), 407–436.

Mitra, D. L. (2009c). The role of intermediary organizations in sustaining student voice initiatives. *Teachers College Record, 111*(7), 1834–1868.

Mitra, D. L., & Kirshner, B. (forthcoming). Insiders versus outsiders — Examining variability in student voice initiatives and their consequences for school change. In: B. McMahon & J. Portelli (Eds.), *Student engagement in urban schools: Beyond neoliberal discourses*. Charlotte, NC: Information Age Publishing.

Noddings, N. (1984). *Caring: A feminine approach to ethics and moral education*. Berkeley, CA: The Regents of the University of California.

Oakes, J., & Rogers, J. (2006). *Learning power: Organizing for education and justice*. New York, NY: Teachers College Press.

Perkins, D., & Borden, L. (2003). Positive behaviors, problem behaviors, and resiliency in adolescence. In: R. M. Lerner, M. A. Easterbrooks & J. Mistry (Eds), *Handbook of psychology* (pp. 373–394). Hoboken, NJ: Wiley.

Rawls, J. (1971). *A theory of justice*. Cambridge, MA: Belknap Press.

Rose, M. (2009). *Why school? Reclaiming education for all of us*. New York, NY: The New Press.

Rudduck, J., & McIntyre, D. (2007). *Improving learning through consulting pupil*. Routledge: Oxon.

Rudduck, J. (2007). Student voice, student engagement, and school reform. In: D. Thiessen & A. Cook-Sather (Eds), *International handbook of student experience in elementary and secondary school* (pp. 587–610). Dordrecht, The Netherlands: Springer.

Rudduck, J., Day, J., & Wallace, G. (1997). Students' perspectives on school improvement. In: A. Hargreaves (Ed.), *Rethinking educational change with heart and mind (The 1997 ASCD Year Book)*. Alexandria, VA: Association for Supervision and Curriculum Development.

Shapiro, J. P., & Stefkovich, J. A. (2011). *Ethical leadership and decision making in education* (3rd ed.). Mahwah, NJ: Lawrence Erlbaum Associates.

Stefkovich, J. A. (2006). *Best interests of the student: Applying ethical constructs to legal cases in education*. Mahwah, NJ: Lawrence Erlbaum Associates, Inc.

Stefkovich, J. A., & O'Brien, G. M. (2004). Best interests of the student: An ethical model. *Journal of Educational Administration, 42*(2), 197–214.

Starratt, R. J. (1994). *Building an ethical school*. London: Falmer Press.

Strike, K. A., Haller, E. J., & Soltis, J. F. (1998). *The ethics of school administration* (2nd ed.). New York, NY: Teachers College Press.

United Nations. (1989). *Convention on the rights of the child*. Geneva: United Nations.

Walker, K. (1995). The kids' best interests. *The Canadian School Executive, 15*(5), 2–8.

Walker, K. (1998). Jurisprudential and ethical perspectives on the "best interests of children. *Interchange, 29*(3), 283–304.

Warren, M. R., Mira, M., & Nikundiwe, T. (2008). Youth organizing: From youth development to school reform. *New Directions for Youth Development, 2008*, 27–42.

Westheimer, J., Kahne, J. (2004). What kind of citizen? The politics of educating for democracy. Lifelong Citizenship Learning, Participatory Democracy & Social Change Conference, 2003, University of Toronto.

Zeldin, S. (2004). Youth as agents of adult and community development: Mapping the processes and outcomes of youth engaged in organizational governance. *Applied Developmental Science, 8*, 75–90.

Zeldin, S., Camino, L., & Mook, C. (2005). The adoption of innovation in youth organizations: Creating the conditions for youth-adult partnerships. *Journal of Community Psychology, 33*, 121–135.

Chapter 29

Voices for Change: Student Voices on Sexuality and HIV/AIDS Education

Colleen McLaughlin and Susan Kiragu

Abstract

This chapter explores notions of student consultation and involvement in curricula for HIV-related education. The chapter draws on a research project in Kenya, Tanzania and South Africa in 2009–2010 where primary school students in three schools in each country were consulted. The aim of the project was to investigate students' sexual knowledge, using Bernsteinian notions of formal (in-school) and informal (out-of-school) knowledge. The data was analysed to examine the ramifications for HIV education in school. The project used photovoice, videos and focus group discussions with pupils to explore where their sexual knowledge was acquired and how, as well as finding out their views on their current and ideal sexuality education. Dialogues between pupils, teachers and community members were also held. The chapter argues that this form of consultation can be used to transform difficult sociocultural situations that block HIV-related education.

Keywords: Curriculum development; HIV-related education; transformative dialogue

Introduction

This chapter discusses the use of student knowledge and voice to change attitudes and drive changes in practice in a highly sensitive and contentious area of the curriculum: HIV/AIDS education. We argue that the educational issues are sociocultural and explore how we can use students' voices, particularly in research

The Student Voice Handbook: Bridging the Academic/Practitioner Divide
Copyright © 2011 by Emerald Group Publishing Limited
ISBN: 978-1-78052-040-7

and in dialogue with adults, to address such complex sociocultural problems. We are drawing on the first phase of a research study in Kenya, South Africa and Tanzania, which took place in eight primary schools in total in 2009 and 2010. The pupils ranged from 11 to 18 years old, but the majority were 12–14. The project used 'photovoice', videos and focus group discussions with pupils to explore where and how their sexual knowledge was acquired, as well as finding out their views on their current and ideal HIV/AIDS education. The chapter argues that this form of consultation can be used to transform difficult sociocultural situations that block HIV/AIDS education. The study is ongoing and the next phase will engage in curriculum development based on consultation and negotiation with young people.

HIV/AIDS Education and Young People

It is 30 years since AIDS' cases were reported in sub-Saharan Africa and there has been much development; however, it is still the region of the world most affected. In 2008, sub-Saharan Africa accounted for 67% of HIV infections worldwide, 68% of new HIV infections among adults (with 40% of all new adults being children of 15+) and 91% of new HIV infections among children. Fourteen million children have been orphaned in this area. The region also accounted for 72% of the world's AIDS-related deaths in 2008 (UNAIDS, 2009). Young people are at the centre of it for they, especially girls and young women, are disproportionately affected. Schools are engaging with the challenge of orphanhood and a reduced teacher workforce because teachers' mortality rates are rising. Acedo (2009) shows that teachers are dying faster than they can be replaced. The World Bank (2002, p. xviii) estimated that HIV/AIDS would add between $US 450 and 550 million to the cost of achieving the Education for All[1] (i.e. providing basic education for all children, youth and adults) goals in 33 African countries. Therefore, there can be no doubt that this is a serious problem for education and young people.

Conceptions of the Problem

In response to the problem of HIV/AIDS, education has been seen as key — in fact, it has been called the 'social vaccine' (Baker, Collins & Leon, 2008). Countries have addressed the problem by constructing curricula and evaluating interventions. However, many have argued that the sociocultural aspects of sexuality and youth (Allen, 2007; Campbell, 2003; Rivers & Aggleton, 1999) have been ignored and that

---

1. The UNESCO Education for All movement took off at the World Conference on Education for All in 1990. Since then, governments, non-governmental organisations, civil society, bilateral and multilateral donor agencies and the media have taken up the cause of providing basic education for all children, youth and adults.

they, in fact, drive practice. We also believed this and were keen to address some of the sociocultural beliefs that informed the practices in the schools in our study: beliefs such as children are not old enough to know; if you educate young people, they will experiment with sex and that young people are and should remain innocent of sexual matters. Therefore, we set out to find out what children's sexual knowledge in these schools was. We used the Bernsteinian concepts of formal or in-school knowledge and informal or out-of-school knowledge to shape our research (Bernstein, 1999; Taylor, 2000). Bernstein (1999) differentiated two discourses or knowledge forms — the horizontal and the vertical. The horizontal or informal is gained in everyday life and for young people is largely acquired in interaction with peers. The vertical is the more formal discourses and knowledge forms of schooling. We wanted to see the fit or tensions between the knowledges; to see how the young people framed the problem; what they wanted from schools in terms of HIV/AIDS education, and how the adults (teachers and opinion leaders in the community) perceived these elements. We were also interested in the possibility of crossing the boundaries and saw this as central to effective HIV education in schools.

The Underlying Sociocultural Problems — Conceptions of Young People, Sex and Learning

There are different approaches to HIV prevention education. One approach sees individuals as rational and able to have control and bring about change (the bounded rationalists), and another sees human behaviour as contextual and located in the 'economic social and cultural structures' (Boler & Aggleton, 2005, p. 1). Our approach is very firmly in the second category. We were interested to build on the work of researchers such as Campbell (2003) who argue that sexuality and sexual behaviour are socially constructed and we wanted to find out more about this. The sociocultural context is complex. We know that in recent times, there is a tradition of silence around sexual matters in some communities in Africa, that there are very specific views of knowledge and authority, what young people should know and when, of pedagogy and of the role of the school (McLaughlin, Swartz, Kiragu, Walli, & Mohammed, forthcoming, 2011) and that the contexts of urban, rural, poor or more affluent make a difference. These themes and views are discussed further in later sections of this chapter but are encapsulated in this extract from a discussion with a group of South African primary students:

Naledi:	The teachers are careful with us because they think we are still young.
Buyelwa:	They think we can be able to process these things [better] in Grade seven or Grade eight.
Sisa:	[Last year] they said we were going to learn more in Grade six but they have not taught us as much.
Pinky:	They think we are too young to know.
Interviewer:	What do you think they think of you?

ALL:	They think we are going to be naughty or sometimes experiment with what they told us.
Zama:	Just like in Generations [a TV soap opera].
Interviewer:	Would you try to experiment with what you are told?
ALL:	No, who wants to experiment with AIDS?!

Sexuality and young people are highly contentious and sensitive topics, not ones that can be addressed without engaging with deep culturally bound understandings of young people, adults and education. As Foucault (1976, p. 4) has observed, there is a conception that sex is not a territory for young people: 'Everyone knows that 'children have no sex', which is why they are forbidden to talk about it, why one closes one's eyes and stops one's ears whenever they show evidence to the contrary'. However, the problem of HIV/AIDS makes it urgent to do so. We wanted to know if we could use young people and the results of consultation with them to address these deep and sensitive sociocultural issues. Therefore, the first task was to find out what their sexual knowledge is and where it is gained from. The aim in this research was to see if we could interrogate the understandings of young people, teachers and opinion leaders in the community, share these between these groups and explore whether this brought about reflection and change, as others who have used participatory approaches have suggested is possible (Freire, 1970).

Using Photovoice and Mini Documentaries to Consult

Therefore, we chose eight primary schools in total in the three countries: Kenya, South Africa and Tanzania. We deliberately chose upper primary classes, that is, year 6, because the pupils would be at the onset of puberty, and it is also an age that is under researched in terms of HIV/AIDS education. It was not difficult to gain access to the schools, but it was necessary to gain permits and permissions. We approached the relevant national or district ministries and gave a detailed report of our research design and gained permission to research. Local officers who were knowledgeable aided us in approaching schools. Only one school declined on the grounds of 'busyness'. Table 29.1 summarises the number of study participants and data collected.

We used photovoice to explore where young people got their sexual knowledge and its content. Photovoice is a method of consulting young people through taking photographs similar to autoethnography and was used by Swartz (2010) to engage with the views of young people. We trained the young people to use a digital camera, gave it to them for 2–7 days and asked them to take photographs of the people, places and things from which they learned about sex, love, AIDS and relationships. The training consisted of technical use of the camera as well as training in approaching people to ask to take their photos and discussion of more difficult scenarios, for example, if they wanted to take a sensitive or controversial photos, for example, of a prostitute or of how to handle a difficult reaction from someone when permission was asked. This did not stop children having difficulties. In South Africa,

Table 29.1: Research methods and participants per country.

	South Africa	Kenya	Tanzania	Total
Schools	2	3	3	8
Lesson observations	9	48	9	66
Child[a] participants aged (11–18 years)	38	45	42	125
Photos[b]	380	450	420	1250
Photo[c] interviews	38	45	42	125
Mini documentaries	4 groups	13 groups	4 groups	21
Teacher[d] participants	11	19	15	45
Community opinion leaders	13	14	13	40

[a]We aimed at working with 20 pupils per school in South Africa (therefore a planned total of 40) and 15 pupils per school in Kenya and Tanzania (a planned total of 45 per country).
[b]Ten photos per pupil.
[c]One interview per pupil.
[d]We aimed at six teachers per school.

in particular, the safety of the camera and the children using them was a big concern. In Kenya and Tanzania, all the cameras were returned safely. Children also took photos of their family and friends and many ran out of batteries. This meant it took longer in some places. The children were then interviewed about the photos they had taken. The interviews were then analysed using NVivo. The data and the photos were very rich and powerful indeed. They showed starkly the sites and sources as well as the content of sexual knowledge.

Using the same cameras, we asked the children to make mini documentaries of HIV/AIDS education as it is in their schools (current practice) and HIV/AIDS education as they would want it to be (desired practice). These were made by groups of children and ran to about 3–5 minutes. These videos were then discussed in groups and the desired HIV/AIDS education video was shown to the teachers and they discussed it too.

Table 29.2 details the main sources of the children's knowledge. Young people were highly sexually aware: they observed and reflected upon the sexual aspects of their social and personal worlds. Their photographs and comments were explicit and comprehensive. We have included some detail on one of the sources of sexual learning — sex for money. In all three sites, pupils were aware of the exchange of sex for money. Fathiya, a girl from Kenya, summed it well, 'when there is no food at home because of drought, a man will give you money and you will accept'. Hakika a girl from Tanzania added, 'you have expenses at home, life is hard. Maybe you don't have examination fees'. Campbell (2003, p. 63) describes this as 'gift sex' and explains that it is not shrouded with the shame and stigma associated with prostitution, but is seen as a means of survival. Achieng from Kenya talked of how girls in Mombasa were attracted to the white male tourists who frequented the beach. She gave an example of sex for money at the beach by assembling her dolls (as shown in Figure 29.1) and giving them roles, that is, a white man (tourist) with two schoolgirls.

Table 29.2: The primary sources of knowledge for young people.

Adults' social worlds — bars, beer dens, discos	Their homes and their relatives	Their schools — teachers, lessons and clubs
Observing adults social worlds — adults having sex in public places, adults drunk	Their peers' sexual behaviour — parties and observations of sexual behaviour, drugs and alcohol related sex, sex without and with consent	Their community organisations — NGOs, village elders, mosques and churches
Informal sexuality and the media — pornography, TV and films and books	Social messages about HIV/AIDS — posters, banners and wall paintings	Health organisations — hospitals and voluntary counselling and testing centres

Figure 29.1: Sex for money. An older man (white male tourist) with two 'beach' girls.

Sex for money or intergenerational sex were practiced by both sexes. For some pupils, sex for money was personal, as it was right in the home. Anna from South Africa shared how a boy in her class had a mother who was a drug addict and went as far as sleeping with her own brother to get money. A much more comprehensive report and discussion can be found in McLaughlin et al. (forthcoming, 2011).

The children learned very different things from the different sources. Table 29.3 gives a brief summary of the main differences. In discussing what they wanted from HIV/AIDS education, they were very clear that they wanted constructive honest and open dialogues with adults about their questions and their agendas. They perceived

Table 29.3: The content of the sexual knowledge.

From the school	From the streets
They seem to have been given mainly information on:	They gained their knowledge from what they saw and experienced in the communities. They witnessed:
• Facts about what HIV/AIDS — for example, definitions, symptoms, transmission, prevention, it has no cure, testing and stigma • Facts about transmission — through breast milk, a cut or wound, deep kissing, mother to child, a razor, sex, a syringe or injection or needle and sharing a toothbrush • How to protect themselves — abstinence, being faithful to one partner and condoms. Using condoms is not advocated • The need to avoid having sex with 'sugar daddies/mummies' or to get into prostitution • The consequences of unwanted pregnancy and drug abuse	• Themselves or others having sex on the streets, sometimes group sex • Themselves or others taking drugs and blacking out on the streets • Hearing and speaking 'dirty' language that they would not normally speak at school • Young people and adults having sex and relationships for money • Young people and adults engaging in same sex relationships • Sexual assault from peers. Especially from male youth who are drug addicts and have dropped out of school

adults to be scared as is clear in the earlier quotation from the South African pupils. They saw adults as running away from explicit and difficult discussions with them. They also saw the teachers' fear of explicit discussion and make the connection to the cultural issues of shame around sexual discussions.

> There is no need for teachers to be shy because we children already knew about sex. We see it on TV and some of us are already doing it. They must not be ashamed and say we are children, they had the same experience and their teachers were ashamed to speak about these things-but now they must talk to us because AIDS it is the most infectious disease in SA. They must be firm when they talk us, and they must tell our parents to believe in us as we also believe in them. (Naledi, girl, age 13, South Africa)

Using Students' Voices to Bring About Change

These two methods proved to be highly effective in providing data about the social worlds, attitudes and sexual learning of the children and young people in our study.

We were highly engaged by the results of the consultation and wanted to see how the other adults in the study — the teachers and community opinion leaders — would respond. We produced a collage on PowerPoint of the photos and we edited an all inclusive video with data from all three countries. We then showed this to a meeting called a community dialogue. We invited four to six community opinion leaders (including the ones interviewed early on in the process), four to six teachers from each school and four to six pupils. In addition to the prime purpose of seeing what would happen when all the participants engaged in the dialogue and understood one another's positions, we were aiming to find out:

- What their reactions were to the young people's sexual knowledge and more of their views on HIV/AIDS education.
- What they saw as the difficulties, challenges and benefits in integrating the informal and school knowledge of young people.
- What the participants thought was the potential to use this data to develop the curriculum for HIV/AIDS education.

As will be presented later, there was evidence of an attitudinal shift in the adults during the final dialogues. There were also some adults who seemed to experience a form of cognitive dissonance and were unable to accept that the children were so sophisticated in their knowledge and in their desire for constructive, open dialogues with the adults. There was also an open debate within these dialogues of the pressures and dilemmas of the different parties as is voiced by the Tanzanian male teacher in the following:

> Traditions and culture are compelling teachers not to speak freely on the issues of HIV/AIDS. Children living in risk environment can easily understand but those living in good residential areas cannot understand [so] straightforwardly. [Mr Omar, Tanzania]

There were powerful examples of children daring to ask questions and adults seriously answering them, thus enacting the processes that the pupils had asked for. There was also a joint expression from all participants of a desire to create a different situation in the future. The following quote is one example.

> HIV/AIDS education should not be a secret; we should all collaborate from all peerages. [Ms Kafumu, Tanzania]

Conclusion

The data showed that young people were astute observers of their communities and of the sexual aspects of community and family life. There were some adults in our study who articulated that they were aware of this. Others preferred not to engage with this or if they did wanted to be protective. In the data, the cultural tensions were evident and therefore the complexity of HIV education in schools. What was also clear was that there was a possibility of change. We felt that there was enough evidence for us to continue to pursue this notion of consulting pupils as a way of developing the curriculum. The dialogues had shown that on those occasions, teachers, community leaders and young people could engage in honest and authentic conversations about HIV/AIDS and sexual matters, Therefore, we feel that through processes of consultation and dialogue with all parties, it may be possible to create local understandings of what HIV/AIDS education should be like and thus support curriculum development.

We are now embarking upon an extension of this work in six sub-Saharan countries (Botswana, Ghana, Kenya, South Africa, Swaziland and Tanzania). We have established curriculum development groups of four pupils, two community members and a HIV/AIDS consultant to work with a class teacher in each country. They will engage in a process of consultation and through action research explore the development of a curriculum for HIV/AIDS education.

Acknowledgements

Dr Sharlene Swartz at The Human Sciences Research Council (HSRC), Cape Town, South Africa. Ms Shelina Walli and Mr Mussa Mohamed at The Aga Khan University Institute for Educational Development, East Africa (AKU-IED), Dar es Salaam, Tanzania.

References

Acedo, C. (2009). Editorial. *Prospects, 39*(4), 307–309.

Allen, L. (2007). Denying the school subject: Schools' regulation of student sexuality. *British Educational Research Journal, 33*(2), 221–234.

Baker, D. P., Collins, J. M., & Leon, J. (2008). Risk factor or social vaccine? The historical progression of the role of education in HIV and AIDS infection in sub-Saharan Africa. *Prospects, 38*, 467–486.

Bernstein, B. (1999). Vertical and horizontal discourse: An essay. *British Journal of Sociology of Education, 20*(2), 157–173.

Boler, T., & Aggleton, P. (2005). *Life skills-based education for HIV prevention: A critical analysis.* London: UK working group on education and HIV/AIDS.

Campbell, C. (2003). *Letting them die: Why HIV/AIDS intervention programmes fail.* Bloomington and Indianapolis, IN: Indiana University Press.

Foucault, M. (1976). *The will to knowledge: The history of sexuality (vol. 1).* London: Penguin Books.

Freire, P. (1970). *Pedagogy of the oppressed.* New York, NY: Seabury.

McLaughlin, C., Swartz, S., Kiragu, S., Walli, S., & Mohammed, M. (forthcoming, 2011). *Old enough to know: Consulting children about sex and HIV/ADS education.* Cape Town: HSRC Press.

Rivers, K., & Aggleton, P. (1999). *Adolescent sexuality, gender and the HIV epidemic*. UN Development Programme, HIV Development Programme.

Swartz, S. (2010). *Ikasi: The moral ecology of South Africa's township youth*. Johannesburg: Witwatersrand University Press.

Taylor, N. (2000). Schooling and everyday life. In: J. Muller (Ed.), *Reclaiming knowledge: Social theory curriculum and education policy*. London: RoutledgeFalmer.

UNAIDS. (2009). *AIDS epidemic update*. Geneva: UNAIDS.

World Bank. (2002). *Education and HIV/AIDS: A window of hope*. Washington, DC: World Bank.

Chapter 30

Marginalised Students and Insider Knowledge

Derek Bland

Abstract

One of the claims made for valuing the voices of marginalised students is that an insider perspective can be revealed on student issues and the ways in which education policies and systems impact on them. This chapter examines the ways in which participants in an Australian 'students-as-researchers' (SaR) project were able to raise knowledge of and address, to some extent, long-standing issues of racism in their schools. The SaR project has operated in more than 30 schools for periods of 1–5 years. Based on a participatory action research model, groups of secondary school students from schools serving socio-economically disadvantaged communities have worked with nominated teachers and university researchers to identify and research local issues relating to low academic outcomes and to develop and enact responses to the identified concerns.

The voices of marginalised students quoted in this chapter illustrate that important insider knowledge can be revealed through the SaR process. Where student views have been acknowledged and acted on by the schools, significant change to student–teacher relationships and school culture has been achieved; the participants have been personally empowered and academic improvements across the schools have been noted. For such change to occur, however, a culture of mutual respect must be created in which teachers and school administrators value students' views and are open to the possibility of unfavourable criticism.

Keywords: Students-as-researchers; educational disadvantage; racism; school improvement; participatory action research

The Student Voice Handbook: Bridging the Academic/Practitioner Divide
Copyright © 2011 by Emerald Group Publishing Limited
All rights of reproduction in any form reserved
ISBN: 978-1-78052-040-7

Introduction

Students' perceptions have a great capacity to 'alert schools to shortcomings of their current performance and possible ways of addressing the deficiencies' (Fielding 2001, p. 123). Although this can pose challenges for schools and teachers, valuing the voices of marginalised students has particular benefits. An 'insider perspective' can be revealed on ways in which education policies and systems impact on the most disengaged (Atweh & Dornan, 1999), excavating the meanings of concepts such as disengagement from the inside and using these new understandings to help make a difference to the lives of the most disadvantaged (Smyth, 2006, p. 288). Kincheloe and Steinberg (1998, p. 233) noted that the students-as-researchers model, through which students work with professional researchers and teachers, 'can be used especially effectively with marginalised students'. The scaffolded process can assist students to 'figure out ways of overcoming the obstacles that block their success'.

This chapter will, first, discuss a project in which secondary school students in a number of schools have investigated issues of educational importance to themselves and their peers. Secondly, it will consider examples of the insider perspectives that the students were able to make known to their schools. Finally, some of the problematics for teachers and schools in listening to the voices of disadvantaged students will be considered.

Students-as-Researchers

The students-as-researchers (SaR) project that is the focus of this chapter developed from a conversation in 1991 between a concerned teacher and an inquisitive academic. It was intended to be a short-term collaboration to obtain the views of students at one secondary school relating to apparent low aspiration for tertiary entrance. The success of SaR in that original project school in generating tertiary aspiration saw the number of students applying for and successfully gaining university entrance go from 0 to 20 in just two years. Following this result, a number of other schools requested assistance from the university.

Over the ensuing 20 years the project has been embraced by over 30 schools, involving several hundred secondary school students and dozens of teachers. Throughout the process, students' voices have remained central to the research and have, at times, revealed insights that may not have been otherwise evident to their schools. On occasion, their views have been challenging to teachers and school administrators.

Although the project has developed through several iterations and name changes, participatory action research has been maintained as the core process. The project is facilitated by academics from the host university's Faculty of Education. Each year, up to five schools participate in the SaR project, nominating around 10–20 students each, generally drawn from the middle years (aged around 13–15). Some schools have participated in the project for up to five years while others have remained for only one or two years, depending on perceived needs.

The project is designed on an annual cycle, commencing with an on-campus introductory workshop for the student researchers and their support teachers. At this workshop, students engage in deep reflection on aspects of educational disadvantage affecting themselves and their peers and are introduced to various data-gathering techniques. By the end of the workshop, each student group is expected to complete an action plan for school-based research. The students' research is assisted by the university facilitators as well as each school's support teacher. Following the data analysis, in accordance with action research procedures, they develop and implement potential solutions to identified problems.

Throughout the life of the SaR project, the focus has continued to be on students in schools that serve some of the most educationally disadvantaged communities around the city of Brisbane, Australia. These communities are mostly located in outer-suburban areas following the gentrification of what were once working-class inner suburbs, requiring low-income families to relocate further from the city centre to more affordable housing. Many of the communities are rich in cultural diversity but are also characterised by low income, high levels of unemployment and distance from cultural facilities such as museums and art galleries. Traditionally, the schools have had strong ties with vocational education providers and limited interaction with universities. Hence, students considering post-school options have few role models to encourage them in the direction of university study.

Over the years, the age and background of participating students has been re-focused: where earlier participants were recruited from senior years, the focus is now on middle year students. Also, where it was first suggested that participants should have a desire to attend university, experience has shown that one of the project's greatest strengths is its ability to create aspiration among students from backgrounds that are under-represented in higher education and those who are disengaged or at-risk of early school-leaving. Although student selection is entirely the prerogative of the schools, they are advised that special consideration be given to those students who may not demonstrate the expected academic signs of potential university students. There is, of course, a responsibility to avoid 'setting up students to fail'. For this reason, easy exit from the project must be assured where participants feel the tasks are unrealistic or uninteresting for them. Project experience demonstrates that it is preferable for a student to have some exposure to the project and make a decision to leave voluntarily than to exclude students on the basis of apparent lack of academic merit. As one such student commented: 'my attitude has changed and I'm not so much of a problem student as some teachers might call you — they see me as someone they can have a friendship with' (Year 10 male).

Some schools specifically nominate Indigenous (Australian Aboriginal) students and others have nominated Pacific Islander (mostly Samoan) groups. These students are, statistically, the least likely to complete formal education: a poor retention rate is reflected in university entrance with 5% of Indigenous people aged between 18 and 24 attending university in 2001 compared with 23% of non-Indigenous people (Monash University, 2007). Further, there is a 'disproportionately high' rate of suspension of Indigenous students in most Australian States (Fullarton, Walker, Ainley, & Hillman, 2003, p. 13).

For these students, the opportunity to have input into the ways that schooling impacts their lives is rare and they are among the least likely to be heard on issues that directly affect their educational outcomes (Riley & Rustique-Forrester, 2002; Thomson, 2004).

Insider Information

As well as opening up opportunities for the previously silent voices of young people to be heard, SaR participation benefits schools as the young people involved in researching a social practice or a problem are in a better position to know the 'inside story' (Atweh, 2003). The SaR project proposed to 'excavate the meanings' (Smyth, 2006, p. 288) of concepts such as disengagement from the inside. The students' 'insider perspective' (Atweh & Dornan, 1997) was frequently candid and revealed information that is unlikely to have been disclosed other than to peers.

In 1995, for example, one school used the SaR model to investigate issues of tertiary aspiration and access among their Indigenous student population. The research disclosed disturbing findings relating to racism in the school:

> About one third of the students indicated that some teachers have shown some racist attitudes and about one half said that other students had racist attitudes. (Atweh et al., 1995, p. vi)[1]

Further, it revealed that the highest level of racism, a staggering 48%, was experienced by lower grade students (Atweh et al., 1995). The study also investigated the experiences of Indigenous ex-students, 44% of whom reported racist attitudes of teachers. A survey of male Indigenous students who had left the school disclosed that

> more than half of the young men (56%) indicated that some teachers had encouraged them to leave school. (Atweh et al., 1995, p. 17)

This research provided insights from a student perspective that may have been discomforting but were essential data in addressing the early school-leaving of Indigenous students. Following a recommendation of the research group, the school established a more rigorous system for dealing with complaints of discrimination and ensuring increased cultural understanding.

Students have often been in a privileged position to recognise the local significance of the data gathered in relation to a particular line of inquiry. For example, two later studies of Polynesian and Samoan groups (Bethel, Fui, Leati, & Tauilo, 2000; Terapo et al., 2001) identified data that were very helpful to their schools in communicating with parents. These studies highlighted an obvious but not previously considered

---

1. Student quotations are taken from focus group interviews with the student researchers and, where indicated, from research reports compiled by them.

disadvantage in the school's use of English only to keep the community informed about school matters. Another group identified a lack of recognition by their school of the diversity of cultures and religions among the student population and revealed discriminative practice displayed by teachers and students against 'asylum seekers' and refugees. The students' findings prompted a swift revision of policy on these issues in their school.

Data has been obtained by some students from their peers that may not have been readily tendered to teachers or external researchers. One SaR group, for example, investigated the reasons for a seemingly large transfer of students to another school. They found that 'a lot of students ... were encouraged to do so by their friends at other schools' (Bloomfield et al., 1996, p. 11). This insight, revealing the importance and influence of friendship groups, resulted from the researchers' cultural under-standings and from the willingness of the respondents to share their lifeworld views with the researchers. The insight helped the school to consider new ways to address the issue.

Generally, students' negative observations have been phrased constructively, such as from a group investigating the problems facing Pacific Islander boys in their school, who noted that adverse behaviour and inappropriate classroom humour often masks students' resentment of teachers' lack of cultural understanding. This group recommended the establishment of a forum to discuss discipline and teaching issues with the staff. Assisting marginalised students to become more aware of the social and political conditions that pervade school decision-making and affect their educational opportunities can, though, lead to uncomfortable questioning about perceived injustices and, as Kincheloe and Steinberg (1998, p. 14) point out, 'questions are dangerous, often perceived as an attack on authority'.

Such a situation was exemplified by the comments of one student research group following the rejection of their recommendations by the school's administration. The student group had little confidence that their project would be successful as they regarded the administration of the school as being aloof, as one student commented:

> our school doesn't really listen to us ... we knew it wasn't going to help anything, like it wasn't going to do anything. But that's our school.

Listening to Students' Voices

Fielding and Bragg (2003) observed that students need assurance that their work will not be 'hijacked' by others and that this must form part of the initial shared understanding between all participants in the project, adding that, if their proposal is in fact not viable, students will understand if a clear rationale is given. In the above case, however, the students questioning of the school administration led to their project being given to a more 'trusted group' of students. The student researchers commented in a focus group that they had anticipated failure due to past experience, expressing the view that 'our school's crap' and likening the administration to

Orwell's *1984*. Criticisms then spread to many other staff members. For these students, the situation was summed up by one of the group who commented:

> How can you respect someone if they don't respect you back.

This view was replicated by another school's Indigenous SaR group. One student in particular, who was in danger of expulsion for continued misbehaviour, felt that his teachers had no respect for him or his culture and, therefore could see no reason why he should show respect for the teachers. For this student, it was his involvement in the SaR project that saved him from suspension and kept him involved in mainstream education for a number of years. The group to which he belonged, conducted research with other Indigenous students at their school that led to a proposal for an Indigenous room which would be a quiet space for homework and additional tuition. There was quite a deal of trepidation among the students in approaching the principal with their recommendation as they generally interacted with him only on matters of misbehaviour. Having gathered the courage, however, they were faced with disappointment, feeling that their school administrators had prevaricated and effectively wasted their time, as indicated in a focus group discussion:

Izzie: He doesn't like anything new, and he likes everything by the book, and he stays by the book.

Jean: Yeah, every room that we'd get, we'd be like, yeah, finally get a room, start to go to work in that room, and then we'll get told 'no you can't have that room'. So then we're back to square one again ... Indigenous people don't really have a big thing in the school, and we don't really ask for much at all ... we asked for one room, one little room ... out of how many rooms in the frigging school, and they couldn't do it, and then we, I got really cut, because they're so stupid.

In discussing this situation and the prevailing attitudes of teachers, the students' views indicated on-going racial stereotyping:

> There are teachers in this school that will judge us. And that's what a lot of people fire up about as well because you won't even do nothing wrong but they will find the most worst thing out of it and they will just, they'll despise you as a student ...

Through the persistent efforts of the group's support teacher, however, a room was eventually obtained as a safe space for the Indigenous students and their friends. A later student research group used the facility when exploring the identity of Indigenous students within the school through document analysis. They discovered that the successes of Indigenous students tended to receive little or any recognition, whether in academic, sporting, cultural or social areas. For example, the failure of the school to publicly acknowledge the achievement of one of the project students who obtained a place at a local university, although praising non-Indigenous students, was an unfortunate message to the students about who was or was not deserving of praise in the eyes of the school.

After a few years of exposure to the work of the student research teams, the culture of the school began to change; the students' support teacher cited grade 8 (12–13 year old) Indigenous students receiving academic awards as evidence of the impact of the project. At a subsequent student conference, the achievements of dozens of Indigenous students were celebrated through a PowerPoint display presented by the student researchers which was later screened at the school, encouraging staff discussion on how Indigenous culture could be recognised within the school curriculum.

Conclusion

As the earlier examples demonstrate, working with students as equals and partners in research opens the door for challenges as well as new opportunities to work in productive ways but is not without its risks (Atweh, Cobb, & Dornan, 1997). It challenges the normal demarcations of power between teachers and students. There is also an inherent risk for schools and teachers in that they may receive unwelcome feedback through the SaR process. Commenting on early examples of SaR projects, Atweh and Burton (1995) noted 'mismatches' between the novice researchers and their professional co-participants. They believed work must be done in the establishment stage to overcome any cynicism, assure the students of the principle of 'parity of esteem' (Grundy, 1998), and reduce the possibility of conflict between the duty-of-care requirement of the adult participants and the rights of students to express their own voices in authentic ways.

Frequently, where the views of the student researchers have been acknowledged and acted on by their schools, significant change to student–teacher relationships and school culture has been achieved. This was particularly notable in the school where the Indigenous room was eventually established. The experience of this project suggests that transformation begins with the students. Their immersion in the SaR projects, demonstrating high levels of motivation to achieve socially useful outcomes creates new perceptions in the minds of teachers, quite often reversing negative expectations. This has led to a culture of mutual respect in which teachers and school administrators value students' views and accept the possibility of unfavourable criticism.

Being a novice researcher from a background of educational disadvantage presents certain risks for students entering the project and the unknown territory of a university campus. The potential risk of failure can be minimised during the introductory workshop, as can the other identified risks for students. Although protecting students from unnecessary risk is essential, the action research cycle provides students with the opportunity to take risks in their project work through trialling ideas, re-evaluating them and working out where things need to be re-thought. As one student said

> I think, if we just do what we think we should do, you know, you can see if it helps. If it doesn't we can do it again and do it a bit differently. It's all good.

Schools that agree to commit to such projects need to assure students that they have the support of the executive of the school in order that the work is regarded as serious learning and that tokenistic participation is avoided. As illustrated earlier, where the students believe they lack that support, the experience can risk a reinforcement of the experience of failure that so often underscores the education journey of at-risk students. The question for schools and teachers is whether, in the interests of working with marginalised students to obtain essential insider knowledge to address problems, they are willing to accept the attendant risks of criticism.

References

Atweh, B. (2003). On PAR with young people: Learnings from the SARUA Project. *Educational Action Research, 11*(1), 23–40.

Atweh, B., Cobb, A., Crouch, T., Curtis-Silk, V., Delaney, M., Hemsworth, B., Jarrett, L., Riley, M., & Towney, J. (1995). Dalipie and Dalinkua project – 1995. Research report. QUT, Brisbane.

Atweh, B., Cobb, A., Dornan, L. (1999). Students as partners: Potentials and dilemmas in action research. Paper presented at the annual conference of the Australian Association for Educational Research. Brisbane, Hilton Hotel.

Atweh, B., & Dornan, L. (1997). *SARUA: Project training and resource manual.* Brisbane: Centre for Mathematics and Science Education, Queensland University of Technology.

Atweh, W., & Burton, L. (1995). Students as researchers: Rationale and critique. *British Educational Research Journal, 21*(5), 561–575.

Bethel, T., Fui, A., Leati, R., & Tauilo, D. (2000). Making links. Research report. QUT, Brisbane.

Bloomfield, N., Kitzelman, D., O'Grady, M., Parsons, D., Proctor, A., & Leshke, J. (1996). Have you found the road to success? A report of the SARUA project for Bundamba State High School. QUT, Brisbane.

Fielding, M. (2001). Students as radical agents of change. *Journal of Educational Change, 2*(2), 123–141.

Fielding, M., & Bragg, S. (2003). *Students as researchers: Making a difference.* Cambridge, UK: Pearson Publishing.

Fullarton, S., Walker, M., Ainley, J., & Hillman, K. (2003). Patterns of participation in year 12. Research Report 33, Australian Council for Educational Research, Camberwell, Victoria.

Grundy, S. (1998). Research partnerships: Principles and possibilities. In: B. Atweh, S. Kemmis & P. Weeks (Eds), *Action research in practice: Partnerships for social justice in education.* London: Routledge.

Kincheloe, J., & Steinberg, S. (1998). In: *Students-as-researchers: Creating classrooms that matter* (pp. 2–19). London: Falmer Press.

Monash University. (2007). Facts and statistics about indigenous education. Retrieved from http://www.education.monash.edu.au/indigenous-ed/viewinfo.html?id=2. Accessed on 28 January 2011.

Riley, K., & Rustique-Forrester, E. (2002). *Working with disaffected students.* London: Paul Chapman Publishing.

Smyth, J. (2006). When students have power: student engagement, student voice, and the possibilities for school reform around 'dropping out' of school. *International Journal of Leadership in Education, 9*(4), 285–298.

Terapo, R., Tongia, M., Nisa, C., Fetoa, F., Toma, G., Winterstein, M., Seve, S., Laula, Q., Faaee, I., & Fau, S. (2001). SARUA 2000: The Glenala students' report. Research report. QUT, Brisbane.

Thomson, P. (2004). Unpopular voices: Listening to pupils 'at risk'. Paper delivered to the International Networking for Educational Transformation on-line conference on student voice, 20–26 September. Retrieved from http://www.cybertext.net.au/inet/focus_papers/f5_14.htm. Accessed on 25 September 2004.

Chapter 31

Developing the 'Tact of Researching': The Ethically Aware Researcher Giving 'Voice to Students' — a Swedish Context

Ulrika Bergmark and Catrine Kostenius

Abstract

From a Swedish perspective, the concept of student voice can be linked to the idea of adults listening to students and giving them voice. It also involves inviting students to actively participate in decision-making in school, as well as fostering democratic citizenship. Our interest in student voice initiatives in schools have motivated us, as researchers, to engage in participatory research with students. This chapter focuses on student voice within the context of educational research in Sweden. Voicing students' experiences has ethical connotations for the overall well-being of students. In addition to protecting children from harm, ethical student voice research should offer children opportunities to have a say in matters affecting them, as well as showing respect for their views and trusting their competence. Thus, the nature of voicing students' experiences in research implies demands regarding how research is conducted, putting the researcher's role under pressure and scrutiny. This chapter explores the issues researchers need to consider when researching the idea of student voice from a Swedish perspective.

In conclusion, we argue for 'tact of researching' when adhering to student voice research: the development of ethical research practice, which affirms participants. We emphasise relationships in research that are oriented towards students' experiences, their self-understanding and individual agency, accompanied by the researchers' self-awareness and sensitivity. The 'tact of researching' involves a striving to become an enabling one, researcher aware of one's role and using critical reflection regarding ethical values; ensuring empowerment throughout the research process. This offers possibilities for being an ethically aware researcher working within the field of student voice.

Keywords: Participatory research; researcher's role; relationships; ethics; well-being

Introduction

From a Swedish perspective, the concept of student voice can be linked to the idea of adults listening to students and thereby 'giving them voice' (Alerby, 2000, 2003; Bergmark, 2009; Kostenius, 2008; Sehlberg, 1999) as explained by Cook-Sather (2006) as well as Roberts and Nash (2009). Another tenet of student voice used by Swedish researchers echoes Rudduck and Flutter's (2004) declaration of not underestimating students' abilities when it comes to participating in school activities, as well as in decision-making (Almqvist, Eriksson, & Granlund, 2004; Danell, 2006; Elvstrand, 2009; Näsman, 2004). The interwoven connection between students' participation and their influence on education is often used in Sweden as an example of democratic values (Biesta, 2006; Lindahl, 2005; Roth, 2000). This is in-line with Mitra (2008) who connects student voice to civic engagement and active citizenship. Adopting a local and national context, it has been suggested that the Swedish school represents an important place for the education of citizenship and it also has democratic influence on society (Elvstrand, 2009), an assertion that mirrors that made by many writers in other national contexts — in particular, the United Kingdom and the United States. One underpinning notion of student participation in Swedish schools, as elsewhere, is the United Nations Conventions on the Rights of the Child (CRC, 1989). Children's rights are evident in the managerial documents for the national school system in Sweden. They stress the importance of taking students' voices and experiences as starting point in educational settings, with the aims of increasing students' achievements, as well as developing their ability to be responsible citizens (Swedish National Agency for Education, 2010). Children's rights are also frequently discussed and practiced in curriculum development, as well as in classroom activities (Hägglund, 2001; Quennerstedt, 2009).

In Sweden, children's rights are interpreted as viewing children as competent, trustworthy and capable (Kostenius & Öhrling, 2008; Näsman, 2004). The core of the concept 'student voice', such as listening to students, encouraging active participation in schooling and being engaged citizens, has been explored by a number of Swedish researchers, although the specific term 'student voice' is not frequently used. One reason for the components of student voice being positioned in Swedish schools is based on cultural values. One major responsibility in the Swedish educational system has historically been, and continues to be, to foster democratic citizens who participate in schooling and in society as a whole (Englund, 2005; Quennerstedt, 2009). This strong emphasis on the link between education and democracy can be traced back to educational policy documents established after the Second World War, which expressed student influence as a human right of the child. The precedence of student influence as an important children's rights issue in education can therefore be understood in relation to a historical and political background. It also reflects the emphasis that Swedish society puts on education being a fundamental role in upholding and maintaining democracy (Quennerstedt, 2010).

Our interest in student voice initiatives in schools have motivated us as researchers to engage in participatory research with students. This chapter focuses on issues researchers need to consider when researching student voice — from a Swedish perspective. The discussion we develop here is linked to the concept of an 'ethically aware researcher', an attitude which we call 'tact of researching'. Firstly, however, we examine the links between student voice, schools as a site for research knowledge and the adoption of participatory research.

Links between Student Voice in Schools and Participatory Research

Increasingly schools have become a meaningful site for research — research involving students, teachers and school leaders (Bergmark, 2009; Coad & Evans, 2007). Such research often adopts an ethically aware and qualitative enquiry. It is research *with* people rather than research *on* someone (Heron & Reason, 2001; Kostenius, 2008). The prerequisite for such participatory research is building relationships between participants and researchers. When changing the research focus to *with* from *on* it 'requires and constitutes a change in the role of both researcher and student and a change of relationship between them' (Cook-Sather, 2007, p. 850). A researcher's role can vary considerably; from occupying a position as someone who builds active, collaborative relationships with students to that of a researcher who adopts a more detached and traditionally academic approach (*ibid.*). When undertaking research together with students, underpinning notions of student voice, such as children's rights, participation, empowering children and demonstrating democratic values, have inspired us. In the following section, we explore our understanding of student voice research, as well as issues of ethics and well-being, related to this kind of research.

Dimensions of Ethics and Well-Being in Student Voice Research

The issue of voicing students' experiences involves dimensions of ethics and well-being, due to mutual impact in the relationship between students and researchers. According to UNESCO (2011), researchers have to handle ethical, at times even legal, issues from competing values, obligations and conflicts of interest. Therefore, the social science research society has developed ethical codes of conduct, which serve as guidelines for research practice (UNESCO, 2011). The ethical code of research in Sweden and around the world includes obtaining informed consent from participants, ensuring confidentiality, autonomy and preventing participants from harm (SFS, 2008). However, there is still a need to critically reflect upon and evaluate problematic situations in research to enact the ethical guidelines.

When researching issues pertaining to student voice, dimensions of well-being can involve providing students with a safe environment and offering opportunities to have a say in matters affecting them. As researchers, showing respect for students' views and trusting their competence are also issues relating to well-being. In a reciprocal research relationship where students feel welcome and are treated with respect and recognition both as individuals and also as a whole group, possibilities for the students to experience a high level of well-being are created (Kostenius & Öhrling, 2006). Thus, the aforementioned understanding of voicing students' experiences in research make demands for how research is conducted, putting the researcher's role under pressure. The researcher's role in assessing student voice is therefore explored later.

Exploring the Researcher's Role in Student Voice Research

During our research involving student voice, we have naturally reflected upon our role as researchers as we have built relationships with students in the Swedish compulsory school. Our experience is based on research within the areas of ethics and health in learning processes (Bergmark, 2009; Kostenius, 2008). In conducting our enquiries focusing on articulating children's voice, one question that has arisen is: How can we act as ethical researchers when voicing students' experiences? Peshkin (1988) argues that subjectivity in research is inevitable. Researchers should strive for explicit exploration and presentation of one's experiences concerning the researcher's role in, for example, research articles and dissertations. Cook-Sather (2007) emphasises the importance for researchers voicing students' experiences to conceptualise themselves differently compared to a researcher's role constituted by a hierarchical and distanced approach. This means that the interactions between the researcher and the participants become non-hierarchical and based on close relationships. Reflecting on a researcher's role throughout the research process may create an awareness — a sensibility — about the nature of the relationship between researchers and students and how to perform ethically as researchers. In the following section, we explore different ways of acting as ethically aware researchers when giving voice to students, guided by the following questions: In what ways can a researcher deal with sensitive and problematic experiences brought forward in research? What are the different ways of dealing with relationships in research?

The Ethically Aware Researcher in Student Voice Research

We have reflected on the researcher's role in student voice research. The relationship with the students is affected, consciously or unconsciously, depending on how a researcher conceptualises himself or herself. The role of the ethically aware researcher in student voice research which we wish to emphasise is based on two concepts relating to education and philosophy: van Manen's (1991) 'tact of teaching' and Lévinas' (1969) 'being-for-the-world'. 'Tact of teaching' means a will to meet and touch others, openness for student experience, improvisation and flexibility. van Manen (1991) provides insights in terms of what *tact* can bring: it defends what is vulnerable, prevents hurt, heals what is broken, strengthens what is good, amplifies the unique and encourages personal development and learning. Tact is, according to van Manen (1991), something a teacher shows. We stress that tact can also be connected to the researcher's role in student voice research. If a researcher, for example, interviews a student about stressful situations in life, thereby evoking sad memories that make the student unhappy, it calls for the attention of a response from the researcher's side. The tactful researcher takes responsibility for the situations that his or her research has caused, by addressing other professionals, with the student's consent, asking for help in solving a problematic situation. This researcher is seeking ways to see, hear and support the participants without trying to solve the participants' problems, echoing the words of van Manen (1991): 'A tactful pedagogy, therefore, tries to prevent the circumstances and factors that make an experience injurious and hurtful to children' (p. 194). Most importantly, when people feel heard and valued, they may be encouraged to improve their own efforts. Oliver (2003) describes how a research participant can benefit from being part of a study when he stresses that the research can 'help people understand more about dilemmas and conflicts which confront us in life' (p. 67). The process of reflection that is included in voicing one's own experiences can help students to clarify their own thoughts, express them and by that learn about themselves and others.

We argue that Lévinas' (1969) notion of 'being-for-the-world' can be seen as a way of acting as an ethically aware researcher due to its emphasis on treating others with respect and appreciation. This is about seeing the value of others and being responsible for communicating in appreciative terms to them. 'Being-for-the-world' includes actively meeting others. Researchers exploring student voice can contribute to relationships between students, teachers and researchers signified by a 'we'. This 'we' can be created through inviting the students to set the agenda, letting them influence a project, from the beginning, and being a part of the goal setting. Individuals can help and learn from one another (Kirby, 2001). This approach is supported by Cook-Sather (2007) when she writes, 'Researchers who seriously engage in the work of seeking out, taking up, and re-presenting students' experiences of school not only translate what they gather but are also translated by it' (p. 829). Lévinas' notion of 'being-for-the-world' involves a movement forward to another person, as an expression of responsibility. As we have interpreted Lévinas, this means that a person cannot expect another person to take the first step when meeting one another. However, an individual has to take responsibility when actively meeting another person. People can choose their actions, but they cannot force others to act as they want. Student voice research can in this sense involve meeting students with respect, for example, actively inviting them to be involved in data creation and analysis, thus letting their voices be heard. If listened to and offered the possibility to participate, students can enrich a research process, which consequently can offer important components of a democratic education, such as the right to voice ones experiences and views, and freedom to act on the opportunity offered to take part in society (cf. Quennerstedt, 2010).

The ideas of 'tact of teaching' and 'being-for-the-world' can be connected to student voice, ethics and well-being, due to their emphasis on listening to students' experiences, creating respectful relations, having responsibility for others and promoting students' development and growth. Morrow and Richards (1996) state that ethical concerns in research represent ways to protect participants from harm and respect their views. The aforementioned authors stress the importance of developing 'strategies that are fair and respectful to the subjects of our research' (p. 91). If research is conducted in a participatory way, it has the potential to empower those involved through a democratic process. Empowerment can be defined as a process of focusing on human rights and human beings' capacity to actively participate in and influence their own lives (Melander-Wikman, 2007). Booth et al. (1991) concluded that 'power can be healthy' (p. 31) and this power enables human beings to be active participants. A researcher who undertakes research by involving students is actively promoting student well-being (cf. Eder & Fingerson, 2002; Kostenius, 2008). One the basis of the earlier exploration of 'tact of teaching' and 'being-for-the-world', we argue for the value of 'tact of researching' when giving voice to students, something that is further reflected upon in the next section.

'Tact of Researching' When Giving Voice to Students

'Tact of researching' involves critical reflection on how to conduct research ethically when voicing students' experiences. This research attitude can be connected to underpinning notions of student voice, for example, listening to students, giving them voice, inviting them to actively participate and fostering democratic citizenship (cf. Cook-Sather, 2006; Mitra, 2008; Roberts & Nash, 2009). 'Tact of researching' can include a balancing act between being a distanced and authoritative researcher and a researcher who is close and deeply involved in the students' lives, creating mutual relationships characterised by care and trust (cf. Cook-Sather, 2007; Reinharz, 1979). The hierarchal and authoritative researcher does not focus on the relationships he or she has built during the research and does not wish to have further relationships with the participants, an approach that does not help the students. Such a researcher wants to draw a sharp line between themselves and the participating students. According to this approach, the belief is that it is not a researcher's responsibility to console and care about sad or bullied students, it is the teachers' or school nurses' job. This can seem harsh, but this is a way for the researcher to act professionally and not confuse roles. The caring and deeply involved researcher is characterised by someone who maintains the relationships with the participating students during and after the research. The involved researcher becomes deeply committed with the students, sharing sadness and anxiety, as well as joy and companionship. He or she takes on the role of a therapist and tries to actively solve those students' problems that have arisen during the research. On the basis of the previous argumentation, the distant and authoritative role and the close and deeply involved role can raise ethical issues.

Sensitivity to the research field, relationships between researcher and participant, as well as the researcher's impact on the research setting are some ethical concerns to consider in research (Oliver, 2003). The first role can, from a participatory research paradigm, be seen as being too distant and involves not being sensitive to the participants' views and being (cf. Heron & Reason, 2001). Alternatively, the second role can, from an ethical research standpoint, be viewed as creating overly intimate relationships with participants, with the risk of affecting the research negatively (Oliver, 2003). The researcher's ability to be critical of research findings may be limited and the researcher can confuse the roles of a professional researcher and a private person, resulting in poor scientific research (Forsman, 2002). Involvement and interest in the research topic are important abilities when conducting rigorous research. However, there is a risk of distortions appearing when the researcher's own or others' interests are focused upon at the expense of the research results (*ibid.*). As a response to the preceding described opposing research roles, we want to emphasise that 'tact of researching' denotes flexibility and humility. It involves finding ways to act in the middle ground between the distant and authoritative researcher and the close and involved researcher. This entails listening to students and inviting their participation. It also involves adjusting to the needs and circumstances of the students and at the same time being responsible for undertaking rigorous research.

Conclusion

The student voice movement in Sweden is connected to the general idea of research participants being empowered rather than exploited, particularly if there is a genuine desire from the researcher to listen to what they have to say and thereby showing a concern with the issue at hand (Bergmark & Kostenius, 2009, Taguchi, 2010; Wennergren, 2007). The ideals contained in the United Nations Convention on the Rights of the Child (CRC, 1989) fit well with the value of democratic fostering, which is deeply rooted in the Swedish culture (Englund, 2005; Quennerstedt, 2009, 2010). The awareness of article no. 12 in the convention about the obligation and importance of taking on children's perspectives and listening to them is also well anchored in the field of educational research in Sweden. Nevertheless, the fact that researchers are aware of, and agree with, the basic message in the convention does not imply that researchers in Sweden focus on actively inviting students to participate in and influence the research process. In this sense, it involves transforming the intentions of the conventions into research practice within the educational field. There are certainly a number of reasons why this transformation is frequently not achieved. These can, for example, involve economic constraints and time limits, which lead students to be assigned the role of informants rather than active participants (Alerby & Kostenius, 2011).

As seen in this chapter, the focus on voicing students' experiences and active participation as well as citizenship in Swedish schools has a cultural, historical and political background. Underpinning notions of student voice are, as expressed earlier, common features in the Swedish educational system, with its emphasis on education as a place for fostering democratic principles. This calls attention to the importance of exploring cultural fundamental values of education and educational research in different countries. Such a reflection can increase knowledge of how to find new ways for voicing students' experiences within and outside national borders, as well as within education and educational research. Teachers, researchers and students can learn from one another through bringing forward different cultural characteristics enriching the diverse body of student voice.

To conclude, we argue for the value of 'tact of researching' when adhering to student voice research. Using 'tact of researching' encourages acting as an enabling researcher, which includes awareness of one's role and critical reflection in connection to ethical values such as empowerment issues. This, in combination with actively meeting participants and taking individual responsibility for situations arising from the research process are the core of the proposed research attitude in this chapter. In line with Graham and Fitzgerald (2010) we emphasise relationships in research that are oriented towards students' experiences, their self-understanding and individual agency, accompanied by the researchers' self-awareness and sensitivity. 'Tact of researching' entails conscious reflection and action, which can take place regardless of cultural context. Interestingly, there has been an increase in the number of researchers around the world who see the benefit of involving students in research (Ghaye et al., 2008; Mitra, 2005; Robinson & Taylor, 2007; Rudduck & Flutter, 2004). This offers opportunities for being an ethically aware researcher working within the field of student voice both nationally and internationally.

References

Alerby, E. (2000). A way of visualising children's and young people's thoughts about the environment: A study of drawings. *Environmental Education Research, 6*, 205–222.

Alerby, E. (2003). During the break we had fun: A study concerning pupil's experience of school. *Educational Research, 45*, 17–28.

Alerby, E., & Kostenius, C. (2011). 'Dammed Taxi Cab' — How silent communication in questionnaires can be understood and used to give voice to children's experiences. *International Journal of Research & Method in Education, 34*(2), 1–14.

Almqvist, L., Eriksson, L., & Granlund, M. (2004). Delaktighet i skolaktiviteter: Ett systemteoretisk perspektiv [Partcipation in school activities: A system theoretical perspective]. In: A. Gustavsson (Ed.), *Delaktighetens språk [The language of participation]*. Lund: Studentlitteratur.

Bergmark, U. (2009). *Building an ethical learning community in schools*. Doctoral thesis, Luleå University of Technology, Luleå.

Bergmark, U., & Kostenius, C. (2009). Listen to me when I have something to say: Students' participation in research for sustainable school improvement. *Improving Schools, 12*(3), 249–260.

Biesta, G. (2006). *Bortom lärandet: Demokratisk utbildning för en mänsklig framtid [Beyond learning: Democratic education for a human future]*. Lund: Studentlitteratur.

Booth, B., Faugier, J., Rundell, S., Fawcett-Henesy, A., Pitkeathley, J., & Andrews, J. (1991). Power can be healthy. *Nursing Times, 38*, 31.

Coad, J., & Evans, R. (2007). Reflections on practical approaches to involving children and young people in the data analysis process. *Children & Society, 22,* 41–52.

Cook-Sather, A. (2006). Sound, presence, and power: "Student voice" in educational research and reform. *Curriculum Inquiry, 36*(4), 359–390.

Cook-Sather, A. (2007). Translating researchers: Re-imagining the work of investigating students' experiences in school. In: D. Thiessen & A. Cook-Sather (Eds), *International handbook of student experience in elementary and secondary school.* Dordrecht: Springer.

CRC. (1989). United Nations Conventions on the Rights of the Child. Retrieved from http://www2.ohchr.org/english/law/crc.htm. Accessed on March 18, 2011.

Danell, M. (2006). *På tal om elevinflytande — Hur elevers inflytande formas i pedagogers samtal [The speech of student participation — How students' influence is shaped in teachers' conversations].* Doctoral thesis, Luleå University of Technology, Luleå.

Eder, D., & Fingerson, L. (2002). Interviewing children and adolescents. In: J. K. Gubrium & J. A. Holstein (Eds), *Handbook of interview research.* London: Sage.

Elvstrand, H. (2009). *Delaktighet i skolans vardagsarbete [Participation in every-day practice in schools].* Doctorial thesis, Linköping University, Linköping.

Englund, T. (2005). *Läroplanens och skolkunskapens politiska dimension [The political dimensions of curricula and school knowledge].* Lund: Studentlitteratur.

Forsman, B. (2002). *Vetenskap och moral [Science and morality].* Nora: Nya Doxa.

Ghaye, T., Melander-Wikman, A., Kisare, M., Chambers, P., Bergmark, U., Kostenius, C., & Lillyman, S. (2008). Participatory and appreciative action and reflection (PAAR) — Democratizing reflective practices. *Reflective Practice, 9*(4), 361–397.

Graham, A., & Fitzgerald, R. (2010). Progressing children's participation: Exploring the potential of a dialogical turn. *Childhood, 17,* 343–359.

Hägglund, S. (2001). FN:s konvention om barnets rättigheter — En källa till forskningsfrågor om barns villkor [UN Conventions on the Rights of the Child — A source for research questions about children's conditions]. *Utbildning & Demokrati, 10,* 3–8.

Heron, J., & Reason, P. (2001). The practice of co-operative inquiry: Research 'with' rather than 'on' people. In: P. Reason & H. Bradbury (Eds), *Handbook of action research: Participative inquiry and practice.* London: Sage.

Kirby, P. (2001). Participatory research in schools. *Forum, 43*(2), 74–77.

Kostenius, C. (2008). *Giving voice and space to children in health promotion.* Doctoral thesis, Luleå University of Technology, Luleå.

Kostenius, C., & Öhrling, K. (2006). Schoolchildren from the north sharing their lived experience of health and well-being. *Journal of Qualitative Studies of Health and Well-Being, 1,* 226–235.

Kostenius, C., & Öhrling, K. (2008). Friendship is like an extra parachute: Reflections on the way schoolchildren share their lived experiences of well-being through drawings. *Reflective Practice, 9*(1), 23–35.

Lévinas, E. (1969). *Totality and infinity: An essay on exteriority.* Pittsburgh, PA: Duquesne University Press.

Lindahl, M. (2005). Children's right to democratic upbringings. *International Journal of Early Childhood, 37,* 33–47.

Melander-Wikman, A. (2007). *Empowerment in living practice. Mobile ICT a tool for empowerment of elderly people in home health care.* Licentiate thesis, Luleå University of Technology, Luleå.

Mitra, D. L. (2005). Adults advising youth: Leading while getting out of the way. *Educational Administration Quarterly, 41*(3), 520–553.

Mitra, D. L. (2008). Balancing power in communities of practice: An examination of increasing student voice through school-based youth-adult partnerships. *Journal of Educational Change, 9*(3), 221–324.

Morrow, V., & Richards, M. (1996). The ethics of social research with children: An overview. *Children & Society, 10*, 90–105.

Näsman, E. (2004). Barn, barndom och barns rättigheter [Children, youth and children's rights]. In: L. Olsen (Ed.), *Barns makt [The power of children]*. Uppsala: Justus förlag.

Oliver, P. (2003). *The student's guide to research ethics*. Berkshire: Open University Press.

Peshkin, A. (1988). In search of subjectivity. One's own. *Educational Researcher, 17*(7), 17–21.

Quennerstedt, A. (2009). The rights of the child and the rights of parents — An act of balance in the Convention on the Rights of the Child. *Journal of Human Rights, 8*(2), 162–176.

Quennerstedt, A. (2010). Den politiska konstruktionen av barnets rättigheter i utbildning [The political construction of children's rights in education]. *Pedagogisk forskning i Sverige [Pedagogical Research in Sweden], 15*(3/4), 119–141.

Reinharz, S. (1979). *On becoming a social scientist: From survey research and participant observation to experiential analysis*. San Francisco, CA: Jossey-Bass.

Roberts, A., & Nash, J. (2009). Enabling students to participate in school improvement through a students as researchers programme. *Improving Schools, 12*(2), 174–187.

Robinson, C., & Taylor, C. (2007). Theorizing student voice: Values and perspectives. *Improving Schools, 10*(5), 5–17.

Roth, K. (2000). *Democracy, education and citizenship: Towards a theory on the education of deliberative democratic citizens*. Stockholm: HLS Förlag.

Rudduck, J., & Flutter, J. (2004). *How to improve your school: Giving pupils a voice*. London: Continuum.

Sehlberg, G. (1999). *Elevinflytande i lärandet [Student participation in learning processes]*. Luleå: Luleå University of Technology.

SFS. (2008). SFS 2008:192 Lag om ändring i lagen (2003:460) om etikprövning av forskning som avser människor [Law on change in law (2003:460) about ethical review of research concerning human beings].

Swedish National Agency for Education. (2010). Läroplan för grundskolan, förskoleklassen och fritidshemmet, Lgr2011 (U2010/5865/S) [Curriculum for the compulsory school, preschool class and leisure-time centres], Stockholm, Ministry of Education.

Taguchi, H. L. (2010). *Going beyond the theory/practice divide in early childhood education: Introducing an intra-active pedagogy*. London; New York, NY: Routledge.

UNESCO. (2011). Code of conduct social science research UNESCO. Retrieved from http://www.unesco.org/new/fileadmin/MULTIMEDIA/HQ/SHS/pdf/Soc_Sci_Code.pdf. Accessed on January 25, 2011.

van Manen, M. (1991). *The tact of teaching: The meaning of pedagogical thoughtfulness*. Albany, NY: State University of New York Press.

Wennergren, A.-C. (2007). *Dialogkompetens i skolans vardag. En aktionsforskningsstudie i hörselklassmiljö [Dialogue competence in every-day practice in schools. An action research study in classes for children with impaired hearing]*. Doctoral thesis, Luleå University of Technology, Luleå.

Chapter 32

Students' Experiences of Enquiry-Based Learning: Chinese Student Voices on Changing Pedagogies

Wei Kan

Abstract

It is clear that while much has been written about the achievements and doubts of current educational reforms in China — particularly the introduction of inquiry-based learning — little is known about what students make of these changes. This chapter reports on a qualitative study, conducted in 2008, which explored 15 pupils who were mostly aged between 15 and 16 and their views of the pedagogy change in Beijing. The study enlisted the students as 'co-researchers', who were both the subjects of the enquiry, and partners in its processes. A focus group research method has been employed, in which students from each of the three different types of high school in Beijing were given 'voices'. The research reveals that there appears to have been little real change in teaching and learning methods in urban and rural school classrooms. Students themselves, teachers and parents from 'ordinary' school (see footnote 2 on page 410) systems were resistant to the changes, which did not meet their needs for entry into higher education and to the professions. In contrast, new teaching and learning methods were found to be better accepted, though it was only regarded as an individual improvement strategy, rather than a co-operative learning approach, by those top high schools students in Beijing, where it bestowed further advantages on an already privileged group. The students' voices indicated that, in the context of Chinese schools, there is a powerful pedagogical culture that is so ingrained that it is resistant to change.

Keywords: China; pedagogy; constructivism; institutional change

Introduction

Over the past 10 years, curriculum reform in China has been centrally implemented to address the competing needs of the country as the previous pedagogy in China was regarded as having 'excessive emphasis … upon learning by rote and neglect of practical studies and of acquisition and application of skills" (MoEd, 2001, p. 7). New pedagogic changes focus on producing cooperative ability, an interest in inquiry and intellectual curiosity, to meet the needs of a technological society. 'Symposium on Curriculum Reform of School Education (trial edition)' (p. 12), issued by the Ministry of Education in China in 2001 calling for a change in the pupil–teacher relationship, in the case of China, has been found to be very teacher dominated. This change could only take place, as new pedagogic ways, such as inquiry-based instructional methods,[1] learner-centred pedagogy were to be adopted by teachers and used in lessons. It further suggests that: 'wherever possible throughout the curriculum, instruction should include project work and an applied approach to solving problems' (Zhong, 2002).

Influenced by constructivism, the notion of inquiry-based learning that has emerged emphasizes Chinese pupils' active construction of knowledge by relating new elements of knowledge to already existing cognitive structures. As the symposium states, 'inquiry-based instruction is a new challenge for teachers and pupils … It requires pupils to actively participate in realistic problem situations reflecting the kind of experiences typically encountered in the discipline in classrooms and conduct research according to the theme they choose, the plan they make and, then draw conclusions on their own, with instruction from teachers as needed' (MoEd, 2001, p. 24).

Since inquiry-based learning was launched, most classroom research stressed the rationality and the necessity of the new pedagogy, which claimed would radically shift the ways that teaching and learning are enacted. However, this study shows that any expectations on pedagogic changes are remote from present practice.

It is not surprising that pupils from different level schools in Beijing[2] would come to express diverse opinions and experiences. One common strand that

---

1. Educational reform in China had attempted to introduce a series of new pedagogic concepts, such as inquiry-based learning, group work and projects design. Inquiry-based learning could be described as: (a) emphasizing interaction between pupils and teachers in class, e.g. by encouraging pupils to engage in group discussion, team work and (b) highlighting autonomy of learning and positive inquiry through all kinds of resources such as the Internet and libraries, and through activities such as social research (MoEd, 2001).

2. Secondary schools in China are divided into 'top' and 'ordinary' schools. Designated key schools are schools distinguished from ordinary schools by their academic reputation and are generally located in the urban areas. Their original purpose was to quicken the training of highly needed talent for China's modernization since 1950s, but another purpose was to set up exemplary schools to improve teaching in all schools. This stratified structure has given key schools numerous privileges on enrolling pupils with high scores and assigning high-quality teachers during 1980s and 1990s. Although MoEd implored educationalists to stop using the term 'key schools' at the end of 1990s, for those top schools, accounting for 20% of that among secondary schools nationwide are still maintained under the name of 'demonstration schools' which are given more resources, enabled to provide higher standards of facilities, assigned better school buildings and allocated more academically able students. Meanwhile, namely, those 'ordinary schools' had been renamed as 'characteristic schools' and they are still confronted with the obvious differences on pupils' achievements and the quality of teachers.

interweaves the interview transcripts and pupils' comments is that they were all expressed by students' experiences on pedagogic change rather than the views of curriculum reform from teachers, school administrators or researchers. In this qualitative study, students' experiences of inquiry-based learning in two different types of secondary schools (so-called the 'top schools' and 'ordinary schools' with the gaps on pupils' achievements and the quality of staff) were examined. The goal of this investigation was to provide the entire school community with insights into reasons that the extent and direction of curriculum change is not always consistent with the intentions of policy initiatives. Specifically, the study was guided by the following research questions: (a) How has the introduction of the new pedagogy altered the students' learning experiences; (b) in what ways has the teaching and learning strategy affected students' needs and teachers' roles and (c) what are the broader implications of the change to the new pedagogy?

Student Voices Studies in Mainland China

Echoing studies on pupil voice in the United Kingdom and the United States, some Chinese researchers in recent years have begun to rethink pupils' perspectives, albeit in a limited way. Lai (2003) advocates that in the new curriculum should be linked with pupils' own experiences. Other studies lend further weight to the need to place greater emphasis on the views of pupils and teachers (Ding, 2002). In particular, some studies (e.g. Zhong, 2004) of pupil needs from the perspectives of educational psychology have emerged in China, which argue that pupils come to the class with a pre-existing view of what 'appropriate' teaching and learning should be like in their classroom, which has been shown to apply also in some western studies (Morgan, 2007; Rudduck & McIntyre, 2007). Pupils tend to evaluate new teaching methods in the light of their own preconceptions and expectancies, which is part of their classroom needs (Feng, 2001). Dissonance or inconsistency is likely to occur, if the introduced pedagogic innovations are inconsistent with previously held beliefs.

Underpinning the ignorance of student voice by Chinese educationists and researchers are challenges to the ingrained dualistic acceptance of 'teacher' and 'pupil' and to the assumption that 'educators stand above their pupils and young people themselves have no correct judgment from their own "voice"' (Hao, 2005). Studies of pupil voice, particularly empirical research, are noticeably sparse in Chinese educational literature. Questions not yet addressed include the means by which researchers might use the breadth of pupils' voices that are heard, and the proposed outcomes of seeking pupil voice. Therefore, it has significance for Chinese educational reform that this study places emphasis on the role of pupil experience and response during curriculum reform and the implementation of the new teaching strategy.

Methodology

Participants

Fielding (2007) emphasizes that there is a need now to move beyond the notion of 'voice', which has several limitations as 'a metaphor for student engagement' (p. 306). Also, Arnot and Reay observe that pupils talk differently about their learning in response to particular teaching methodologies in front of researchers (Arnot & Reay, 2007, p. 317). In this respect, adults will often act as the gatekeepers for children's voices, the quality of their mediation determining the form in which those pupil voices can be expressed (Thompsona, 2009, p. 672).

The present study, however, is different with those studies that borrow pupils' voice as adult researchers' message. It is a multi-site qualitative study exploring pupils' perspectives on pedagogical change. Inspired by the contemporary 'pupil voice' movement, the researcher has attempted to encourage pupils to investigate the practice in their own classrooms. The form of research is the involvement of high school pupils as co-researchers with the researcher himself.

Procedures

This research project studied the introduction of inquiry-based learning under the conditions of curriculum reform. Fifteen pupils who come from two 13–18 secondary schools were involved in the research process. School A is a top-school with a high reputation. In contrast, School B lay within the city boundaries and was known as a challenging school. There is little sense in which these 15 participating young people (7 pupils from School A organized as Focus group No. 1 and 8 pupils from B formed the Focus group No. 2) could be said to represent the full range of opinion about pupils in Beijing. Focus group discussion began in the middle of September, 2008, after the researcher spent two weeks on getting acquainted with the members of an inquiry-based learning group at each school. As Krueger and Casey (2000) point out, the priority for focus group research strategies is to create a permissive environment so that pupils can share their ideas and comment on their own experiences or others stories.

Gradually, pupils were interested in participating in this co-research initiative after the researcher explained the whole scheme and research questions. It took the researcher nearly 40 min on each day to develop sub-questions with focus group pupils at the end of September 2008. The step was for the pupils to clearly understand what they need to know and make sure the pupils are involved in the research process.

Data Analysis

The data analysis began in the middle of December 2008, after the researcher spent two months getting acquainted with the members of the inquiry-based learning group at each school. The step was for the students to clearly understand what they need to know and make sure the students are involved in the research process. In the following month, the researcher observed these focus group students in science and mathematics classes and then interviewed them individually. These interviews generated different perspectives on the same issues which took place in the classroom and group activities. The 15 student researchers subsequently read over transcribed interviews and their own journals and highlighted comments that seemed to best represent the experiences in the new pedagogy when they were asked to design the projects, collect the data and present their studies. They also provided a written summary analysis in which they identified prevalent themes and patterns across all the interviews they conducted. However, the notion of 'student as co-researcher' did present several potential limitations. Although the students were trained in conducting interviews, the possibility that interviewees may have provided biased responses because of their relationships with the student researchers should be noted. Also, the students selected for interviews may not be reflective of the experiences of typical students' learning experience at three schools.

Findings

Since the primary focus of this study is on pupils' experiences of the changed teaching/learning approach, the co-research results are reported here. Pupils from School A explained how inquiry-based learning stimulated and enhanced their learning by valuing personal opinion. Lessons became more enjoyable and less boring when they were not continually directed down set learning pathways. Designing the project and solving the real problems in their life offered a broader range of ideas and rich opportunities for School A pupils.

However, to those low-attainers in School B, inquiry-based learning seemed to work as the 'superficial alternative' (Interview/Yu/29/Oct/2008) for them. They did not entirely engage in the inquiry-based learning and lacked enthusiasm.

It took the two focus groups nearly two months to complete the analysis of the selected material with the researcher. More than 20 topics were summarized by the student co-researchers, covering the three research questions, concerning pupils' experiences, their needs and teachers' roles and the broader implications for education.

Students' Needs

> Now, the class is not controlled by teachers and we are seen as ... researchers, right? Because we have time to discuss our own questions. Mr. Cheng, Mrs. Qi, they are excellent and encourage you to put your individual views and then others could add their ideas or change it in some way to come to a more satisfying result. [Interview/Li/27/Oct/2008]

The School A pupils who were successful and interested in inquiry-based learning defined themselves as 'scientists' and 'researchers', who liked to conduct research working with groups. The independent thinking and discussion, in this sense, gave them space to feel good about themselves as learners and to see themselves as 'capable' in a learning community. Meanwhile, students said they sensed the low expectations that certain teachers held of them when they were involved in group discussions. One of the pupils discussed her experiences with a student co-researcher:

> It seems that some teachers always care about those high-score students. They made me see that I could not do well [Interview/Ai, Year 11, top-level high school/24/Nov/2008]

In ordinary schools, teachers who were successful in orchestrating inquiry-based learning pushed students to develop greater confidence in teaching. Students challenged the classroom context when they were involved in inquiry-based learning. They needed to maintain their motivations and responsibilities to succeed. They also asked for some teacher abandon traditional teacher-centered instructional methods for more participatory practices, the suggestions most frequently provided by the students' co-researchers including: (1) more group work, (2) more discussion and freedom of asking questions and (3) more activities and projects designed by students themselves.

Teachers' Role

According to the requirement of inquiry-based learning, teachers should play the roles of 'collaborators', 'facilitators' and 'friends' of students in classroom (Mcnallya & Martinb, 1998). Although the majority of focus group pupils from top school found that their teachers' role had changed, the summaries from co-researchers have indicated that pupils from ordinary schools thought that the principle roles of teachers were still that of a 'guru of knowledge':

> It appears that they know about the small-group discussions not being useful, so we only had a few group-work activities this semester. Mostly, we just take notes from the blackboard, and teachers say we should grasp the basic knowledge rather than spending too much time on inquiring, which is not a strategy to get high marks in the test. [Interview/Zhao, Year 12, ordinary high school/25/Sep/2008]

This perspective on the teacher's role was congruent with the ordinary school context, where an abundance of prescriptive rules and regulations appeared to be improving pupils' marks. This context may be counter-productive in affecting the shift of teachers' roles in inquiry-based learning.

Educational Context

The third research question concerns the broader implications of the change to inquiry-based learning. Curriculum experts and teachers attempt to transform teaching/learning approaches by coming up with 'empowering' alternatives to traditional learning strategy, but they appear to have neglected the context of learning. Students themselves pointed out that those high attainers from top schools were more likely to be engaged in inquiry-based learning than those of ordinary schools, because the school context reinforced their identities as 'good students' and their performances were acknowledged by teachers. As Yu, one of school co-researchers commented:

> To be honest, this new teaching way (inquired-based learning) might be designed for us, as we are the top school students. We have opportunities to participate in project and access to all kinds of resources [Yu, Year 12, ordinary high school /15/Nov/2008]

The classroom context guaranteed that these able pupils obtained immediate and frequent feedback on their work. Since they frequently had to report the results of their work in front of the class, or to engage in dialogue with the teacher, the opportunity for feedback was effectively built into the new learner identities they developed.

Conclusion

The study has the potential to make a significant contribution to an understanding of complex pedagogic change by studying how students make sense of inquiry-based learning, which had been introduced into the Chinese classroom. In particular, focusing on the student voice has demonstrated the importance of investigating the perspectives of learners themselves who bring experiences and attitudes that indicate the risk of oversimplification of curriculum reform.

How can the voices of students inform teachers and school administrators in ways that will promote pedagogic change? The findings from this study were presented to schools at the beginning of 2009. Although some teachers and administrators felt that the research framed young people's views as unwarranted attacks on new teaching approaches, most said the studies were thought provoking explanations on how students were experiencing their classrooms. Some teachers admitted that it was the first time for them to rethink their roles and performances in classrooms after they read students' views.

Not only is the process of listening to student voices important for studying the various responses of implementation to new pedagogic strategies but it is also vital as a research methodology to promote curriculum reform. Secondary schools must work with students to be more actively improving inquiry-based learning. The school will need to consider the quality of teachers and evaluation systems that students called for, which could entail significant effort to implement. The introduction of inquiry-based learning must reconcile students' purposes and preferences for learning, the social context, differing role expectations and the conceptualization of learning — all having potential for disagreement and clashes, yet all having powerful influences upon learning outcomes. Any attempt to change the process of 'cultural production' and to alter students' classroom experiences may result in varied responses from them, even including some being seriously hampered by learner resistance. The success of inquiry-based learning depends on pupils' capacity for accommodation and change. Possible resistance and problems should be considered and investigated by school administrators and curriculum experts. Without an understanding of the reasons for resistance to the implementation of inquiry-based learning, attempts to enforce it may be extremely harmful to educational reform.

References

Arnot, M., & Reay, D. (2007). A sociology of pedagogic voice: power, inequality and pupil consultation. *Discourse: Studies in the Cultural Politics of Education, 28*(3), 311–325.

Ding, G. (2002). Narrative research in educational reform. *China Educational Research Quarter, 3*(2), 3–14.

Feng, T. S. (2001). Objectives of current curriculum reform in secondary school. Educational Reference, Shanghai, Vol. 7, No. 3, pp. 92–106.

Fielding, M. (2007). Beyond 'voice': New roles, relations and contexts in researching with young people. *Discourse: Studies in the Cultural Politics of Education, 28*(3), 301–310.

Hao, J. R. (2005). Learning to listening pupils' voices. Education in Shanxi, No. 9. pp. 17–19.

Krueger, R. A., & Casey, M. A. (2000). *Focus groups: A practical guide for applied research* (3rd ed.). Thousand Oaks, CA: Sage Publications.

Lai, X. Q. (2003). The inquiry-based learning assessment and new idea. *Academic Journal of Guangxi Educational Institute, 14*(1): 24–27.

Mcnallya, P., & Martinb, S. (1998). Support and challenge in learning to teach: The role of the mentor. *Asia-Pacific Journal of Teacher Education, 26*(1).

Morgan, B. (2007). *Consulting pupils about classroom teaching and learning; policy, practice and response in one school.* Doctor of Philosophy thesis, University of Cambridge.

MoEd (Ministry of Education) (2001). *China education development statistics 2005.* Beijing: High Education Press.

Rudduck, J., & McIntyre, D. (2007). *Improving learning through consulting pupils.* London: Routledge.

Thompsona, P. (2009). Consulting secondary school pupils about their learning. *Oxford Review of Education, 35*(6), 671–687.

Zhong, Q. Q. (2002). Inquiry based learning: significance, values and misunderstanding. *Education Research, 21*(6): 4–7.

Zhong, Q. Q. (2004). Debate about the old pedagogy with some specialists. *Academic Journal of Northeast Normal University, 7*(4), 4–11.

Chapter 33

Political Learning through the Prefigurative: The Case of the Brazilian Landless Movement

Tristan McCowan

Abstract

Latin America has been the site of a number of experiments in participatory democracy in recent years, involving social movements, progressive local governments and community organisations. This chapter explores one of these experiences, the Landless Movement of Brazil, which works for agrarian reform and has established a large number of rural communities based on principles of cooperativism and egalitarianism. The movement also runs a large number of schools, following the ideas of Paulo Freire, and aiming to develop political awareness among students as a means to social transformation. This case is assessed through the lens of the 'prefigurative' — the embodiment of political ideals within action and organisation in the here and now. Educational work in the Landless Movement shows high levels of integration of the fundamental values of radical democracy within its everyday processes, with students playing a meaningful role in shaping pedagogy, curriculum and management, as well as forging opportunities for political participation outside the school. Nevertheless, there are some constraints on students' participation and construction of their own distinctive political vision, both from the influence of patterns of traditional schooling, and the distinctive dynamics of the movement. Despite these constraints, the Landless Movement provides a significant illustration of radical transformations that can be achieved within formal education.

Keywords: Brazil; democratic education; participation; prefigurative; social movements

Introduction

If Latin America is a region of contradictions, this is no less true in the sphere of participation. Although the countries comprising this region have historically been characterised by colonisation, rule by small elites and systematic marginalisation of workers and indigenous peoples, they have also been sites of radical democracy and participatory innovations that have been focal points of worldwide attention. In some ways, the latter can be viewed as a response to the former, and certainly the vigorous assertion of civil society and democratic processes from the 1980s was a direct response to the removal of democracy during the military dictatorships that spread across the region in the 1970s.

Education has been a particularly dynamic sphere of participatory action. Community groups, political movements, trades unions, local authorities and in some cases national governments have developed innovative forms both within and outside the mainstream education system (Barrón Pastor, 2010; Kane, 2001; Portillo & Reyes, 2006; Starr, Martínez-Torres, & Rosset, 2011). In some cases these participatory approaches have stemmed from constructivist views of learning, whereas in others they have been based on a more radical political vision, aiming for social transformation and the emancipation of oppressed groups. In the latter cases, the ideas of Paulo Freire (1972; 1994) have been particularly significant, and his notions of *dialogue* and *conscientization* have underpinned the work of numerous experiences of 'popular education' across the region.

Brazil, the birthplace of Freire, has seen many examples of radical participatory practice in education (e.g. Gandin, 2006; Ghanem, 1998; King-Calnek, 2006; Myers, 2008). This chapter will focus on the Landless Movement, the most influential of the Brazilian social movements emerging since the end of the dictatorship in 1985.

Prefigurative Lens

Why should we value student voice and participation in school affairs? Justifications vary between instrumental approaches (such as positive effects on academic performance) and intrinsic approaches (such as the entitlement to have a say in decision-making that affects an individual or group in question). One approach that questions the basis of purely instrumental rationales is to view participation through a *prefigurative* lens. In this approach, strategies are not adopted so as to bring about a democratic society at some future point in time: instead participatory democracy is practised in the here and now.

As Boggs (1978, p. 2) states: prefiguration is 'the embodiment, within the ongoing political practice of a movement, of those forms of social relations, decision-making, culture and human experience that are the ultimate goal'. In consequentialist forms of political action, means can be in tension with the ends, in that hierarchical organisation and violence are used to achieve a peaceful, non-hierarchical society. In contrast, prefigurative forms of political organisation aim to embody the values of the desired society within their activities, with 'the pursuit of utopian goals ... recursively built into the movement's operation and organisational style' (Buechler, 2000, p. 207).

Prefigurative practice has been evident in a range of experiences, particularly since the 1960s, including feminist, anarchist and peace movements (e.g. Breines, 1982; Epstein, 1991; Franks, 2006; Rowbotham, 1979; Woodin, 2007). Although school represents a challenging context in which to introduce these forms of practice, there have also been experiences in formal education, as documented by Fielding (1997, 2007) for example. This chapter assesses one current experience of the prefigurative in formal education — the schools of the Landless Movement — drawing on findings from a qualitative study (McCowan, 2010) of the movement in the state of Rio Grande do Sul. This state — the southernmost of Brazil, with a strong agricultural tradition — was the location for the founding of the movement, and is still a key locus of its activity. Two focus schools were selected as sites for in-depth research: the first, 'Treviso', located in a remote rural area of the state, and the second, 'Salinas', also in a rural area, but near the state capital.

The Landless Movement

The Movement of Landless Rural Workers (MST-*Movimento dos Trabalhadores Rurais Sem Terra*) has grown rapidly since its official founding in 1984, moving out from the south to cover the full expanse of the Brazilian territory. The main aim of the movement is to bring about agrarian reform, addressing the severe inequalities of land ownership (1.6% of owners control 47% of the land, whereas there are some 4.5 million landless peasants [Brandford & Rocha, 2002; Caldart, 2000]). Central to the movement's activities is land occupation, whereby a group of families squats on unused agricultural land in one of the large estates. An *acampamento* (camp) is formed, in which high levels of organisation and co-operation are required to sustain the itinerant community. If the families win the right to stay, the *acampamento* then becomes an *assentamento* (settlement) and they can begin to farm their own land, which they do either individually or collectively.

Soon after the first settlements were established it became clear that some form of educational provision would be necessary for the children of the landless. Furthermore, a large proportion of the adults were themselves illiterate and needed to develop basic skills to improve their agricultural work and enable effective political participation. A few primary schools emerged, along with adult literacy classes, staffed mainly by those few members of the community who had completed school. After struggles with local authorities, communities managed to have their schools officially recognised, and thereby gain state funding and provision of teachers and materials. Today there exists a network of more than 1,500 schools which have provided for 160,000 children, many of whom otherwise could have expected no more than a few years of poor quality primary education (MST, 2004). There are also many thousands of students in youth and adult education, and provision in pre-school education, technical secondary courses, teacher education and other HE courses in partnership with established universities. (This chapter, however, will focus on primary/lower secondary schools.)

These quantitative gains are significant in themselves. Yet the aim of the MST is to transform the fundamental nature of education as well:

> Faced with the tradition of an elitist, authoritarian, bureaucratic, content-heavy, 'banking' school, with a narrow and pragmatist conception of education, [we have] the challenge of constructing a popular, democratic, flexible, dialogical school, a space for a holistic human development in movement. (MST, 2004, p. 15)

Participatory Approaches in MST education

Participation for the MST is linked to the Freirean notion of becoming 'subjects of history', of having the capacity for transforming the world, and being aware of that capacity. In accordance with this commitment, a fundamental principle of MST education is that the students are fully involved in the educational process, not only in terms of expressing their views in the classroom, but also of participating in the processes of decision-making within the institution:

> The big and even the little activities of day-to-day life in the school must be planned collectively ... Where the planning is concentrated in a few heads (from top to bottom) there is no democracy ... (MST, 1995, p. 8)

The most radical examples of student participation are seen in the MST teacher education courses (Caldart, 1997), but it is also evident in primary education (McCowan, 2003, 2009). Ideally there is election of headteachers and a school council, although these features depend on municipal or state legislation. The school council, which has teacher, student and community representatives, is the highest body of management, with responsibilities for financial resources, the school calendar, accountability and the elaboration of the politico-pedagogical plan.

This emphasis on participation is also built into the pedagogy. *Dialogue* — in the Freirean sense — is one of the principles on which MST educational activities are built:

> [N]o one learns through somebody else, but also nobody is educated alone ... [I]t is not only the teacher-student relationship which educates: it is also the relationship between students and between teachers ... Everybody learning and teaching amongst themselves ... The collective educates the collective. (MST, 1999a, p. 23)

Yet how does the MST fare in implementing this vision of participation in practice? Aline,[1] a 14-year-old student, who had studied in other schools in the local town, gave a good indication of the distinctive atmosphere of an MST school:

Aline: I think that if I continued … studying at that school, I wouldn't think in this way … It's like they, they don't teach right, you know. They don't want the children to have a clear vision of what's happening in the country … And here in the [MST] school, it's different. Here in the school you can speak to teachers in the hallway. You can say what you think, you can ask anything about politics and the political parties and so forth … That's why, that's why I like it here more. I think that this school made me grow a lot as a person.

Class councils in the school enable students to resolve their own problems of disputes and disruptive behaviour. Raiza, the student representative at Treviso School, related that the voice of the students was increasingly heard in relation to the facilities and decorations in the school, yet also in bringing changes in teaching styles. She is an example of someone who had developed considerable levels of knowledge and skills through her role in the school (although not all students had such an active role).

Salinas School has two representatives for each class who meet once or twice a month with the headteacher and deputy to discuss student issues. According to deputy headteacher Horácio, 'they have total freedom to criticise the leadership of the school'. However, there were some limits on student influence. Aline describes her experience as class representative in the following way:

Aline: So they [the head and deputy] held a meeting, to see everything that we wanted to change in the school. So we [the students] sat in the classroom, we set aside some time, half an hour … Everyone said what they wanted, so we noted it down and took it to the meeting and discussed it with the teachers there. It was like that.
TM: And did you manage to change anything?
Aline: Yes, we did, we got them to ring the bell for break earlier [laughs]

This does represent a form of student victory, but, as indicated by the student's reaction, represents only a small change in power relations. The limitations of student power are backed up by comments by the younger children at Salinas School:

Cristina: They have a meeting, and we put forward everything, like, the problems of the class. We speak, we discuss everything and gradually find a solution to the problems of the class.

---

1. Pseudonyms have been used for students, staff and schools.

TM: Do they do what you ask for?
Cristina: If it's something okay, here inside which is possible without much
             problem, then they do it.
Paulo: But not everything!
Cristina: Now if we expect something more, I mean, out of the ordinary, then that
             won't do.
TM: Can you give an example of the types of things you ask for in meetings?
Sara: Like, we ask for the day that we're going to celebrate the June festival.

In restricting student action to recreational events, therefore, the structures for
student representation can at times be little different in practise from the less than
radical experiences of school councils in the United Kingdom and elsewhere.

Students also organise themselves in 'work teams'. Time is set aside in the school
day for them to engage in cooperative work such as tending to the vegetable plot and
flowerbeds. The work undertaken both inside and outside school is intended to foster
positive rural values and identity, and for them to gain skills and knowledge in
agricultural techniques. This serves:

> [T]o break the individualist culture in which we are submerged,
> through new relations of work, through sharing out tasks and thinking
> of the welfare of all the families, and not everyone for him or herself.
> (MST, 1999b, p. 7)

In addition, students take responsibility for cleaning their classrooms at the end of
the day. There was a naturalness, efficiency and even enjoyment with which the
students tidied and swept their room after the bell went in Treviso School. There
were also other spaces for participation, such as the 'self-organisation' period in
which students would gather to organise events and other activities, with careful
processes of debate and recording of discussions.

In relation to the gender dimension of participation, classroom observation
showed equal or greater participation of girls than boys in discussions, and
proportions of girls in representative positions were higher than those of boys.
Although there were cases of stereotyping of gender roles, in general MST schools
were challenging the low representation of women in positions of political power in
the wider society. The strong participation of girls was particularly surprising given
the machista values of traditional culture in Rio Grande do Sul.

There are other forms of active political development aside from these instances of
student self-organisation. The MST is emphatic that 'education' cannot be confined
to schools:

> But it is good to bear in mind that the pedagogy which forms new
> social subjects, and which educates human beings, goes beyond the
> school. It is much bigger and involves life as a whole. Some educational
> processes which sustain the Landless identity could never be realised
> within the school. (MST, 1999b, p. 6)

Community involvement is one example of this reaching beyond school. Students are involved in organising cultural activities, contributing to the preservation of community history and visiting other settlements, camps, schools, cooperatives and historical sites. In addition, students participate in 'pedagogical camps', which model the land occupations engaged in by their parents and allow a space to reflect on the history of the community and discuss overarching aims for the school. However, the MST is distinctive in its encouragement not just of community involvement but also political activity at local and national levels. Examples of this form of activity are participation in the occupation of land and establishment of *acampamentos*, occupation of public buildings and participation in protest marches. The participation of students in MST mobilizations is justified by the need to 'provide students with the means to widen their horizons, thereby allowing a different reading of their own reality' (MST, 1999b, p. 43). In view of the importance of activities conducted outside the school, the MST urges schools to organise themselves in such a way that students are not disadvantaged through possible absences, and that the experiences outside the school are shared with the other students.

The headteacher Ruth highlighted participation in the movement's mobilisations:

> The school does not distance itself from this struggle. Children initiate campaigns … the school is in constant movement. Always campaigning for teachers, for the quality of school transport, the widening of the civic space, our children are always in this debate.

During the period of research, students at Salinas organised their own protest at the town hall to obtain reliable transport to and from the school. Another example was a drama presentation prepared in Treviso School for the celebration of the founding of the local town, aiming to help those outside the landless community understand the struggle.

Student participation in the MST, therefore, is strong in relation to the community's collective construction of the curriculum and in instances such as the work teams. There are also democratic representative bodies, although these encounter limitations on their power in practice. Schools have a very strong engagement with political action outside.

Conclusion

The MST, therefore, shows prefiguration clearly in its educational practice, by embodying democratic relations and structures in the school experience, rather than only equipping students with the knowledge and skills needed for future participation. Importantly, representative bodies for students are embedded in a deeper democratisation, involving fundamental aspects of teacher–student relations and decision-making over teaching and learning, in conjunction with participatory structures for teachers and the local community. This is important in order to avoid fragmented instances of student participation leading to trivialisation and tokenism. It is also important that democratic experiences within the school are linked to wider political action outside it. Lastly, the democratisation is based on a vision of social transformation, rather than the insertion of young people into a rigid and unchangeable political and economic system.

However, as shown earlier, these initiatives are not without their problems. There is always a risk of representative bodies channelling student demands towards less threatening areas such as recreation times and clothing, rather than curriculum and management. In addition, the initiatives have other challenges of implementation — such as gaining the active support of parents and local communities — that this chapter has not been able to address. Nevertheless, they serve to illustrate an orientation for student participation that goes beyond tokenistic forms and instrumental, non-democratic rationales.

Given that MST schools are located within the public system, and funded by local governments, this experience also shows what is possible within mainstream education. Latin America provides contradictory evidence in this regard: at the same time scenarios of neglect and discrimination on the part of the authorities, and others of extraordinary popular innovation and courage. It is the challenge of the prefigurative that we grasp in this way the nettle of the undemocratic school systems in which we find ourselves, and create pockets of democratic experience that with time will grow.

References

Barrón Pastor, J. (2010). Globalisation perspectives and cultural exclusion in Mexican higher education. In: E. Unterhalter & V. Carpentier (Eds), *Global inequalities and higher education: Whose interests are we serving?* London: Palgrave Macmillan.

Boggs, C. (1978). Marxism, prefigurative communism, and the problem of workers' control. *Radical America*, 11/12(1), 99–122.

Brandford, S., & Rocha, J. (2002). *Cutting the wire*. London: Latin American Bureau.

Breines, W. (1982). *Community and organization in the New Left, 1962–1968: The great refusal.* New York: Praeger.

Buechler, S. (2000). *Social movements in advanced capitalism: The political economy and cultural construction of social activism.* Oxford: Oxford University Press.

Caldart, R. S. (1997). *Educação em Movimento: Formação de Educadoras e Educadores no MST*. Petrópolis: Editora Vozes.

Caldart, R. S. (2000). *Pedagogia do Movimento Sem Terra: a Escola é Mais que Escola.* Petrópolis: Editora Vozes.

Epstein, B. (1991). *Political protest and cultural revolution: Nonviolent direct action in the 1970s and 1980s.* Berkeley, CA: University of California Press.

Fielding, M. (1997). Beyond school effectiveness and school improvement: Lighting the slow fuse of possibility. *Curriculum Journal*, 8(1), 7–27.

Fielding, M. (2007). On the necessity of radical state education: Democracy and the common school. *Journal of Philosophy of Education*, 41(4), 539–558.

Franks, B. (2006). *Rebel alliances: The means and ends of contemporary British anarchisms.* Edinburgh: AK Press.

Freire, P. (1972). *Pedagogy of the oppressed.* London: Sheed and Ward.

Freire, P. (1994). *Pedagogy of hope: Reliving pedagogy of the oppressed.* New York: Continuum.

Gandin, L. A. (2006). Creating real alternatives to neo-liberal policies in education: The citizen school project. In: M. W. Apple & K. Buras (Eds), *The subaltern speak: Curriculum, power, and educational struggles.* New York: Routledge.

Ghanem, E. (1998). Social movements in Brazil and their educational work. *International Review of Education, 44*(2–3), 177–189.

Kane, L. (2001). *Popular education and social change in Latin America.* London: Latin American Bureau.

King-Calnek, J. (2006). Education for citizenship: Interethnic pedagogy and formal education at Escola Criativa Olodum. *Urban Review, 38*(2), 145.

McCowan, T. (2003). Participation and education in the landless people's movement of Brazil. *Journal for Critical Education Policy Studies, 1*(1)http://www.jceps.com/index.php?pageID= article&articleID=6.

McCowan, T. (2009). *Rethinking citizenship education: A curriculum for participatory democracy.* London: Continuum.

McCowan, T. (2010). School democratization in prefigurative form: Two Brazilian experiences. *Education, Citizenship and Social Justice, 5*(1), 21–41.

MST (1995). *Como Fazer a Escola que Queremos: o Planejamento (Caderno de Educação no. 6).* São Paulo: MST Setor de Educação.

MST (1999a). *Princípios da Educação no MST (Caderno de Educação no. 8).* São Paulo: MST Setor de Educação.

MST (1999b). *Como Fazemos a Escola de Educação Fundamental (Caderno de Educação no. 9).* Veranópolis: ITERRA.

MST (2004). *Educação no MST: Balanço 20 Anos (Boletim da Educação no. 9).* São Paulo: MST Setor de Educação.

Myers, J. (2008). Democratizing school authority: Brazilian teachers' perceptions of the election of principals. *Teaching and Teacher Education, 24,* 952–966.

Portillo, T. G., & Reyes, C. C. (2006). *Revolución Pinguina: La Primera Gran Movilización del Siglo XXI en Chile. [The Penguin Revolution: The First Large Mobilization in the 21st Century in Chile].* Santiago, Chile: Editorial Ayun.

Rowbotham, S. (1979). *Beyond the fragments.* London: Merlin.

Starr, A., Martínez-Torres, M. E., & Rosset, P. (2011). Participatory democracy in action: Practices of the Zapatistas and the Movimento Sem Terra. *Latin American Perspectives, 38*(1), 102–119.

Woodin, T. (2007). 'Chuck out the teacher': Radical pedagogy in the community. *International Journal of Lifelong Education, 26*(1), 89–104.

CONCLUSION

Chapter 34

Conclusion: From Blackboard, to Whiteboard, to 'Smart Board™' — Where Are We Heading?

Gerry Czerniawski and Warren Kidd

The 'tradesman's entrance', the 'servants staircase', 'gentlemen and players': for most of us these are concepts confined to days gone by. Is it not then strange to think that when going to school in the morning, most young people enter the building through a different door to that used by staff, parents, governors and the occasional 'VIP'. From sports trophies in glass cabinets to photos of students predicting academic excellence to come, to the carefully displayed picture of a visiting dignitary, the symbolic contrived distance that typifies relationships between so many teachers and students in schools and colleges is cultivated-physically, emotionally and intellectually on entry to the institution and is firmly embedded in the formal and informal curriculum. Moreover, politicians, policy makers and head teachers remind learners of the importance of 'citizenship' as a statutory subject on the curriculum, expressing concerns about those young people apparently 'switched off' from politics. So is it not also curious then that the very first socializing 'state' institution that many young people experience, one that, supposedly, has been specifically designed with them in mind, offers little or no democratic say in how it is operationalised, run and administered?

Of course, since the introduction of formal state education during the 19th century, things have moved on considerably. A century that, in many Anglo-Saxon countries, constructed the child as one that should be 'seen and not heard' was replaced by a century that espoused, through Article 12 of the United Nation's Convention on the Rights of the Child, a child's right to:

> express those views freely in all matters affecting the child, the views of the child being given due weight in accordance with the age and maturity of the child (United Nations (UN), 1989, *Convention on the rights of the child. UN document A/44/25*, UN, Geneva).

Moving into the second decade of the 21st century, one might argue that the Student Voice movement in schools and colleges in many countries is on the rise. This book offers outstanding evidence to support these developments from leading practitioners in primary, secondary and lifelong learning sectors. Supporting evidence includes the growth in student councils; students as co-researchers in school improvement strategies; student participation in the training of teachers; student involvement in the appointment and continuing professional development of teachers; student consultation in curriculum development initiatives; their advice and guidance in the design of new buildings and the construction and operation of timetables and many other exciting initiatives. Scratch below the surface however and while these initiatives are indeed exciting when led, facilitated, and initiated by passionate practitioners, in many cases only a minority of young people, very often the so-called gifted and talented or good students have an opportunity to voice their opinions. These leaves many others frustrated, marginalized and alienated from student voice, education and any understanding of democratic participation. In the United Kingdom just short of one million young people, at the time of writing, carry the ubiquitous identity marker 'NEET' (*Not in Employment, Education or Training*) and are what (Barber, 1997) has referred to as the 'disappointed, disillusioned and the disappeared'. Many of these young people drift from school, to street, to prison. Not listening — *really listening* — to those who could have a powerful voice in creating and shaping an alternative and far more inclusive and exciting educational environment — can have disastrous consequences for some and represents a lost opportunity for many. Formal state education, a project of the enlightenment, would seem then to contain within it a perverse contradiction. Structurally, while its socializing institutions promote notions of democracy, accountability and citizenship it simultaneously manages to violate the very rights of many of those who are in a position to carry that project forward.

The gravitational pull of conservative forces influencing so many teachers, head teachers and policy makers rests, in part, in the inescapable fact that school systems conceived, built and implemented today, despite huge advances, are founded on outdated notions of youth identity. Changes in patterns of employment combined with the influences of different forms of globalization and the continued rise in female educational achievement at primary, secondary and lifelong learning sectors spell out very different conditions in which young people emerge as citizens compared to their 19th century counterparts. If one function of formal education is to prepare young people for future employment, then the lack of trust and contrived distance that permeate many school cultures would seem an unrealistic site for such preparation. Many young people in the United Kingdom find themselves caught between two contradictory narratives. The first relates to societal expectations about the nature of childhood and its commercialization where children are positioned at the nexus of an array of industrial discourses (e.g. from the media, fashion houses, the cosmetic industry) demanding that they acquire adult norms and values. The second relates to the symbolic relationships and mores that make up school life (e.g. the wearing of uniform, the use of the term 'sir'/'miss') that, for many, bear little resemblance to their understanding of what the world is outside the school.

Despite enormous progress made within the sociology and psychology of education and the exciting insights that neuroscience offers; despite huge advances in the planning, construction and layout of new school buildings; despite a vast array of emerging technologies engulfing students, teachers, schools and colleges; despite substantial developments in our understanding of the nature and purpose of assessment, it is perhaps disappointing how little has changed in classrooms since the end of the 19th century. Most young people study in relatively cramped environments, in large hierarchical institutions and with little opportunity to get to know, really know, the teachers who teach them or their peers, other than at a relatively superficial level. The academic/vocational divide that typified many institutions over a century ago remains, as does the entrenched division in educational attainment between middle-class and working-class learners. And while teachers are increasingly better educated, trained, and professionally developed, many exit a career they have chosen burnt out, disillusioned and frustrated.

But there is cause for hope — even if that hope is unstable, complex and inchoate. In addition to some truly inspirational student voice initiatives taking place in the primary (e.g. Kenworthy, Chapter 7; Waller, Chapter 8), secondary (e.g. McLellan, Kirckman, Cartwright, & Millington, Chapter 9; Morgan & Porter, Chapter 10) and lifelong learning sectors (e.g. Pope & Joslin, Chapter 12; Baldry Currens, Chapter 15), this book has drawn attention to the international appeal of student voice (see Mitra, Frick, & Crawford, Chapter 28; McLaughlin & Kiragu, Chapter 29; Bland, Chapter 30; Kan, Chapter 32; McCowan, Chapter 33). These initiatives rest on one overwhelming common denominator. In all cases, although to varying degrees, the young people discussed in this book have been trusted. Trusted by their peers, their teachers, their head teachers and the researchers from the universities where many research projects were conceived. But this observation comes with a health warning. Different forms of professional trust are said to range from relatively high degrees in social democratic countries such as Sweden (see Bergmark & Kostenius, Chapter 31), to extremely low in more free-market liberal countries such as England (Czerniawski, 2010). In many schools professional trust has been battered by neo-liberal accountability rituals of monitoring, reporting, recording and surveillance strongly associated with pervasive forms of quasi-market educational practices. While these practices are particularly common place in England they represent powerful trends within social welfare regimes internationally and informed by the discourses of economic globalisation (Ball, 1999; Ritzer, 1993). If left unchecked this pervasiveness threatens to restrict the fostering of trust required for successful implementation of student voice initiatives or at least reduce student voice to the tokenism and instrumentalism that some commentators in this book have drawn attention (e.g. Fielding, Chapter 1; Wisby, Chapter 3; Thomson, Chapter 2).

Opportunities to develop a passion for learning in young people (and teachers) are frequently tarnished by the cultures of performativity that increasingly characterize formal education in the 21st century. And while all professionals are said to have an 'ethics of care' (Noddings, 2005) where caring forms the foundation for any ethical decision making that the job entails, how this is worked through in terms of what it is to be a teacher, is context-specific and culturally situated. We recognize that bringing about the transformation argued for by many of the contributors in this book will require substantial changes in the nested cultures permeating schools, colleges and teacher education institutions. Such transformation will take time but must happen. In conclusion we offer the following suggestions for transforming schools and colleges that take into consideration the ethics of care that motivate most teachers. In so doing we recognize the transformational potential of student voice and hope that in another 100 years the 'board'/bored component that typifies the educational experiences of so many young people is brought to an end:

1. Extend the period of time spent on the training and education of teachers, in part, to ensure that theoretical conceptions regarding the nature and purpose of education underpin the preparation of all teachers. All too often beginning teachers are on the receiving end of courses designed to meet governmental expectations of what an outstanding teacher should be with less emphasis placed on the humanitarian values that attract people into the teaching professions. It is, therefore, essential that critical, reflective practitioners have alternative conceptions of education at the heart of their emerging professional identities if they are to avoid narrow and conservative conceptions about what it means to be a teacher.

2. Ensure that critical pedagogy becomes a significant pillar within the theoretical foundations of the teaching profession. What is taught, when and how are decisions to be shared by learners and teachers in a classroom viewed as a microcosm of an idealized egalitarian view of society. While, for some, critical pedagogy might appear not to be relevant to many classrooms — particularly in the UK context — it is in fact an approach to teaching and learning that resonates with elements of current educational policy thinking (albeit instrumentally), for example, student voice, personalized learning, student-centered teaching, negotiated curriculums, etc.

3. Embed Student Voice in the recruitment and preparation of those entering the teaching profession. While many schools involve students in recruitment procedures (e.g. young people on interview panels; observing micro-teaching), this practice is not widespread. Neither is there evidence to show that university schools of education involve pupils at interview stage when considering who should or should not be accepted on teacher education courses. Ensuring that school and college students are prominent at the start of teacher preparation courses raises the importance of young people in the eyes of future cohorts of trainee teachers and their professional development.

4. Greater emphasis is needed on understanding what it means to be a teacher in different national contexts pivotally positioning this understanding at the heart of the initial preparation and continuing professional development of all teachers. The 'look and feel' (Ibarra, 2003) of teaching varies significantly from one national context to the next as do the sorts of relationships that teachers cultivate with young people in schools and colleges. An understanding of these differences is essential if teachers are to avoid the siloed cultures that often restrict the potential for alternative conceptions of the nature and purpose of education.

5. Bring to an end the contrived distance that typifies the relationships between so many teachers and young people. Recognizing and eradicating the pervasiveness of the 'ideology of immaturity' (Grace, 1995) that exists in many schools can increase hope in an increasingly convoluted world. The default position that many schools and colleges adopt in relation to students is a deficit model in which young people are assumed to lack the maturity, integrity and honesty that, it is supposed,

their adult counterparts develop later in life. This flawed position restricts the ability of young people to nurture and develop traits they already possess but have little opportunity to rehearse. If the transition from secondary (education) to tertiary (employment) socialization is to be managed by educationalists and young people more successfully, then schools and colleges need to re-examine their practices, policies, norms and values and eradicate this pervasive and damaging ideology.

6. All educational institutions need to recognize, understand and embrace 21st century youth identities and reject outdated conceptions of childhood. Young people (and all members of the teaching profession) need to be, as well as feel, valued and comfortable to change, experiment and take risks. For Student Voice initiatives to be effective and truly transformative, all communities of practice and social spaces (Gee, 2000) in schools and colleges need to be ones in which trust forms the cornerstone of all professional relationships and where language and all symbolic systems used are non-threatening. In this way, greater synergy between the world of school and work can be achieved, enriching the former and vitalizing the latter. In so doing, schools and colleges will minimize the transition shock that many young people experience as they enter the world of employment.

This book celebrates the integrity and passion of the practitioners and academics who have contributed to this body of work and the student voice movement as a whole. It is, nevertheless, important to remind ourselves that material conditions partially determine and constrain student voice initiatives, as do the values and the existing commitments of young people and the teachers who teach them. Accompanying huge improvements in so many aspects of education, including the student voice movement, is a pervasive form of instrumentalism. We need to move away from student voice being viewed as a tool to improve measurable outcomes, 'Student Voice-by-numbers' if you like, to one in which the voices of young people shape and determine new institutions of education, redefining current and future generations' conceptions of the importance and substance of both formal and informal education.

References

Ball, S. J. (1999). Global trends in educational reform and the struggle for the soul of the teacher. Paper presented at the British Educational Research Association Annual Conference, University of Sussex at Brighton, September 2–5, 1999 (Centre for Public Policy Research – Kings College London).

Barber, M. (1997). *The learning game: Arguments for an education revolution*. London: Indigo.

Czerniawski, G. (2010). *Emerging teachers and globalisation*. New York, NY: Routledge/ Taylor Frances.

Gee, J. P. (2000). New people in new worlds: Networks, the new capitalism and schools. In: B. Cope & M. Kalantizis (Eds), *Multiliteracies: Literacy, learning and the design of social futures*. London: Routledge.

Grace, G. R. (1995). *School leadership: Beyond education management: An essay in policy scholarship.* London: Falmer.

Ibarra, H. (2003). *Working identities.* Harvard: Harvard Business School Press.

Noddings, N. (2005). *Caring in Education.* Infed. Retrieved from www.infed.org/biblio/ noddings_caring_in_education.htm

Ritzer, G. (1993). *The McDonaldization of society.* London: Sage.

United Nations (UN). (1989). *Convention on the rights of the child.* UN document A/44/25, UN, Geneva.

Subject Index

Page numbers followed by "n" indicate footnotes.